Children in the New Media Landscape

Games • Pornography • Perceptions

Children in the New Media Landscape

Games Pornography Perceptions

Editors:
Cecilia von Feilitzen and
Ulla Carlsson

Children and Media Violence • Yearbook 2000

The UNESCO
International Clearinghouse
on Children and Violence
on the Screen
at Nordicom

Published by
The UNESCO International Clearinghouse on Children and Violence on the Screen
Nordicom
Göteborg University
Box 713
SE 405 30 GÖTEBORG
Sweden

Editors
Cecilia von Feilitzen and Ulla Carlsson

Cover by Roger Palmqvist
Printed by Livréna Grafiska AB, Kungälv, Sweden, 2000

ISSN 1403-4700
ISBN 91-89471-01-6

Contents

Violence in Video and Computer Games

Pornography and Sex in the Media

Audience Perceptions of Violence and Sex in the Media

Foreword

A new media landscape and a new media order are emerging. Media cultures are changing, in both the public and the private sphere. Information flows ever more freely, and with ever looser ties to time and place. The volume of information conveyed via new media technologies continues to expand, while the distinctions between computers, television, radio, the press, books and telephony gradually dissolve. We speak of fragmentation and individualization. Media culture today is intensive and all-pervasive.

We also witness a comprehensive restructuring of media markets around the world. National markets, once distinct, are becoming integrated into a global power structure. National frontiers are, for that matter, fading away in other respects, as well. The new order allows people all over the globe to hear sounds and see images from many different places, near and distant. At the same time, we note that a very few global media corporations, principally headquartered in the USA, Europe and Japan, deliver products of mass culture to larger, broader and more far-flung audiences than ever before.

Digitalization is advancing into new phases of development, which have palpable effects on our cultures. Digital technology changes the conditions of media consumption. Internet is often considered the most salient example of the digital revolution. Increasingly, Internet serves as a sort of mass medium, accessible to many in a continuous flow, unbound by the constraints of time. Internet is in many respects a young people's medium.

Viewed in the longer term, new media technology and the changes we note in the media order have a profound influence on the conditions and cultures of children and young people. For many children in the world today culture is something they partake of via electronic media. What is the nature of the content in this burgeoning media output? Whose values and judgements does it represent?

Many voice concern about the media's influence on their audiences, and not least the youngest of them. Mediated violence is the object of especial concern. The media's role is not unequivocal. A frequently debated question is to what extent children are helpless victims in the glow of the television screen or, alternatively, can master the challenges contemporary content poses. To answer the question requires a greater understanding of children, of the media, and of children and the media in a variety of perspectives, and particularly an understanding of the influence of mediated violence on children and youth.

In 1997, Nordicom began building up *the UNESCO International Clearinghouse on Children and Violence on the Screen*, whose operations are financed jointly by the Swedish Government and UNESCO. The overall point of departure for the work of the Clearinghouse on the subject of children and violence in mass media is the UN Convention on the Rights of the Child (cf. Articles 13 and 17).

The work of the Clearinghouse *aims* to increase our understanding of children and media violence, particularly in the light of new media like satellite television and Internet, with a view to informing relevant policy decisions and contributing to a constructive discussion of the subject. Greater knowledge can also help to heighten children's media literacy and competence as media users. Further research in the area is a key factor, and stimulating such research is naturally a central objective of our work.

The International Clearinghouse on Children and Violence on the Screen informs various groups of users – policy-makers, journalists, media representatives, teachers, interest organizations, researchers, students – about current research and research findings on media violence, about children's access to the media and their media use, about media education and children's participation in media productions, and about pertinent legislation and self-regulating initiatives.

The Clearinghouse is *user-oriented*, which means that the information we publish is adapted to our users' needs. Central to our work has been the creation of an effective network. Today the network links about 800 participants in different user groups: the research community, the media industry, politics, public authorities, voluntary organzations, and so forth. About 150 countries are represented in the network.

The Clearinghouse publishes a *newsletter*. Issues generally have a theme in addition to reporting notices and articles of current interest. Examples of the subjects treated to date include: *Internet, Fear* and *Emotional Responses, Children's Programmes,* and *Paedophilia on Internet*. The newsletter reaches roughly 2,000 subscribers in about 150 countries.

Our *bibliographical programme* got under way in 1997 in conjunction with work on the first Yearbook. It has since been further developed, with respect to both the documentation system and entry content. In Spring of 1999 we published our first bibliography in hard copy. The documentation work continues and is accessible via Internet on Nordicom's and the Clearinghouse' home page (www.nordicom.gu.se).

A *register of institutions and organizations* has also been compiled. This, too, is accessible via the home page. An initial version was included in the 1999 Yearbook. An updated hard copy edition will be published in spring this year. The register comprises more than 240 entries.

One of the most important tasks of *the International Clearinghouse on Children and Violence on the Screen* is the publication of a *Yearbook*. The first volume, *Children and Media Violence*, appeared in 1998. The focus that year was research on the influences on children of depictions of violence in the media. This first volume may be said to relate to the first goal toward which we work: to *report what is known about children and media violence after decades of research* on the subject.

The next Yearbook, in 1999, focused on the second of the Clearinghouse' goals: to highlight *initiatives and activities aiming to bolster children's competence as users of the media.* Here we sought to gather researchers, teachers and media practitioners around the world who are involved in the development of programmes in the areas of *media education* and *media participation.*

Now we are pleased to present a third Yearbook. *The 2000 Yearbook* treats two themes, both of which relate to newer features of the media landscape: *violence in video and computer games,* and *pornography on television and on Internet.* Some articles in the Yearbook also discuss findings on *audience perceptions of violence and sex in the media.* The choice of these themes has to do with the marked increase in the availability of such content to children and youth via new media technologies.

The first theme treated in this year's volume concerns *video and computer games.* Games of this type have been on the market for over a decade, and as more and more homes acquire game consoles and computers, the market has mushroomed. These interactive games have achieved permanence as a favourite children's leisure activity. Acts of violence are not uncommon in these games; at the same time, computer games can be valuable educational tools. We know that many children and adolescents prefer violent games, but our knowledge of the contents of games is limited. And we know very little about the influences. The articles presented in this year's volume highlight selected aspects and point out areas for further research.

The second theme treated concerns *pornography* in the media. Another form of violence has become more common in both satellite television and Internet, namely, violence in pornographic films and images. The acts of violence depicted in such images are important components of a social order predicated on the notion of women's subordinance to men. It is a form of violence that requires some new approaches alongside those followed in traditional studies of media violence.

There has been rather little research on how pornography influences its audiences, and we know even less about how it might affect children. Studies of sadistic pornography are even rarer. Here it is important to stress that we know very little about how depictions of sex in the media influence children. We do know, however, that they are much more common on television and in films today than was the case only a couple of decades ago. How has this change affected young people's attitudes, values and behaviour? Knowledge of this sort must reasonably be a necessary prerequisite to studies of the influences of watching pornography.

An inventory of the literature on sex and pornography in the media was conducted in conjunction with the work on this Yearbook, which presents articles based on some of the more interesting studies in this area. The articles give us a comprehensive picture of the state of our knowledge and the lacunae in it. Thus, they provide a fruitful point of departure for further study.

Whenever one considers pornography on Internet, the subject of child pornography presents itself. Because it is condemned in virtually all cultures, child pornography is considerably less accessible than other pornographic material on the Net. Maintaining one's anonymity is a priority to those who deal in illicit material, even in the 'virtual' world. Nonetheless, studies have found that even a moderately competent user of the Net can gain access to images of child pornography. The book contains articles on this subject, as well.

The problem complex raised in these articles is, of course, considerably broader than the presence of such images in the media. How does the presence and accessibility of child pornography on Internet relate to the underlying problem of sexual exploitation and abuse of children in the world today? This is a serious problem worldwide: Is the presence of child pornography on Internet responsible for an increase in the sexual abuse of minors? The answer to this question must be sought in numerous disciplines: psychology, sociology, media sciences, criminology, law, political science, theology, philosophy. Media researchers are but one – in this context perhaps even peripheral – discipline among many that can cast light on such a complex problem as child pornography.

In conjunction with the work on the third yearbook considerable effort has been put into the compilation of specialized bibliographies on the subjects treated in this yearbook – *children and computer games* and, *children and sex/ pornography on the screen*. These special bibliographies are presented in separate volumes.

Stimulating further research on these new phenomena relating to children and the media has been an overriding objective in our work with this year's book. We find major gaps in our knowledge relating to computer games and to sex and pornography in the media. Filling these gaps will to some extent require new research methods, and the Clearinghouse hopes to help in the 'bridge-building' efforts between innovative and traditional media research methods.

Let me conclude by thanking all the contributors who have made this Yearbook possible and whose articles put the focus on these important areas of research. Thanks, also, to the Swedish Government and UNESCO without whose financial support the book would never have seen the light of day.

Göteborg in May 2000

Ulla Carlsson
Director

Electronic Games, Pornography, Perceptions

Introduction by Cecilia von Feilitzen, Scientific Co-ordinator of the UNESCO International Clearinghouse on Children and Violence on the Screen

New technology, more and more globally spread media contents produced for an international audience, and deregulation of media in many countries have led to an increasingly changing media landscape. The 1990's can be summarised as a decade when ever larger parts of the world were flooded by TV and satellite TV, and also when electronic games and computers with CD-ROM and Internet connection were spread among well-to-do households.

In 1996, 7 out of 10 households in the world were estimated to own a TV set – far more than had a telephone. This was a 100 per cent increase of channel expansion, hours of television watched and television ownership since the end of the 1980's. With that, TV reinforced its position as the most important mass medium besides radio, which is still more essential in large rural areas in Africa, Asia and Latin America. Satellite TV channels reached every country where there was television, while transnational satellite channels with miscellaneous contents multiplied, and an abundance of niche channels were launched with contents focused for special target groups, not least children and young people. With few exceptions, the pattern of prime-time television viewing among populations as a whole is similar throughout the world – entertainment, live action, sports and news. However, the output of national broadcasters attracts most viewers, and the general demand is for more local programming (Lamb 1997).

The video and computer game industry has become the fastest growing and most profitable children's entertainment business, in 1998 earning an estimated $18 billion world-wide for the corporations that manufacture, design and sell console game systems, domestic computers, Internet play sites, and gaming arcades. In the U.S., digital entertainment won shares of the toy market in 1998 larger than the Hollywood box-office gross and ten times the amount spent on the production of children's television (*Stephen Kline* in this book). However, Japan is leading the world in the video game industry. In 1999, this

Japanese industry sold over ten million machines and about one hundred million copies of software only on the domestic market. The total market sizes were about two hundred billion yen ($ two billion) for machines and over five hundred billion yen ($ five billion) for software (*Akira Sakamoto* in this book).

The Internet is an even younger medium. It is true that the Internet has been available since the early 60's, when it was developed and established to protect military communication from external interference. However, it was when a new generation of software – the World Wide Web (WWW) browsers – was presented in the beginning of the 1990's, that the Internet became widespread (*Tor A. Evjen & Ragnhild T. Bjørnebekk* in this book). The spread is now explosive. In early 2000, the number of Internet users in the world was estimated to have almost doubled compared to only one year before, from 159 million people in March 1999 to 305 million in March 2000, that is, from less than 4 per cent of the world population to more than 7 per cent (http://www.nua.net/surveys April 2000). The figures represent both adults and children who had accessed the Internet at least once during the three months prior to the survey. However, almost three-quarters of the Internet users are estimated to live in North America and Europe (ibid.), areas inhabited by only 17 per cent of the world population.

In countries with few media, collective listening and viewing are common. Many people gather in front of, for instance, the only television or video set in the village, if such a set exists. In countries where TV has become more common, as, for example, in recent years in India, radio has lost much of its previous glamour, especially for children, but children's TV viewing in India occurs almost exclusively within the family circle (Agrawar in press). With more and more media, individual media use becomes more frequent. If the household owns several TV sets, for example, one is often moved into the child's room and, consequently, children and adults often choose to watch different programmes. Children and parents use the media together less often, talk about the media contents less often, and parents are less likely to have rules for children's media use. To a greater extent than for TV, this seems to be true for video and computer games (e.g., *Ferran Casas* in this book). At the same time, it should be underlined that both in countries with more collective media use and in countries with more individualised media use, children, to a high degree, watch programmes and use other media contents that are aimed primarily at adults.

In regions with many media, children and young people as a rule use new media more than older generations do. This is not only a result of the fact that young people are fascinated by new media, curious about them, or find them more "natural", since they are growing up with them, but also of purposeful marketing by the industry. By directing media contents and advertising to the young, it is easier to attain penetration among adults, now and in the future.

Hopes and fears

With new media – just as with the advent of books, press, film, radio, etc. – come both hopes and concerns. Satellite television has aroused expectations of greater freedom of choice and equal access to information for all, but also fear of standardisation, more violent entertainment, advertising, pornography and discriminating portrayals of gender, social groups, cultures and nations.

These hopes and fears are not altogether the same for all media, but depend on the output and character of the medium. Video and computer games are not only an extension of moving images on film and television, but also of play. The electronic games form an *interactive* medium in the sense that the player in several respects can steer the course and outcome of the game. Optimists, therefore, believe that video and computer games mean an educational revolution and a different socialisation. The games are regarded as a fabulous gateway to the future, training children and youth to cope with virtual reality in cyberspace – training that increases young people's perceptual-motor skills and social competence, as well as providing them with a greater sense of agency and control of the changing digital environment, yes, empowering them in their lives. Pessimists, however, remark that the contents of video and computer games are overwhelmingly violent, sexist and racist, leading to possible aggression, desensitisation, fear, decreased empathy – even destroying the mental processes, social relations and culture that are essential for humanity (e.g., *Stephen Kline* in this book).

Hopes and concerns about the Internet, computer-mediated communication and cyberspace are, in turn, somewhat different. Optimists point out that the Internet offers gateways to education, culture, self-improvement and social contacts, that the Net is a means for enlightenment and increased democracy. Others wonder if the Internet does not cause user addiction and isolation, and it is a fact that many children and adults have come across material on the Net that they do not want to be acquainted with. The Internet not only involves interactivity; much of the Net's possibilities and contents also depend on its *anonymity, easy availability, immediate world-wide distribution* and *lack of control.* And this is a mixed blessing. The Internet may enable breach of privacy and economic crime by unknown perpetrators. The surfer may also encounter oppression in the form of hate speech, racism and political propaganda, discrimination of gender and cultures, gratuitous depictions of violence, incitement to illegal acts, recipes for drugs and weaponry, violent pornography and child pornography.

During the 1990's, the inherent risks with the ever intensifying transnational flow of satellite TV channels, electronic games and Internet have given rise to several discussions about what international means might exist to counteract undesired media contents and to support media that both guarantee freedom of expression for adults as well as children and that respect children's right to receive material that is good for them, while protecting them from harmful influences.

The research

Hopes and fears are important incentives for research. Questions about the influences of media violence have been with us as long as the media have existed, but have intensified internationally with the global spread of TV and satellite TV. Recently, similar questions about the digital media have also become more and more common: How are children affected by violent video and computer games? What risks are connected with the Internet, not least when it comes to violent pornography and child pornography? What are, after all, the audiences' views of violence and sex in the media generally, and what can be done about such contents?

These are the questions the Clearinghouse wants to highlight in this, its third yearbook. In addition, two separate bibliographies have been compiled by *Johan Cronström*, one about research on video and computer games and one about research on pornography and sex in the media. Particularly with respect to violent aspects of video and computer games, and violent pornography and child pornography, the yearbook and the bibliographies combined cover a great deal of the research available world-wide.

In the public debate and in the press, far-reaching conclusions are often willingly drawn about the impact of media violence. However, many also turn to research to learn what has been established, and concerning electronic games and the risks of Internet pornography, pressure on the research community has become increasingly great. Hence, let me stress, in sum:

- *Research on video and computer games, as well as research on children's relations to pornography and sex in the media, is very novel and, accordingly, scanty.* One reason for this is that electronic games and the Internet are young – and research takes time. Thus, the knowledge we have gathered in this book, containing both reviews of the state of research and presentations of new, concrete studies, provides more questions than answers. Much more research is needed on both video and computer games and on children's relations to pornography and sex, as well as on the risks of the Internet in this context.

- *The research on electronic games and the Internet is practically only performed in richer countries, one reason being that these media are most widely spread there.* In spite of the fact that we addressed persons on all continents asking for contributions, the research picture we are able to present is, unfortunately, skewed. In this regard, it is important to remember that research conducted in one country or one culture often cannot be generalised to other cultures. Consequently, there is a need for corresponding research in more countries and from more perspectives. There is a particular need for international comparative research.

- We have found it essential with this yearbook, in combination with the two bibliographies, not only to give an orientation to much of the extant research on video and computer games, and pornography and sex in the media, but also to ask questions revealing gaps in the research. *One of the aim of the publications is, therefore, to stimulate ideas about where the future research focus within these areas should be placed.* Several of the authors themselves give recommendations for further research.

- With respect to the third area dealt with in the yearbook, audience perceptions of violence and sex in the media, it appears from the articles – which are slightly better distributed over the world than those treating digital games and children and pornography – that *violence and sex in the media are issues of most concern in many countries.* However, it also appears that the perceptions, opinions and attitudes are culturally shaped. So, within this area, too, more countries should carry out research on their own terms and within their own cultural context, and we should see more international comparative research.

Video and computer games

The Clearinghouse's separate bibliography of research on video and computer games indicates, among other things, that hopes for benefits of these games are represented by relatively extensive research on use of games and multimedia for specific learning purposes in school situations, and research on the possible contribution of the games to cognitive development, perceptual-motor skills, and social interaction. Electronic games have also been tested for therapeutic purposes. Regarding concerns, on the other hand, research has focused on possible harmful influences, such as increased player acceptance of violence as a useful means to solve conflicts, desensitisation to violence, increased aggression, addiction, isolation, disregard for homework and outdoor activities, certain cognitive-emotional influences, as well as health issues, such as epileptic fits, cramps, and the like.

Concerning possible aggression as a consequence of playing, some people work from the hypothesis that the essence of electronic games is their relations to children's play, pleasure and fantasy. Accordingly, the fictive violence the player engages in is just for fun and does not entail the desire or inclination to hurt or kill (e.g., *Birgitte Holm Sørensen & Carsten Jessen* in this book). There are also speculations that playing the games might serve as a vent for inner aggression, or at least facilitate the satisfaction of desires that are not allowed to turn into behaviour in everyday life (e.g., Goldstein 1998). Others start instead from the hypothesis that game violence, just as film and TV violence, contributes to increased aggression, due to, e.g., social learning or competition. In this connection, some people point to the fact that games are *more* effective training in desensitisation and aggression than TV viewing precisely because they involve play – combined with the factors of game interactivity, individual practice, repetition, engagement, as well as the rewards for violent actions and the fact that play is pleasurable and enjoyable (e.g., Grossman & DeGaetano 1999).

In the yearbook, the central feature is what research has shown about the violent aspects of video and computer games.

It is evident from the articles that electronic games are popular among children and young people, and also among young adults, in countries where the games are spread. In 1998-99, more than 80 per cent of school-aged children in the U.S. had at least one game console for video games, more than half had access to a home computer with CD-ROM, and almost half access to the Internet (Roberts et al. 1999), of which the last-mentioned platforms have hitherto been more or less requirements for playing computer games and games online, respectively. In Sweden, children's home access to computers and the Internet was even more common in 1999 (Nordicom-Sveriges Mediebarometer 1999). In 1999 in Japan, about 90 per cent of elementary school children possessed video game machines for their own exclusive use (*Akira Sakamoto* in this book).

When children have computers at home, they use them more often for recreational and entertainment purposes than for schoolwork. Playing digital games, and using the Internet, is a particularly male occupation – boys more often own or have access to electronic games, video game consoles, computer and Internet connection than do girls, and boys use these media much more frequently. Technology is also primarily developed by, and the contents of these media produced by, men (e.g., *Peter Petrov* in this book; Roberts et al. 1999; *Akira Sakamoto* in this book).

There is a great variety of video and computer games. Nowhere near all games contain violence (*Lisbeth Schierbeck & Bo Carstens* in this book). The electronic games that children and young people, above all boys, prefer, however, belong to the genres of 'action/combat', 'sports/racing', 'strategy' and 'adventure' (*Peter Petrov* in this book, Roberts et al. 1999), genres that more often contain violence. The 'action/combat' genre contains most violence, which is often aimed at figures representing human beings (as opposed to machines, monsters, and the like). Salient sub-genres within the 'action/combat' genre are 'first person shooters', that is, violence perpetrated from the perspective of the player, and 'fighting games' (*Jan Christofferson; Lisbeth Schierbeck & Bo Carstens*, all in this book). A recent trend is also various meta-genres that mix previous genres.

What, then, are the most fascinating characteristics of the digital games? Approaching the problem from different angles, several researchers in the book show that what players themselves find most motivating is not the violence *per se*, but the challenge, i.e., learning how to advance in the game, overcoming difficult situations, solving problems, and competing, something due to the interactive nature of the games. Essential is also the emotional excitement and immersion that the games give rise to. However, the violence in the games is a motivating factor, too, primarily for boys (*Jan Christofferson; Birgitte Holm Sørensen & Carsten Jessen*; *Stephen Kline*; *Peter Nikken*, all in this book).

Regarding influences of the violence in electronic games, there is reason to repeat that this research is still in its infancy – most research on these games has been performed during the 1990's, and only some of the studies focus on the impact of violence. In comparison, research on film and TV has been in progress since the 1930's, and studies on specifically violent contents and their consequences amount to at least two thousand, according to some statements, four thousand. Furthermore, these studies employ different theories, complexes of questions, methods, materials and populations, and have been performed both in the short and long term, that is, certain investigations have followed the same individuals over many years. Taken together, this means that conclusions can be based on a variety of studies whose findings point in the same direction. Several authors in this book emphasise precisely the fact that inquiries on influences of the violence in electronic games are very few and have employed a limited number of methods. According to some studies, young children become more aggressive in their subsequent play, but these studies have used only one type of method. Among the very few studies that have included the newer, more violent electronic games, there are some, both in the West and East, indicating that the games can contribute to aggression also among older children and young people. At the same time, however, other studies have provided conflicting or inconclusive findings (e.g., *Alexander Ask et al.; Mark Griffiths; Stephen Kline; Akira Sakamoto*, all in this book).

Thus, in certain respects, research on digital games is similar to the early research on film and TV violence. Apart from the fact that more research is needed using different methods, the authors emphasise that the studies have insufficiently theorised the difference between watching moving images in film and on television and the activity connected to playing the games – interactivity may, for example, contribute to another kind of identification than does TV, and this and other emotional experiences are in all likelihood different for boys and girls. In addition, extremely few studies have dealt with the long-term influences of the games – the only such studies we have found are presented in the Japanese article (by *Akira Sakamoto*) in this book. Thus, it is not possible to simply translate the findings on the impact of film and TV violence into the impact of violent electronic games. Moreover, the research needs to distinguish more explicitly between different types of games and different types of harmful influences. Furthermore, the fact that the games continuously change means that research findings on video and computer games during the 1980's and early 1990's cannot be generalised to the new generation of games today, which are based on much more advanced technology and contain much more advanced and realistically portrayed violent elements.

Children's relations to pornography and sex in the media

Research on children's and young people's relations to pornography and sex in the media is even sparser than research on video and computer games. As an introduction to this second section of the book, we have included a few articles treating young people's encounters with, uses and impressions of pornography and sexually explicit media content in general. Much seems to indicate that pornography and sex in the media do influence young individuals' thoughts, ideas, attitudes and behaviour, not least since they are in a period when curiosity about sex is great (*Ellen Wartella et al.; Margareta Forsberg*, all in this book), and since TV glamorises sex, seldom showing its risks (*Dale Kunkel et al.* in this book).

Pornography research in general, in other words with adults, is much more comprehensive. This is evident from the separate research bibliography on pornography and sex in the media that the Clearinghouse has compiled. However, the bibliography also shows that research on both violent pornography and child pornography seems to have increased during the 1980's and even more in the 1990's, whereas research on contents, uses, and effects of 'ordinary' pornography seems to have decreased proportionally, compared to the 1970's and 1980's. Meanwhile, there is a tendency towards an increase in material discussing regulations and policy matters in this context, something that in all likelihood has to do with the development of the Internet.

Nevertheless, qualified research on violent pornography and child pornography is difficult to find. A few such examples are presented in the yearbook.

As mentioned, the world of electronic games as well as Internet is male dominated. This is certainly valid also for pornography. Young women seldom actively search for pornography on the Net, whereas many young men confess that they do so, at least occasionally (*Peter Petrov* in this book). Pornography on the Internet has become a very lucrative branch. *Mark Griffiths* (in this book) refers to an estimation stating that over half of all spending on the Net is sex-related, and underlines that pornographers have always been among the first to exploit new publishing technologies (e.g., photography, film, videotape, satellite TV, Internet). Cyberspace is, thus, largely utilised by mainly male producers and mainly male consumers of pornography – due to easy availability, anonymity, speedy global distribution and the lack of control. This not only means oppression of women, but also that many children have come across content on the Internet that has upset or embarrassed them. What is worse, it also means that sex-related Internet crime is on the rise (*Mark Griffiths* in this book). Child pornography is one of the media's worst crimes against children, a crime justifying child sex myths and actual child sex abuse, as well as helping paedophiles to, via the Internet, make appointments with children. Child pornography is, thus, not only an expression of certain individuals' sexual fantasies, but may lead to a growing evil spiral of child abuse in practice (*Rachel O'Connell* in this book). In a similar vein, other forms of violent pornography can have a legitimising function. Also, studies with young adults generally find that pornography combined with violence leads to more callous attitudes towards rape and sexual coercion on the part of men (*Ellen Wartella et al.* in this book).

The research on violent pornography and child pornography on the Internet has largely focused on its availability, prevalence and different forms of expression. The few analyses performed evince that violent pornographic material is very likely increasing on the Internet, and that, with time, it has become easier to find and download (*Ragnhild T. Bjørnebekk & Tor A. Evjen* in this book). Child pornography is illegal in most countries, but despite the efforts of law-enforcement agencies and voluntary organisations, newsgroups for paedophiles, for instance, have not decreased on the Internet, rather the opposite (*Rachel O'Connell* in this book).

Ellen Wartella and co-authors comment on the lack of research concerning children, young people and sex in the media generally, but their words are valid for research on violent pornography and child pornography on the Internet, as well: "There is need for an accumulated body of systematic studies using a variety of methods, interdisciplinary teams of investigators, and a variety of populations. Given the paucity of available studies and the need to develop a systematic research base ... the answers ... will not be obtained simply or quickly. Nonetheless, we must begin to accumulate a serious, systematic research base that could serve as a catalyst to stimulate further research and provide a solid foundation for understanding media sexual content effects." Several authors in the book put forward concrete suggestions for future research in this area.

Audience perceptions of violence and sex in the media

One question is, then, if access to and use of electronic games and the Internet have resulted in children abandoning television – such assertions often turn up in the press. The studies we are acquainted with do not support such assumptions. Children's and young people's TV viewing has not decreased over time, and there are also relationships showing that, on average, those who watch a great deal of television are also avid computer users (e.g., Johnsson-Smaragdi 1998; Nordicom-Sveriges Mediebarometer 1999; Roberts et al. 1999).

Accordingly, TV is still the medium that dominates children's media leisure in large regions of the world, and in the – far fewer – regions where children also have electronic games, computer and access to Internet, the use of these media is, if anything, added to that of television.

More media and purposeful global marketing in a situation of increasing media competition have led to more, and more intensive, media violence – violence that takes partly different shapes in the different media. We know from research that film and TV violence has multiple influences on viewers. Besides some desirable influences, media violence contributes to undesirable fear, erroneous conceptions of violence in reality, habituation to violence in the media, imitation and, to some extent, destructive aggression – if other and far more decisive factors promoting destructive aggressiveness are also present (e.g., von Feilitzen 1994). We asked several outstanding researchers throughout the world to summarise the research on influences of media violence for the Clearinghouse's first yearbook (Carlsson & von Feilitzen 1998). How do, then, audiences perceive TV's and other media's violent contents?

In the third section of this yearbook, several studies – with the total adult population in various countries, with parents, and sometimes also with children and young people themselves – provide examples of what people in different cultures perceive to be violence in the media. The studies also show whether people think that something should be done about media violence, and, if so, what type of violence should be taken into consideration (e.g., *André H. Caron & Letizia Caronia; Margaret Cupitt; Ingrid Geretschlaeger; Andrea Millwood Hargrave; Joseph Turow,* all in this book). Of course, findings from these studies cannot be generalised across frontiers. The questions, methods and cultural contexts of the studies vary greatly. More countries need to ascertain their audiences' thoughts on what – on TV, the Internet and in other media – is problematic, who might be negatively influenced, who profits by it, and on what can be done. There are also general traps in opinion research, such as, for instance, the fact that people expect media content to have a greater negative influence on others than on themselves (*Albert C. Gunther & Peng Hwa Ang* in this book).

Nevertheless, it is remarkable that, in spite of the fact that violence and sex are important ingredients in people's lives and therefore for many may be exciting as media contents, violence and pornography in the media that are perceived as contextually inappropriate seem to be issues of great concern among audiences in many countries. In those countries where such research questions have been asked, the majority also find that there is an augmenting and disturbing trend towards more problematic media contents (e.g., *Veronica Silva & Maria Dolores Souza; Jens Waltermann & Marcel Machill,* all in this book). At least according to a few studies, there also seems to be a tendency among new media audiences to widen the definition of what media violence is – for example, to include racism and child pornography. From the investigations we have seen, there is also an explicit wish to change the situation.

Perceptions of what types of media content are problematic are, as noted, dependent on the culture. The culture as a whole, the media system, the available media output and how it is regulated, the audiences' wishes to use different programmes, games, web sites, etc., and, not least, earlier experience of traditional as well as new media and what they offer, are some of the factors affecting perceptions of media contents. However, what is clear generally is that audience perceptions of and relations to the media are essential and should be taken into account when each country chooses to realise regulations and/or self-regulations on national and international levels.

Concluding words

To make solutions possible, there is also need for extended research on power mechanisms and states of ownership, as well as on the economic, industrial-technological and political interests underlying the ever-increasing media output. If large parts of the audience are concerned about the development, it is not only popularity, or a desire to watch violence and pornography on TV or to search for it on the Net, that guides media production, but marketing and a desire for profit on the part of media owners and distributors. In order to realise solutions, the audience, global media corporations, other media professionals, politicians, voluntary organisations and researchers must meet.

The realisation of solutions particularly concerns children in the new media landscape. According to the United Nations Convention on the Rights of the Child, ratified by all member states but two, the child, too, shall have the right to freedom of expression (article 13), which in today's society means, among other things, the right for children to appear and participate in the media. The child shall also have access to information and material from a diversity of national and international sources, especially those aimed at the promotion of his or her social, spiritual or moral well-being and physical and mental health, at the same time as the child shall be protected from information and material injurious to his or her well-being (article 17 about the mass media). And several articles state that children have the right not to be exploited or abused.

Lastly, we want to extend our warm thanks to both the authors contributing to the yearbook and to all persons and organisations all over the world who answered the Clearinghouse questionnaire during Summer 1999. This questionnaire was an attempt to establish who had conducted and was currently conducting research within the above-mentioned areas. The answers were invaluable to us in identifying research literature for the bibliographies and finding authors for the yearbook.

References (besides the authors' articles in this book)

Agrawar, B (in press) "Children's Media Use in India. A Current Scenario", *Newsletter from The UNESCO International Clearinghouse on Children and Violence on the Screen*, Vol. 4, No. 1, 2000

Carlsson, U & von Feilitzen, C (Eds.) (1998) *Children and Media Violence. Yearbook from the UNESCO International Clearinghouse on Children and Violence on the Screen*. Göteborg University, Nordicom

von Feilitzen, C (1994) "Media Violence – Research Perspectives in the 1980s", in Hamelink, C J & Linné, O (Eds.) *Mass Communication Research: On Problems and Policies. The Art of Asking the Right Questions*. Norwood, N J: Ablex Publishing Corporation, pp. 147-170

Goldstein, J H (Ed.) (1998) *Why We Watch: The Attractions of Violent Entertainment*. New York: Oxford University Press

Grossman, D & DeGaetano, G (1999) *Stop Teaching Our Kids to Kill. A Call to Action Against TV, Movie & Video Game Violence*. New York: Crown Publishers

http://www.nua.net/surveys, April 2000

Johnsson-Smaragdi, U (1998) "Barn och ungdomar i 90-talets föränderliga medievärld [Children and Young People in the Changing Media World of the 90's], in *Barn och ungdomar i det nya medielandskapet. Statistik och analys*. MedieNotiser. Nordicom-Sverige, Göteborg University, No. 2, 1998, pp. 5-23

Lamb, R (1997) *The Bigger Picture: Audio-visual survey and recommendations*. New York, UNICEF. (Parts from this survey are reproduced in the Clearinghouse Yearbook 1998)

Nordicom-Sveriges Mediebarometer 1999 [The Media Barometer 1999] (2000). Nordicom, Göteborg University

Roberts, D F, Foehr, U G, Rideout, V J & Brodie, M (1999) *Kids & Media @ The New Millennium. A Comprehensive National Analysis of Children's Media Use*. Menlo Park, CA, Kaiser Family Foundation

Violence in Video and Computer Games

The Monster Massacre
or What Is a Violent Electronic Game?

Jan Christofferson

The report *The Monster Massacre*[1] is an introduction to electronic interactive gaming for the uninitiated with emphasis on games with violent content. In the public debate, the most discussed aspect of video- and computer games is violence and the possible negative influence of use of such material. *The Monster Massacre* report tries to explore and explain what the player experiences when playing games of this kind. The book is not an empirical study, but a personal and subjective description of the games and what they offer. This brief article contains excerpts from selected book chapters and deals with the absolute basics of action gaming.

Various platforms

Electronic interactive games come in different forms. We have computer games, video games, on-line games, etc. The term computer game refers to games that you play on a PC – IBM compatible or Macintosh. The term video game refers to games played on a game console, such as Sony Playstation, Nintendo 64 and Sega Dreamcast. All video games require a television set, which acts as a display for the game. Until recently, on-line gaming was only possible with computers via a connection to the Internet, but the new generation of video game consoles, such as Playstation II and Dreamcast also have on-line possibilities.

For the most part, computer games are designed to be played either as single player games, i.e., against the computer, or as multiplayer games, which means that you play against one or, usually, several human opponents via the Internet or a Local Area Network (LAN). In both cases, you play alone in front of the computer. Video games, on the other hand, are often designed to be played one-on-one, which means that there are at least two people in the same room doing the same thing. If you arrange a homemade tournament in, for example, hockey, which is a very popular kind of video game, as many people as desired can participate. Today, video games are being converted to PC-format, but this social way of playing is in the *nature* of video games, and original computer games are not designed in this way. This is probably related to the normal TV-viewing situation, which often is a social activity, whereas sitting in front of a computer is not (for one thing, you sit much closer to a computer, making it difficult and uncomfortable to be many). Paradoxically, even though you play computer games alone, sometimes the activity itself can be said to be much more social than video game playing because of the sheer number of people you communicate with during a multiplayer game over the Internet. Personal contact is often made through multiplayer gaming on the Internet, resulting in gaming clubs, among other things.

Game genres

The most accepted and well-known categorisation of game genres is probably the following:

- Action
- Strategy
- Adventure
- RPG (Role Playing Game)
- Sports
- Sim (Simulators)

Many of these genre names speak for themselves, like sports, strategy and simulators; others can be a bit unclear. Adventure games, for example, refers to a specific type of game where the main focus is on solving riddles and intellectual activity; this category does not refer to games only containing "adventure" in a broader sense.

These genres can be divided into more specialised sub-groups, but there will always be games that cannot readily be categorised into any of the major genres mentioned above. The action genre includes, by definition, the most "violent" games. By "most violent" is meant the amount of violent content, not necessarily the quality or explicitness of violence. Some of the most graphic violence can be found in "adult" adventure games like *Phantasmagoria*.

Action games

One of the most popular sub-genres of the action genre is "first person shooters". The name describes the perspective of the game. The action takes place from the player's point of view – as a player you see your own hands and the weapon you happen to wield at the time. Your surroundings and enemies take up the rest of the screen. Well-known titles are, among others, *Quake*, *Quake II* and *III*, *Unreal*, *Half-life* and *Kingpin*. All of the popular first person shooters have a distinct "animated" look. Animated does not mean that they are "childish", but that they can be compared to an advanced superhero comic with exaggerated proportions and movements. The animation has advanced lighting effects and even gives a certain illusion of realism. First person shooters are also distinguished by their extreme tempo, especially when played as a multiplayer game via the Internet or LAN. This means that the violence (however brutal) mainly flickers by and that lingering scenes of death or mutilation are extremely rare. The absence of slow deaths probably has little to do with the constructors' good taste; it is simply that such scenes would be an unacceptable hiatus in gameplay and would work against the essence of the game.

What is then the primary attraction of these games if it is not the violence itself? The attraction primarily lies in the challenge of overcoming difficult situations. The games are designed in such a way that they become more difficult the farther you advance in the game. As a player you will meet your death many times in situations that seem impossible the first time you experience them. As you try them repeatedly, you will become more accomplished and learn how to succeed in getting past them. The goal for the player is to move on and "beat" the game and its challenges. The attraction of first person shooters is essentially the same as the attraction of child-oriented games like *Donkey Kong 64* (where you shoot coconuts at your opponents) or *Super Mario Bros.* (where you have a vast arsenal of "funny" weapons and martial techniques), but with the added element of blood and guns. This added element, though apparent, could probably be compared to the difference between a *Roadrunner* or *Tom & Jerry* cartoon and a violent car chase movie like *Mad Max*. The former are aimed at children, the latter at adolescents and adults, but the violent content remains essentially the same albeit with differences in visualisation.

There are other sub-genres of the action genre. One violent and much-discussed genre is "fighting games". This term refers to games that exclude everything except the fighting (and violence) itself and that often have a martial arts backdrop of some sort. Well-known games of this kind are *Mortal Kombat* and its successors, the *Street Fighter* series, the *Killer Instinct* series, the *Tekken* series, and the *Virtua Fighter* series, among others. There are many differences between these games and first person shooters, the main ones being perhaps the perspective and playing situation. Instead of a first person perspective you have a third person perspective and the action often takes place in a single environment, as the action is restricted to the fight itself. These games are largely developed as video games meant for two players in a one-on-one situation. You can play them by yourself, too, but then you have to play against the "game", which is generally regarded as much less entertaining than playing against a human opponent. Whereas multiplayer is quite popular with first person shooters, there is little point in having a multiplayer "fighting game" due to the one-on-one nature of a "stand off" fight.

Gameplay in fighting games is simple: with different combinations of button pushing you kick, punch, and grapple with your opponent until there is a winner. Sometimes there are weapons available, never guns but sometimes swords, chains, sticks, and so on. There are variations in backgrounds and appearances of the opponents, but it is the fights themselves that supply the main attraction of these games. Because every fight is different and you are not dependent on a "story" (that can become irritatingly familiar in first person shooter games), the fighting games have a long life. The violence is largely illustrated in the style of "Kung Fu-, Karate-, Hong-Kong-" movies, with exaggerated sound effects, shouting and sprays of blood. Similar to first person shooters, they are also distinctly animated at this point in time – and they always have been, something that should be taken into consideration when discussing their absolute violent content.

Note

1. Christofferson, Jan (1999) *Monstermassakern* [The Monster Massacre]. Stockholm, Council on Media Violence, Ministry of Culture.

Video Game Violence and Aggression

A Review of Research

Mark Griffiths

One of the main concerns that has constantly been raised against video and computer games is that most of the games are claimed to feature aggressive elements. This has led some people to state that children become more aggressive after playing such games. However, these assertions have been made without the backup of empirical evidence. Despite the continuing controversy for over 15 years, there has been relatively little systematic research. The issue is ever more important because new games are using more explicit representations of extreme and realistic violence.

Theoretical concerns

Theoretically, video games might have the capacity to promote aggressive tendencies (as predicted by, among other theories, social learning theory) or to release aggressive tendencies (as predicted by catharsis theory). Put more simply, social learning theory (Bandura, 1986) would hypothesise that playing aggressive video games would lead to the stimulation of aggressive behaviour, i.e., children will imitate or in other ways learn what they see on screen. In direct contradiction to this, catharsis theory (Feshbach & Singer, 1971). would hypothesise that playing aggressive video games would have a relaxing effect by channelling latent aggression and therefore have a positive effect on a child's behaviour. The rest of this article briefly examines the growing body of research that has been carried out in order to put the debate into an empirical context.

Areas of research on video game violence

Self-report methods

The presence of increased aggression has been measured by self-report questionnaires in a number of studies (e.g., Lin & Lepper, 1987; Fling et al, 1992; Griffiths & Hunt, 1995). Many of the results are contradictory with some showing violent video games have a calming effect whereas others claim violent video games increase aggression and/or hostility scores. The problem with all questionnaire research is that correlational evidence is unconvincing not only because correlations may be due to backward causation (i.e., aggressive children may be drawn to video games rather than and/or in addition to their aggression being a result of this activity), but for the more plausible reason that the correlations may not be directly causal at all but may result from mediating factors (e.g., low educational attainment, low socio-economic status, etc.) that may themselves be causally related both to video game playing and to aggressive behaviour.

Experimental studies

There have been a number of experimental studies (e.g., Lynch, 1994; Scott, 1995;

Ballard & West, 1996) looking at the relationship between aggression and video game playing although a number of these studies use video games as an experimental paradigm to investigate other theoretical concerns. Only experimental studies can hope to provide persuasive evidence regarding causality. However, the laboratory studies to date have examined fantasy aggression rather than real aggression. This is somewhat irrelevant, and the increased aggression in the fantasy and role-play measures, far from confirming the hypothesis that games cause aggression, is entirely consistent with the catharsis hypothesis, i.e., it might be precisely the fantasy aggression that releases the energy that would otherwise be expressed as aggressive behaviour. Since laboratory studies cannot study serious aggressive behaviour for ethical reasons, what is required are naturalistic field experiments. However, such field experiments have been non-existent up to now in the field of video game research.

Observational studies

A number of studies have examined the differences in children's behaviour after playing an aggressive video game by observing the child's free play (e.g., Schutte et al, 1988; Irwin & Gross, 1995). These studies, all of which were carried out on young children, do seem to suggest that the playing of violent video games has the effect of increasing a child's aggressive behaviour – at least in the short term. It is possible that this particular methodology (i.e., the observational analysis of children's free play) may itself be contributing to the effect. For instance, the novelty of the play room with new toys (including those associated with aggression) may be played with more than if it was done in the child's own setting. Alternatively, this may be a genuine effect which mirrors research showing that young children imitate what they see on television as a common way of reacting and learning (behaviour which diminishes as they get older).

Other studies (projective tests, case studies)

Other studies have used a mixture of methodologies (self-report, experiment and observation) and have suggested that video games may have short-term beneficial effects for children (e.g., Graybill et al., 1987). These authors have concluded that their results tended to be more consistent with catharsis theory (i.e., the release of aggressive tendencies), that violent video games discharge aggressive impulses in a socially acceptable way and that playing violent video games may have a short-term beneficial effect for the children playing them. However, longer-term negative effects were not ruled out in any of these studies.

General concluding comments

All the studies that have examined the effects of video games on aggression have only involved measures of possible short-term aggressive consequences. The majority of the studies on very young children – as opposed to those in their teens upwards – tend to show that children do become more aggressive after either playing or watching a violent video game but all these studies were based on the observation of a child's free play after playing a violent video game. Such evidence suggests that at a theoretical level, there is more empirical evidence supporting social learning theory than catharsis theory – particularly in younger children. However, there is much speculation as to whether the procedures to measure aggression levels are methodologically valid and reliable.

There is also the very important question of developmental effects, i.e., do video games have the same effect regardless of age? It could well be the case – and is probably the case in reviewing the research evidence – that violent video games have a more pronounced effect in young children but less of an effect, if any, once they have reached their teenage years. There is no evidence that violent video games have any effect in adult behaviour (although it must be pointed out that there are very few studies using adult samples as most of the research has concentrated on children and adolescents).

Another important factor is the social context of playing, i.e., if playing in groups or individually, with or against each other may affect the results. The findings of some researchers (Anderson & Morrow, 1995) suggest that competitiveness increases aggression. There are also problems concerning the definition of "violent" or "aggressive" as there are numerous television cartoons such as *Tom and Jerry* which may not be regarded as violent within the operational definitions employed in mass media research. Since all video games are animated, the same argument might be used for them also. Research into the effects of long-term exposure to video games on subsequent aggressive behaviour is noticeably lacking and at present remains speculative.

References

Anderson, C.A. & Morrow, M. (1995). Competitive aggression without interaction: Effects of competitive versus cooperative instructions on aggressive behavior in video games. *Personality and Social Psychology Bulletin, 21,* 1020-1030.

Ballard, M.E. & West, J.R. (1996). The effects of violent videogame play on males' hostility and cardiovascular responding. *The Journal of Applied Social Psychology, 26*, 717-730.

Bandura, A. (1986). *Social Foundations of Thought and Action: A Social Cognitive Theory*. Englewood Cliffs, NJ: Prentice Hall.

Feshbach, S. & Singer, R.D. (1971). *Television and aggression: An experimental field study*. San Francisco, CA: Jossey-Bass.

Fling, S., Smith, L., Rodriguez, T., Thornton, D., Atkins, E. & Nixon, K. (1992). Video games, aggression, and self-esteem: A survey. *Social Behavior and Personality, 20,* 39-46.

Graybill, D., Strawniak, M., Hunter, T. & O'Leary, M. (1987). Effects of playing versus observing violent versus non-violent video games on children's aggression. *Psychology, A Quarterly Journal of Human Behavior, 24,* 1-7.

Griffiths, M.D. & Hunt, N. (1995). Computer game playing in adolescence: Prevalence and demographic indicators. *Journal of Community and Applied Social Psychology, 5,* 189-193.

Irwin, A.R. & Gross, A.M. (1995). Cognitive tempo, violent video games, and aggressive behavior. *Journal of Family Violence, 10,* 337-350.

Lin, S. & Lepper, M.R. (1987). Correlates of children's usage of video games and computers. *Journal of Applied Social Psychology, 17,* 72-93.

Lynch, P. (1994). Type A behaviour, hostility, and cardiovascular function at rest after playing video games in teenagers. *Psychosomatic Medicine, 56,* 152.

Schutte, N.S., Malouff, J.M., Post-Gorden, J.C. & Rodasta, A.L. (1988). Effects of playing video games on children's aggressive and other behaviors. *Journal of Applied Social Psychology, 18,* 454-460.

Scott, D. (1995). The effect of video games on feelings of aggression. *Journal of Psychology, 129* (2), 121-132.

Killing Time?

A Canadian Meditation on Video Game Culture

Stephen Kline

After an introduction noting the explosive growth in the video and computer games industry, this article reviews some international literature about possible harmful influences of video game play on children and young people, adding Canadian research findings from studies of the role of video games in adolescents' lives.

The coming out of interactive entertainment

As industry legend has it, the first video game *Space Wars* took a multi-million dollar, room size computer in the basement of M.I.T (Massachusetts Institute of Technology) to play. By applying the same cybernetic principles of 'feedback' – originally associated with automation and office technology – to children's entertainment, Steve Russell created an entirely new medium out of the TV screen. Because it demonstrated the novel possibility of using computers for fun, this innovation in computer programming has had a profound impact on contemporary children's culture around the world (Herz, 1997). Three decades after its invention, the video game industry it founded has become the fastest growing and most profitable children's entertainment business which earned an estimated $18 billion in the world (1998) for the corporations that manufacture, design and sell domestic computers, console game systems, Internet play sites, and gaming arcades. Given the scope of this industry, video gaming has also periodically been subjected to critical examination for its growing impact on children and youth.

It is important to realize that from the 1970's on, this industry's astounding growth arises from successive waves of innovation in technology and programming design. Home consoles like a Nintendo 64 (sold in 1996 for under $200 in Canada) pack more than 10 times the processing capacity of the original Pentium PCs. Industry sources claimed that by 1998, video games had already been incorporated into the daily routines of 65 percent of all US households, and 85 percent of those with male children. The recently release Sega Dreamcast is the first of a new generation of even more powerful processors which – when augmented by recent advances in 3D graphics chips, DVD (Digital Video Disc) storage devices and fast modems – means that future kids will be playing *Doom, Mortal Kombat* and *Final Fantasy* on extremely advanced consoles with computational speeds and graphics display chips exceeding those of most engineering workstations. This is why, in his book *Being Digital* (1995), Nicholas Negroponte of the M.I.T. media lab claimed that video games are the clearest indication how computers will be transforming the specter of human communication:

> We are not waiting on any invention. It is here. It is now. It is almost genetic in its nature, in that each generation will become more digital than the preceding one. The control bits of that digital future are more than ever before in the hands of the young. Nothing could make me happier. (Negroponte, 1995: 231)

Douglas Rushkoff in his book *Playing the Future* (1996) similarly writes optimistically about the effects of this new wave of interactive entertainment on youth:

> While their parents may condemn Nintendo as mindless and masturbatory, kids who have mastered video gaming early on stand a better chance of exploiting the real but mediated interactivity that will make itself available to them by the time they hit techno-puberty in their teens. (Rushkoff 1996: 31)

He quotes Timothy Leary to support his optimism about interactivity:

> The importance of the Nintendo phenomenon is about equal to that of the Gutenberg printing press. Here you had a new generation of kids who grew up knowing that they could change what's on the screen. (Rushkoff, 1996: 30)

To techno-enthusiasts like Rushkoff and Negroponte, video gaming is a perfect preparation for the high-tech cybernetic future that awaits the 'screenager': "The games he plays are simulated drives through the very real data networks he will access later on with his computer and modem. ... Thanks to video games, kids have a fundamentally different appreciation of the television image than their parents. ... Rather than simply receiving media they are changing images on the screen" (Rushkoff, 1996: 182). 'Screenagers' will attain a greater sense of agency and control in their ever changing lives, Rushkoff assures us, because they are learning to live with a changing digital environment. Or as Herz writes in her book *Joystick Nation* (1997):

> Video games are perfect training for life in fin de siècle America, where daily existence demands the ability to parse sixteen kinds of information being fired at you simultaneously... Kids weaned on video games are not attention-deficient, morally stunted, illiterate little zombies who massacre people en masse after playing too much *Mortal Kombat*. They're simply acclimated to a world that increasingly resembles some kind of arcade experience. (Herz 1997: 2-3)

Enthusiasm for digital technology has, thus, been forged into a promotional strategy for technologizing children's socialization in an 'information age'. Digital megacorps promise a pedagogical revolution of 'interactive multimedia' proportionate to their own stake in the 'digital economy':

> Multimedia has the potential to revolutionize certain aspects of how educators manage education... TV in its time was going to do the same thing. They didn't because they couldn't. Unlike these earlier technologies, multimedia is interactive. It has the ability therefore to replicate some teacher/learner interaction. It also has the ability to link the student with tutors, his or her peers in other places, and with remote sources of information. (Henry & McLennan, 1994: 3)

To today's youths, *Commander Keen* and *Crash Bandicoot* are as familiar as *Mickey Mouse* and *Ninja Turtles* were in previous generations, reflecting the current corporate repositioning around the digital channels of communication distribution. The $100 million launch of the Sega Dreamcast in North America in 1999 reminds us that the video game industry is becoming the most active and dynamic merchandisers of entertainment products to the young with promotional budgets exceeding those of the toy or movie industries. Digital entertainment has already won 30 percent of the US playthings market, earning $8.8 billion in the US (1998) – winning an increasing share of entertainment spending – larger than the Hollywood box-office gross ($5.2 billion) and ten times the amount spent on the production of children's television (Haynes & Dinsey, 1995).

Digitalization has extended the capacities of the global media industries by adding interactivity to television. And with the increasing push of global marketing campaigns video game culture has been developing a similar loyal following around the world – mostly young and male, who prefer interacting with avatars in cyberspace to 'vegging-out' in front of the television, hanging around with friends, or playing street sports. Recent studies of children's media use have documented that a global 'gamer' culture focused on digital adventure is taking shape around interactive entertainment technologies (Livingstone et al., 1999). Indeed, just as contemporary parents were becoming accustomed to their kids spending close to three hours a day with television – much of it violent – the video game came along and began changing the contours of children's leisure. While technophiles like Negroponte celebrate this new digital youth culture as empowering, parents, teachers, and researchers remain concerned about what the growth of interactive entertainment media means for their kids. The comparisons of video games with television are obvious, because the interactive entertainment industry emerged at the point of convergence of the twentieth century's two most important communication technologies – the computer and television. Moreover, as Eugene Provenzo (1991) notes, this hybrid technology is a new medium, which fuses TV's *spectatorship* with cybernetic *play control*. This is why Provenzo wrote in his examination of this industry, that the real significance of video game technology for contemporary childhood is that:

> It represents the first stages in the creation of a new type of television – an interactive medium as different from traditional television as television is from radio. The remaining years of this decade will see the emergence and definition of this new medium form in much the same way the late 1940's and early 1950's saw television emerge as a powerful social and cultural force. (Provenzo, 1991: 105)

The video game industry is a hybrid because it not only cultivates new uses of interactive technology, but is also a unique "entertainment experience". This experience has already changed how many kids allocate and spend their leisure time. And children's attachment to this hybrid medium is confusing – at least to parents – because although the computer chips makes technology more "dynamic" and "engaging", the contents and themes of these games and entertainment appear to be extensions of escapist TV fare at its worst. A quick look at *Messiah*, *Resident Evil II* or *Splatterhouse* will leave anyone wondering whether we really have transcended the age of television in this new digital playground, when so much of the contents promote testosterone fantasy and grotesquely cartooned violence. Noting that the largest single target audience will no doubt be children, Provenzo (1991) worries that the video game industry is simply extending the troubled TV culture of the past:

> If the video game industry is going to provide the foundation for the development of interactive television, then concerned parents and educators have cause for considerable alarm. During the past decade, the video game industry has developed games whose social content has been overwhelmingly violent, sexist, and even racist. (Provenzo, 1991: 105)

There can be no doubt that this 'hybrid' technology is poised to change the way children play and learn. Yet media analysts are only beginning to understand the implications of 'interactivity' for how children use and respond to the screen.

Technophobes like Neil Postman (1993) have already warned that the emergence of interactive or computerized communication technologies possesses a serious threat to children's culture: "A new technology does not add or subtract something. It changes everything" (Postman, 1993: 18). He goes on to state his opposition to interactive media, which like television he sees "breaking a four-hundred year old truce between gregariousness and openness fostered by orality and the introspection and isolation fostered by the printed word". He continues:

> Stated in the most dramatic terms, the accusation can be made that the uncontrolled growth of technology destroys the vital sources of our humanity. It creates a culture without a moral foundation. It undermines certain mental processes and social relations that make human life worth living. (Postman 1993: xiii)

Postman's opposition, it turns out, is based less on his concerns about interactivity than about the way it will be used:

> Surrounding every technology are institutions whose organization – not to mention their reason for being – reflects the world view promoted by the technology. Therefore when a technology is assaulted by a new one, institutions are threatened. When institutions are threatened, a culture finds itself in crisis. (Postman 1993: 19)

Postman believes that our literate culture is in crisis because we have left this powerful new medium in the hands of the entertainment industry that has failed to develop new media in a way that is beneficial and helpful to children.

Whether we agree with the technological optimists or pessimists about the consequences of digitalization, as media researchers it is clearly time we realized that our children's popular entertainment is becoming increasingly confusing to us. As cultural critic Allucquère Rosanne Stone (1995) recently observed:

> There seems no question that a significant proportion of young people will spend a significant and increasing proportion of their waking-hours playing computer based games. ... It is entirely possible that computer-based games will turn out to be the major unacknowledged source of socialization and education in industrialized countries before the 1990's have run their course. (Stone, 1995: 26-27)

Yet, despite its ascent as the fastest growing and most profitable entertainment industry, there is remarkably little commentary on the development and acceptance of this new medium, on the range of games and their ratings, let alone studies of their impact on children's socialization and growth. Stone argues that we have very little understanding of the unique features of virtual presence and interactivity that make video gaming a unique cultural experience, comparing our ignorance about this medium "to holding a cocktail party in a house that is already ablaze".

A house ablaze? What the research says

Stone is right. Compared with television, academic research on the impact of video games on young people amounts to little more than cocktail party chit-chat. Reviewing this literature one finds that there are almost as many reviews as there are original studies on the question of video games and aggression in youth. The 'moral panic' concerning the teen arcade culture of the late 1970's and early 1980's has been quelled by such repeated assurances that computerized play is empowering the digital generation, because these technologies provide opportunities for exploring, learning, developing eye-hand coordination and connecting with diverse sources of information (Greenfield & Cocking, 1996). Moreover, much of the supportive research has been undertaken in the context of schools' use of educational video games (Greenfield, 1984; Kafai, 1995) with little regard for the growth of arcade and domestic video game cultures which are arising in young males (Funk, 1993).

There does exist a small and slowly growing body of evidence concerning the potential negative effects of video games and the question of violence and addiction. Subsuming Albert Bandura's (1986) social learning paradigm, most is focused on whether the interactivity and realism of video games are likely to intensify identification with and modeling of violent behaviors.

Durkin's (1995) review of these early studies for the Australian Office of Film and Literature Classification acknowledges that, like television violence, violence in interactive entertainment is of concern. There are a few studies which demonstrate the possibility of social learning from video games, he finds, but this constitutes very limited evidence concerning the causation of aggressiveness: "Evidence does not lend strong support to the suggestion that computer game play promotes aggression in children." Overall he concludes: "Although the research is not exhaustive and by no means conclusive, it indicates that the stronger negative claims are not supported. Computer games have not led to the development of a generation of isolated, antisocial, compulsive computer users with strong propensities for aggression. To the contrary, some evidence indicates that there may be cognitive and perceptual-motor skill gains as a result of computer game practice… and reviving patterns of family togetherness in leisure" (Durkin 1995: 71).

Durkin notes two reasons why video game play may not result in violent behavior in kids: Firstly, by age 8 most kids understand the 'virtual' nature of video games and therefore the aggressive behaviors enacted in video games are playful and cognitively distinct from real aggressive behaviors in daily conflicts or interactions. One of the key problems in attempts to compare the effects of television violence and that of video game play is the difference between playing and watching. He points out that identification is a complex process that has been scarcely studied in relationship to computer game play, especially in respect of aggressive content. Secondly, many heavy players report that they enjoy the experience of conflict and competition – since playing makes them happy and relaxed rather than angry and hostile it is not likely to result in aggression.

In their more recent contribution to this Clearinghouse's Yearbook 1998 Durkin and Low note that problems in research methods makes it difficult to draw any conclusions on video games contribution to violent behavior: "There were only a small number of studies and these had yielded weak or inconsistent findings" (Durkin & Low, 1998: 111). In this overview of Australian and New Zealand research they note that the limitations in design and measurement of effects are serious. Even more recent studies in Australia reveal that "aggressive responses are not an inevitable consequence of playing video games" (ibid.: 112) because studies often confuse conflict with aggression, and hostile feelings with aggressive behavior. Durkin and Low note that laboratory studies of effects are especially inconsistent in their results. Moreover, as in television research generally, correlations between judged aggressiveness and time spent playing video games are confounded by interpretations of causal direction. Durkin and Low also point out that most of the original research into the effects utilized earlier gaming technologies whose graphic capacity and game control bear little resemblance to the current and coming generations of young gamers.

Dill and Dill (1998) in their review of the literature weigh the evidence similarly: "Overall the majority of investigations have supported the predicted relationship between violent video game or violent virtual reality play and increases in aggression or aggression related outcomes… two studies show decreased pro-social behavior as a function of violent video game play" (Dill & Dill, 1998: 409). These two researchers have noted that only four studies have used the 'current generation of video games' (i.e., recognizing the important changes in the graphic qualities and design of the new 64 bit video game systems) and of these three did show effects on "aggressive behavior, hostility or aggressive thoughts". So they conclude: "The preponderance of the evidence from the existing literature suggests that exposure to video game violence increases aggressive behavior and other aggression-related phenomena. However, the paucity of empirical data coupled with a variety of methodological problems and inconsistencies in these data, clearly demonstrate the need for additional research" (ibid.: 410).

Dill and Dill go on to cite the same reservations about this research as Durkin and Low (1998): "Precious few true experiments have been done to assess the effects of playing violent video games on aggression-related outcomes; too much has focused on very young children and used aggressive free play" and the studies of "aggressive affect studies often uses undergraduates". Moreover there is a failure to deal with the gender differences cogently, and to properly theorize the aggression effect or distinguish between hostile feelings, aggressive thoughts or fantasies, and behavior. They conclude that "there are a number of methodological problems in this literature, the majority of which were in efforts that found no differences or that failed to support their own hypotheses" (Dill & Dill, 1998: 420).

Dill and Dill see the need for a more sophisticated theorization of the effects of media – one which might better accommodate the growing diversity and realism of contemporary video games, the sophistication of our understanding of social learning, the gender and other individual differences that lead to susceptibility, and other external factors that mediate the processes of aggressiveness. Dill and Dill note the growing complexity in the theorization of TV violence, arguing: "A similar relationship should exist because the same conceptual variables are involved. Specifically, video game violence effects should operate through elaboration and priming of aggressive thought networks, weakening of inhibitions against antisocial behavior, modeling, reinforcement, decreased empathy for others and the creation of a more violent world view" as well as the possibility of catharsis and arousal effects (ibid.: 409).

They go on to note, following Huesmann's theory, that playing violent games may prime in two ways: 1) by either exposing children to aggression which "can trigger related feeling and can bring to mind knowledge of aggression-related skills, memories and beliefs" or 2) by exposing children to aggression which "weakens inhibitions against engaging in aggressive behavior…

changing individual perception of what is normal or acceptable behavior". Noting that the video games generally "reward" violent responses as opposed to other means of solving problems, they argue this may lead children to "chose aggressive responses to conflict situations in their own lives". Dill and Dill also note that the increasing realism in the games is of consequence, because the similarity of aggressive clues "most particularly the weapons, and moves used in fighting can be translated into real life". They state: "The child playing an aggressive video game may learn that hitting or even shooting another person is the appropriate response in a conflict situation and that this type of aggression is likely to be reinforced" (ibid.: 410).

These two researchers also mean that the active participation of video game play where players choose and then manipulate characters from first person point of view, may accentuate the identification with his aggressor: "Identification with the video game character may be stronger than identification with television or movie characters, in part because players choose a character and play the character's role in the video game scenario" (ibid.: 413). For this reason desensitization effects may be accentuated. They point out that empathy has been found to be lower among known aggressors than non-aggressive persons. The degree that plots justify the aggression also plays a role, that is, if violent video games depict victims as deserving attacks, and if these video games tend to portray other humans as targets, then reduced empathy is likely to be a consequence of violent video game play. Dill and Dill observe that many of the problems in these studies arise from limited theorization of the differences between video game play and television watching.

Three general issues arise from this literature: the difference between watching TV and playing video games; the need for new research that recognizes that video games have dramatically changed; and a need for an expanded theory of how playing aggressive games may have long-term effects on children.

Funk et al. (1999), reviewing the body of literature, note the positive health, educational and therapeutic implications of video games, stating that "edutainment is one of the most positive applications of electronic games, but one whose impact has yet to be demonstrated through longitudinal research" (Funk et al. 1999: 117). They go on to say that many are more concerned about violent video games than films because "on a theoretical basis playing violent electronic games may influence behavior through observational learning, practice and reinforcement... The critical dimension of active participation may increase the impact of electronic games relative to time spent" (ibid.: 120-121). They find that surveys have identified various negative correlations between playing electronic games and various target measures, such as aggression and self-concept, yet these results are correlational and do not at this point establish causality. As a whole, however, laboratory and survey results suggest that game-playing, particularly playing violent games, "may not be entirely benign for all players" (ibid.: 124). These authors have also observed there is consistent evidence of gender differences in use of and response to video games, as well as in aggressive predisposition, which create problems for generalizing the effects of playing violent video games.

As in the TV violence issue, the confounding of aggressive predisposition with preferences for aggressive entertainment makes it hard to explain both correlations between playing violent video games and real violence or its absence. As Dill and Dill (1998) note, the correlation between aggressiveness and video game play 1) might have a social learning explanation – video games cause aggression (or its absence indicates catharsis); 2) might have a disposition explanation – aggressive disposition leads to preference for more violent video game play; or 3) might relate to an underlying factor (e.g., low self esteem, social isolation) which leads to both aggressiveness and video game play.

So the same problem of interpreting survey studies is endemic in this literature, too, because correlations cannot reveal the causal relations between gender, amount of violent play, and aggressiveness or hostility that researchers measure. And this is of concern because the 'experience' of those simulated conflict situations seems to be crucial to the mood altering qualities of the play experience that male gamers seek and that young females avoid (Kubey, 1996; Goldstein, 1998). As Goldstein and Jukes (1993) have noted, there is strong evidence that boys develop a preference for aggressive toys and games and that this is related to arousal levels and chronic aggressiveness. Highly aggressive boys find war toys more appealing than other toys – and prefer violent sports films and video games and television programs (Goldsten, 1998). "Both war and war play may reflect the prevailing values of the cultures in which they flourish, values that stress aggression, assertion and dominance" (ibid.: 67). Given the consistent evidence of gender differences in both aggressiveness and play preferences, correlations are theoretically problematic for media effects surveys, Goldstein points out, because it confuses issues of male aggressiveness and male entertainment preferences with those of media effects. Commenting on the evidence of a relationship between aggressive play and war in children, he notes: "The reasoning underlying this research is that exposure to violence activates aggressive associations and images. These in turn heighten the preference for further exposure to violence" (ibid.: 59).

Goldstein argues that it is crucial to understand why and how young males develop their preferences for violent entertainment generally. Real violence is different from play violence, he says, because there is the absence of intent to hurt another. Entertainment violence is consumed for distraction and mood management, to increase excitement and arousal, and to express emotions. Goldstein believes therefore that we must differentiate between violence experienced for its own sake and violence experienced as play and entertainment. He underlines that individuals differ in their need for excitement and tolerance for stimulation; those with a moderately high need for sensation find portrayals of violence more enjoyable than those with a lesser need. He cites a number of studies that reveal that enjoyment is the male response to violent entertainment, not hostility. And in order to experience anything like pleasure from exposure to violent or threatening images, the audience must feel relatively safe and secure in their surroundings. Furthermore, there must be cues that the violent images are produced for purposes of entertainment and consumption. In relation to video game violence he believes that interactivity may make video games seem less violent than similar images in film; since "video gamers have more control over the images, perhaps the effects of violent images are reduced" (ibid.: 60). The implications of this are that we need to better understand the developmental processes through which simulated aggressiveness is socialized and turned into a form of pleasure for males.

Griffiths (1999), who also has reviewed the research literature on video and computer games, recently concluded: "The one consistent finding is that the majority of the studies on very young children – as opposed to those in their teens upwards – tend to show that children do become more aggressive after either playing or watching a violent video game" (Griffiths, 1999: 210) but all the evidence is based on one research method observing children's free play. In this sense claims about aggression effects are based on observations of energized conflict play. Griffiths is scathing on the design and measurement issues, arguing that all the published studies on video game violence have methodological problems and that they only include possible short-term measures of aggressive consequences. Differentiating between the modeling and catharsis explanations is especially difficult in correlational studies using self-report measures of hostility, he notes, and because subjects vary in their predisposition to aggressiveness.

He argues that not all video games are violent or aggressive in the same way. There is confusion in the literature between cartoon-like violence and more realistic games (as in TV shows) and also between competitive hostility (sports or racing) and aggressive contest (fighting, shooting). There is therefore "a need for a general taxonomy of video games as it could be the case that particular games have very positive effects while other types are not so positive" (Griffiths, 1999: 210). He goes on to conclude that the question of whether video games promote aggressiveness cannot be answered for the present because the available literature is relatively sparse and conflicting, and there are many different types of video games which probably have different effects. He notes that it is evident that video games can have both positive and negative aspects. If care is taken in the design, and if games are put in the right context, they have the potential to be used as training aids in classrooms and therapeutic settings – and to provide skills in psychomotor coordination in simulations of real life events, for example, training recruits for the armed forces.

Video games as military training?

Bathed in a maniacal aggressiveness, filled with a postmodern cynicism and urging a new tribalism of virtual comradery, the contemporary multimedia entertainment industries have once again caught the eye of the popular press precisely because, as Griffiths notes, they are effective in training recruits to the armed forces. Unfortunately it was a series of school shootings in Paducah, Jonesboro and Littleton, in the USA, and in Tabart Alberta, Canada, that once again catapulted the long simmering debates about North America's media industry's contribution to the 'cultures of violence' into the public limelight, when some avid gamers on the fringe of their schools' social life exacted vengeance on their peers with well planned and executed shootings. Perhaps not coincidentally, Jonesboro was also the place where Dave Grossman, author of *On Killing* (1996), had retired. Grossman was a lieutenant colonel who had devoted his career to figuring out how to train soldiers to kill. Recently he has become a leading US critic of the interactive entertainment industry, arguing that the main concern is that these violent video games are providing military quality training to children (Grossman & DeGaetano, 1999).

Grossman's arguments are helpful in broadening our understanding of how video games influence kids. As a retired US army officer, he is well positioned to comment on the similarity between the tactics used in the army to train soldiers and the use of violent video games among children today. The US military has long used simulation training for its soldiers because the "repetition and desensitization" of simulated killing effect kill rates (the actual percentage of soldiers that will pull the trigger in real life combat). Grossman has trained elite fighting soldiers and police officers how to kill, by adapting fighting simulations for training purposes. What he found was that by eliminating the blood, gore and emotions of the 'victims' on the computer screen, the soldiers begin to treat their training as more of a game. According to Grossman, the soldier's training is designed to be both practical and psychological. Simulation training enhances familiarity and physical skills with weapons while decreasing the soldiers' empathy towards their enemies. By firing at the computer-simulated images of enemies who die without blood and gore, the fighting simulation can sharpen the marksmanship of these soldiers at the same time as it trains them to see enemies as targets rather than humans. In desensitizing the soldier to the act of killing, the trainee becomes more capable of actually pulling the trigger effectively (Discovery Channel, 1999). It also shifts researchers' attention to the cognitive and emotional mechanisms by which violence is disinhibited.

Like the training of these soldiers, Grossman believes that violent video games may have a similar effect on young people who play them a lot because they help break down the psychological barriers that prevent killing: "Children don't naturally kill; they learn it from violence in the home and… from violence as entertainment in television, movies and interactive video games" (Grossman, 1998). Like in the army, the repeated shooting at targets in the video games may not only enhance weapons skills, but also desensitize some young people to the horror of killing by turning enemies into targets. Like the soldiers, with constant practice players of violent video games will eventually have extremely low or even no empathy towards victims of violence. The engagement process from video games will decrease the players' empathy and negative reaction towards violent acts. The disturbing blend of participation, engagement, rewards and practice that video games encourage, is a perfect instructional environment. One of the central thrusts of Grossman's argument is that we see the rise of violent video gaming as more of a concern than violence in movies and on television. In other words, aggression training is more effective to the degree it is experienced as not really violent – even pleasurable and enjoyable – which is the case for most gamers.

Video game research in Canada

In Canada research on anti-social and aggressive implications of the emerging video game industry is far outweighed by the massive promotional investment justifying the next generation of multimedia, and research facilitating their incorporation into schools (CANARIE project). The Canadian government prides itself on wiring children into the digital future, and on cooperating with private media corporations to link classrooms through the Internet, although evidence of educational benefits and efficiencies from such investment is scarce. So although projects supporting the use of interactive media in schools are plentiful in Canada, there is remarkably little research into the negative implications of video games.

In a recent review of the extant literature Canadian psychiatrist Craig Emes (1997) examines the thirteen outstanding US studies concluding that aggressive behavior may result from playing video games among younger children. As he notes, the evidence confirms that, like TV, video game research reveals that a majority of these studies showed that especially young children become more aggressive after either playing or watching violent video games. Yet, as he goes on to point out, like the TV violence literature, there are contradictory finds and the reliability and validity of the procedures used to measure aggression levels are questionable. And research into the long-term effects of video game playing is lacking.

Given the limited data, Emes believes that video games have some adverse effects based on the scientific weight of evidence: 1) the physiologic response of playing video games is similar to mild intensity exercise but not aerobic for fitness; 2) issues of seizures in susceptible children; 3) many children do become aggressive after playing but not consistently so. But at the same time he finds that studies concerning the generalizability of these effects are questionable. Emes also feels there is no support for arguments concerning psychopathology associated with video game play, or clear causal relationship to academic performance. But there is some indication, he finds, that video games may be also valuable learning tools and useful for job training and management of mental illness. Like most other reviewers of this very limited literature, Emes calls for more and better research, particularly on the long-term effects of heavy video game play.

Arcade play

Since the arcade craze of the late 1970's and early 1980's, public concern about what excessive video game play did to children has from time to time piqued the public interest (Brody, 1992). Braun and Giroux (1989) were among the early researchers to explore interactive media naturalistically, observing young people's play in eighteen Montreal arcades to assess the social issues presented by interactive media. They note, given the growth of the industry, that parents, school teachers, school administrators and legislators are confronted with the challenge of making well-informed decisions regarding whether, or the extent to which, youngsters will be allowed access to video games, and also regarding control of the video game industry. They lay out the arguments both for and against video gaming, pointing out that the proponents argue that video games are rich in tasks that demand perceptual, motor and cognitive skills which imply psychological enrichment and skilling from playing. They also point out that the critics claim: potential addictiveness of video games; the preponderance of male players; the potential isolation of this play form; the promotion of competitive values; as well as the 'antisocial and aggressive content' of the games.

In an observational "proxemic" study of arcade play they find strong evidence 1) that the most played games are dynamic and intensely engaging; 2) that players and themes are disproportionately male; 3) that players are mostly solitary; 4) that games are never cooperative and mostly sequentially competitive; and 5) that 80 percent of the game play is with violent and aggressive themes (war 35%, sport 20%, adventure 15%, crime 10%).

On observing players in the eighteen arcades they conclude that video game play is a social occasion or point of congregation for adolescents and "there is reason to believe that skill acquisition and generalization, which have been demonstrated to occur on a small scale, may underestimate the benefits of video game play" (Braun & Giroux, 1989: 101). But they note that their data also warns that "we, the public, should be critical of arcade video games and attempt to exert some control on children's access to these games and on the video game industry". Their study supports the arguments that "reinforcement theory has been applied to the letter by video game designers" and that the "reinforcement parameters" of video games "represent the perfect paradigm for induction of 'addictive' behavior"; "there does not seem to be a safe arcade video game in this respect, at least not among the most popular ones" (ibid.: 103). They go on to comment that "it seems unfortunate, however, that microcomputers have not been used more to promote pro-social or cooperative behavior among youth" and this might especially encourage more female players. Moreover "the extreme saturation of arcade video games by violent content is to be deplored". They conclude that "more public concern about and awareness of, the video arcade phenomenon might also in turn influence legislators and decision makers in and around the industry to intervene in favor of improving the quality of life of youth, with regard to video arcades" (ibid.: 104).

Video game play and gambling

Gupta and Deverensky (1996), noting the high incidence of gambling among school children, argue that video games and gambling activities have similar attractive features and intermittent reinforcement schedules which may lead to a relationship between them. Since gambling has been associated with "criminal involvement, delinquency, truancy and poor academic achievement" it was important to understand this relationship. "Like gambling, video games are reinforcing because they sharpen the contingencies of winning and losing", they argue. Video games and games of chance share several properties: "Both are exciting, contain elements of randomness and operate on schedules of intermittent reinforcement." They argue that "if the compulsive behaviors of gamblers and video game players are the result of similar mechanisms of reinforcement, then one might hypothesize that sophisticated video game players will transfer their relentless effort to exert control in a video game over to a gambling situation" (Gupta & Deverensky, 1996: 380).

Their study had 104 children aged 9-14 fill out a questionnaire, exploring issues related to video game playing and gambling behavior, respectively; subsequently they observed the youths as they played a computerized blackjack game. Surprisingly, 70 percent of the sample had gambled, and 53 percent gamble at least once a week. Frequent video game players are more likely to see themselves as skillful, go to arcades, and gamble more – but males disproportionately so. 55 percent of female video game players also gamble once a week, compared to 10 percent of the infrequent video game players. Motivations for gambling are also largely the same as for gaming, such as enjoyment, excitement and pass time. It turned out that males report more excitement than females. Moreover, gamblers find video games more exciting than non-gamblers. And frequent video game players wagered more money in the blackjack game, although there was no difference in their gross winnings. Males also exhibited greater risk taking tendencies on the blackjack task than females.

The findings generally suggest that frequent video game players gamble more, report that gambling makes them feel more important, and take greater risks on the blackjack gambling task than infrequent video game players, although no overall differences in success were found. However, Gupta and Deverensky state that although the relationship between video gaming and gambling is significant, it still remains unclear whether experience with video games leads one to gamble, or whether both activities attract the same children due to their shared properties. They go on to note that it is plausible that the widespread gambling behavior noted in Canadian youth is related to the rise of video game arcades.

Gupta and Deverensky base their conclusions on the similarities between the reward structures of video gaming and gambling: "Sporadic reinforcement schedules, excitement while playing, and an atmosphere of risk are important aspects of video gaming as they are of gambling and other addictions." They also note that although the majority of the youths see video games as more skill driven than luck driven, many (especially gamers) also see gambling as requiring skill (56%). Playing video games involves a progression through induction of rules and skilling of coordination, such that "child establishes a sense of mastery as randomness turns into order" (ibid.: 380); "games lead to continually and sometimes compulsively attempt to improve one's performance" (ibid.: 379). It is possible therefore that, as in video games, a "false belief in control" leads the youthful gambler mistakenly "to establish a sense of master while playing" the blackjack game. For high video game players, "their tendency to wager more could be viewed as an indication of a false sense of security and confidence that they are exerting control over the gambling situation. This illusion of control suggests that the players' cognitions may be driven by the intermittent schedule of reinforcement in the game similar to those found in video games. ... they believe that reinforcement has something to do with their ability to control outcomes... It appears as though they get so caught up on the excitement of the game (physiological arousal) that their ability to think rationally is lost" (ibid.: 380).

A new generation of video games...

Kline (1996) has noted researchers must understand the tremendous growth and sophistication of design within the video game industry. Early studies of video game 'effects' involving *Pac Man*, *Space Invaders* and even racing games are so primitive that few researchers now consider them relevant to today's much more realistic, more dynamic and much more 'violent' games. As Herz (1997) also notes, games like *Street Fighter* and *Mortal Kombat* are generations away from those designed in the 1980's. They have catapulted from total abstraction to full frontal gore and realism. Games like *Syphon Filter* (a recent top 10 selling game for the Playstation) captures the essence:

> The action unfolds with heated non-stop gunfire... a conspiracy that deepens as the bodycount rises. Plunge into this suspenseful thriller where enemies are taken on in a hail of bullets or taken out with a stealthy click of the silencer's trigger.

Kline (1997) argued a new generation of video games has emerged as game designers learned to target their primary audience of male aficionados with more intensely engaging game experiences. From interviews with game designers he notices how they focused on producing games with good graphics, lots of action, and play control that increased immersion and intensity of the play experience. The new action adventure meta-genre often combines elements of conflict, including combat, with other forms of competition and problem solving. For example, racing and sports games that involve fighting scenes (*Road Rage, NHL Hockey*), or Role Play Games that include shooting, combat and war (*Age of Empires, Golden Eye*), or action adventure meta-genre which can blend several aspects of game play (strategy, fighting, mastery, etc.), all have become the leading sellers for both home computers and console games in North America. Games like *Golden Eye* in which the player gets to be James

Bond in the movie also has ensured realism so that where you shoot the approaching enemy soldiers (knee or shoulder) they die differently. And it is the specter of the evolving game systems and emerging game genres that use first person point of view to situate an imaginary player within a simulated brutal environment, that has drawn the attention of US senators and regulators.

... provides a dramatic focus of excitement

Noting the historical shift of popular arcade games to the home systems taking place in the early 1990's with the successful promotion of Nintendo and Sega 16 bit systems, de Waal (1995) states that "within the technological cycle of obsolescence and new technology there remains a continuous stream of development. The primary male audience and the violent games they enjoy are continually developed, moving from one video game platform to another" (de Waal, 1995: 95). De Waal predicts that games will continue to become more violent: "The violent characteristic of video games is likely to remain due to structural industry constraints. New game platforms are in development to create even more realistic three-dimensional fighting games patterned on the concept of the *Mortal Kombat* type game. The industry has found a solid money-generating machine in the fighting game. As my study demonstrated, these violent games provide a dramatic focus of excitement for the player" (ibid.: 118).

De Waal undertook a study of the physiological responses of 28 players while playing a violent game *(Mortal Kombat)* and an adventure game *(Bubsy)*, using the ICARUS© system to simultaneously monitor blood flow (BF), heart rate (HR), eye muscle tension (EMG), and galvanic skin responses (GSR) of two youths alternating between playing and watching each game in sessions of up to 10 minutes. Through a video record of the sessions, de Waal was able to monitor social interaction between them, as well as construct a time-based record of game events (kills, mistakes, etc.). He also pre-interviewed his subjects, asking them about their play histories and play preferences, as well as questioning them about their play experiences after the sessions. The factorial design allowed de Waal to compare violent and non-violent play experiences, and different subjects playing and watching the same game.

This study demonstrates potentially different physiological response to video games between male and female subjects whose heart rate readings were consistently and significantly higher than those of their male counterparts – but differed between playing and watching only for the violent game (Table 1). Heart rate measures provided the clearest evidence that playing was more exciting than watching for all male subjects across games, and that playing and watching violent games is more arousing than playing and watching adventure games. Moreover males were relatively less excited by the violent games than females. The GSR readings only reflected a gender difference when playing *Mortal Kombat*.

Table 1. Heart rate while playing and watching the video games *Mortal Kombat* and *Bubsy*, respectively, by gender

		Playing video games	Watching video games
Boys	*Mortal Kombat*	121	87.5
	Bubsy	102	90
Girls	*Mortal Kombat*	157	135
	Bubsy	120	118
Total	*Mortal Kombat*	126	93
	Bubsy	105	94

Source: de Waal, 1995.

De Waal states that the study clearly shows that video game players are experiencing significantly different levels of excitement and arousal between playing and watching conditions. This would suggest that the content of the video game is secondary to the interactivity. However, players' reactions to the two different games were almost identical when watching, yet quite different when playing, so one is forced to re-examine the role of content in interactive media. Noting his subjects expressed a general excitement and desire to play with friends whenever possible, de Waal suggests the next research step would be to compare the physiological reaction of solitary play to multi-player play. He goes on to note that kills were rarely mentioned as motivational: Score was not a motivating factor to play. Players expressed advancing in levels, solving problems and life left as the primary forms of gauging their progress through a game. These factors, not kill score, provided motivation and desire to continue playing. Once a player passes all the levels of a game, their interest and motivation to play disappears or is sharply reduced unless a game that can produce the same emotional intensity is discovered. The de Waal study then indicates that both the symbolic structure of conflict and the challenge of violent games are crucial to the pleasure of the play experience.

Interestingly, those who played violent games more frequently and liked them more, were relatively less aroused when playing the violent video game *Mortal Kombat*. Interviews also revealed that the same intensity that makes the gamer want more violent games, can also be experienced as frustrating and overwhelming by female players or those less skilled or habituated to such intense experiences. The girls seemed to have more trouble experiencing the intense emotional fighting games as pleasurable especially, possibly because they were less habituated to the excitement and possibly because they were less good at them. Overall, however, the implications of this finding are consonant with an emotional desensitization effect and also suggest that there is greater need to understand why heavy gamers play them and how they experience the various representations of conflict and fighting.

Kline (1997) notes that interactivity has also enabled game designers to 'narrativize' the conflict situation and context with more complex and vivid lifelike graphics, more complete character backstories, and by adding elements of voice and character construction from Role Play Games. The implications of this new narrativity make game play less like solving puzzles and more like a participatory experience in a conflict situation. Video games are not just about representation of conflict as much as about experiencing it. Immersion defines the paradoxical quality of gaming experience in which realism is heightened by disbelief – a perception which Herz (1997) argues arises from a kind of social contract in which as a player "you have accepted the designers values and assumptions, at least for the duration of the game. ... Once you're in the game, you've agreed to let someone else define the parameters" (Herz, 1997: 223). Kline notes that the latest generation of games have seen new qualities of immersion which arise from designs that allow players the illusion of reality through navigation, choice of characters, settings and point of view, all of which strengthen role-taking and identification.

Video games in the lives of Canadian youth

The general ascendance of video game media has not therefore been widely acknowledged or studied in Canada either, compared with that on television violence and the V-chip. In spite of the continuing Canadian debate about violence in media, only a very few researchers have investigated domestic and arcade play at all. This is surprising, given the extensive exposure of Canadian children to this medium. With 80 percent of households with children having some sort of game system for console or computer (40% of Canadian households have computers, 20% access to the Internet), the video game appears to be by far the more important communication medium, rivaling television in its acceptance into children's lives. More importantly, as home use of computer studies show, gaming is a significant use of computers, especially among young males 10 and over (MediaMetrix, 2000). Rather than booking hotel rooms, doing homework, or reading news, this wired generation of Canadian young males, just like their US counterparts, prefer playing *Doom* and *Quake* online or off.

Kline (1997) argues therefore, that the heavy promotion of digital technologies, the web, and computers have lead many parents to see all interactive media as educational or benign. He concludes that, in the light of promotional publicity surrounding computers, it is not surprising that many parents adopt an uncritical attitude towards video game play which they see as emphasizing computer literacy. Less than 25 percent of the teens had experienced restrictions from their families with regard to video games, whereas 43 percent had television restrictions. Most of those restrictions were concerned with homework, or the lateness and duration of the play, rather than the content of the games, and heavy players were no more likely to experience censorship than light players. Kline notes that like US and Australian parents (Sneed & Runco, 1992; Cupitt & Stockbridge, 1996) Canadians do not monitor their children's video game play and generally think that computers are good for children.

Kline (1996) has recently documented the growing role that action packed video games play in young people's lives which he thinks constitutes an important new sub-culture of youth. Based on his survey of 650 students aged 11-18, he found that 93 percent of his sample had played video games. Of these slightly more than half were light players, whereas about one fourth were moderate players and nearly one fourth heavy players. The heavy players were disproportionately male; 32 percent of males and 8 percent of females were 'gamers' playing 1 hour per day or more. Light and moderate players said that they had few friends who played video games, while heavy players were split: 49 percent said they played games with lots or most of their friends and 51 percent were playing with few of their friends. There were also striking differences in the leisure preferences and solitary activities of the players (Table 2).

Table 2. Rank order of favorite solitary activities, by player (%)

Light players		Moderate players		Heavy players	
Listening to music	30	Watching TV	22	Video games	41
Outdoor activities	27	Video games	23	Watching TV	25
Watching TV	25	Listening to music	21	Listening to music	15
Video games	8	Outdoor activities	17	Outdoor activities	13
Reading	8	Reading	9	Reading	3
n =	322		141		131

The male gamers (i.e., heavy players) were especially electronic in their entertainment preferences, watching an average of 20 hours of television a week, almost double the amount that moderate and light players watched. Keeping in mind that heavy players were those that spent at least 7 hours a week playing games, the combined activities of television and video game play took up nearly 30 hours per week, if not more. For these individuals, viewership and gaming complemented each other and, most likely, occupied the majority of their leisure time. It was also the case that the male heavy players preferred the cartoon genre on TV, suggesting a graphic link that was important. Kline (1997) speculates that what seems to differentiate the gamer is the absence of friends and alternative leisure opportunities; heavy players resort to solitary media for distraction and entertainment. The evidence is rather limited on this point but, clearly, video games are an activity, which, like watching TV and videos, is something kids prefer to do when they have no other more social options. Family and sibling play is infrequent, mostly involving play with brothers, and is more frequent in the occasional player groups. Solitary video game play is especially attractive to the younger high school age males who are most interested in the great graphics, cool characters and exciting distractions this medium provides. Their favorite games are the ones that most create the combined experience of action, fantasy and simulation. A good game must have most of these attributes, although the heaviest players privileged action, fighting and cool themes. Older males often report a decrease in both their fascination with video games and time spent in video game play, as other social activities outside the home begin to attract them more.

Although most children rate video games positively, gamers find this form of play extremely pleasurable and involving. They said that playing video games was exciting (98% of heavy players), interesting (96%), pleasant (92%) and involving (90%). 60 percent of the heavy players characterized gaming as *very* pleasurable and *very* exciting compared to 30 percent of light players and 40 percent of moderate players. Heavy players also found game play to be less frustrating than light players but tended to rate their own ability as higher.

The survey also revealed that certain aspects of video games were more important for heavy players than for light players. For instance, gamers were significantly more likely to say that a good game had to have good characters, lots of excitement, good weapons, be challenging, responsive, and provide lots of action. These features were all less important to other teens. However, also for females the importance of weapons was found to be dependant on how much they played (74% of female gamers said that good weapons were important for a game to be fun compared to 54% of female light players). When gamers rated eight given genre categories it was clear that male gamers rated the fighting and/or combat genre most enthusiastically (61% vs. 35% of female gamers), followed by racing (60% vs. 42%) and action (60% vs. 35%). On the other hand, female heavy players (71%) expressed a strong preference for action games compared to female light players (49%).

The intensity, repetitiveness and immersion in the game's play distinguish the heavy player's experience from the more moderate play of the majority. One participant said that he "could play video games for hours and not notice" the passage of time (Kline, 1997). Flow experience is not only valued by gamers, but reflects a dependency behavior that the kids themselves call 'addictive' because it indicates a loss of subjective control and a distortion in the sense of time (Kubey, 1996). Indeed, over 80 percent of the young people in the survey felt that video games can be described as compelling or like an addiction, and over 50 percent agreed that there could be harmful effects of playing them too much. Moreover, the survey revealed that heavy players were more likely to report that they sometimes displaced homework and chores than light players were. In particular, heavy players were more likely to put off doing homework and chores (37%) and family activities (18%) than leisure activities (13%) or spending time with their friends (10%) (Table 3).

As regards perceptions of addiction, more than one third of heavy players (37%) agreed with the statement that "some kids played games too much", a further 27 percent felt that "some kids played them obsessively", and 19 percent believed that many were "totally dependent on their video game fix". 10 percent of heavy players said that games were not addictive. Heavy players were more likely to say that games were not addictive compared to light players.

Table 3. Activities that young people missed out on to play, by player (%)

Activities displaced	Total	Light players	Moderate players	Heavy players
Homework or household chores**	21	15	22	37
Family activities**	8	7	7	18
Leisure activities**	7	6	7	13
Friends**	5	3	5	10
n =	611	310	137	128

Note: ** = p<0.01 (the chance that the difference is not significant is 1 out of 100).

When asked to comment on the effects of violent games, only 15 percent of all young people felt that video games had no bad influence. 24 percent felt that the negative influence was confined to vulnerable kids, 33 percent felt the influence was not that serious, and 25 percent thought the negative influence was both significant and widespread. Most strikingly, 20 percent of heavy players felt that violent games had no bad influence at all, compared to 12 percent of light players.

Teens generally agreed on those aspects that make games violent; regardless of how much they played they saw above all incidents of sexual assault, gore, weapons and shooting, as well as punching and kicking, as making for violence. If desensitization is revealed through the willingness to use the word 'violence' to characterize aggressive acts, then the result might reflect the changing meaning of the term violence as it applies to representational acts. Heavy players found rape, gore, verbal abuse, military content, and kidnapping as less 'violent' (Table 4).

Table 4. Characteristics that make a game violent, by player (%)

Characteristic of violent game	Total	Light players	Moderate players	Heavy players
Sexual assault**	85	93	79	78
Gore (blood and guts)	83	85	81	79
Weapons and shooting	65	65	70	64
Punching and kicking	57	59	54	58
Verbal abuse*	53	59	51	50
Realistic graphics and sound	53	51	60	53
Military setting	46	49	45	40
Any aggressive action where characters contact and get hurt	40	42	34	40
Kidnapping**	33	42	30	25
n =	611	312	134	126

Note: * = p<0.05, ** = p<0.01 (the chance that the difference is not significant is 5 out of 100, and 1 out of 100, respectively).

Gender differences for sexual assault, kidnapping and verbal abuse accounted for much of the significant differences in the ratings of violence between heavy and light gamers. Female light players (91%) were more likely than female heavy players (79%) to say that the occurrence of sexual assault made a game violent.

Conclusion

In North America, the video game has arrived as the adolescence witch-hunt of the next century. So rather than television, the moral panic of today is focusing on violent video games and their potential harmful influences on aggression and desensitization. As children's culture commentator Henry Jenkins (1999) stated: "When the Littleton shootings occurred calls from the media increased dramatically. Suddenly, we are finding ourselves in a national witch-hunt to determine which form of popular culture is to blame for the mass murders, and video games seemed like a better candidate than most."

The moral panic has also spread to Canada. In a recent case where five teens were accused of brutally murdering an 81 year-old woman in her home, the press reported statements by the town mayor who claimed: "Young people play Nintendo with scenes of violence and flowing blood" (Peritz, 1999). The article also cites: "A group of local teenaged boys who hung around with one of those charged said the boy in recent months became increasingly withdrawn, spending hours playing video games or surfing the Net on his home computer. 'He used to get into crazy Web sites – murder, pedophilia, there were no exceptions', said one boy in a baseball cap and cargo pants. It's like there were fantasies at work." Jenkins rebuffs this hysteria as a moral panic and in his 1999 statement to Senate committee argues: "We are afraid of our children. We are afraid of their reactions to digital media. And we suddenly can't avoid either." In recent series of interviews with parents, however, we have found that there is growing tension in the family and growing uncertainty about the role that video gaming (on PCs, the Net, or game consoles) plays in children's lives.

Yet unlike television and films, where violence and cultural content have been categorized and regulated by the CRTC (Canadian Radio-Telecommunications Commission), video games and the Internet have been treated as a different kind of medium, more like telecommunications. There are no restrictions on video games beyond the criminal code. Like the Internet, video gaming is emerging as a self-regulated global media industry, largely because that is how the Americans have viewed it. In the digital global marketplace Americans make world policy. Although Canada has been a leading advocate in television regulation of 'gratuitous violence' on TV, this has not extended to video gaming industry. The classification standards most widely used are those of the ESRB's (Electronic Standards Review Board) self-regulation categories, created when the US gaming industry was threatened by a Senate investigation. Indeed, in a

1994 decision the CRTC allowed cable companies to distribute Sega video games (many of them violent and thus violating the 9 o'clock watershed) over the protests of advocacy groups, and recently CRTC decided not to regulate the Internet – indications that the potentially harmful consequences of video games are of decreasing importance on Canada's public policy agenda.

As this review of the literature revealed, there is in Canada very little reliable public data on the distribution of video games, on their use or the reasons why children choose to play them, let alone their implications and effects. As mentioned, what I discovered as I set out to take stock of this evidence is that on a global basis there are almost as many reviews of the literature on violence and video games as there are actual studies. Cultural critic Stone (1995) attributes this oversight to the feeling on the part of many academics that computer games are inherently educational, or, instead, are an entertainment medium beneath serious contemplation. Additionally, the promotional hype enveloping the Internet and computer literacy seems to have produced a naive faith among many Canadians that interactive media are empowering youth for the 'digital era'. Yet the evidence is already available, that like television and films, this interactive entertainment industry may require guidelines for the sale and marketing of gratuitously violent entertainment to children and young people. Although the bleating call for more research is all too familiar, it is time someone sounded the fire alarms.

References

Anderson, C.A. & Ford, C. (1986) "Affect of the Game Player: Short-term Effects of Highly and Mildly Aggressive Video Games." *Personality and Social Psychology Bulletin*, Vol. 12(4): 390-402.

Ballard, M.E. & Wiest, J.R. (1996) "Mortal Kombat: The Effects of Violent Videogame Play on Males' Hostility and Cardiovascular Responding." *Journal of Applied Social Psychology*, Vol. 26(8): 717-730.

Bandura, A. (1986) *Social Foundations of Thought and Action: A Social Cognitive Theory*. Englewood Cliffs, NJ: Prentice-Hall.

Braun, C.M. & Giroux, J. (1989) "Arcade Video Games: Proxemic, Cognitive and Content Analyses." *Journal of Leisure Research*, Vol. 21(2): 92-105.

Brody, H. (1992) "The Pleasure Machine." *Technology Review*, April, 31-36.

Calvert, S.L. & Tan, S.L. (1994) "Impact of Virtual Reality on Young Adults' Physiological Arousal and Aggressive Thoughts: Interaction versus Observation." *Journal of Applied Developmental Psychology*, Vol. 15(1).

Cupitt, M. & Stockbridge, S. (1996) *Families and Electronic Entertainment*. Sydney: Australian Broadcasting Authority and the Office of Film and Literature Classification.

De Waal, B. (1995) *Motivations for Video Game Play: A Study of Social, Cultural and Physiological factors*. MA Thesis, School of Communication, Simon Fraser University.

DFC Intelligence (1999) *Year in Review: 1998*. Internet information: www.dfcint.com/game_article/yearreview98.html

Dill, K. & Dill, J. (1998) "Video Game Violence: A Review of the Empirical Literature." *Aggression and Violent Behavior*, Vol. 3(4): 407-428.

Discovery Channel (1999) *Game Violence*. 17/08/1999, Episode S35.

Durkin, K. (1995) *Computer Games: Their Effects on Young People – A Review*. Sydney: Office of Film and Literature Classification.

Durkin, K. & Low, J. (1998) "Children, Media and Aggression. Current Research in Australia and New Zealand." In *Children and Media Violence*. Eds. U. Carlsson & C. von Feilitzen. Yearbook 1998 from The UNESCO International Clearinghouse on Children and Violence on the Screen, Nordicom, Göteborg University: 107-124.

Egli, E. & Myers, L. (1984) "The Role of Video Game Playing in Adolescent Life: Is There Reason to Be Concerned?" *Bulletin of the Psychonomic Society*, 22.

Emes, C. (1997) "Is Mr. Pac Man Eating Our Children? A Review of the Effect of Video Games on Children." *Canadian Journal of Psychiatry*, Vol. 42, May: 409-414.

Funk, J.B. (1993) "Re-evaluating the Impact of Video Game Play." *Clinical Pediatrics*, Vol. 32(2): 86-90.

Funk, J.B., Flores, G., Buchman, D.D. & Germann, J.N. (1999) "Rating Electronic Games: Violence Is in the Eye of the Beholder." *Youth and Society*, Vol. 30(3): 283-312.

Goldstein, J.H. (1994) "Sex Differences in Toy Play and Use of Video Games." In *Toys, Play and Child Development*. Ed. J.H. Goldstein. New York: Cambridge University Press.

Goldstein, J.H. (Ed.) (1998) *Why We Watch: The Attractions of Violent Entertainment*. New York: Oxford University Press.

Goldstein, J.H. & Jukes, J. (1993) "Preference for Aggressive Toys." *International Play Journal*, Vol. 1: 81-91.

Graybill, D., Kirsch, J.R. & Esselman, E.D. (1985) "Effects of Playing Violent versus Non-violent Video Games on the Aggressive Ideation of Aggressive and Non-aggressive Children." *Child Study Journal*, Vol. 15(3): 199-205.

Graybill, D., Strawniak, M., Hunter, T. & O'Leary, M. (1987) "Effects of Playing versus Observing Violent versus Non-violent Video Games on Children's Aggression." *Psychology: A Journal of Human Behavior*, Vol. 24(3): 1-8.

Greenfield, P.M. (1984) *Mind and Media: The effects of Television, Video Games and Computers*. Massachusetts: Harvard University Press.

Greenfield, P.M. (1994) "Video Games as Cultural Artifacts." *Journal of Applied Developmental Psychology*, Vol. 15(1): 3-12.

Greenfield, P.M. & Cocking, R.C. (Eds.) (1996) *Interacting with Video*. Norwood, NJ: Ablex.

Griffiths, M.D. (1999) "Violent Video Games and Aggression. A Review of the Literature." *Aggression and Violent Behavior*, Vol. 4 (2): 1359-1389.

Grossman, D. (1996) *On Killing: The Psychological Cost of Learning to Kill in War and Society*. Boston: Little, Brown & Co.

Grossman, D. (1998) "Trained to Kill." *Christianity Today*, 10/08/1998.

Grossman, D. & DeGaetano, G. (1999) *Stop Teaching Our Kids to Kill. A Call to Action Against TV, Movie & Video Game Violence*. New York: Crown Publishers.

Gupta, R. & Derevensky, J. (1996) "The Relationship between Gambling and Video Game Playing Behavior in Children and Adolescents." *Journal of Gambling Studies*, Vol. 12(4).

Hamilton, J.T. (1998) *Channeling Violence: The Economic Market for Violent Television Programming*. Princeton, NJ: Princeton University Press.

Hayes, M. & Dinsey, S. (1995) *Games War*. London: Inbook.

Henry, D. & McLennan, K. (1994) "There Are No Brakes, so Who's Steering: A paper on issues for educators." Presented at Griffith University *Media Futures: Policy and Performance*, Australia: Telstra Corp.

Herz, J.C. (1997) *Joystick Nation: How Videogames Ate Our Quarters, Won Our Hearts, and Rewired Our Minds*. Boston: Little, Brown & Co.

Huesmann, L.R., Moise, J.F., Podolski, C.L. (1997) "The Effects of Media Violence on the Development of Antisocial Behavior." In *Handbook of Antisocial Behavior*. Eds. D.M. Stoff & J. Breiling. New York: John Wiley & Sons Inc.: 181-193.

Irwin, A.R. & Gross, M.A. (1995) "Cognitive Tempo, Violent Video Games and Aggressive Behavior in Young Boys." *Journal of Family Violence*, Vol. 10 (3): 337-350.

Jenkins, H. (1999) Personal communication. Published e-mail letter.

Kafai, Y.B. (1995) *Minds in Play: Computer Game Design as a Context for Children's Learning.* Cambridge, Mass.: M.I.T. Press.

Kalamas, A. & Gruber, M. (1998) "Electrodermal Responses to Implied versus Actual Violence on Television." *The Journal of General Psychology*, Vol. 125 (1): 31-37.

Kinder, M. (1996) "Contextualizing Video Game Violence: From Teenage Mutant Ninja Turtles 1 to Mortal Kombat 2." In *Interacting with Video*. Eds. P.M. Greenfield & R.C. Cocking. Norwood, NJ: Ablex: 25-38.

Kline, S. (1996) [with Albert Banerjee]. *Video Game Culture: Leisure and Play Preferences of BC Teens.* MAL SFU: Vancouver.

Kline, S. (1997) "Pleasures of the Screen: Why Young People Play Video Games". Proceedings of the *International Toy Research Conference*, Angouleme, France, November.

Krish, S. (1998) "Seeing the World through Mortal Kombat-colored Glasses: Violent Video Games and the Development of a Short-term Hostile Attribution Bias." *Childhood: A Global Journal of Child Research*, 5.

Kubey, R.W. (1996) "Television Dependence, Diagnosis, and Prevention: With Commentary on Video Games, Pornography, and Media Education." In *Tuning in to Young Viewers: Social Science Perspectives on Television*. Ed. T.M. MacBeth. Thousand Oaks, CA: Sage: 221-260.

Livingstone, S., Holden, K. & Bovill, M. (1999) "Children's Changing Media Environments: Overview of a European Comparative Study." In *Children and Media: Image Education Participation.* Eds. C. von Feilitzen & U. Carlsson. Yearbook 1999 from The UNESCO International Clearinghouse on Children and Violence on the Screen, Nordicom: Göteborg University: 39-59.

McIlwraith R., Jacobvitz, R.S., Kubey, R. & Alexander, A. (1991) "Television Addiction: Theories and Data Behind the Ubiquitous Metaphor." *American Behavioral Scientist*, Vol. 36(2): 104-121.

MediaMetrix (2000) http://www.mediametrix.com/Methodology/Convergence.html

Negroponte, N. (1995) *Being Digital.* Cambridge, Mass.: M.I.T. Press.

Owens, A.M. (1999) "Site of Massacre Littered with Booby Traps." *National Post,* Canada, 22/04/1999.

Peritz, I. (1999) "Crown Wants 3 Murder Suspects Tried as Adults: One of five teens charged in elderly woman's death spent hours playing violent video games, surfing 'crazy Web sites', friend says." *Globe and Mail,* 28/09/1999, A3.

Postman, N. (1993) *Technopoly.* New York: Vintage.

Provenzo, E.F.Jr. (1991) *Video Kids: Making Sense of Nintendo!* Cambridge, Mass: Harvard University Press.

Provenzo, E.F.Jr. (1992) "What Do Video Games Teach?" *Education Digest,* Vol. 58 (4).

Quittner, J. (1999) "Families: Are Video Games Really So Bad? They mesmerize children. They frighten parents. But take heart: there are ways to tame the monsters in the box." *Time,* 10/05/1999.

Rushkoff, D. (1996) *Playing the Future.* New York: Harper Collins.

Scheff, D. (1993). *Game Over.* New York: Random House.

Schutte, N., Malouff, J., Post-Gordon, J. & Rodasta, A. (1998) "Effects of Playing Video Games on Children's Aggression and Other Behaviors." *Journal of Applied Social Psychology,* 18.

Silvern, S.B. & Williamson, P.A. (1987) "The Effects of Video Game Play on Young Children's Aggression, Fantasy, and Prosocial behavior." *Journal of Applied Developmental Psychology,* Vol. 8(4): 453-462.

Sneed, C. & Runco, M.A. (1992) "The Beliefs Adults and Children Hold about Television and Video Games." *Journal of Psychology,* Vol. 126(3): 273-284.

Steinberg, S. & Kincheloe, J. (1997) *KinderKulture.* Colorado: Westview Press.

Stone, A.R. (1995) *The War of Desire and Technology at the Close of the Mechanical Age.* Cambridge, MA: M.I.T Press.

van der Voort, T. (1998) "The Effects of Television on Children. Parental Perceptions and Mediation." In *Trends in Communication 2.* Eds. T. van der Voort & J. Beentjes. The Netherlands: Boom Publishers: 5-29.

Video Games and Violence

Controversy and Research in Japan

Akira Sakamoto

Japan is now leading the world in the video game industry. In the 1990's, Japan experienced a severe recession, and consequently many industries have declined. Only the video game and animation industries have the highest level of international competitiveness even now.

Japanese video game companies are quite strong, and video games have been very popular among Japanese people since the mid-1980's. Thus, the Japanese have long been interested in the effects of video game use, and actually many arguments concerning this issue have often been found in the Japanese press. Some empirical studies, though not many, have also been conducted on the issue. Since Japanese researchers only infrequently write their papers in English, it seems that the Japanese debate and empirical studies on the effects of video games are relatively unknown outside Japan. It would, therefore, be meaningful to introduce this work to an international readership.

Thus, in the present article, Japanese debate and studies are described. First, however, the current situation as regards the popularity of video games and children's use of the games in Japan is described.

The popularity of video games

Home video games began to be popular in Japan in 1983 when Nintendo Co., Ltd. introduced a video game machine called Family Computer or Famicom on to the market (Family Computer was often called "Nintendo" outside Japan). Prior to this, people could not play video games unless they went to a game arcade or a coffee house where machines were available or unless they wrote their own game programs on a computer. Family Computer made it much easier to enjoy video games.

Even when they began to sell Family Computer, the staff at Nintendo did not predict that it would become so popular (Kurihara, 1993). However, the number of sold machines dramatically increased, and with the appearance of an action game named *Super Mario Brothers* in 1985, Family Computer became remarkably popular. At this time, many children came home as soon as their classes in school were over, because they wanted to play video games as early as possible. This was called the "Express Return", and drew people's attention. Video games became the most-wanted toys among boys, and in 1986, 3.9 million machines were sold in Japan (cf. Dentsu Institute for Human Studies, 1998). At about this time, half of the children possessed video game machines, and it was said that Family Computer had become a full-fledged member of the family (Kurihara, 1993).

Subsequently, the number of sold machines temporarily decreased, but video games quickly recovered their popularity, and children's enthusiasm reached its peak in 1988 when a role-playing game named *Dragon Quest III* appeared (also called *Dragon Warrior III* outside Japan). When this game came on to the market, many children queued outside shops all night long waiting for them to open. In addition, some children who could not buy the game threatened those who did with violence and robbed them of the game. This was called the "Dorakue Affair" in Japan, and Japanese journalists enthusiastically reported it (Dorakue is an abbreviation of *Dragon Quest* pronounced in Japanese).

After 1987, in addition to Family Computer, many video game machines appeared, for example, PC Engine, Mega Drive, Game Boy, Super Famicon, Sega Saturn, Nintendo 64, Play Station, and Sega Dreamcast. Video game machines attained variety and sophistication, and more firmly attracted children. Since 1988, the number of sold machines has greatly increased, and in 1992, the interests of Nintendo Co., Ltd. surpassed those of Toyota Motor Co., a representative Japanese automobile company (*Yomiuri Shimbum*, 1999, August 11). In 1996, over twelve million machines were sold only in Japan (cf. Dentsu Institute for Human Studies, 1998). This number is about one-tenth of the total Japanese population. At present, the Japanese video game industry sells over ten million machines and about one hundred million copies of software per year only in domestic markets. The total market sizes are now about two hundred billion yen (two billion US dollars) for machines and over five hundred billion yen (five billion US dollars) for software. About 90 percent of Japanese elementary school children possess video game machines for their own exclusive use (cf. Dentsu Institute for Human Studies, 1998).

Children's use of video games

With the increasing number of sold machines in Japan, children's use of video games also increased.

NHK Broadcasting Culture Research Institute has often conducted survey research on children's play. Elementary school students were asked, "what they often played" in 1984, 1989, and 1994 (Janamoto, 1985, 1990, 1995). The sample size was about 1,500 at each occasion. Mori (1997) summarized these results

(Table 1). As is seen in the table, video games did not take a high rank in 1984. However, in 1989, they ranked second for boys. As for girls, they still did not rank high in 1989, but they ranked second in 1994. While the rank for boys did not change for the period 1989 to 1994, the percentage often playing video games increased. The proportions for 1989 and 1994 were 34 and 42 percent, respectively.

Table 1. What elementary school students often play (% of students)

Ranks	1984	1989	1994
Boys 1st	Baseball 55	Baseball 49	Football 59
2nd	Football 43	**Video games** 34	**Video games** 42
3rd	Dodge ball 27	Football 28	Baseball 25
4th	Tag, hide-and-seek 21	Dodge ball 24	Basketball 19
5th	Playing with a ball 14	Tag, hide-and-seek 20	Tag, hide-and-seek 15 Dodge ball 15
Girls 1st	Tag, hide-and-seek 31	Tag, hide-and-seek 30	Tag, hide-and-seek 23
2nd	Dodge ball 26	Dodge ball 17	**Video games** 18
3rd	Elastic cord jumping 14	Cards 14	Books and comics 17
4th	Chatting 14	Books and comics 11	Talking with friends 15
5th	Swings, slides, playing with sand 13	Talking with friends 10	Dodge ball 13

NHK Broadcasting Culture Research Institute has also conducted other survey research (Shiraishi, 1998). Elementary school children ranging from third to sixth grade (from 8 to 12 years of age) were asked, "how long they played a video game" in 1987 and 1997. The sample size was about 1,500 at each occasion. The children were provided five alternatives, that is, "I always play it", "I sometimes play it", "I do not often play it", "I do not play it at all", and "I do not know of it". In 1987, 58 percent of children answered "always" or "sometimes", while 77 percent answered so in 1997. Thus, the proportion increased by almost 20 percent. In particular, the increase is remarkable for girls. The proportions for girls in 1987 and 1997 were 40 and 64 percent, respectively. As for boys, they were 75 and 89 percent. In addition, the children in this survey were asked, "what they played before dinner". As is shown in Table 2, a dramatic increase is found for video games. The proportion playing video games before dinner grew by 25 percent, but no other activities showed a great increase. On the other hand, decreases are found for outdoor activities, such as playing with balls and riding bicycles.

Table 2. What elementary school students play (or do) before dinner (% of students)

	1987	1997	Change
Watch television	55	59	+4
Play video games	**25**	**50**	**+25**
Read comics, books, magazines for hobbies	35	33	-2
Play balls, such as baseball and football	31	20	-11
Chat	18	17	-1
Play games such as cards, toys	14	12	-2
Ride bicycles	20	11	-9
Listen to records, tapes, CDs	6	9	+3
Play tag	7	7	0
Do rope jumping, elastic cord jumping	8	4	-4
Swing, slide	4	3	-1

It should be noted that the Dorakue Affair occurred in 1988, and children's enthusiasm for video games was already regarded as a serious problem at that time. As is suggested from the data mentioned above, children's current use of video games is probably greater than in 1988. Therefore, the current situation should be regarded as more serious.

Thus, children's use of video games has increased, and the games are now very important in their daily lives. In particular, the recent increase for girls was remarkable. Nowadays, as concerns male elementary school students, 59 percent play a video game for over one hour per day on weekdays and 23 percent for over two hours. As for female students, 20 and 6 percent spend over one and two hours, respectively (Shiraishi, 1998).

Arguments for the harmfulness of video games

In recent years in Japan, children's social problems – such as violence, bullying, schoolphobia, drugs, and prostitution – have become still more serious, and therefore, their causes and methods for coping with them are often discussed. Considered as possible causes are children's frustration due to the so-called "controlled school" and "entrance examination war" and the lack of teaching by parents and people in the immediate community. The harmful effects of media, especially video games, are also fervently regarded as one of the causes. For example, in February 1998, the following passage was found in *Asahi Shimbum*, a representative Japanese newspaper selling eight million copies daily:

> A male teacher living in the Tohoku district says that the brutal crimes of secondary and high school students are caused by video games. "Everyone says they were quiet and gentle. It is natural. They have avoided keeping company with others, and have murdered others only in their own world every

> night. Imagine what happens to children who have been living under such circumstances for ten years." (*Asahi Shimbun*, 1998, February 2)

This teacher argued that video games are seriously harmful in that they cause violence, but video games are also argued to generate various other problems in children. For example, worsening eyesight and epileptic fits are typical of the physical problems, and social maladjustment – such as withdrawal and lack of interpersonal skills – as well as declining academic achievement are typical of the psychological problems. In some cases, such complexes of problems are considered in arguments for the harmfulness of video games, and a particular problem such as violence is considered in other cases. Recently, because of the violent crimes children have committed from 1997 to 1998, violence has been stressed as a serious deleterious effect.

The rationale behind the arguments

The arguments for the harmfulness of video games contain an underlying plausible logic explaining why video games can generate each problem. For example, as to violence, Sakamoto (1999a) summarized the rationale behind the arguments, and presented three characteristics of video games that were likely to promote children's violence.

First, in video games, players' own violence is rewarded. When the players conquer the enemy, they can obtain a variety of rewards such as high scores, new stories, and impressive images and music. Many empirical studies have been conducted on the effects of violent scenes on television, and their harmfulness has often been shown. These researchers believe that the harmful effects of violent scenes on television derive partly from the fact that violence is often rewarded, teaching viewers that violence is an acceptable means. For example, television programs for children in which heroes beat the enemy are typical. These heroes are respected and loved by everyone. The researchers believe that this reward pattern makes children regard violence as an acceptable means and consequently even behave violently themselves. However, on television, the violence of *others*, such as heroes, is rewarded (this is called "indirect reinforcement"). In video games, on the other hand, players' *own* violence is rewarded (this is called "direct reinforcement"). Since a reward for one's own behavior is more pleasant than that for others' behavior, the acceptability of violent behavior should be learned more effectively through video games than through television.

Second, in video games, players are accustomed to displaying violence. When people feel anger toward someone in real life, they never show violence if it is not an available behavioral option. When they are accustomed to it in video games, it might become an option. If so, they should more often show violence in real-life contexts when angry. Thus, it is possible that video games are the instruments with which people learn that violence is an available option.

Third, the setting of virtual reality provided by video games is similar to real life. It is therefore possible that the learned advantages and availability of violence in video games are transferred to the context of everyday life, causing people to use violence toward others. Nowadays, a phrase like "the ambiguity of borders between reality and fiction" is often found among the arguments for the harmfulness of video games in terms of violence.

The influence of arguments

The arguments concerning the harmfulness of video games have become heated every fifth year (Sakamoto, 1999a).

The first peak was in 1988. As mentioned earlier, in 1983 when Nintendo began to sell Family Computer, people did not realize that Family Computer would become so important in children's daily lives, and there was no controversy. However, as its popularity increased dramatically, some people began to debate the issue, and after about 1985, arguments for the harmfulness of video games were often presented. Children's enthusiasm for video games reached its peak at the time of the Dorakue Affair in 1988. The heat of the arguments also reached its first peak at this point.

The second peak was in 1993, five years after the first. In the end of 1992, a fourteen-year-old boy living in the United Kingdom died of an epileptic fit when he was playing a video game. The heat of the arguments in 1993 originated from this affair. The affair was often reported in the Japanese press, and many people fervently expressed a fear that video game use could lead to not only an epileptic fit, but also to a variety of serious physiological and psychological problems.

The arguments were also heated from 1997 to 1998. This peak was spawned by the frequent occurrence of children's violent crimes. For example, in May 1997, a murder occurred in Kobe. A fourteen-year-old male secondary school student killed a boy in the 6th grade, cut off his head, and placed the head at the gate of the student's own school for display. Before this, the student had already killed one girl and injured three. In addition, from January to March 1998, acts of violence in which a knife was used were frequent. Students often killed and injured their classmates. On January 28, 1998, a boy in the 7th grade even killed his teacher with a knife. These incidents led to a sensation, and consequently the possible causes of children's violent crimes were intensively discussed. In this discussion, the use of video games was often regarded as one of the causes, and therefore arguments surrounding the harmfulness of video games were heated.

The arguments of 1997 to 1998 were very strong, making them influential in reality. In Japan, there is a large organization for the video game software industry called the Computer Entertainment Software Association or CESA, to which over a hundred companies belong. In July 1997, the organization took notice of the arguments, and produced a written code for the voluntary restraint of harmful software. The code consisted of 25 items (for example, "You may not express murder, injury, and violence or suggest a way of accomplishing them in a stimulated manner.") and the organization decided to demand that companies not sell software that violated the code. CESA can give the companies certain punishments, such as an oral warning, a written warning, up to two years' deprivation of the right to vote, recommendation of withdrawal from the organization, and expulsion from the organization, when they sell software that violates the code. Up to the present, CESA has actually judged that some products of software violate the code, and demanded their companies not to sell them, unless the contents are modified. In addition, CESA has given an oral warning to two companies that sold unaccepted software. In September 1999, it was decided that software with severe violence must be labeled in order to inform the consumers. So far, about ten products have been labeled.

The influence of the arguments is found not only in the world of the video game industry, but also in the fields of justice and administration. On March 18, 1998, the Family Courts of Japan made a severe judgment on a boy in the ninth grade who had tried to rob a policeman of his pistol by threatening him with a knife. He was ordered to go to a reformatory. In making this judgment, the harmfulness of video games was considered. The judge's explanation was as follows: "His behavior is not due to an impulse, but to his own disposition developed through the use of media such as video games. Therefore, intensive teaching and training by experts are necessary for his reformation, and it is appropriate that he be sent to a reformatory." On June 30, 1998, the Central Council for Education of the Ministry of Education, Science and Culture presented a document, entitled "Cultivating the sound minds of children who will develop a new era: A crisis of losing confidence in bringing up the next generation." This document was written to guide mainly parents in the education of children's morality and sociality, and it was one of the Ministry's policies for coping with the frequent occurrence of children's violent crimes. In the document, one instruction reads: "You should avoid the endless exposure of children to television and video games."

The arguments may have become a little calmer during the past year, but it seems that they remain influential. As mentioned below, arguments for the harmfulness of video games have not received great support from empirical research. Therefore, the strong influence of the arguments is not caused by research, but rather by their plausible logic.

Research on video games and violence

The occurrence of brutal crimes has long been low and therefore unremarkable in Japan. It seems that, due to this infrequency, the Japanese have not been greatly interested in media violence, and consequently only a few researchers have been trained as experts on this issue. As mentioned earlier, arguments for the harmfulness of video games in terms of violence are heated in Japan, but empirical research on this issue has not often been conducted. This may be due to a lack of expertise in media violence.

Before 1992, no studies on video games had been conducted in Japan, and in addition, the findings of studies conducted in other countries such as the United States had not been systematically introduced. Therefore, Japanese researchers did not fully understand that previous research had not shown negative effects of video games. Consequently, even academic researchers often supported the more popular arguments for such effects. Their enthusiastic comments were frequently found in the press.

Sakamoto (1993) reviewed empirical studies that had been conducted mainly in the United Sates, and introduced their findings in Japan. He wrote that: (1) Some studies had been conducted in the United States; (2) in experimental studies, the short-term effects of video game use on violent *behavior* had been detected only for infants and at most preadolescents, but no such effects had been clearly detected beyond these ages; and (3) in survey studies, even significant correlations between the frequency of video game use and violent tendencies had not been detected, and therefore it was difficult to regard the two variables as being causally related. Based on these findings, Sakamoto (1993) concluded that there was no evidence for serious negative effects of video games. This article had an impact on Japanese researchers, and it has frequently been cited. It seems that since this article was published, at least academic researchers such as social psychologists have not simply supported the argument for the harmfulness of video games.

However, the situation changed again recently. After the mid-1990's, Japanese researchers began to conduct empirical studies of their own. In these studies, serious harmful effects of video games have sometimes been detected. Based on these findings and other new evidence, some researchers argue that it is possible that video game use has deleterious effects.

In the following parts of the present article, empirical research conducted in Japan is introduced. Experimental studies are first described, and, subsequently, survey studies. After this description, Sakamoto's (1999b) recent view on the harmfulness of video games is introduced. This is based on the findings of recent studies and other new evidence.

Most studies mentioned below were conducted by the Ochanomizu University group, consisting of Akira Sakamoto and his co-researchers. Unfortunately, this is the state of Japanese research. However, the Tsukuba University group, consisting of Shintaro Yukawa, Tetsuhiro Miyamoto, and Toshio Yoshida, has recently initiated research on this issue, and it seems that other groups have begun to show an interest. Thus, there is hope for change in the near future.

Experimental studies

Most previous research conducted in the world has not examined the effects of video game use on violent *behavior* in adolescents and adults. In the research on adolescents and adults, violent behavior was not measured, although hostility and aggressive *thoughts* were. In the research on violent behavior, only infants and preadolescents have commonly been used. However, research on the violent behavior of adolescents and adults is perhaps most important. If video game use affects only their hostility and aggressive thought and does not affect their violent behavior, the effects cannot be regarded as serious, because they do not lead to actual physical harm to people. In addition, if video game use affects the violent behavior of infants and preadolescents, the effects cannot be regarded as serious, because their behavior seldom leads to brutal crimes.

Thus, Sakamoto and his co-researchers conducted two experimental studies to examine the effects of video game use on violent behavior in adolescents and adults (Sakamoto et al., 1998a; Sakamoto et al., 1999). They also tried to examine the moderators and mediating processes associated with such effects.

In the first study, Sakamoto et al. (1998a) randomly assigned 52 female students at Ochanomizu University to one of five conditions. In these conditions subjects: (1) played a realistic game (*Virtua Cop*), (2) played an unrealistic game (*Space Invader*), (3) merely watched the realistic game, (4) merely watched the unrealistic game, and (5) watched a neutral film (*Ann of Green Gables* or *A Symphony of Forests*). After the subjects played or watched the game or film, they were given opportunities to subject a confederate to electrical shocks. The strength and length of the electrical shocks they gave were used as measures of their violent behavior. In addition, their blood pressures and heart rates were measured before and after exposure to the various media.

Sakamoto and his co-researchers conducted the next study (Sakamoto et al., 1999) to validate and expand their previous findings. The procedures of the first study were modified in the following manner. In order to enhance the illusion of reality, the realistic game *Virtua Cop* was in the second study replaced by *Area 51*, which has a virtual gun. In addition, a condition was added in which the subjects played a fist-fighting game, and a measurement of violent behavior was based on how long and strongly they subjected a confederate to white noise. Furthermore, the condition in which they merely watched a game was not used. Thus, the researchers used four conditions in the second study in which the subjects: (1) played a realistic game (*Area 51*), (2) played an unrealistic game (*Space Invader*), (3) played a fist-fighting game (*Tekken 2*), and (4) watched a neutral film (*Ann of Green Gables*). The researchers randomly assigned 41 female students at Ochanomizu University to one of these conditions.

The findings of these two studies were as follows:

(a) The subjects who had played a game sometimes subjected a confederate to more intense electric shocks and white noise than did those in the control group. This implies that adolescents' and adults' use of video games can promote their violent behavior.

(b) However, the sizes of such effects were different between video games. The effects were detected for *Area 51*, but not for *Virtua Cop*. As for *Space Invader*, the results of the two experiments were inconsistent. The degree of reality and reward found in video games can be regarded as moderators leading to these differences between the games, although more systematic research is needed on this issue.

(c) The subjects who had played a video game showed more intense violent behavior than did those who merely watched. This suggests that the effects of video game use on violence could be due to the interactivity of the games.

(d) The effects of video game use were not changed when the mediating effects of blood pressure and heart rate were controlled for. This might indicate that effects on violent behavior are not due to physiological arousal generated by the video game use, but due to cognitive processes such as the learning of violence.

Thus, these studies show that adolescents' and adults' use of video games can promote their violent behavior, and therefore, that the negative effects of video games can be serious. If so, however, the results also show that this is only true of a limited range of games.

Yukawa et al. (1999) also conducted an experimental study. Based on the results of their own factor analysis, they divided violent video games into two types, that is, role-internalizing games (for example, role-playing games) and stimulus-responding games (for example, shooting games), and examined the effects of each type. Like Sakamoto et al. (1998a), they also examined the effects of interactivity. In Yukawa et al. (1999), 60 male students were used as subjects and divided into two groups. One group of subjects played a video game, while the other group merely watched it, and the subjects in each group were assigned to one of three conditions. In these conditions the subjects: (1) played or merely watched a role-internalizing game (*Biohazard 2*), (2) played or merely watched a stimulus-responding game (*Lay Storm*), and (3) played or merely watched a non-violent game (*Puyopuyo*, a game similar to *Tetris*). Yukawa et al. (1999) measured the subjects' aggressive thoughts, negative affect (such as discomfort and hostility), physiological responses, and violent behavior, after the subjects had played or watched the video game.

Their results showed that the role-internalizing game generated more aggressive thought and negative affect than did the non-violent game, and the stimulus-responding game also generated aggressive thought, although not to the same degree as the role-internalizing game. As for physiological responses and violent behavior, no significant differences were found between the violent and non-violent games. In addition, no differences were found between the conditions of playing and watching, and therefore, effects of interactivity were not revealed.

Thus, Yukawa et al. (1999) show that violent video games can lead to aggressive thought and negative affect, but do not reveal their influence on violent behavior and the moderating effects of interactivity. In this regard, the findings of Yukawa et al. are different from those of Sakamoto and co-researchers. Some methodological factors might explain these differences, for example, subject gender. The subjects of Sakamoto and co-researchers' studies are female, whereas those of Yukawa et al. are male. In addition, the procedure and software used in the experiments are different. In any case, further research is needed to explain the different outcomes.

Thus, although there are mixed findings, effects of video game use have been detected in some cases. It therefore seems that video game use can affect even violent behavior, at least under particular conditions. However, in the studies mentioned above, only the short-term effects of video game use have been detected, but their long-term effects have not been examined. Although experimental studies have the advantage of revealing causality, it is usually difficult to examine long-term effects. However, when long-term effects of video game use are revealed, the harmfulness of the games can be regarded as more serious. Survey research is useful for examining such long-term effects, although it makes observing actual behavior difficult.

Survey studies

Some Japanese researchers have conducted survey studies on relationships between video game use and violence. However, most of the studies were one-shot surveys, which reveal correlations but not causality. It is therefore possible to say that these studies have not revealed the effects of video game use on violent behavior.

On the other hand, when researchers use a survey method, they can reveal causality to some extent, if they conduct a panel study. In the panel study, the same variables are measured on several occasions over time. It is possible to reveal causality to some extent by analyzing obtained data in particular ways. Actually, Sakamoto (1994) examined causality between video game use and social maladjustment.

As for video game use and violence, Sakamoto and co-researchers have conducted three panel studies. Panel studies on this issue seem to be rare not only in Japan but also in the international literature.

Kobayashi et al. (1998) conducted a panel study of 210 elementary school students attending fourth to sixth grades (111 boys and 99 girls between nine and twelve years of age). Their frequency of video game use and violent tendencies were measured twice, in October 1993 and February 1994. As for video game use, the frequencies of seven types of games – action, simulation, adventure, role-playing, sport, puzzle, and board games – were measured. Five-point scales ranging from "I very often play it" to "I do not play it at all" were used. Violent tendencies were measured with thirteen five-point scales. For these data, regression analyses and synchronous effects model analyses were conducted. The synchronous effects model analyses can be realized using structural equation modeling. When the same results were obtained from both analyses, the researchers regarded them as credible and important. Results indicated that board games lowered boys' violent tendencies, and sport games lowered those of the girls.

Kobayashi et al. (1999) conducted the same kind of panel study five years after the above-mentioned one. They measured the frequency of video game use and violent tendencies of 764 children attending fifth to sixth grades (367 boys and 397 girls) twice, in July 1998 and from November to December 1998. As for video game use, the frequencies of eight types of games – fist-fighting action, action, action role-playing, shooting, adventure, simulation, sport, and panel games – were measured. As for violent tendencies, its six components – physical violence, hostility, irritation, verbal aggression, indirect aggression, and replacement – were measured on 54 five-point scales. The results obtained from both regression analyses and synchronous effects model analyses indicated that (1) action role-playing games promoted boys' hostility, (2) action games promoted girls' hostility, and (3) fist-fighting action games promoted girls' indirect aggression. As for the other components – physical violence, irritation, and verbal aggression – no effects were found.

Naito et al. (1999) conducted the same kind of panel study for 192 secondary school students in grade eight (98 boys and 94 girls aged 13-14). The researchers measured the students' frequency of video game use and violent tendencies twice, in December 1998 and March 1999. The frequencies of the same eight types of games as used in Kobayashi et al. (1999) were measured. As for violent tendencies, 24 five-point scales were used. The results obtained from both regression analyses and synchronous effects model analyses indicated that action games promoted boys' verbal aggression. No other effects were significant.

Thus, Kobayashi et al. (1998) did not show that video game use promotes violent tendencies, but even that it lowers them. It cannot be said that this study supports the arguments for the harmfulness of video games. On the other hand, Kobayashi et al. (1999) and Naito et al. (1999) showed that fist-fighting action, action, and action role-playing games promoted some components of violent tendencies, although these effects were not found for both genders. Therefore, it can be said that the results of these studies support the arguments to some extent, though not greatly. Since fist-fighting action, action, and action role-playing games often include violent contents, it seems plausible that only these games could promote children's violent tendencies. This enhances the credibility of those studies.

As noted above, the studies produced different results. The difference in the period of survey can be regarded as a possible explanation. Data from 1993 to 1994 were used in Kobayashi et al. (1998), whereas data from 1998 to 1999 were used in Kobayashi et al. (1999) and in Naito et al. (1999). The latter data are fairly newer than the former. Recently, video game technology has dramatically developed, and has provided a very realistic world to users. When the degree of reality is high, i.e., when the world found in video games is similar to the real world, violence learned in video games might easily appear even in real-life contexts. This implies the possibility that the effects of video games have recently been augmented. In addition, as mentioned earlier, the frequency of video game use has recently increased, and this has the same implications.

Given this line of reasoning, it is possible that the effects of video game use are more easily detected when newer data are analyzed, and this could be the reason why the effects were detected in the studies by Kobayashi et al. (1999) and Naito et al. (1999), but not in the study by Kobayashi et al. (1998). If so, it could be said that the findings of Kobayashi et al. (1999) and Naito et al. (1999) are more important, and that children's use of video games can increase their violent behavior. In addition, these are long-term effects, which can be regarded as serious. In any case, further research is necessary to reconcile the inconsistencies of the studies.

Current arguments

As mentioned earlier, Sakamoto (1993) did not think that video game use could have serious effects on violent behavior. Some researchers, however, are now changing their opinions. Actually, Sakamoto (1999b) states that video game use might cause increased violence under particular conditions. This shift in opinion is due to the observation of recent changes in the four issues described below.

First, changes in research findings have been observed. As mentioned earlier, previous studies conducted mainly in the United States did not provide evidence for the deleterious effects of video games. However, as seen above, recent Japanese studies have sometimes shown harmful influence that can be serious. Of course, since there are differences in the results, it is impossible to say that negative effects are clearly proved. However, the existence of some results supporting such effects means that the issue cannot be neglected.

Second, changes in the reality of video games have been observed. It is likely that realistic games more easily promote violence. As mentioned earlier, since video games have recently become still more realistic, it seems possible that current video game use has quite harmful effects on violence. Previous experiments and surveys in the United States did not show such effects, but in these studies, the unrealistic games that were popular at that time were used. It is impossible to generalize from such unrealistic games to today's super-realistic ones. And thus it would seem that these results – based on unrealistic games – no longer are applicable.

Third, changes in the frequency of video game use have been observed. When use is frequent, its effects are arguably greater. As mentioned earlier, since the frequency of children's video game use has recently increased, its effects may now be larger than previously. As also mentioned, no correlations between video game use and violent tendencies were found in previous survey studies conducted in the United States and Japan (for example, Kobayashi et al., 1998). This may be because children of that time used video games for relatively shorter periods or more infrequently. This fact also decreases the applicability of findings obtained in the previous studies.

Fourth, changes in the occurrence of violent crimes have been observed. It seems that the frequency of violent crimes that might be related to video game use has recently increased. For example, in March 1994, an act of violence perpetrated by a group of children occurred at Nagoya. On this occasion, fourteen secondary school students attacked two secondary school students, causing them serious injury. In the police examination, a boy from the offender group said: "You ask me why we did that? We just wanted to know how effective the punches and kicks we learned in fist-fighting games were." Actually, the violence was perpetrated in the following manner. The group first made the victims select their opponent. The selected boy identified with the heroes of fist-fighting games, and using their punches and kicks, he attacked a victim who could not resist because the group had him surrounded. The unselected boys formed the audience and gave joyous shouts every time the selected boy gave showy punches and kicks to the victims. The selection was repeated, and many boys eventually perpetrated violence on the victims. A boy even went to a game arcade that was located 200 meters away to make sure of the punches and kicks he wanted to give (*Nihon Keizai Shimbum*, 1995, January 4). This incident seems to have been caused by video game use. Although credible statistics are unavailable, it appears that recently such incidents are more common than previously.

The changes in research findings and the occurrence of violent crimes may be caused by the augmentation of effects of video game use, which are in turn due to changes in the degree of realism in video games and the frequency of their use. In any case, considering these developments, some researchers are changing their minds (Sakamoto, 1999b).

Final remarks

As found in the present article, although only a few studies have been conducted in Japan, each study seems to be fairly well constructed. For example, violent behavior has been measured in experimental studies. In addition, some panel studies have been conducted. These are probably not so common in the rest of the world, and could therefore be regarded as important contributions to the research field on video games and violence.

However, the scarcity of studies is problematic. At present, some unsolved inconsistencies are found between Japanese studies, leading to unclear conclusions. This is partly due to the small number of studies. In addition, the quality of research is usually improved by frequently exchanging opinions with other research groups, but today, such exchanges are difficult in Japan, because there are only a few research groups, although the number is increasing. It is not easy for Japanese researchers to exchange opinions with foreign groups because of the language. Thus, several groups are necessary in Japan.

Japan is now leading the world in the video game industry, and therefore, it should take responsibility for issues concerning deleterious effects of video games. Japanese researchers should conduct many studies. Actually, they have a lot of advantages for conducting research in this area.

First, it seems that in Japan, ethical standards for psychological research are still not as severe as in other countries such as the United States. As mentioned earlier, violent behavior has been measured directly in Japanese experimental studies. This is made possible by the generosity of the standards.

Second, since the popularity of video games began early in Japan, many Japanese people are now using the games and they have accumulated experience with them. This is useful in examining the effects of video game use with survey research. If the survey sample does not include the subjects who have used video games often, it is impossible to detect the effects of the games.

Third, Japan has a lot of game software companies, and therefore it is not difficult for Japanese researchers to cooperate with the companies on research projects. For example, it would be relatively easy for Japanese researchers to ask companies to make or modify software used in experiments.

Many questions can be identified for future research on video games and violence. First, does video game use affect violence? Do the effects continue over time? Are the effects serious? Second, what kinds of variables moderate the effects of video game use? What kinds of games have larger effects? What kinds of use have larger effects? Third, what are the processes underlying the effects of video game use on violence? How related is the interactivity of video games to such processes? Fourth, what kinds of interventions are useful in avoiding the harmfulness of video games? And many other questions can be found.

Japanese researchers should make efforts to help in answering these questions by conducting much more research than they have previously, and their possibilities for doing so are good.

Summary

In Japan, since 1983 when Nintendo began to sell Family Computer, the number of sold video game machines and software has continued to increase, and the frequency of children's video game use has also increased. Nowadays, 59 percent of male elementary school students play a video game for over one hour per day on weekdays and 23 percent of them for over two hours. 20 and 6 percent of female students spend over one and two hours, respectively.

Given such popularization, many people in the Japanese press have argued that children's use of video games could have serious harmful effects on their violent behavior. Before 1992, previous studies conducted mainly in the United States had not been systematically introduced to the Japanese, and therefore, even academic researchers in Japan often fervently supported arguments for the harmfulness of video games. However, after 1993, considering the findings of US research, Japanese academic researchers did not simply support the arguments.

From the mid-1990's, empirical research on video games and violence began in Japan. Japanese empirical research can be regarded as unique because violent behavior has often been directly measured in experimental studies and because some panel studies have been conducted, measuring the influence of video games over time. In these studies, the deleterious effects of video game use on violence have sometimes been detected, and based on this, some researchers are now beginning to believe that video games can be harmful.

Despite these studies, Japanese research is still rare. Japan is now leading the world in the video game industry, and as such it should take responsibility for the games' possible negative effects. In addition, Japanese researchers are in a particularly good position to work on these issues, and therefore their work should be expanded in the future.

References

Asahi Shimbun (1998, February 2). Wareware no Jinken ha, Kyoushi tachi no mikata [Our human rights?: Teachers' views]. Morning edition, p. 34. (in Japanese)

Dentsu Institute for Human Studies (Ed.) (1998). *Research for information and media society 1999.* Tokyo: Dentsu Institute for Human Studies. (in Japanese)

Janamoto, K. (1985). The current world of elementary school children: From the survey of elementary school children (1). *The NHK Monthly Report on Broadcast Research,* 35(1), 43-58.

Janamoto, K. (1990). Tired children: From the second NHK survey of the "Elementary School Children's Life and Mind". *The NHK Monthly Report on Broadcast Research,* 40(2), 2-11.

Janamoto, K. (1995). Elementary school children's life and cultures: From the third survey of the "Elementary School Children's Life and Cultures". *The NHK Monthly Report on Broadcast Research,* 45(1), 12-23.

Kobayashi, K., Kimura, F., & Sakamoto, A. (1999). *Causal relationships between video game use and aggressiveness: A panel study of Japanese elementary school students.* Paper presented at the third conference of the Asian Association of Social Psychology, Academia Sinica, Taipei. (in English)

Kobayashi, K., Sakamoto, K., Hinokuchi, Y., & Sakamoto, A. (1998). Terebigeimu shiyou to kougekisei no ingakankei no kentou: Syougakusei ni taisuru paneru kenkyuu [The examination of causality between video game use and aggressiveness: A panel study of elementary school students]. *Proceedings for the 39th annual conference of the Japanese Society of Social Psychology, Tsukuba University, Tsukuba,* 326-327. (in Japanese) (Sakamoto, K., Sakamoto, Kobayashi, & Hinokuchi (1998) is the early version of this paper, which was written in English.)

Kobayashi, K., Sakamoto, A., Kimura, F., & Hasebe, M. (1999). Terebigeimu shiyou to kougekisei no ingakankei no kentou (2): Syougakusei ni taisuru paneru kenkyuu [The examination of causality between video game use and aggressiveness (2): A panel study of elementary school students]. *Proceedings from the 40th annual conference of the Japanese Society of Social Psychology, Keio University, Tokyo,* 286-287. (in Japanese) (Kobayashi, Kimura, & Sakamoto (1999) is the early version of this paper, which was written in English.)

Kurihara, T. (1993). Bideo geimu no syakaiteki hankyou [The social impact of video games]. In T. Sato (Ed.), *Jouhouka to taisyuu bunka: Bideogeimu to karaoke* [Informationization and popular cultures: Video games and Karaoke] (pp. 83-95). Tokyo: Shibundou. (in Japanese)

Mori, Y. (1997). Terebigeimu no komyunikeisyon [Communication in video games]. In Y. Hashimoto (Ed.), *Komyunikeisyon gaku heno syoutai* [An introduction to communication science] (pp. 184-202). Tokyo: Taisyuukan Syoten. (in Japanese)

Naito, M., Kobayashi, K., & Sakamoto, A. (1999). Terebigeimu shiyou to kougekisei no ingakankei no kentou (2): Syougakusei ni taisuru paneru kenkyuu [The examination of causality between video game use and aggressiveness (2): A panel study of elementary school students]. *Proceed-*

ings for the 40th annual conference of the Japanese Society of Social Psychology, Keio University, Tokyo, 288-289. (in Japanese)

Nihon Keizai Shimbum (1995, January 4). Kakutou gamen, rinchi de saigen [Fighting on screens realized by group violence]. Morning edition, p. 30. (in Japanese)

Sakamoto, A. (1993). "Terebigeimu no akueikyou" ha hontouka?: Kougekisei to syakaiteki hutekiou nikansuru syakaisinrigaku-teki kenkyuu no gaikan [Are "the harmful effects of video games" true?: A review of socio-psychological research on aggression and social maladjustment]. In T. Sato (Ed.), *Jouhouka to taisyuu bunka: Bideogeimu to karaoke* [Informationization and popular cultures: Video games and Karaoke] (pp. 64-82). Tokyo: Shibundou. (in Japanese)

Sakamoto, A. (1994). Video game use and the development of socio-cognitive abilities in children: Three surveys of elementary school students. *Journal of Applied Social Psychology, 24*, 21-42. (in English)

Sakamoto, A. (1999a). Terebigeimu wo meguru shakai gensyou [Social phenomena related to video games]. *Child Study, 53*(1), 112-120. (in Japanese)

Sakamoto, A. (1999b). Terebigeimu ha bouryokusei wo takameruka? [Do video games promote violence?] *Child Study, 53*(2), 105-112. (in Japanese)

Sakamoto, A., Narushima, R., Sakamoto, K., Takahira, M., Suzuki, K., & Izumi, M. (1999). Terebigeimu asobi ga ningen no bouryoku ni oyobosu eikyou: Genjitsusei no chousei kouka [The effects of video game play on human violence: The moderating effects of reality]. *Proceedings for the 63th annual convention of Japanese Psychological Association, Chukyo University, Nagoya*, 897. (in Japanese)

Sakamoto, A., Ozaki, M., Mori, T., Takahira, M., & Ibe, N. (1998a). Video games and human violence: Impacts of interactivity in media. *Proceedings from the Interaction '98 symposiums of the Information Processing Society of Japan, the University of Tokyo, Tokyo,* 109-116. (in Japanese) (Sakamoto, Ozaki, Mori, Takahira, & Ibe (1998b) is the short version of this paper, which was written in English.)

Sakamoto, A., Ozaki, M., Mori, T., Takahira, M., & Ibe, N. (1998b). Human aggression caused by virtual reality and multimedia. In H. Thwaites (Ed.), *Future fusion: Application realities for the virtual age* (pp. 416-421). Burke, VA: IOS Press. (in English)

Sakamoto, K., Sakamoto, A., Kobayashi, K., & Hinokuchi, Y. (1998). *Causal relationships between aggressiveness and various types of video game use in Japanese elementary school students.* Paper presented at the 15th biennial meeting of International Society for the Study of Behavioural Development, Berne. (in English)

Shiraishi, N. (1998). The important role of TV and video games in children's friendship: From the survey of the "Elementary School Children and TV '97." *The NHK Monthly Report on Broadcast Research*, 48(4), 2-19. (in Japanese)

Yomiuri Shimbun (1999, August 11). Kasougenjitsu samayou doushin [Children's mind wandering virtual reality]. Morning edition, p. 12.

Yukawa, S., Miyamoto, T., & Yoshida, F. (1999). Bouryokuteki terebigeimu ga kougekikoudou ni oyobosu eikyou: Yakuwari-douka-gata geimu to sigeki-hannou-gata geimu no hikaku: Sankasei no kouka wo kuwaete [The effects of violent video games on aggressive behavior: The comparison of role-internalizing and stimulus-responding games: Adding the effects of participation]. *Proceedings from the 40th annual conference of the Japanese Society of Social Psychology, Keio University, Tokyo*, 132-133. (in Japanese)

Computer Games and Aggression

Research in Australia and New Zealand (-1998)

Kevin Durkin & Jason Low

There has been considerable interest in Australia and New Zealand in the uses of new media, especially computer games, by young people. In Australia, computer games are classified by the Office of Film and Literature Classification following guidelines similar to those employed in the classification of films, with the difference that material which would receive an 'R' in the movies (Restricted to persons over the age of 18) is refused classification in computer games (see Bedford, 1995, for a discussion of adults' rights in this context).

Durkin (1995) undertook a commissioned review of the available (international) literature investigating the place of computer games in the lives of contemporary children and adolescents, considering both negative effects (such as 'addiction', learning or encouragement of aggressive behaviour, impairment of family life and school performance, health consequences) and positive effects (such as cognitive and perceptuo-motor skill enhancement, heightened peer interaction, development of familiarity with computers).

Durkin concluded that the research did not justify assumptions of widespread ill effects. Incidence of obsessive involvement in computer game play is low in most surveys of children's leisure time use, and there is little evidence of deleterious consequences for social life or educational progress. On the topic of aggression, Durkin stressed that there were only a small number of studies published (in contrast to the large literature on television and aggression), and that these had yielded weak or inconsistent findings. Some studies pointed to an association between *arcade* play and aggressiveness, but not between home play and aggressiveness; surprisingly little success had been obtained in experimental studies attempting to find greater aggressiveness following labora-

---

Excerpt from Kevin Durkin & Jason Low (1998): Children, Media and Aggression. Current Research in Australia and New Zealand, the passage 'Computer games', pp. 111-113, *in Ulla Carlsson & Cecilia von Feilitzen (Eds.) Children and Media Violence. Yearbook from the UNESCO International Clearinghouse on Children and Violence on the Screen 1998, Nordicom, Göteborg University.*

tory exposure to violent games. However, Durkin noted that most of this literature was reporting work conducted in America and Britain in the 1980s, and it remains possible that the picture could change in the light of new research and in response to changes in the games themselves (such as greater realism and higher levels of violence). He suggested also that there is a need for research appropriate to the Australian cultural context (for example, Australia scores lower on most indices of real-life violence than the US and this may interact with any influence due to game content).

This report resulted in some debate in the national media. Some commentators have interpreted the literature differently from Durkin, and argued that "We have no proof of no harm from video games, and we have some proof of harm" (Biggins, 1995, p. 85). Biggins argues that where researchers have failed to find proof of harm, it may be because of general deficiencies in social science research, or of sloppy methodology. Biggins holds also that the parental community is "ill-equipped to guide and take responsibility for children's access to video games" (p. 89) and therefore favours conservative classification of this medium. Biggins makes the general point that the information superhighway could helpfully be flagged: "Proceed with caution – children crossing."

Most parties to this debate tend to agree that the amount of research available is limited. Since the Durkin (1995) report, some new Australian research has been completed. Ask, Winefield, and Augoustinos (1997) drew on competition-aggression theory to argue that violent video games can elicit aggressive behaviours because of their competitive themes. Essentially, the thesis is that when placed in a competitive situation, people are prone to become angry, hostile and aggressive. The authors propose also, along lines similar to Huesmann (1986, 1988) and Sanson and Di Muccio (1993), that people may develop from earlier experiences schemas in which competitive environments become associated with particular cognitions, most notably hostile and aggressive patterns of thought. In a preliminary test with high school students, Ask et al. (1997) found that children do perceive competitive situations as more aggressive than cooperative situations. The investigators then conducted an experiment with other male and female adolescents in which participants played a video game in pairs, such that some individuals were competing against their partner, and others were cooperating with their partner. The hypothesis was that participants in the more competitive situation should demonstrate more aggressive responses, which were defined here as the proportion of 'kills' of adversaries on screen (computed as the ratio of kills over kills + avoidance responses). Earlier American research by Anderson and Morrow (1995), with college students as participants, had obtained such an effect, though Ask et al. saw that study as confounded because the participants gained points for 'killing'.

In the Ask et al. study, the participants were not rewarded with points for killing. The participants' mean kill ratios were virtually identical in the competitive and cooperative situations (.67 and .66, respectively). The researchers also solicited participants' evaluations of their partners, to test the hypothesis that competing against someone was more likely to evoke hostile reactions than cooperating with someone. No difference was obtained. Although these findings might be taken as contradicting the competition-aggression account, Ask et al. note that their participants reported enjoying the game played (*Donkey Kong*), found it easy and not very frustrating. Hence, the game – if it is perceived as 'fun' rather than 'battle' – may not provide an optimal test of the theory. Certainly, it does indicate that aggressive responses are not an inevitable consequence of playing competitive video games.

Ask (1996) reports a variant of the experiment using a more ostensibly aggressive game (*Mortal Kombat III*), with male high school students as participants (their female peers did not want to play). In this study, participants played initially in a series of trials and then, a week later, took part in a knock-out 'tournament' with financial prizes at stake. The game allows the possibility of aggressive types of moves and nonviolent moves. During the trials, the winners tended to use more violent moves and during the tournament, aggressive moves increased. Ask concludes that participants 'had an inclination to produce violent moves when there was more competition'. He cautions, however, against oversimplistic interpretations that this demonstrates an effect of video games on social behaviour, and points out that the experiment does not test transfer effects (i.e., learning about the efficacy of violence in a game context which is then transferred to 'real life' contexts). His current research is addressed to this issue. (*Editors' remark:* For findings of the last-mentioned current research, see the article by Ask, Augoustinos and Winefield in this book.)

In sum, interest in the effects of violent media content remains an active research area. Studies of children reacting to television and adolescents playing with computer games yield complex but provocative findings. Much remains to be settled about causal relations and about the meaning of aggression in these contexts, but recent studies underline the need for continuing investigation and point to new methodological developments and refinements that could usefully be exploited by other researchers.

References

Anderson, C. A., & Morrow, M. (1995). Competitive aggression without interaction: Effects of competitive versus cooperative instructions on aggressive behavior in video games. *Personality and Social Psychology Bulletin, 21,* 1020 - 1030.

Ask, A. (1996). The behavioural effect of violent video games during competition. Paper presented at the 1996 Australian Psychological Society Conference, Sydney.

Ask, A., Winefield, A. H., & Augoustinos, M. (1997). *Competition, aggression, and violent video games.* Manuscript submitted for publication, Department of Psychology, University of Adelaide.

Bedford, R. (1995). Contributions to 'Interactive games. What about adults?' Symposium in *Regulation and entertainment media. Proceedings of the Censorship Conference, 1995.* Sydney, NSW: Office of Film and Literature Classification.

Biggins, B. (1995). Contributions to 'Interactive games. What about adults?' Symposium in *Regulation and entertainment media. Proceedings of the Censorship Conference, 1995.* Sydney, NSW: Office of Film and Literature Classification.

Durkin, K. (1995). *Computer games: Their effects on young people— A review.* Sydney: Office of Film and Literature Classification.

Huesmann, L. R. (1986). Psychological processes promoting the relation between exposure to media violence and aggressive behavior by the viewer. *Journal of Social Issues, 42,* 125 - 139.

Huesmann, L. R. (1988). An information processing model for the development of aggression. *Aggressive Behavior, 14,* 13 - 24.

Sanson, A., & Di Muccio, C. (1993). The influence of aggressive and neutral cartoon and toys on the behaviour of preschool children. *Australian Psychologist, 28,* 93 - 99.

To Kill or Not To Kill

Competitive Aggression in Australian Adolescent Males during Videogame Play

Alexander Ask, Martha Augoustinos & Anthony H. Winefield[1]

In recent years in Australia, media debate about the potential negative effects of violent videogames, and the implementation of a stringent classification system, has been carried out with limited scientific evidence derived from the Australian context (see Durkin, 1995, and Durkin & Low, 1998, for an outline of studies from Australia). We set out to fill this knowledge gap by conducting a series of studies in a 'middle-class' Adelaide suburban high school. The first section in this article summarises information on the extent of videogame use amongst males and females, whilst the second section outlines a series of ecological studies[2] conducted on a self-selected sample of experienced male *Mortal Kombat* players. This series of studies examined whether a competitive situation leads to aggressive behaviour within the videogame context. They should not be interpreted as showing that videogames with competitive-violent themes cause aggressive behaviour in other social contexts. The last section is devoted to recommendations for further videogames research.

Videogame use amongst Australian adolescents

There are no published data on the prevalence of videogame use amongst adolescent Australians. We conducted a survey to evaluate the extent to which adolescents play videogames across a number of different domains (e.g., personal computer and games systems at home, arcade parlour, and at a friend's house). Data for this study were collected during 1995-96.

214 high school students were given a short survey to complete during class. There were approximately 750 students in the school, that is, nearly 1/3rd of the school were sampled. The survey requested students to state the number of sessions per week that they played videogames on the personal computer and games system (e.g., Super Nintendo) at home, and at a friend's house and

arcade parlour. They were also requested to estimate the amount of time they spent playing videogames during an average session.

Eleven questionnaires were excluded from the data set because they contained a large number of missing answers. An examination of the raw data showed that some students reported playing for 40-50 hours per week which may have constituted over-estimations of their experience. Thus, a trim was performed on the remaining data (of 5%) in order to exclude students who may have grossly over-estimated playing time. The estimates after the trim are conservative. The trim excluded 8 males and 2 females from the data set. Thus, findings are reported for 193 students.

The responses are presented separately for males and females. A total of 108 males completed the survey. They had an average age of 14.2 years (range = 12-17). Sixty percent of males were 14 years old or younger. A total of 85 females completed the survey. They had an average age of 14 years (range = 12-18). Seventy-five percent of females were 14 years or younger.

Table 1 shows the number of sessions indicated by males and females across the four domains. Males indicated four sessions or more on the personal computer and games system, and played less than two sessions at the arcade parlour and at a friend's house, in an average week. Males spent a total number of 11.4 sessions playing videogames across all domains each week. Females also indicated an inclination towards the personal computer and games systems, although, in comparison to males, they reported fewer sessions per week across all domains (of 3 to 4 times less).

The pattern of average minutes across the domains were consistent with the sessions data for males and females. Males indicated spending nearly four hours on the personal computer per week, three hours on the games system, and 20 minutes at the arcade parlour and friend's house. Total time spent playing videogames exceeded seven hours for males. Females reported spending over one hour on the personal computer, one and a half hours on a games system, and less than 10 minutes at the arcade parlour and at a friend's house. Total time spent playing videogames for females (of nearly 3 hours) was approximately half of that reported by males.

Table 1. Mean videogame play each week in several domains for males and females

	Males		Females	
Domain	Average No. of sessions a week	Average minutes a week	Average No. of sessions a week	Average minutes a week
Personal computer	4.2	224.0	1.6	61.0
Games system at home	4.0	180.0	1.7	91.0
Arcade parlour	1.6	20.0	.4	7.0
Friend's house	1.6	20.0	.5	8.0
Total	11.4	444.0	4.2	167.0
n =	108		85	

Competitive aggression: Mortal Kombat studies with male adolescents

The competition-aggression hypothesis is the idea that competitive situations increase the likelihood of observing aggressive forms of behaviour, and is based on anecdotes of elite athletes, historical accounts of sports violence, academic conjecture (e.g., *On Aggression* by Konrad Lorenz, 1963), and people's everyday conversation. There have been a number of investigations in psychology on the competition-aggression link (e.g., Deutsch, 1949; Sherif, 1967). However, there has been only one study on adolescents, and there is no evidence from the Australian context. Moreover, there has been a recent spate of violence by children and adolescents (e.g., Columbine School massacre in the U.S.) which may be attributed to the way competitive environments (e.g., sports settings, schools) are structured. The studies we report in this section examine the notion of competitive aggression using a videogame task as a tool to demonstrate the link. Our research question was: Do adolescents demonstrate more simulated aggressive behaviour (i.e., within a videogame) when placed in an ecological competitive situation (i.e., a tournament for prizes) in comparison to a less competitive situation (i.e., a trial period). Participants were all males.

Mortal Kombat 3

The videogame we used during our studies was *Mortal Kombat 3*, © 1995. The Australian Office of Film and Literature Classification (OFLC) has classified *Mortal Kombat 3* (*MK3*) for Mature Audiences (MA) suggesting that the videogame "contains elements likely to disturb, harm or offend those under 15 years to the extent that it should be restricted to those 15 years and over" (OFLC, 1994, p. 7). The OFLC further writes about the MA classification: "Elements which might warrant this category would include: Depictions of realistic violence of medium intensity (e.g., impactful punches, kicks, blows and blood-shed to realistic animated characters or real-life images)" (OFLC, 1994, p. 7).

MK3 is the third game in a series of martial arts simulations where two players fight against each other in the videogame. The videogame manual describes the fictitious history of the Mortal Kombat tournament:

> The Shaolin Tournament for Martial Arts, better known as Mortal Kombat, was, for countless ages, a noble institution that tested the metal of the very best Warriors. Years ago, the Tournament was corrupted by the evil sorcerer Shang Tsung who dared to take not only the lives of his opponents, but their very souls. Eventually, it became known that Shang Tsung was acting at the behest of his diabolical master Shao Khan, Emperor of the Outworld, who planned to claim all the souls on earth. The Champions of Earth: Liu Kang, Kung Lao, their Ancestors and others have, so far, thwarted this plan. For centuries, Earth has used Mortal Kombat to defend itself against the Outworld's Emperor, Shao Kahn. (Super Nintendo, 1996, p. 5)

The player, in the context of this Tournament, chooses between 15 mortal fighters. Each fighter has basic moves (e.g., punch, low kick, sweep). The *Mortal Kombat* manual outlines the importance of perfecting these basic moves: "Each kontestant invited to the Tournament has spent years in practice and meditation to perfect his/her martial arts skills. Before challenging these Warriors in Kombat, you too, should practice the martial arts by meditating on these lessons" (Super Nintendo, 1996, p. 17).

Each fighter has unique playing moves in addition to these basic moves. There are two types of unique playing moves. 'Special moves' are performed by the player during a round and are executed by pressing a complex combination of buttons on the joypad. The *MK3* manual suggests that: "All of the *Mortal Kombat* Warriors possess expert fighting skills. In that respect, they are equal to thousands of other Warriors around the universe. What raises them above their peers are the special moves which they have created and perfected" (Super Nintendo, 1996, p. 18). These complex combination of button presses for each fighter are obtained from videogame magazines or from the Internet. For example, Cyrax, a fighter in *MK3*, releases a net that entraps the other game character when the player presses backwards twice on the joypad and then performs a low kick.

In contrast, 'finishing moves' are executed by pressing a combination of buttons on the joypad but only after the round has ended, i.e., when one character has no energy or health remaining. At this point, the winning player, who is prompted by the videogame to "Finish Him (Her)", has the choice of performing either a violent or a non-violent finishing move. There are two types of non-violent moves, namely, 'babality', where the losing fighter is converted to a baby, and a 'friendship', where the winning fighter offers a gift to the losing fighter. There are two types of violent moves, namely, 'fatality', where the winning fighter kills the losing fighter, and an 'animality', where the winning fighter transforms into an animal and mauls the losing fighter to death. All 15 fighters have two different types of fatalities. Unlike special moves, that are performed during a round in order to move a player towards victory, finishing moves are inconsequential to the fight's outcome because they are performed by the winning player, at the end of a round, when the other player is defeated.

Thus, the winning player has the opportunity either 'to kill or not kill' the opponent's fighter at the end of each round. Our studies focussed on the frequency of these killing versus non-killing finishing moves across two types of competitive situations, i.e., low and high competition. The rationale for focussing on finishing moves instead of other playing moves (e.g., special moves) was based on the authors' observations that the latter type of moves are stereotyped because each player develops a style of play that is developed from hours of practice on the videogame. In contrast, finishing moves are less stereotyped because they do not affect the fight's outcome. The outcome measure utilised in this study (which was assumed to represent aggressive behaviour in the videogame context) is called the 'kill ratio'. The kill ratio was first developed by Anderson and Morrow (1995). The kill ratio is a fraction of the total number of killing responses by the winning player divided by the total number of all responses (i.e., killing + non-killing finishing moves).

Experiment 1

Experiment 1 was conducted over a three-week period. All sessions were held during lunch periods.

During the first week, male students, who were very skilled at *MK3*, were invited to attend an information session. It just so happened that 16 males attended this session (which was a sufficient number to conduct the tournament). During this session, the nature of the tournament was described in detail. For the remainder of the first week, informal practice sessions took place with all 16 males and the first author of this article observed their relative abilities at *MK3*. At the end of the week, all 16 competitors were ranked roughly from best to worst and a schedule was devised for the trial period conducted in the following week. The top four ranks were placed into four different groups (i.e., Monday Trial Group, Tuesday Trial Group, Wednesday Trial Group, and Thursday Trial Group). The next four ranks were, again, placed into the four separate trial groups, and so on, until all 16 competitors had been allocated to a trial group session. Participants were not permitted to change their fighter during the study because a strategy amongst good players is to observe what fighter their opponent has chosen for a bout and then choose a fighter who is relatively stronger (in order to maximise the chances of winning). Forcing participants to adhere to their chosen fighter prevented unnecessary debate between competitors as to who would choose their fighter first before a match.

The trial groups were run during the week following the information session. When a trial group arrived on the nominated day, competitors were paired and rotated so that they played each other once only. Thus, there were six matches played over the lunch hour. Each match between a given pair was conducted as the best of three games (where a game was the best of three rounds). The remaining pair, who were not competing for the purpose of the trial, were allowed to practice *MK3* in an adjacent room on another Super Nintendo games system. Competitors were told at the start of the lunch period that the trials served to rank competitors for the tournament. The trials were recorded on videotape.

At the completion of the second week, when all had participated in a trial group session, participants were ranked on the basis of their performances. A tournament draw was devised based on these ranks. The tournament draw was constructed so that the top-ranked player was assigned to play the bottom-ranked player during Round 1, the second-ranked player was assigned to play the fifteenth-ranked player, the third-ranked player was assigned to play the fourteenth-ranked player, and so on, until all players were paired with another player. In addition, the draw was designed so that a high ranked player did not meet another high ranked player until late in the tournament. This meant that the top-ranked player did not meet the second-ranked player until the Final, assuming that both players progressed that far in the tournament.

The tournament was conducted during three lunch periods in the week following the trials. The tournament was conducted like a tennis event. During Round 1, the first pair was escorted from the classroom into a practice room, which was adjacent to the experimental room, in which the two players were allowed to practice for approximately 5 minutes on a spare Super Nintendo system. At the end of the practice session, the second pair was escorted into the practice room and the first pair, who had now ended its practice session, was escorted into the experimental room in order to compete proper. Matches were played as the best of three games (where a game was the best of three rounds). The match was terminated when the first player reached two games. Thus, if a player was leading 2 games to nil, the match was terminated and the losing player was eliminated from the tournament. The winning player progressed into the Quarter Final round. The third pair of Round 1 was subsequently escorted from the class room into the practice room, and the second pair was escorted into the experimental area in order to compete proper. This procedure was repeated until all pairs from Round 1 had competed in the experimental area. When Round 1 matches had ended, the same procedure was employed for Quarter Final matches. There were eight matches during Round 1, four matches during the Quarter Finals, two matches during the Semi Finals, and the Final. Round 1 matches were conducted on Monday, Quarter Final and Semi Final matches were conducted on Tuesday, and the Final was conducted on Wednesday. The tournament was recorded on videotape.

To increase the competitive nature of the tournament, matches were transmitted from the experimental room to a closed circuit television in the class room. The tournament attracted nearly 40 spectators for the Final on Wednesday. All spectators were high school students who did not participate in the tournament.

Prizes were offered to increase the competitive nature of the tournament. Losing semi-finalists were each awarded a $10 gift voucher, the losing finalist was awarded a $25 gift voucher and a trophy, and the winner was awarded a $40 voucher and a larger trophy. Competitors were aware that they were playing for prizes at the commencement of the study.

Results and discussion

Six competitors did not produce a finishing move in the trial period or tournament situation and were thus excluded from the data analysis. Table 2 displays the kill ratios for the sample of 10 competitors who produced a finishing move in the trial period and tournament situations. Competitors are identified as their fighter, rather than by their given name. During the trial period, the average kill ratio for the sample was .67 which suggests that the competitors tended to kill their opponent's game character nearly 7 out of 10 times. In comparison, the average kill ratio during the tournament rose to .84 which suggests that the competitors tended to kill nearly 8.5 out of 10 times.

An examination of the kill ratios across the sample reveals that seven competitors had a higher kill ratio in the tournament relative to the trial period, two competitors had a lower kill ratio in the tournament relative to the trial period, and one competitor displayed no change at all. A one-tailed Wilcoxon Signed-Ranks test was performed on these data in order to test the experimental hypothesis that the sample would display a higher kill ratio in the tournament than in the trial period. The Wilcoxon T-statistic was statistically significant, $T=2$, $p<.01$, thus supporting the experimental hypothesis.

Table 2. Kill ratios (%) for the trial and tournament for 10 participants during the first study

Participant's game character	Trial		Tournament	
	Kill ratio	(%)	Kill ratio	(%)
Smoke #	7/12	(58)	12/16	(75)
Sindel	11/13	(85)	10/12	(83)
Kabal #1	8/10	(80)	5/6	(83)
Kabal #2	4/9	(44)	10/10	(100)
Sonja	3/11	(27)	1/4	(25)
Smoke #2	8/9	(89)	8/9	(89)
Cyrax	5/7	(71)	4/4	(100)
Sub Zero #1	5/7	(71)	5/5	(100)
Sub Zero #2	7/8	(88)	1/1	(100)
Sub Zero #3	1/2	(50)	1/1	(100)
Total	59/88	(67)	57/68	(84)

Experiments 2 and 3

A major shortcoming of Experiment 1 was the complex nature of the experimental design. A number of factors could have caused the increase in kill ratios during the tournament situation, e.g., the reward, tournament-type situation, and/or audience. We conducted two further studies that explored the potential influence of two situational factors, namely, the reward and the tournament.

Experiment 2 was conducted six months after Experiment 1. The same methodology was employed except that the male students did not play for prizes and trophies. Instead, all 16 competitors were given a $5 gift voucher at the end of the study for participating in the tournament event. Ten competitors in this tournament had participated in the previous study.

An analysis of these data showed that the average kill ratio during the trial period, for the 11 competitors who produced at least one finishing move in both the trial period and tournament, was .77. The average kill ratio during the tournament situation rose slightly to .83. Seven competitors had a higher kill ratio in the tournament relative to the trial period, three competitors had a lower kill ratio, and one competitor displayed no change at all. A one-tailed Wilcoxon Signed-Ranks test was performed on these data in order to test the experimental hypothesis that the sample would display a higher kill ratio in the tournament than in the trial period. The Wilcoxon T-statistic was not statistically significant, T=19.5. That is, the absence of a reward failed to produce the link demonstrated in the previous study.

Experiment 3 examined the idea that the link demonstrated in Experiment 1 was partially caused by the presence of an audience. Past research from the aggression field has shown that the mere presence of an audience increases the chances of observing competitive aggression, particularly when the audience is composed of peers (e.g., Borden & Taylor, 1973). The tournament-type event was abandoned for this study in place of a competitive situation that contained no audience (except the experimenter).

Twenty-two male students, who were proficient at *Ultimate Mortal Kombat 3* (the next videogame in the series), were paired off. Pairs were of equal ability (which was determined by conducting preliminary trial sessions). Each pair participated in a 'challenge'. The challenge was to pit each individual in the pair against the other for a $10 gift voucher. Pairs practiced for 15 minutes and were then instructed that the 'challenge' period had begun in which they were competing against each other for 15 minutes. The winner of the 'challenge' was the individual who won more rounds than his opponent at the completion of the 15-minute period. The practice period acted as the baseline measure, whilst the 'challenge' period was a competitive situation with a reward.

Twenty-one competitors produced at least one finishing move both during the baseline and challenge periods. During the baseline period, the average kill ratio was .58, whilst the average kill ratio during the challenge period increased to .71. Sixteen males demonstrated a higher kill ratio during the challenge period in comparison to the baseline, three competitors had a lower kill ratio in the challenge period relative to the baseline, and two competitors displayed no change at all. The difference was statistically significant, $t\ (19) = -2.68$, $p<.01$. That is, on average, competitors demonstrated a significant increase in the tendency to kill the opponent's game character during the challenge period.

In addition to playing in the 'challenge', competitors in experiment 3 completed a mood-state inventory at three time periods, i.e., pre-practice period, post-practice period, and post-challenge period. The mood-state inventory contained three scales. The scales measured angry feelings, and negative and positive feelings. An analysis of these scales across the three time periods showed very little change across the sample. That is, the higher competitive aggression demonstrated during the 'challenge' period was not accompanied by feelings of anger or negative emotions. However, there was an association between the eventual winners of the 'challenge' period and self-reported feeling states. Winners were more likely to report lower levels of anger and negative feelings, and higher levels of positive feelings, during the post-challenge period, relative to losers. That is, the euphoria of winning the $10 gift voucher was associated with self-reports of positive feelings; however, the aggressive videogame behaviour by competitors was performed without feeling angry.

Finally, we tested the underlying assumption that the 'kill ratio' measure represents 'social' aggressive behaviour by asking two teachers, who knew the competitors well, to rate each male's tendency to display aggressive behaviour towards peers and teachers in the school context. Both teachers rated each male on a 10-point scale. Each male received two aggression scores, i.e., one for aggression towards peers and another for aggression towards teachers. These data showed that the teachers' ratings of the competitors' aggression (towards peers and teachers) were significantly associated with male's baseline kill ratios derived from the 'challenge' study. That is, the competitor's tendency to kill their opponent's videogame character upon winning was associated with their aggressive behaviour at school. Males who displayed a high level of aggression towards peers and teachers were more likely to have a higher kill ratio. It is emphasised that the aggressive ratings made by teachers were *not* repeated through time (i.e., before and after the study) in order to measure whether competitors' aggressive tendencies changed by playing a videogame with a competitive-violent theme. Rather, teacher ratings were a validity check. They show that participant's videogame play was associated with aggressive tendencies in the 'real world', implying that *Mortal Kombat* play is an aggressive behaviour.

Conclusions

On the basis of these studies, a number of conclusions can be drawn:

1. Australian adolescent males are more likely to display simulated aggressive behaviour under a competitive videogame situation with a reward, i.e., our findings support the competition-aggression hypothesis in a play context;
2. This competitive aggression is displayed in the absence of negative feelings like anger;
3. The competition-aggression effect can be demonstrated in a life-like tournament situation, but it can also be demonstrated in a less life-like competitive situation (i.e., without an audience); and
4. Competitors' aggressive play within a videogame (namely, *Mortal Kombat*) is associated with aggressive tendencies at school both towards teachers and peers.

Recommendations

Australian adolescent males' high exposure to videogames may raise issues over the potential negative effects of playing competitive-violent videogames (e.g., *Mortal Kombat*) on competitors' *social* aggression. However, our findings are a far cry from these issues. We have shown that adolescents spend a large amount of time playing videogames, and that adolescent males, who were experienced at a competitive-violent videogame, were more likely to display aggressive behaviour within the videogame context. We have *not* studied whether playing videogames with competitive-violent themes cause young males either to behave more aggressively *after* a playing session (i.e., short-term effects), or raises their tendency to behave aggressively in *other* competitive contexts, e.g., sports match, classroom (i.e., long-term effects). Further research is required in these areas. Two studies that may be carried out include: 1. A content analysis of videogames on the Australian market in order to explore the extent to which popular titles have competitive-violent themes; and 2. Demonstrating that videogames with competitive-violent themes increase competitive (and even non-competitive) *social* aggression in players over the short-term and/or long-term.

Notes

1. Research conducted by the first author under the supervision of the second and third authors as a part of doctorate work. Please address correspondence to Dr. Alexander Ask, Department of Psychology, University of Adelaide, South Australia, 5005 (E-mail: alex.ask@flinders.edu.au).
2. Ecological study: An experimental design in which the participant is placed in a setting that simulates the 'real world' (e.g., a tournament for prizes) and is afforded the opportunity to behave 'naturally' (i.e., videogame play).

Further readings

Anderson, C. A., & Morrow, M. (1995). Competitive aggression without interaction: Effects of competitive versus cooperative instructions on aggressive behaviour in videogames. *Personality and Social Psychology Bulletin, 21,* 1020-1030.

Ask, A. (1999). *To kill or not to kill: Competition, aggression, and videogames, in adolescents.* Thesis submitted for the degree of Doctor of Philosophy, University of Adelaide.

Borden, R., & Taylor, S. P. (1973). The social instigation and control of physical aggression. *Journal of Applied Social Psychology, 3,* 354-361.

Deutsch, M. (1949). An experimental study of the effects of co-operation and competition upon group process. *Human Relations, 2,* 199-231.

Durkin, K. (1995). *Computer games: Their effects on young people.* Australian Office of Film and Literature Classification, Sydney.

Durkin, K., & Low, J. (1998). Children, media and aggression: Current research in Australian and New Zealand. In: U. Carlsson, & C. von Feilitzen (Eds.). *Children and media violence* (pp. 107-124). UNESCO International Clearinghouse on Children and Violence on the Screen, Nordicom, Göteborg University.

Lorenz, K. (1963). *On Aggression.* Great Britain: Cox & Wyman Limited, Norfolk.

Office of Film and Literature Classification (1994, July 22). *Computer games and images: Classification guidelines and industry code.* Sydney: Office of Film and Literature Classification (Inc. the Film Censorship Board).

Sherif, M. (1967). *Group conflict and co-operation: Their social psychology.* London: Routledge & Kegan Paul Ltd.

Boys, Girls and Violent Video Games

The Views of Dutch Children

Peter Nikken

Video games receive a lot of publicity nowadays, because they too represent an audio-visual medium that might contribute to violence in society. As with television, the assumption is that video games may have a greater influence on the behaviour and attitudes of children when the portrayed violence in the game is rewarded and when the violent acts are perpetrated by the heroes of the game rather than by the villains. Video games might be even more influential than television, because children are actively involved in the games as players and not just passive viewers. On the other hand, doubts are expressed about the possible effects of violent video games as well, because most games are still far from realistic.

So far, scientific results have not yet led to a final conclusion. Modest correlational relations have been observed between game playing and self- and peer-reports on aggressiveness in the U.S. (Dominick, 1984; Lin & Lepper, 1987), and van Schie and Wiegman (1998) in the Netherlands found that heavy game players were rated as less pro-social. Such studies, however, do not allow us to infer causality. According to Durkin (1995), who cites several experimental studies, there is no firm evidence that playing video games leads to antisocial withdrawal. Others, however, mean that, as a whole, laboratory and survey results do suggest that game-playing, particularly playing violent games, may not be entirely benign for all players (Funk et al., 1997; Griffiths, 1997).

Violent video games more attractive for boys

According to Dutch and British children's estimates of the time spent on media, playing video games amounts to about half an hour per day (Van der Voort et al., 1998). This figure, however, does not apply equally to boys and girls. As a rule, boys spend more time playing video games and are more fond of playing such games than girls are. According to Beentjes, Kruse and Vooijs (1995), the higher proportion of personal computers or video game consoles in households with boys is not the sole reason why boys are more apt to play video games. Comparing boys and girls who have access to the same hardware for video games at home, boys in the Netherlands were still found to play more often and longer than girls did.

It is surmised that the higher attractiveness of video games among boys may in part be explained by the content of video games. Most games do represent an aggressive and competitive male culture, rather than a culture that is adapted to girls' interests. In addition, there are more male characters in video games than female characters, providing girls less possibilities for identification (Provenzo, 1991). Support for this assumption is given by several studies in which it is found that girls prefer non-violent or fantasy-violent video games, whereas boys are more apt to like violent games (Spanhel, 1987; Funk, 1993; Griffiths, 1997; Wiegman & van Schie, 1998).

Cantor (1998) proposes several reasons why children choose violent media, e.g., they are looking for arousal; they want to feel empowered; such media products are interesting because they are forbidden; children want to witness their own aggressive behaviour; or they want to cope with fears in their own lives. In addition, it is assumed that boys like violent media more, partly because gender-specific behaviour is biologically determined, but also because boys and girls each derive their social status and identity from violent media (Goldstein, 1998). This means that boys can feel more at ease when watching a violent movie or playing an aggressive video game and thereby fulfil their role as 'being tough'. The social expectations for girls, on the other hand, are that they should not be tough, but rather vulnerable. Not liking violent media gives them the opportunity to fit in.

What do children think of (violent) video games?

A problem in most studies on violence in video games is defining what constitutes violent and non-violent games. Most studies rely on adult experimenters or experts to define video games as violent or non-violent. Wiegman and Van Schie (1998) in the Netherlands, for example, asked an editor of a video game magazine and two toyshop managers to classify as aggressive or non-aggressive several games mentioned by children. Unfortunately, little is known about what children themselves think about video games. Do they also think in terms of violent and non-violent games? Do they feel that playing video games may be harmful to them? And does such a feeling have an effect on their likes and dislikes for video games? In addition, it is not known whether children, and in particular boys, like to play video games because of the violent content of the games, or just because of the action. As a matter of fact, very little is known about the 'ingredients' that, in the eyes of boys and girls, make a good video game.

What children like about video games

When reading semi-popular books on video games and children, or reports aimed at informing parents about video games, one does encounter several game features that video game experts and educators see as important for the popularity of video games among children (Greenfield, 1984; Selnow, 1984; Spanhel, 1987; Provenzo, 1991; Beierwaltes, Grebe & Naumann-Braun, 1993; Fehr & Fritz, 1993; Funk et al., 1997; Valkenburg, 1997). In a content analysis conducted on features mentioned by video game experts and educators as being important for children's liking or disliking a video game, we found that most of these game features could be categorised in terms of thirteen types of standards for video games. Three types of standards primarily deal with violence, i.e., video games are fun to play because they 'contain action', 'contain aggression', and 'are exciting'. The other video game features children 'should' like, according to the adults, could be categorised in standards such as: 'contain beautiful graphics', 'have good audio', 'are fast', 'are difficult and challenge perseverance', 'give the possibility to improve oneself', 'provide possibilities for identification', 'are educational', 'give possibilities for self-control', 'provide possibilities to compete with others', and 'stimulate curiosity'.

Whether children themselves endorse these features as reasons for liking video games has never been systematically investigated. So far, only a couple of studies have been conducted in which children or teenagers are asked why they like to play video games. Two of these studies, both conducted in the Netherlands (Kruse, 1992; Wiegman et al., 1995), used an open-ended question asking children aged 10 to 14 years what they like about their favourite games. Afterwards, the researchers classified the answers into distinct types like: 'tension', 'entertainment or diversion when you are bored', 'excitement', 'providing variation', 'possibility to improve yourself', 'containing action, fighting and winning', 'providing identification and self control', and 'possibilities for exploring and learning'.

Other studies have been conducted in the U.S. Again, the researchers defined the types of preferable game characteristics, but now before the data were collected. Malone (1981) rated 25 games on ten dimensions that he as a researcher thought were likely to affect the games' motivational value. The study, performed with boys and girls from a private elementary school ranging from kindergarten through eighth grade, showed that the most important feature determining game popularity was that 'the game had a goal'. Other features that correlated with game popularity among the children were: 'computer keeps a score', 'audio effects', and 'randomness involved in a game'. By means of a questionnaire, McClure and Mears (1984) asked high-school students why they played video games, whereas Griffiths (1997) posed the same question to children aged 11 years at a summer camp. The main reasons reported with fixed-choice items were: 'challenge', 'fun', and 'escape outside pressures'. Finally, Barnett et al. (1997) presented high-school and college students between 15 and 19 years of age with a list of statements tapping their attitudes towards video game features. These statements provided by the researchers were then clustered into fifteen characteristics, of which most coincided with the game features mentioned above.

The views of Dutch children on video games

To shed more light on what children themselves think about video games, we have conducted an exploratory study (Nikken, de Leede & Rijkse, 1999). We were specifically interested in whether the video game features put forward by adult experts in the literature, or those found among high-school students, would also be seen in the views of children. In addition, we wanted to know if boys and girls differ in their views on these features for video games, e.g., do boys prefer features like aggression, action, and competition, whereas girls prefer humour, comprehensibility, and education? Next, we established how boys and girls in the Netherlands value playing with video games in their leisure time and whether they see video games as more appropriate for boys than for girls. Finally, we also wanted to know how boys and girls value specific video games and if they make a distinction between violent and non-violent games.

The study was conducted among 152 boys and 143 girls in grades four to six at two primary schools situated in two small cities in the centre of the Netherlands. The children ranged in age from seven to twelve years (mean age was 9.3 years). Children's views on playing video games were measured using a paper and pencil questionnaire pertaining to the research questions involved in the study. Children answered the questions in their classrooms.

Attractiveness of playing video games

Almost all children in the sample indicated that they regularly play video games; only 4 per cent of the children said they had never played a video game. Actually, of ten possible leisure activities, playing video games proved to be the most attractive for children (see Table 1). As compared to girls, boys reported playing video games significantly more often, and gave significantly higher ratings to playing video games in their leisure time than girls did. Girls, on the other hand, were significantly more fond of playing round games, drawing or doing handicraft activities, reading books, and playing instruments, than boys were.

Appropriateness of video games for boys and girls

Although girls expressed less liking for playing video games than boys did, and also said that they played them less often than boys did, girls did not indicate that video games are specifically for boys. On the contrary, all girls said that playing video games is equally appropriate for both girls and boys. A majority of the boys also felt that games can be played by both girls and boys. A fair amount of them (21%), however, believed that video games are 'just for boys'. This view was expressed significantly more often by younger boys.

Table 1. Appreciation of ten leisure activities by boys and girls (mean ratings)

Leisure activity	Boys	Girls	Total
Playing video games	8.97	7.51	8.26 ***
Playing outdoors	7.84	7.70	7.77
Doing sports	7.74	7.68	7.71
Watching television	7.69	7.65	7.67
Playing round games	6.98	7.73	7.34 *
Listening to music	7.01	7.42	7.21
Drawing/doing handicraft	6.05	8.04	7.02 ***
Reading books	5.32	7.52	6.39 ***
Reading comics	6.41	6.23	6.32
Making music	5.31	6.01	5.65 *
n =	152	143	295

Note: Scores varied from 1 (minimal appreciation) to 10 (maximal appreciation). Asterisks indicate whether there are significant differences between boys and girls: * the chance that the difference is not significant is 5 out of 100; *** the chance that the difference is not significant is 1 out of 1000.

Evaluation of video games

We asked children to rate sixteen specific video games on a ten-point scale (where 1 means 'I don't like it at all' and 10 stands for 'I like it very, very much'). As expected, each video game was evaluated significantly more often by boys than by girls, and more often by older children. On average, boys evaluated 7.7 games, whereas girls evaluated only 3.6 video games.

By means of a statistical technique (principal components analysis) applied on the ratings given to the video games, it was found that children tend to make a similar distinction between types of games as adults generally do. Four video games that adult experts have classified as violent games (*Streetfighter*, *Doom*, *Mortal Kombat*, and *Killer Instinct*) were also seen as a distinct type of game by children, and six games labelled by adults as non-violent (*Marioland*, *Supermario*, *Supertetris*, *Pinball*, *Duck Tales*, and *Donkey Kong*) also clustered as a distinct type of game according to the children's evaluations. The remaining six games involved in the study could not be interpreted as belonging to a specific type, probably because they were rated by a minority of the children. In accordance with former studies, we too found that violent video games were rated significantly higher by boys (mean rating 7.8; n = 45) than by girls (5.7; n = 7). Non-violent games, on the other hand, were rated significantly higher by girls (mean rating 8.1; n =17) as compared to boys (6.9; n = 55).

Standards for video games

To find out whether boys are more fond of playing with violent games because of the violence portrayed, we first wanted to know if children see aggression as an important ingredient. Therefore, we asked the boys and girls for their views on the importance of 30 different game features, some of them associated with aggression. Using a five-point scale, the children indicated for each feature to what extent they thought the feature should be present in a game. All features were taken from the literature mentioned above.

Again using principal components analysis, the features were clustered into distinct types of standards for video games. The following five standards (with the comprising features within parentheses) could be formed:

1. *Challenge* (it makes you curious about how the game proceeds; it makes you curious about what will come next; you don't know what will happen next; a lot of things happen; it gets harder all the time; there are different levels);
2. *Aggression* (it contains a lot of blood; it contains a lot of fighting; it contains action; it is spooky);
3. *Control* (it lets me decide what happens; it lets me play better than my friends; everything proceeds as I want it to; I get more and more points);
4. *Technique* (it makes beautiful sounds; it contains funny sounds; it goes fast; it has pace);
5. *Instructiveness* (it is educational; I can learn things from it).

The five standards for video games were identified in an analysis applied to the scores of boys and girls combined. Separate analyses for boys and girls were conducted as well. For girls a solution was found that was highly similar to the one for boys and girls combined. The solution for boys was also similar to the combined solution, although the standards 'instructiveness' and 'technique' were part of the same cluster. In addition, the standard 'challenge' proved for boys to consist of two separate clusters that could be labelled as 'unpredictability of the game' and 'difficulty of the game'. The standard 'aggression' was defined by the same four features in both analyses for girls and boys, indicating that they both saw action and fighting, blood and spookiness as aggressive features.

Importance attached to the standards

'Challenge' was considered the most important video game standard of all. The importance children (boys and girls combined) attached to each of the other four standards ('aggression', 'control', 'technique', and 'instructiveness') did not differ significantly, indicating that children saw these four standards as equally important for video games. With respect to the importance attached by boys and girls separately, significant differences were found (see Figure 1). As compared to girls, boys felt significantly stronger that video games should provide 'a challenge' and 'possibilities for self control'. In addition, boys felt particularly strongly that video games should contain 'aggression', ranking this standard second. Girls attached very little importance to the standard 'aggression', which resulted in it being placed at the bottom of their ranking of the standards.

Figure 1. Importance attached to five standards for video games by boys and girls (mean scores)

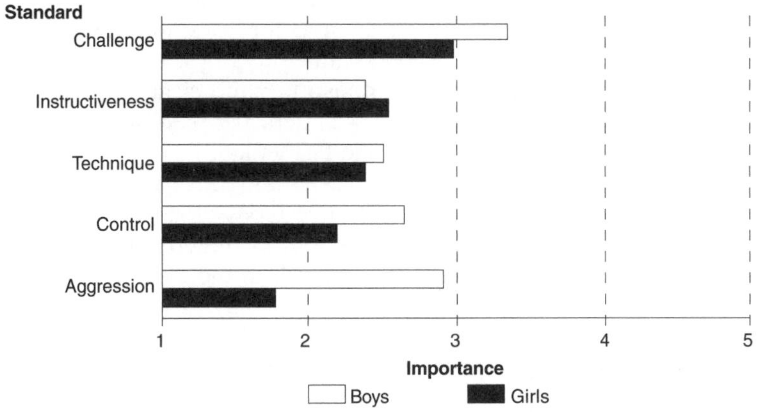

Note: Scores varied from 1 (entirely unimportant) to 5 (very important).

Does aggression enhance the pleasure of playing video games?

In order to find out if an aggressive content makes it more fun to play video games, we looked at the relationship between the *importance* children attached to the five standards, on the one hand, and the extent to which they *liked to play video games* in their leisure time. By means of a multiple regression analysis we determined which standards *predicted* a child's pleasure in playing a video game. We found that children who like to play video games more than others, were significantly more interested in being challenged, in being in control, and in aggressive content. These relations, however, were not the same for boys and girls. For boys, the appreciation of playing video games was significantly predicted by the standards 'challenge' and 'aggression'. In other words, boys prefer to play video games more if the games provide a challenge for them and if they contain aggressive features like blood, fighting, action and spooky elements. Among girls, the pleasure of playing a video game depended significantly on the standards 'instructiveness' and 'control', indicating that girls are more apt to play if the games allow them to learn and to decide the course of the game.

Conclusion

The purpose of our exploratory study was to gain more insight into the determinants of appreciation of video games for boys and girls aged seven to twelve years. The results of the study indicated that playing video games is a highly appreciated leisure time activity in the Netherlands, although boys are far more fond of it than girls are. Boys, specifically younger ones, also tended to see video games as somewhat more appropriate for them than for girls, and they were familiar with more video games. This, however, does not mean that girls had no interest in video games at all. On the contrary, all girls said that video games are just as appropriate for them as for boys, indicating that games may have the potential to attract girls as much as boys. From the ratings children made of a list of specific games, it also became clear that girls do like video games, especially those that are not violent *per se*. Boys, on the other hand, preferred games that may be classified as violent.

In our study, the extent to which boys and girls like to play video games in their leisure time could be related to five types of standards that children discerned for video games. The most *important* ingredient of a video game was the extent to which a 'challenge' is offered. In the eyes of children, this standard encompassed the element of unpredictability as well as encountering difficulties when bringing the game to an end. 'Challenge' proved to be more important than all other standards for both boys and girls. Especially for boys, 'providing a challenge' was also a significant *predictor* of their appreciation of playing video games.

A second standard was 'instructiveness', which means that children want to learn from video games. 'Instructiveness' was the least important standard for boys and did not contribute to their pleasure in playing video games. For girls, however, 'instructiveness' was the second most *important* standard and was also a significant *predictor* of their appreciation of playing video games.

Another standard that boys and girls found equally important for video games dealt with 'technique'. The standard 'technique' encompassed features like interesting sounds and a high pace. But neither for girls nor for boys did the standard 'technique' contribute to a child's appreciation of playing a video game.

Finally, two standards — 'control' and 'aggression' — were both seen as more *important* by boys than by girls. The standard 'control' included actively deciding which course a game takes, as well as being able to compete with playmates or with the computer. In other words, children saw it as important that video games meet and stimulate their feeling of competence. However, the standard 'control' was in particular for girls also a *predictor* of their appreciation of playing video games.

The standard of 'aggression' implies that a video game should be spooky and that it should contain lots of blood, fighting, and action. Thus, contrary to what some experts surmise, in the eyes of children, action and aggression belonged to one and the same standard. In addition, 'aggression' was also different from the standard 'challenge'. The standard of 'aggression' was the second most *important* standard for boys and the least important for girls. In fact, girls preferred the absence rather than presence of this element. For boys, 'aggression' was not only an important standard, it was one of the two significant *predictors* of their appreciation of playing video games (besides 'challenge'). Boys that were more fond of playing video games were more often to be found among children who expected a game to contain aggression than among children who didn't like violence in a game.

Acknowledgement

I am grateful to my colleagues Natalie De Leede and Christa Rijkse for obtaining the data for this study.

References

Barnett, M. A., Vitaglione, G. D., Harper, K. K. G., Quackenbush, S. W., Steadman, L. A. & Valdez, B. S. (1997). Late adolescents' experiences with and attitudes toward video games. *Journal of Applied Social Psychology, 27*, 1316-1334.

Beentjes, J., Kruse, C. & Vooijs, M. (1995). Computerattitude en computergebruik in de vrije tijd: Verschillen tussen jongens en meisjes [Computer attitudes and computer use in leisure time: Differences between boys and girls]. *Nederlands Tijdschrift voor Opvoeding, Vorming en Onderwijs, 11*, 32-47.

Beierwaltes, A., Grebe, B. & Naumann-Braun, K. (1993). Indizierte Computerspiele — Markt und Spieler [Indicated video games — Market and players]. In T. Ernst, W. Fehr, J. Fritz, & S. Hiegemann (Eds.) *Computerspiele* [Video games]. Bonn, Germany: Graphischer Grossbetrieb Possneck.

Cantor, J. (1998). Children's attraction to violent television programming. In J. H. Goldstein (Ed.), *Why we watch: The attractions of violent entertainment* (pp. 88-115). New York: Oxford University Press.

Dominick, Y. R. (1984). Video games, television violence, and aggression in teenagers. *Journal of Communication, 34*, 136-147.

Durkin, K. (1995). *Computer games. Their effects on young people: a review.* Sydney: Office of Film and Literature Classification.

Fehr, W. & Fritz, J. (1993). Videospiele in der Lebenswelt von Kindern und Jugendlichen [Video games in the world of experience of children and youngsters]. In T. Ernst, W. Fehr, J. Fritz, & S. Hiegemann (Eds.) *Computerspiele* [Video games]. Bonn, Germany: Graphischer Grossbetrieb Possneck.

Funk, J. B. (1993) Re-evaluating the impact of video games. *Clinical Paediatrics, 32*, 86-90.

Funk, J. B., Germann J. N. & Buckmann, D. D. (1997). Children and electronic games in the United States. *Trends in Communication, 2*, 111-125.

Goldstein, J. (Ed.). (1998). *Why we watch: The attractions of violent entertainment.* New York: Oxford University Press.

Greenfield, P. M. (1984). *Media and the mind of a child: From print to television, video games and computers.* Cambridge, MA: Harvard University.

Griffiths, M. (1997). Computer game playing in early adolescence. *Youth & Society, 29*, 223-237.

Kruse, C. (1992). *Mam, ik heb nog zeven levens! Kind en computer in de vrije tijd* [Mom, I have another seven lives! Children and computers in leisure time]. The Netherlands: Leiden University.

Lin, S. & Lepper, M. R. (1987). Correlates of children's usage of video games and computers. *Journal of Applied Social Psychology, 17*, 72-93.

Malone, T. W. (1981). Towards a theory of intrinsically motivating instruction. *Cognitive Science, 4*, 333-369.

McClure, R. F. & Mears, F. G. (1984). Video game players: Personality characteristics and demographic variables. *Psychological Reports, 5*, 271-276.

Nikken, P., de Leede, N., & Rijkse, C. (1999). *Game-boys en game-girls: Opvattingen van jongens en meisjes over computerspelletjes* [Game-boys and game-girls: Views of boys and girls on video games].Utrecht, the Netherlands: Stichting Jeugdinformatie Nederland.

Provenzo, E. F. jr. (1991). *Video kids: Making sense of Nintendo*. Cambridge, MA: Harvard University Press.

Selnow, G. W. (1984). Playing video games: the electronic friend. *Journal of Communication, 34*, 148-156.

Spanhel, D. (1987). *Jugendlichen vor dem Bildschirm* [Young people in front of the screen]. Weinheim, Germany: Deutscher Studien Verlag.

Valkenburg, P. M. (1997). *Vierkante ogen: Opgroeien met TV & PC* [Square eyes: Growing up with TV & PCs]. Amsterdam, The Netherlands: Balans.

Van der Voort, T. H. A., Beentjes, J. W. J., Bovill, M., Gaskell, G., Koolstra, C. M., Livingstone, S., & Marseille, N. (1998). Young people's ownership and uses of new and old forms of media in Britain and the Netherlands. *European Journal of Communication, 13*, 457-477.

Van Schie, E. G. M. & Wiegman, O. (1997). Children and video games: Leisure activities, aggression, social integration, and school performance. *Journal of Applied Social Psychology, 27*, 1175-1194.

Wiegman, O., & Van Schie, E. G. M. (1998). Video game playing and its relations with aggressive and prosocial behaviour. *British Journal of Social Psychology, 37*, 367-378.

Wiegman, O., Van Schie, E. G. M., Kuttschreuter, M. W. H., Boer, H., Breedijk, A. Ph., & Wiedijk, C. H. M. (1995). *Kind en computerspelletjes: Relaties met vrijetijdsbesteding, agressie, sociale integratie en schoolvaardigheden* [Children and video games: Relationships with leisure time activities, aggression, social integration, and school performance]. Enschede, The Netherlands: University of Twente.

New Media and Young People in Sweden

Peter Petrov

This article presents figures from an inquiry with 17-year-olds strategically chosen from 12 schools in Stockholm, the capital of Sweden. The focus of the inquiry was young people's use of IT and other media. Two aspects are emphasized here – differences between girls' and boys' use of IT, and Internet as a source of knowledge and information. The data collection was carried out as group inquiries during school hours in the autumn of 1999. The sample is, thus, not representative, which means that, according to statistical theory, the results cannot be generalized to a larger population.

The aim of the study is to find patterns of correlation between the respondents' use of computers and Internet, on the one hand, and other activities and values, on the other. It is hoped that such correlations could serve as an empirical frame for more fundamental explanations of the growth and impact of the new media.

The answers to most of the questions have been measured with interval or ordinal scales, which means that analytical methods presupposing such data, for instance Pearson's correlation coefficient and factor analysis, can well be used, as they are here. The figures commented upon in the text have also been controlled for in terms of the impact of other known background variables, not least those that are unevenly distributed in the sample; the results discussed in the text are, thus, independent of these variables.

IT and gender

Considering that some years ago many researchers questioned Internet's importance and potential for growth, it is interesting to note that about ¾ of the respondents have access to Internet in their homes and that all have access to it in the school. It should be further stressed that more than 90 percent have computers in their homes, most often purchased during the last 2-3 years. However, a considerably larger proportion of the boys has a computer of their own. Based on two other questions not presented here, we can conclude that the boys have generally been connected to the Net in their homes longer and have started using it earlier than the girls. It seems that the presence of a male teenager has often been the decisive factor for the family's acquisition of Internet and other advanced IT-equipment.

It is much more likely that boys consider themselves well informed on IT-questions in general and Internet's different fields of application in particular. Almost two-thirds of the boys (as compared to barely one third of the girls) thought that they were the family members who best mastered IT. A considerably larger proportion of the boys also has a TV-play station of their own (Diagram 1).

Diagram 1. What kind of computer equipment is available in your household? (%)

The vertical lines indicate every 20th percent of the respective group

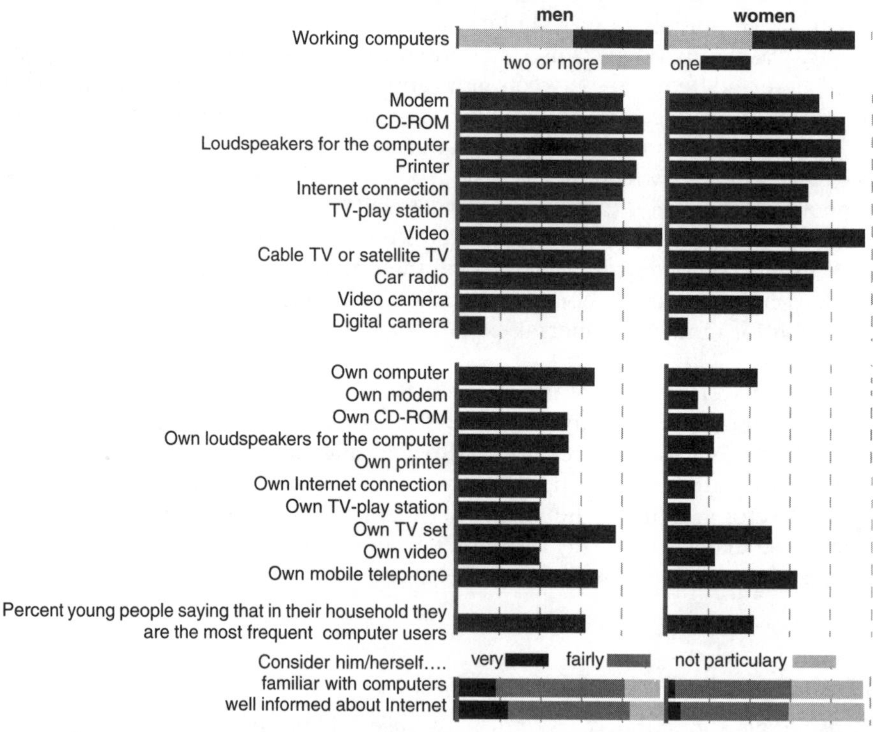

Moreover, boys are more likely to possess IT-equipment and to have access to an Internet connection of their own; in addition they have better self-confidence when it comes to IT know-how. This suggests that they more often have a pronounced interest in IT in general and Internet in particular, something that is reflected in the frequency and duration of their use of these media. The gender differences are striking, especially in terms of IT-use in the home and with friends. In these situations, boys utilize computers and Internet much longer than girls (as a rule, the frequent users run computers and Internet during longer intervals per occasion). The relation between the sexes is more equal as regards use of IT at school (Diagram 2).

Diagram 2. How often do you run... (%)
The vertical lines indicate every 20th percent of the respective group

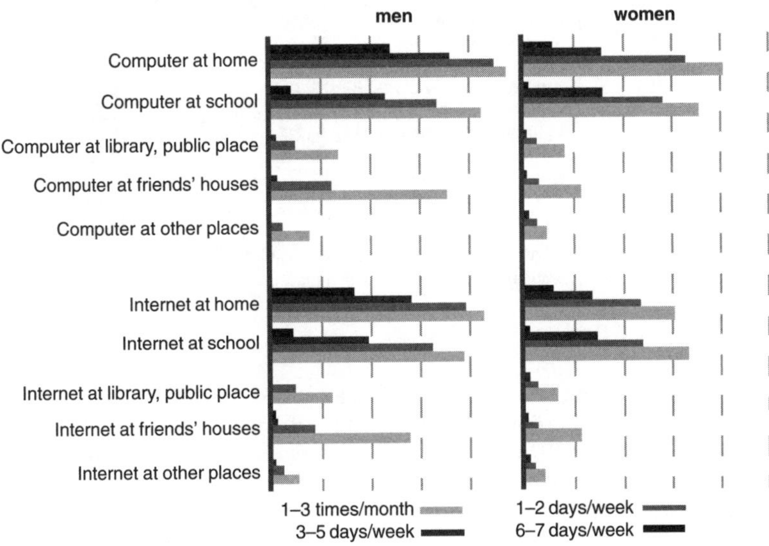

We asked the respondents a number of questions about the character of their use of IT and Internet. From the next diagram, Diagram 3, it appears that computers are used most often, and by most of the young people, for writing school assignments, for Internet, for computer games, and as a substitute for the CD player. The boys dominate in terms of the three latter uses, but there is no substantial difference between boys' and girls' answers when it comes to school assignments. The differences between the two groups are minor also regarding a number of other 'smaller' uses – writing text for personal purposes, using reference books or textbooks on CD-ROM, calculators and statistical programs (Excel is the most frequently used program in this respect) and to some extent also for scanning and designing of pictures. Moreover, it should be mentioned that there are significantly more boys who program or make their own music data files, even though they are a small proportion of the respondents.

The figure to the left of the bar in each row in Diagram 3 shows Pearson's correlation coefficient, which in this and the following examples in this section indicates the strength of the correlation between gender and the variable presented in each row.

Diagram 3. When you run computers, how often do you usually do the following things? (%)

The vertical lines indicate every 20th percent of the respective group

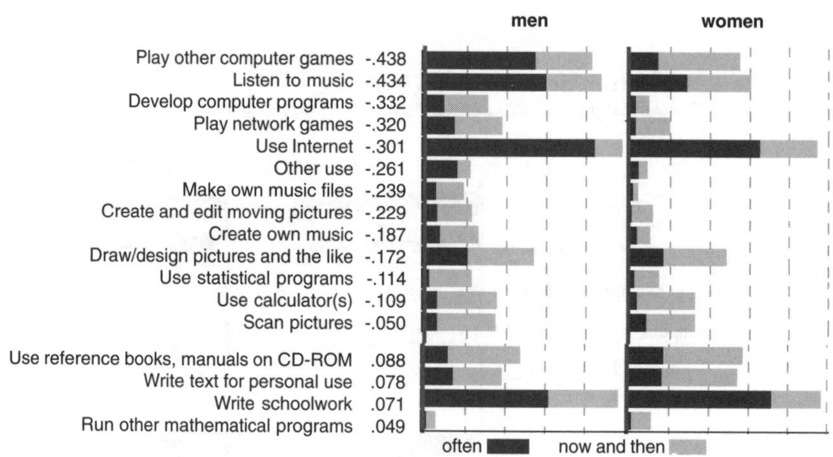

As seen in the following diagram, Diagram 4, many popular areas of Internet application are dominated by men – downloading music files, computer programs or other files from the Net, as well as use of ICQ or IRC. However, more girls than boys – especially if one considers teenagers with Swedish parents – have declared an active participation in chat groups. E-mail as a medium for personal contact is the most popular area of application for both sexes. More than 80 percent of the respondents have reported having an e-mail address of their own. A large proportion of the young people states that they often search information in databases. It should be mentioned that database searching occurs more seldom among girls of foreign origin.

Many results from our study suggest that, for young people, music is the most attractive aspect of Internet. Other analyses show that surfing to music groups' home pages and the like is about equally frequent among boys and girls. But the boys are much more likely to visit and use MP3's and Winamp's sites. Furthermore, it appears that boys are somewhat more likely to visit the sites of public authorities and political parties, whereas girls – to the same extent as boys – visit sites containing entertainment information, celebrities' homepages and also sites of the daily papers.

From the diagrams shown earlier as well as from other surveys, it is evident that boys are generally much more frequent users of computer games and more often have a TV-play station. In order to illustrate this relationship more satisfactorily, we asked a special question about the respondents' preferences for a number of specific games. Diagram 5 shows that video- and computer games are overall a 'male thing', even if more girls than boys like some genres, such as 'fashion and design', 'educational' and 'puzzle' games.

Diagram 4. When you run the Internet, how often do you usually do the following things? (%)
The vertical lines indicate every 20th percent of the respective group

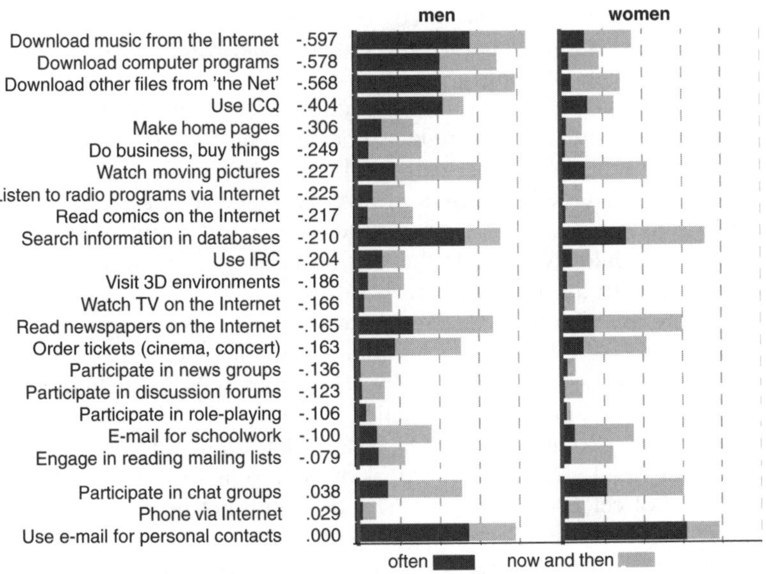

Diagram 5. What kind of computer- or video games do you like most? (%)
The vertical lines indicate every 20th percent of the respective group

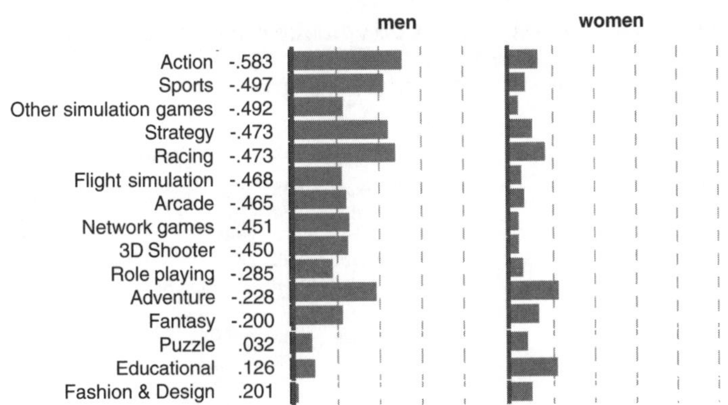

The fact that boys and girls make use of computers and Internet to different extents and, in many respects, in different manners, should not be surprising. Recent as well as previous research shows that there are many activities in 'real life' that could be designated as 'male' or 'female'. Moreover, the field of technology has traditionally been reserved for men, that is to say, created and used mainly by men. Since IT and Internet are male creations, one could presume that their design and content are marked by masculine activities, values and interests. An indirect proof of this statement is the answers to a question asking respondents to evaluate different qualities of IT using a number of adjectives. These responses show that the boys in our study were more likely to perceive IT technology as fun, exciting and comfortable, whereas girls were more likely to experience it as trying.

The quantitative and qualitative differences between boys' and girls' presence in virtual reality also reflect more general differences in young people's values and behavior in the 'real' world. Our survey shows, in accordance with many earlier studies, that girls in Sweden make much more extensive use of books, whereas boys more often watch video and read the comics. We should stress that while TV remains the largest medium, boys more frequently spend their time with the Internet than with radio.

There are also huge differences with respect to young people's interest in several types of content in the traditional media. Here again, we find a larger proportion of boys showing interest in topics such as technology, cars, electronics, and in sports and TV-action (Diagram 6). They also have a marked preference for some music styles, such as hard rock and heavy metal. Girls, on the other hand, are much more likely to report that they like drama fiction, coverage of celebrities, soaps, talk shows and, not least, programs and articles about fashion and beauty (Diagram 6). They also prefer softer music styles. Furthermore, the girls have given more responses indicating that it is important that the media take up welfare topics (such as gender equality, health care, education, school policy, environmental questions, child care, and family policy).

Diagram 6. What content do you like most in papers/magazines/on the radio/on TV? (%)

The vertical lines indicate every 20th percent of the respective group

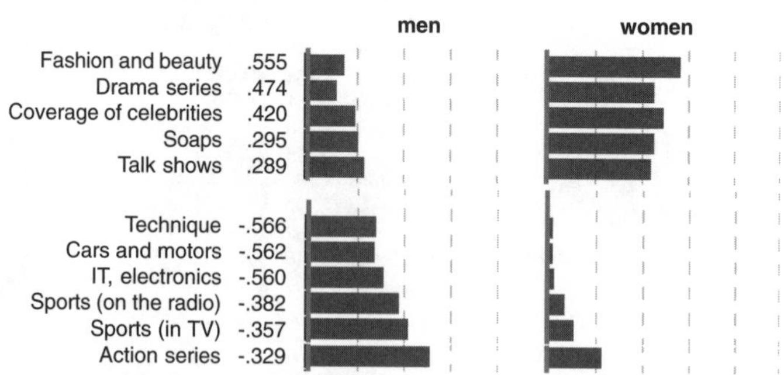

The differences between the sexes also recur in the young people's leisure activities. Girls appear to be much more likely to occupy themselves with writing diaries, beauty care, trying on and buying clothes, and doing different

household activities, such as interior decoration, cooking, sewing and the like. In accordance with their interests, boys devote themselves to a higher degree to cars and motors, fishing, competitions and other sporting events, playing billiards, darts, etc. (Diagram 7).

Diagram 7. How often do you usually...(%)
The vertical lines indicate every 20th percent of the respective group

Much has been written about Internet as a source of knowledge and information. Diagram 8 shows the proportion of respondents in our study that has used Internet for searches within some 30 areas.

Since boys are generally much more diligent Internet users, it is not surprising that they search information – on entertainment, general knowledge or for practical use – within most of the areas more frequently. The gender differences are valid especially for different kinds of computer and technical information, for sports and not least for pornography. Only three girls (out of 134) mentioned that they have checked Net porn at all, whereas almost 60 percent of the boys acknowledged that they do so at least now and then, and one-fifth often or always. Although these results might be expected, they are worth mentioning, since men are the principal producers and users of pornographic content in the traditional media as well. Considerably more boys than girls have also indicated that they seek financial information on the Internet, not least when it comes to stocks, bonds and the like.

It is, on the other hand, worth pointing out that there are no significant differences between boys and girls concerning searches within several fields associated with entertainment and pleasure, as well as within a number of domains of social relevance, such as history, geography, politics, education, etc. We could further mention that news – principally information about trips, public entertainment and film – is also searched on the Net by both sexes.

Diagram 8. How often do you use the Internet for searches when it comes to... (%)

The vertical lines indicate every 20th percent of the respective group

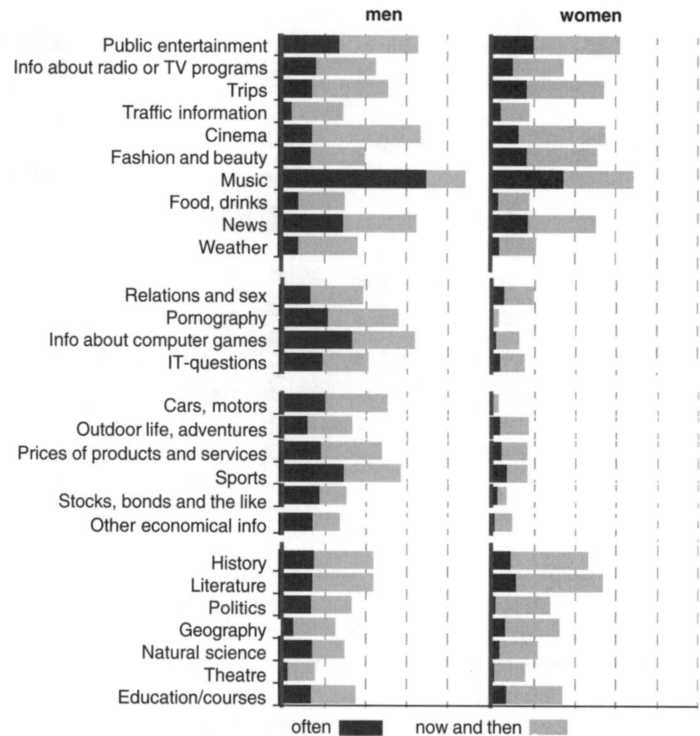

Internet and knowledge

In the preceding diagram, the grouping of the information areas searched on the Internet has been obtained by means of factor analysis conducted on the correlations between the respondents' answers to the separate question items. The fact that certain items have been sorted into the same group indicates that there is a *factor*, a statistical variable, that unites them – correlates with them and thus largely explains the variation in the answers to the original questions. It also means that persons with high scores for a given factor are more likely to search information within several domains sorted under or otherwise correlated with this factor, and vice versa – the lower score a person has for a factor, the lower the probability that (s)he searches information within the fields falling under this factor. This relationship is illustrated in Diagram 9, where two groups are compared – those 20 percent who most often and those 20 percent who (almost) never search *relevant societal information on the Internet (SII)*. SII includes history, politics, literature, natural science, geography, education and theatre, as well as (to some extent) economic information and news – knowledge fields that are associated with the legitimate economic, scientific, symbolic, etc. capital of the society.

Diagram 9. How often do you use the Internet for searches when it comes to... (%)

The vertical lines indicate every 20th percent of the respective group

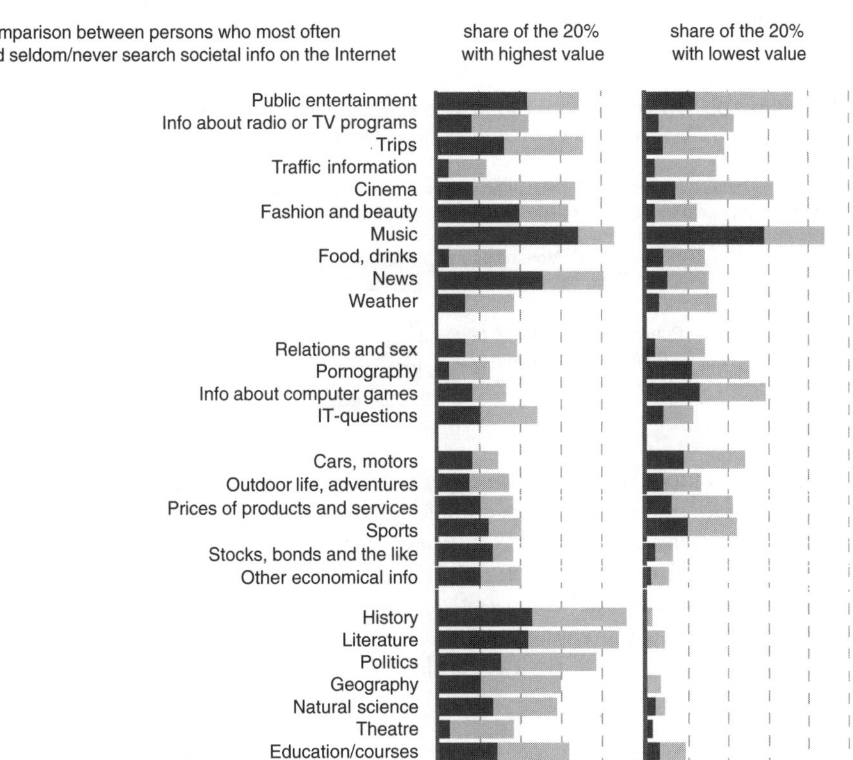

The correlation between the SII factor and the above-mentioned variables is illustrated in the lower part of Diagram 9 above. Here, as well as in the following presentation, the respondents are divided into two groups – the 20 percent with the highest and those with the lowest SII scores. It seems as though access to Internet *per se* – at home and at school – is not decisive for people's searching habits within these fields of knowledge; it is worth stressing that persons with low SII scores have computers and use Internet at least to the same extent as the high SII score group. Both groups are similar also with respect to their general interest in computers, electronics and other technical issues. This is also valid for many entertainment items and for private communication, which, as earlier mentioned, are IT's most popular domains among young people. There are small differences between the groups also regarding use of search engines (Altavista, Yahoo, etc.) and other portals, as well as when it comes to surfing to friends' and celebrities' home pages.

It is, on the other hand, not surprising that persons who often search relevant societal information on Internet are much more likely to surf to sites with corresponding content, such as the web sites of morning papers, government authorities and not least political parties – sites that are practically not visited at all by the low SII-score group (Diagram 10).

Diagram 10. Do you usually visit the following sites on the Internet? (%)
The vertical lines indicate every 20th percent of the respective group

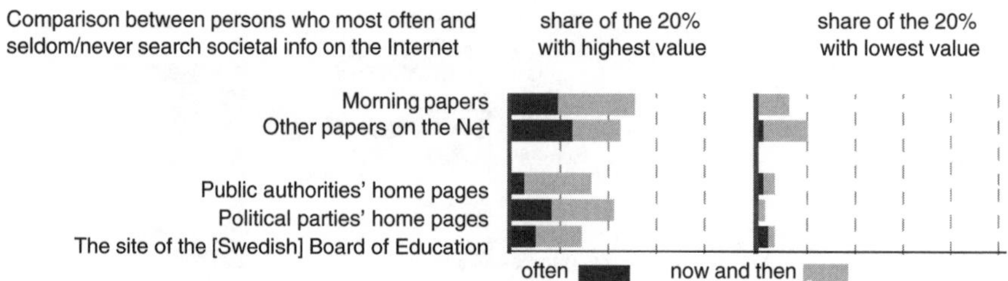

Pupils from elite schools, whose parents have completed higher levels of education or belong to the higher occupational groups, are strongly overrepresented among teenagers who use the Net for acquiring societal information. And these young people also have a strong affinity to corresponding content in the traditional media (public debate, politics, culture, science, etc.), a behavior that corresponds to much greater interest in most of the sciences and relevant societal issues, particularly global political and economic issues (for examples, see Diagram 11 and 12a).

Diagram 11. How interested are you in the following sciences? (%)
The vertical lines indicate every 20th percent of the respective group

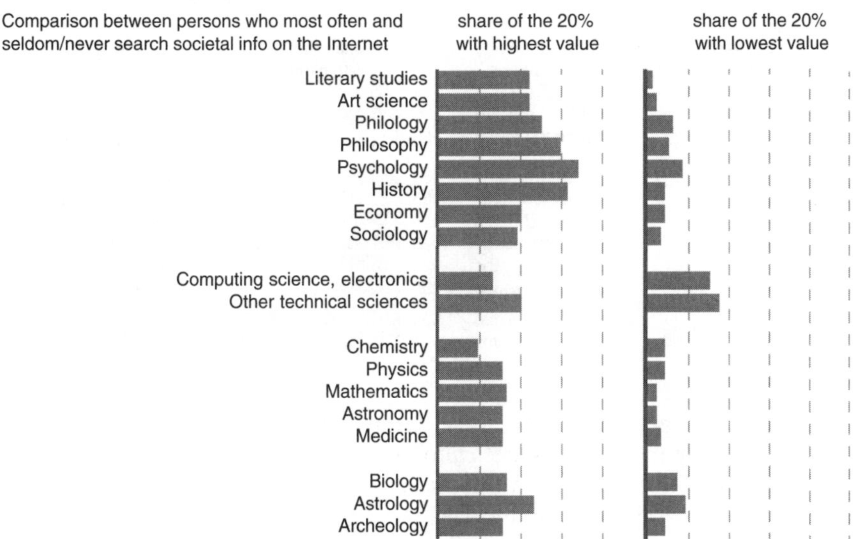

Diagram 12a. What content do you like most in papers/magazines/on the radio/on TV? (%)
The vertical lines indicate every 20th percent of the respective group

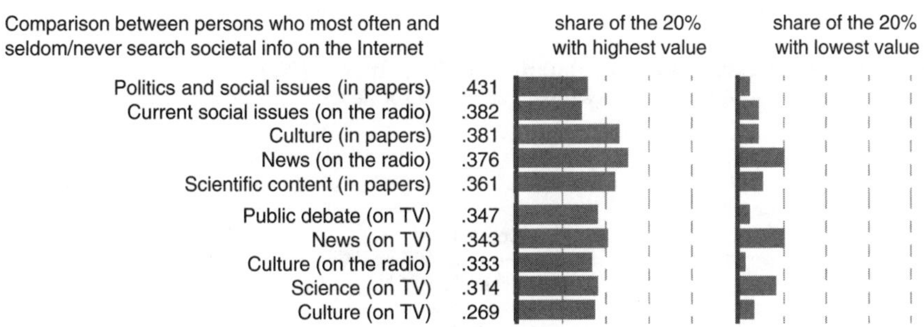

The figure to the left of the bar in each row in Diagram 12a above shows Pearson's correlation coefficient, which in this and in the following examples in this section indicates the strength of the correlation between the SII-factor and the variable presented in each row.

Nevertheless, the two groups are very similar when it comes to the most popular entertainment genres (Diagram 12b).

Diagram 12b. What content do you like most in papers/magazines/on the radio/on TV? (%)
The vertical lines indicate every 20th percent of the respective group

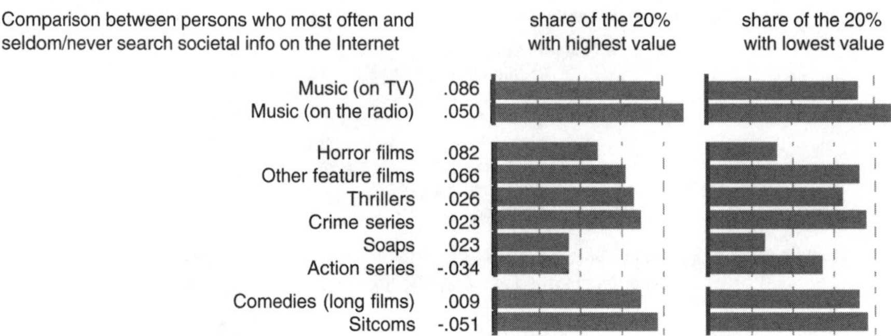

The two extreme groups are also very different in a number of respects connected to 'socially more legitimate' cultural taste and activities. The inclination to search societal information on Internet correlates strongly with the respondents' interest in classical music and jazz (Diagram 13), as well as with several leisure activities such as discussing political topics, going to the theatre, visiting art exhibitions, museums, etc. – activities that are also much more usual among the adult elite of society. Furthermore, these young people are much more likely to use the print media – fiction, factual study books, morning papers (Diagram 14).

Diagram 13. What kind of music do you like most? (%)
The vertical lines indicate every 20th percent of the respective group

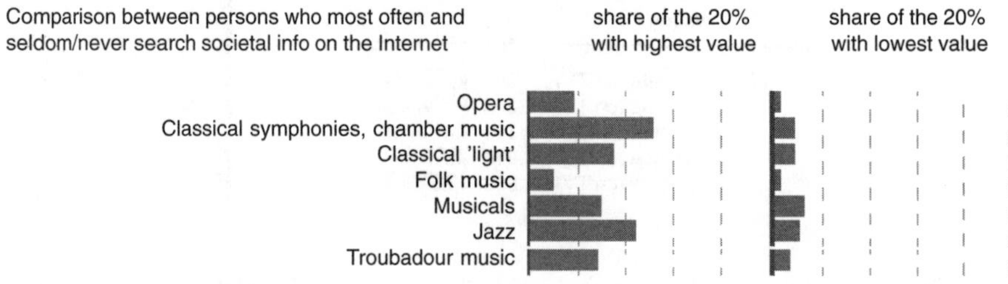

Diagram 14. How often do you usually... (%)

The vertical lines indicate every 20th percent of the respective group

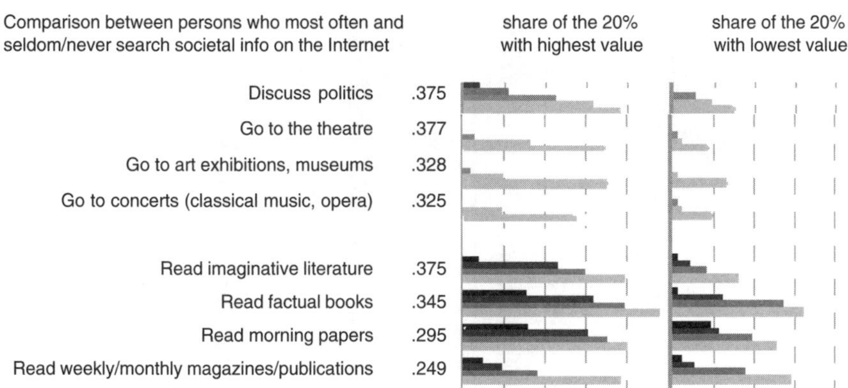

Note: For meanings of the upper set of staples, see Diagram 7; for meanings of the lower set of staples, see Diagram 2.

The last diagram presented here, Diagram 15, deals with the respondents' experienced importance of five given media when it comes to 'knowledge and information' and 'entertainment, pleasure', respectively. The findings provide an interesting ground for discussing Internet's informative function. It is worth mentioning that TV is in a class by itself and the largest entertainment medium for the young people – in spite of the fact that the most popular fields of Internet are associated with pleasure and distraction.

On the other hand, it is evident that Internet is experienced as the most important source of knowledge and information among boys, whereas books are the most popular medium among girls in this respect. Bearing in mind that Internet is singled out as the most important source of information to an even higher degree among boys who are least interested in and (almost) never acquaint themselves with relevant societal information – provided by new as well as old media – it is legitimate to deliberate the possible ambiguity of the concepts of 'knowledge' and 'information'. It seems that the meaning of these words varies across different persons.

Correspondingly, since the tendency to search news on Internet correlates more strongly with a number of entertainment items than with relevant societal information, we might ask what 'news' means for different teenagers. In-depth analyses and follow-up studies can give a clearer insight into these questions. However, in the short-run, it could be difficult to determine whether the different interpretations of the notions of 'knowledge' and 'information' represent a 'normal' condition that could be explained by age, other socio-cultural and life style variables or whether the changing media situation in Sweden during the 1990's has contributed to this variability.

The growth of Internet as a major medium has been preceded by the establishment of a multiplicity of radio and TV-channels for which advertisement is

Diagram 15. Which of the media in the list are most important for you when it comes to…

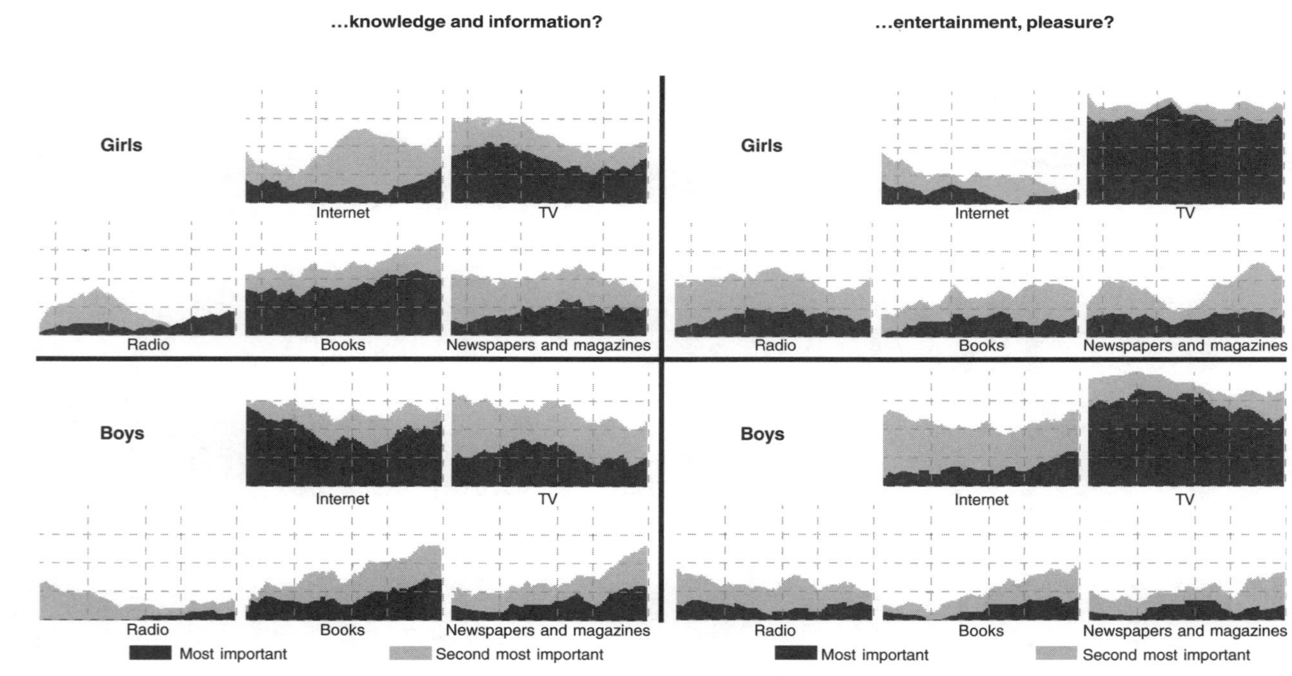

Notes: The curves/surfaces on each diagram show the correlation between the choice of the respondents' favorite media and the SII factor. The respondents have been sorted along the horizontal axes according to their scores on the SII factor. The higher score a person has on this factor the farther to the right the person is placed and vice versa – persons with the lowest SII scores (i.e., those who almost never search societal information on Internet) are placed on the extreme left. The scores for each point are rounded off by sliding mean values.

In the diagrams, the *vertical* lines mark the percent of boys and girls who are part of the cumulative groups (counted from the right) consisting of 20, 50 and 80 percent of all respondents who most often search societal information on the Internet. The *horizontal* lines indicate every 25th percent of the respective group.

the essential information domain. Public service radio and TV (without advertising), upon which the Swedish population was dependent some decade ago, seem, on the other hand, to have marginal importance for the teenagers of today – both as sources of knowledge and of pleasure.

Conclusion

The survey figures presented here show that Internet has become very popular among the Stockholm teenagers in our survey. But only a small proportion of the respondents make use of the medium as a source of societal information (defined as history, politics, literature, natural science, geography, education, theatre and to a significant extent also economy). This result *per se* does not mean that the Net is unsuitable as a platform for enlightenment and debate in the democratic sense – a platform hoped for by many politicians and other debaters.

One objection might be that the persons in our study are too young to devote themselves to knowledge and activities related to societal information. We should not forget that Internet is also a young medium and, according to most experts, in the near future it will experience essential changes that could concern not only its 'physical' aspects, but also its content and functions. Moreover, the future shape of Internet is largely dependent on people's representations of the medium. It is, thus, important to examine what factors are decisive in this respect.

In sum, the large differences in the teenagers' use of computers and Internet – not least in terms of IT's concrete functions and type of media content – depend primarily on factors other than access to IT equipment (which is relatively equally distributed) and do not support the notion that Internet as a medium contributes to increased democracy. Corresponding differences exist in the young people's use of other media, leisure activities as well as cultural and other values, which in their turn could be derived from socio-cultural variables, including the socially constructed gender. Such variables are of more decisive importance for people's dispositions and habits and better explain their interests and activities, including the extent and the direction of their IT-use as well as their engagement in political issues.

It Isn't Real

Children, Computer Games, Violence and Reality

Birgitte Holm Sørensen & Carsten Jessen

In 1999, an investigation was carried out in Denmark, dealing with children's use of violent computer (and video) games. The central question was: What significance does the interaction in violent computer games have for children's fascination with the media and for potential influences, and how do these influences differ from those that children are exposed to through TV, film and video? In relation to this it has been examined whether this fascination is linked to the actual act of playing games, the social situation surrounding them and/or to their violent elements.[1]

The investigation in question employed qualitative methods such as in-depth interviews and observations; the children's statements and actions form the basis for analyses. The purpose was to understand the children's formation of meaning in relation to the computer games. The aim, in particular, was to uncover what significance the interaction between children and computer games has for children's understanding of violent elements and for the relationship between fiction and reality.

A total of 31 children participated in the interview investigation. They were interviewed as well as observed at leisure time institutions or at home. The group consisted of 9 girls and 22 boys between the ages of 5-17. In addition, 17 boys were observed at an Internet café where they played in small groups. Finally, 4 children, aged 15-17, were observed and interviewed while playing network games at a weekend computer camp. Thus, more boys than girls took part in the investigation, the reason being that, among older children, boys spend more time on computer games than girls do.

Findings

The investigation shows that, for many children, the fascination with computer games is closely tied to the actual act of playing. *Competition, challenge* and *achievement*, also known from traditional games, are of crucial importance particularly for the boys. It is especially significant for the children that computer games offer them considerable influence over the course of the game through the game's *interactive* nature. Interaction promotes the challenge, as the player can experience a game as a course of events with no foregone conclusion. The challenges of computer games are enhanced by the fact that they, as a rule, demand that the player practise and develop skills, which is *per se* a positive quality for many children.

The social aspect of playing computer games is another essential reason for the children's interest. This aspect can be seen in relation to the actual act of playing. Children prefer to play computer games along with other children. On the one hand, it promotes experience and excitement, for example in relation to competition and challenges. On the other hand, the social aspect *per se* has an independent significance for children. Children can socialise around the computer. Computer games generate friendship and social events, and computer games can be cultivated as a common interest – an interest that often goes beyond the playing itself. The social situation surrounding the computer constitutes a sort of 'social magnetism' that attracts many children. The social aspect and the play assume a special dimension with respect to network games where the players can challenge each other at Net cafés or at home. In these connections, action games with violent elements seem to be the type of game preferred.

Children's fascination with violent computer games cannot be understood without considering the above-mentioned aspects. *The violent elements* fascinate some children, but this fascination should not be mistaken for a fascination with violence in the real world. On the contrary, all children in the investigation repudiated real-life violence. The violent elements in computer games are attractive as spectacular effects, but also because they prompt excitement and thrill. Computer games are, thus, in line with genres known from the film industry: action movies, animation, thrillers and horror movies. Computer games have inherited the content of violence from a cultural tradition within fiction, as well as genre features, such that spectacular effects are emphasised. Generally, these effects contain an element of exaggeration, which is fully recognised by children. In relation to this, the act of playing violent computer games can be seen as a parallel to the violent and 'rough' play traditionally found among boys.

Generally, the social situation plays an important role for all the children. However, it varies from child to child how much the fascination with computer games ties to the act of playing or to the depicted violence. Most often it is a question of interplay between two of three factors mentioned here.

In the investigation, an important point was to assess how children *distinguish between fiction and reality* and to establish whether they are able to account for this distinction. The children in the investigation, including the youngest who were five years old, are fully aware and can account for the difference between computer games as fiction and computer games as reality. A reason for this is that all computer games belong to a genre in which the indication of the fictitious is distinctive of the genre and takes the form of exaggeration compared to reality. Another reason has to do with the graphic expression of the games. It is also important that this exact feature, which is usually described as a problem in relation to violent computer games – the fact that the player himself must conduct violent deeds – actually makes children aware that their actions take place in a fictitious universe. For children, computer games are in fact 'games' with their own rules. From an early age, they are aware that these rules do not apply outside the realm of the game, with the exception that children can include elements and rules from the games in their play. This is in accordance with knowledge concerning other pictorial media, which often also inspire children to play.

Computer games with powerful violent elements may mean that children *get scared* and have nightmares. Although they get scared, many of them keep playing and seek out new games with action and violence. These are often the types of games that children prefer, and the experience of thrill and excitement is attractive to them. Computer games that depict extreme violence in great detail can frighten the youngest children and those who do not have a clear awareness of the game's genre. Here there is a difference between girls' and boys' attitudes towards violent computer games. Girls dismiss the violence in computer games to a larger extent than boys do. But children do not see computer games as particularly anxiety-provoking compared to, for instance, movies and fiction on TV and video. The children judge violence on TV, film and video to be much worse, more violent and realistic than violence in computer games. All the children who were interviewed told of apprehension related to watching a movie (this does not only apply to actual violent movies). But not everyone reported anxiety-provoking experiences connected to playing computer games. This leads to an essential point which has to do with the difference between identifying with movies and with computer games. Identification is of central importance in relation to many movie experiences where the viewer feels and experiences along with the movie's characters. The psychological level of involvement in relation to the fictitious characters is of a different character when it comes to computer games. In the games, the characters do not react emotionally like they do on film. They are, as a rule, conventionalised types without a (distinct) identity. In computer games, one does not find actual depictions of character that the player can identify with in the same way as in a movie. Thus, the identification with computer games is not as strong as with movies.

The above discussion points to the fact that computer games should not be regarded as a development of the movie genre. Although certain genre characteristics are taken from film, playing computer games does not lead to a sort of intensified movie experience. It is a question of another type of excitement and experience that is more closely *related to game and play experiences* than to fiction genres, such as film or, for that matter, literature. One can say that, for many children, the experience and excitement of playing computer games are more intense than the experience and excitement of other types of games because of the interaction and the visual and graphic space that appeal to children's sensuous experience. The identification is of a different character than that associated with TV, film and video. Playing computer games leads to an active identification that is usually linked to games and play.

Note

[1] This investigation was conducted for the Media Council of Children and Adolescents, The Ministry of Culture in Denmark.

Perceptions of Video Games among Spanish Children and Parents

Ferran Casas

Until recently, video games had only been an object of research interest in Spain because of their possible negative effects on children. However, other research approaches have developed lately. The line of research we will introduce here began with a few simple questions, mainly two: a) What are the most important different perceptions of video games among children and adults? b) How do adults use video games as a topic to communicate with children?

An exploratory research project was conducted with a sample of children and parents from five different schools in the city of Barcelona. An ad-hoc questionnaire was designed in order to pose the same questions to children and then to their parents on separate occasions. Some questions dealt with the parents themselves, others with their perceptions of, or attributions assigned to, the child on whom the questionnaire was focused. Fathers alone answered 28 per cent of the questionnaires, mothers 49 per cent, and 23 per cent were answered by both parents. The children were 11 to 14 years old. A total of 183 pairs of valid questionnaires were obtained – 52.5 per cent referred to boys and 47.5 per cent to girls.

The most outstanding result is that 44 per cent of the parents with children who play video games, *never* play these games with the child and *never* speak with him/her about them. 30 per cent of the parents sometimes play video games with the child, and sometimes speak about them. 16 per cent of the parents speak about the games, but never play them, and 10 per cent sometimes play the games, but never speak about them.

Parents who play video games with their children do have different perceptions of the games in comparison to those who do not play, and they have more positive patterns of communication with their children about that activity.

A set of questions was posed to parents and children about emotions, self-control, fantasy-related thoughts, preferences, and social relationships when playing video games. A few additional questions referred to the utility of playing video games and other opinions about them. Some discrepancies among parents and children have been identified in these regards.

Three discrepancies are particularly interesting: Parents disagree more frequently than their child with the statement "the child plays to forget problems" (Figure 1). Parents agree more frequently than their child with the statement "playing video games is a waste of time" (Figure 2). And children clearly say they "prefer video games when there is fighting and war", while their parents disagree with the statement that their child prefers those kinds of games (Figure 2). The first and second of these discrepancies do not appear in the sub-sample of children not playing regularly, but the third does even in that case.

Figure 1. Emotions when playing video games

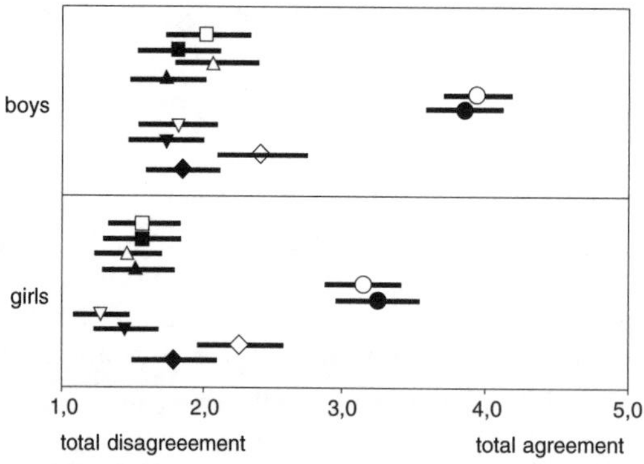

Square: (c) I get anxious to play with video games again.
(p) My child gets anxious to play with video games again.

Triangle: (c) When I must stop playing I often get very angry.
(p) When my child must stop playing he/she often gets very angry.

Circle: (c) I enjoy video games very much.
(p) My child enjoys video games very much.

Invested triangle: (c) I feel more aggressive after playing certain video games.
(p) My child feels more aggressive after playing certain video games.

Rhomb: **(c) I like playing video games to forget problems.**
(p) My child likes to play video games to forget problems.

Note: (c) Reported by the child (empty figures), (p) Attributed by the parent (full figures). The squares, triangles, etc., indicate mean scores of answer values. The length of the bars indicates the standard deviation of answer values. When the children's and parents' bars do not overlap, the difference is significant.

Figure 2. Perceptions of video games

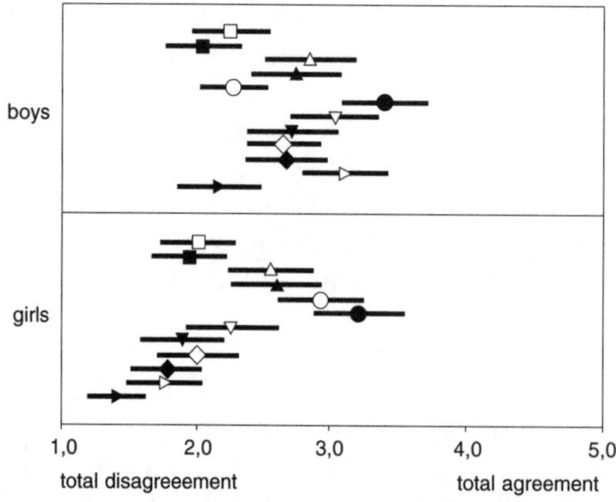

Square: (c) Video games are useful for learning things.
(p) In my opinion, video games are useful for learning things.

Triangle: (c) When you play video games, you get better reflexes and more skills.
(p) In my opinion, when one plays video games, one gets better reflexes and more skills.

Circle: **(c) I believe playing video games is a waste of time.**
(p) I believe playing video games is a waste of time for my child.

Invested triangle: (c) I like video games better than most other games.
(p) My child likes video games better than most other games.

Rhomb: (c) I prefer playing video games to watching television.
(p) My child prefers playing video games to watching television.

Arrow to the right: **(c) I like video games best when there is fighting and war.**
(p) My child prefers video games when there is fighting and war.

Note: (c) Reported by the child (empty figures), (p) Reported/attributed by the parent (full figures). The squares, triangles, etc., indicate mean scores of answer values. The length of the bars indicates the standard deviation of answer values. When the children's and parents' bars do not overlap, the difference is significant.

These discrepancies are statistically significant when we compare the answers of boys with the answers of fathers or mothers referring to their boy, but they do not reach significance when we compare answers referring to girls.[1]

As a consequence of these results, we have started data collection with a larger sample and more extended questionnaires for parents and their children in order to explore their feelings and opinions as concerns all audio-visual media: television, computers, video games, the Internet. We already have a questionnaire sample of more than 2000 "couples", and we plan to develop a cross-national comparative analysis with the support of Childwatch International. This analysis will include data from Norway, India, Brazil, Japan and Thailand.

Note

1. A more detailed analysis of our results will be published in I. Hutchby & J. Moran-Ellis (in press) *Children, Technology and Culture*. Falmer Press.

Violent Elements in Computer Games

An Analysis of Games Published in Denmark

Lisbeth Schierbeck & Bo Carstens

In light of the discussion of a possible Danish system for classification and labelling of computer and video games, the Media Council for Children and Young People at the Danish Ministry of Culture commissioned a study of all such games published in the country during 1998. The aims of the study were, among others, to analyse the content with regard to violence and to analyse the different types of game distribution.[1] This article deals with the violent content.

The study found that 338 titles were published in Denmark during 1998. Eighty-one per cent of these are computer games for a PC, 24 per cent video games for Playstation and 7 per cent video games for Nintendo 64. (Games for playing exclusively online on the Internet were excluded from the study.)

The 338 titles fall into ten main genres. As seen from Table 1, action games and simulators are the two largest genres, together comprising almost half of all titles.

Table 1. Games by genre (%)

Action	30
Simulators	17
Sports	13
Strategy	13
Children	9
Adventure	8
Cards and backgammon	3
Edutainment	3
Role playing	2
Puzzles, riddles, and the like	1
N =	338

The distribution of genres is different for computer and video games. For instance, some genres in the survey exist only as computer games (children, adventure, cards and backgammon, and edutainment). Another difference is that, among video games, the action genre is proportionally much more dominant than among computer games, especially among Playstation video games.

Games with violent elements

The definition of violence used in the study is broad — actions only slightly related to striking and shooting are also included. According to this definition, slightly more than half of the titles (53%) contain some violence.

The proportion of games with some violent elements varies greatly between different genres (Table 2). In particular, action games, strategy games and simulators contain elements of violence; these genres constitute nearly 60 per cent of the published titles. All role-playing games also contain violent elements but these games are few in number.

Table 2. Games with violent elements, % of each genre

	Number of games	Of which contain elements of violence (%)
Action	103	86
Simulators	56	54
Sports	44	9
Strategy	44	89
Children	32	6
Adventure	28	32
Cards and backgammon	11	0
Edutainment	10	0
Role playing	8	100
Puzzles, riddles, and the like	2	0
All games	338	53

The kinds of violent actions also differ greatly between different genres. Strategy games are characterised by decision-making and steering of units on a tactical and strategic level, usually involving little close contact with the opponents. Simulators are characterised largely by learning to technically master a given panel of instruments, and these games are also chiefly of a tactical and strategic nature. In action games, however, the player is often directly involved in close fighting with or shooting at the antagonists, who are often human beings.

Table 3 shows that when there are violent forms of action, human beings are typically the victims, followed by "machines" and other things, whereas animals and monsters are seldom the objects.

Table 3. "Victims" of violent actions, % of all games

Human beings	32
"Machines"	23
Others	22
Animals	8
Monsters	8
Total	53
N =	338

Note: The percentage sum of kinds of victims is larger than the proportion of games containing violent elements, since a single game may contain several kinds of victims.

Table 4 indicates that the most frequent forms of violent action are rule-based actions (that is, actions related to the rules or logic of the game, for instance, aimed at objects, flying saucers, or the like, but normally not at living beings), followed by tactic or strategic use of power. In all, close fighting or shooting is seen in one-sixth of all games.

Table 4. Forms of violent actions, % of all games

Rule-based actions	31
Tactical steering of units	21
Strategic use of power	19
Close fight	18
Shooting	16
Total	53
N =	338

Note: The percentage sum of violent forms of action is larger than the proportion of games containing violent elements, since a single game may contain several violent forms of actions.

There are "often" violent forms of action in one-sixth of all games (56 titles). "Occasional" violent action is more common (Table 5).

Table 5. Frequency of violent elements, % of all games

Seldom	3
Occasional	34
Often	17
Total	53
N =	338

As seen in Table 6, there is relatively little blood in games with violent elements. Most such games contain “no blood”. Six per cent of all games contain “much blood” (20 titles) or “mutilation” (1 title). Titles containing much blood are most often action games, but a few belong to the genres of strategy, role-playing and adventure.

Table 6. Details of violence, % of all games

No blood	32
Camouflaged	9
Some blood	7
Much blood	6
Mutilation	(0,3)
Total	53
N =	338

The complex of violence

Even if there are violent actions in many of the games, these actions are often aimed at more or less impersonal "things" (machines, etc.) and based on the inherent logic or rules of the game, in connection with tactic or strategic steering. Moreover, there is seldom blood in the game. On the other hand, there is obviously a group of games in which violence is salient. Typically, these games contain a high degree of details and frequent use of violent action, and the forms of actions represent close fighting and shooting. These forms of action are also usually aimed at human beings (or possibly at monsters). Overall, 17 games (5%) of the 338 registered show such a combination of different violence criteria that they can clearly be judged as containing a considerable amount of violence. Table 7 presents the games in question:

Table 7. The games with most violent elements

Title	Main category
Blood II, The Chosen	Action
Cardinal Sin	Action
Carmageddon II, Carpocalypse Now	Action
Commandos	Strategy
Die by the Sword	Action
Fallout 2	Role playing
Half-Life	Action
Heretic II	Action
Lands of Lore 2	Role playing
Police Quest SWAT 2	Strategy
Quake	Action
Resident Evil 2	Action
Tenchu, Stealth Assassins	Action
The House of the Dead	Action
Turok, Dinosaur Hunter	Action
Unreal	Action
Wargasm	Action

Note

1. The full report *Gennemgang af computerspil, udgivet i Danmark i 1998* [Survey of Computer Games Published in Denmark in 1998] by Lisbeth Schierbeck and Bo Carstens, 1999, is available on the web site: www.medieraadet.dk (in Danish).

Classifications of Interactive Electronic Media

Jan Christofferson

With the rise of interactive electronic media, such as video- and computer games, national content legislation has become increasingly scarce, due in part to the fact that the forms of distribution defy traditional territorial borders. The Internet, where many games are available, is the most apparent example. Another reason for the relative scarcity of national legislation on interactive electronic games is that they are fundamentally different from traditional media, for example, film and television, in that:

- their content must be unravelled in an active process.
- their content can also vary depending on the player, her/his skill and familiarity with gameplay, etc.
- video- and computer games tend to be massive; certain games can take days, even weeks to complete.

These factors make the classification process extremely time-consuming and place high demands on the persons doing the classifying.

Some countries have included video- and computer games in their traditional film classification and related legislation, one example being Australia, but these countries are in the minority. Australia has incorporated mandatory classification of all video- and computer games — games that are refused classification may not be distributed at all in Australia. If a person should be found guilty of publicly selling or demonstrating a game that has been refused classification – even on a small scale – he or she could spend up to two years in prison. If he or she sells a "commercial quantity" of such a game, a ten-year sentence is possible. (For Australian classification of electronic games, see further the articles by Ask et al. and by Durkin & Low in this book.)

However, Australia's regulated censorship and restrictive legislation in this respect must be considered an exception. Most countries where electronic games have a wide distribution seem to have adapted to the various industry and non-profit organisations that supply content rating globally. There is a multitude of classification providers with varying incentives and motives for their activity. The US has a tradition of strong non-profit organisations based on certain interests. The US is also leading the development of on-line filtering and computer game classification. As for Japan, the leading country of the world in the industry of video games, classification started only recently. In 1997, the Computer Entertainment Software Association (CESA), a large Japanese organisation for the video game software industry, produced a code for voluntary restraint of harmful software and decided to demand that companies not sell software that violated the code unless the contents are modified. In September 1999, CESA also started labelling software products with severe violence (see further the chapter by Sakamoto in this book).

Due to the fact that few countries have a national content rating system and that the games are distributed globally with few variations regarding their actual content, this text will look at the well-known games and the rating symbols appearing on them. Most popular games have more than one classification system represented on their packaging. This is an overview of the most prolific classification organisations in the US and Europe:

ESRB (Entertainment Software Rating Board)

Based in: USA

Type of organisation: "the ESRB is an independent board that has, with the support of the industry, developed a standardized rating system for interactive entertainment software products" (ESRB's website at: http://www.esrb.com, February 2000).

Type of symbols:

Comments: The ESRB classification system is one of the most ambitious and extensive appearing on the market today. In addition to symbols indicating the appropriate consumer ages in relation to content, the system includes "content descriptors" regarding violence, language, sexual content, gaming (i.e., "betting"), use of tobacco and alcohol, use of drugs, informational (i.e., "educational") material and "edutainment". These content descriptors are rated in several steps depending on the level of explicitness and amount of, e.g., sex or violence.

The ESRB classifications appear on many of the most popular games on the American and European markets.

USK (Unterhaltungssoftware SelbstKontrolle)

Based in: Germany

Type of organisation: "The USK is an institution for voluntary self-regulation in the entertainment software industry under the joint responsibility of the Association for the Support of Young People and Social Work (fjs) and the Association of Entertainment Software in Germany (VUD)" (USK's website at: http://www.usk.de, February 2000).

Type of symbols:

Comments: USK utilises simple symbols like ESRB, but instead of using additional content descriptors, all information deemed relevant is incorporated into the symbols. USK claims to cover 90 percent of the sales in PC entertainment software in Germany. In any case, its symbols frequently appear on games for sale in Europe and certainly on those in Germany.

ELSPA (Entertainment Leisure Software Publishers Association)

Based in: Great Britain

Type of organisation: Self-regulation body similar to USK. It is a voluntary industry-based organisation.

Type of symbols:

(old)

(current)

Comments: ELSPA has the highest penetration of all classification organisations in Europe, and its symbols can be found on most games distributed there. The ratings relate only "to the content of the product and its viewing suitability, not its playability or difficulty" (VSC's website at: http://www.videostandards.org.uk, February 2000. VSC, The Video Standards Council, co-operates with and acts as a "father organisation" for ELSPA).

ELSPA has also become the guiding classification system for some European countries, among others Denmark and Sweden. In the case of Denmark, it was recently decided that no additional national rating would be implemented, due to the fact that ELSPA's classification symbols appear on most of the games distributed in Denmark.

MDTS (Multimedia, Dator- och TV-spel)

Based in: Sweden
Type of organisation: union of publishers, producers and distributors of multimedia, computer games and video games in Sweden.

Type of symbols:

Comments: MDTS has only national penetration thus far and they follow ELSPA's ratings.

BBFC (British Board of Film Classification)

Based in: Great Britain
Type of organisation: "The British Board of Film Classification is an independent, non-governmental body, which for over eighty years has exercised responsibilities over the cinema which by law belong exclusively to the local authorities" (BBFC's website at: http://www.bbfc.co.uk, February 2000).

Type of symbols:

Comments: The BBFC is an organisation similar to the MPAA in USA, i.e., it is a non-governmental body, but has come to function as the national standard in film classification and legislative implementation. In addition to film and video classification, the board also supplies ratings for computer games. The BBFC ratings have a considerable penetration in Europe and their symbols can be found alongside ELSPA's on many games distributed in Europe.

A multitude of labels

As can be gathered from this overview, video/computer games often have more than one rating symbol on the packaging. This can be very confusing if the ratings do not match. Considering that the video- and computer games market is relatively "young", this will probably change in the future. Certain classification systems will grow and others will disappear, resulting in a more stable and reliable situation for the consumer. There is little indication of countries applying national legislation in this respect; instead they seem to prefer self-regulation on the part of industry.

Pornography and Sex in the Media

Effects of Sexual Content in the Media on Children and Adolescents

Ellen Wartella, Ronda Scantlin, Jennifer Kotler,
Aletha C. Huston & Edward Donnerstein

In the United States, media effects have been demonstrated for many aspects of social behavior, including aggression, social stereotyping, prosocial behavior, and social attitudes. Effects of television violence have been studied extensively, and most social scientists agree that exposure to violent television has a causal effect on aggressive behavior (cf. Comstock, 1991; Huston et al., 1992). By contrast, the effects of sexual content have received relatively little attention from researchers. Despite only a small body of evidence supporting a link between sex in the media and children and adolescent sexuality, there are strong theoretical reasons to believe that media can play an especially important role in the socialization of sexual knowledge, attitudes and behaviors.

The purpose of this article is to review what is known about the relations of entertainment media to sexual development during childhood and adolescence in the United States. First, we examine what sexual content is available to children in entertainment media in order to understand what types of portrayals may influence sexual development. Second, we briefly review a number of theoretical frameworks in which to approach the study of media effects on sexuality. We then present what is known about the link between media and sexuality based on experimental and correlational studies. Fourth, we consider moderating influences that affect how children respond to sexual content. We conclude with a discussion of the inherent difficulties in doing research on media effects on child and adolescent sexuality.

Sexual content in the media

Children watch a great deal of adult programming, and there has been a steady increase in the frequency and explicitness of sexual content on broadcast television. Young people have access to a much wider range of video content as well as to other entertainment media than they did in the early 1980s. Many of these portrayals show glamorous, young individuals with whom many children and adolescents are likely to identify. Young people in this age range often name media figures as the people whom they would like to emulate. Finally, the United States has not moved very far toward providing sex education or other sources of sexual information for young people, leaving them to get sexual information largely from peers and mass media.

Most researchers who examine sexual content in the media have concentrated on entertainment television, particularly prime-time programming, soap operas, and music videos, but, in recent years, they have expanded to other genres and other media, including talk shows, magazines, advertising, film/ movies, and news. Definitions of sexual content include verbal references to sexual activity, innuendo, implied sexual activity, and visual presentation.

Prime-time television and soap operas

Studies of prime-time television and soap operas have demonstrated that over the last 20 years, references to heterosexual intercourse have increased and have become much more explicit (Kunkel, Cope, & Colvin, 1996). In a recent content analysis of all network prime-time programs, more than two-thirds of the programs contained either talk about sex or actual sexual behavior with an average of more than 5 scenes per hour (Kunkel et al., 1999). Despite the increase in sexual content, the "messages" have remained relatively unchanged: (1) Sexual behavior typically takes place between two adults who are not married to each other (Greenberg, Graef, Fernandez-Collado, Korzenny, & Atkin, 1980; Lowry & Shidler, 1993; Sapolsky, 1982; Sapolsky & Taberlet, 1991). (2) The potential consequences of sexual intercourse are rarely addressed; pregnancy, contraception, and sexually transmitted diseases are generally absent from character dialogue and portrayals are superficial when they are discussed (Greenberg & Busselle, 1996; Kunkel, Cope, & Colvin, 1996; Lowry & Shidler, 1993; Lowry & Towles, 1989a, 1989b; Sapolsky & Taberlet, 1991). In a recent analysis of all programs with sexual content, only 9 percent included any mention of risks and responsibility (Kunkel et al., 1999). (3) Talk about sex is more common than physical depictions, and when instances of sexual intercourse occur, they are often implied rather than being visually portrayed (Kunkel et al., 1999; Kunkel, Cope, & Colvin, 1996). (4) The importance of "physical attractiveness as an asset" is emphasized for both males and females (Ward, 1995).

Music videos

Channels specializing in music videos such as Music Television (MTV), Video-Hits One (VH-1), Black Entertainment Television (BET), and Country Music Television (CMT) target preadolescent, adolescent and young adult audiences. Music videos may be especially influential sources of sexual information for adolescents because they combine visuals of popular musicians with the music;

many of these visual elements are implicitly or explicitly sexual (Brown & Steele, 1995).

Videos frequently combine sexuality with violence or aggression (Baxter, De Riemer, Landini, Leslie, & Singletary, 1985; Sherman & Dominick, 1986), and with objectification and sex-role stereotyping (Seidman, 1992; Sommers-Flanagan, Sommers-Flanagan, & Davis, 1993). Visual presentations of sexual intimacy appeared in more than 75 percent of a sample of "concept" videos. A "concept" video is described as a video mini-movie or mini-melodrama, in which the video interprets or embellishes the song. Eighty-one percent of those concept videos that contained violence also portrayed sexual imagery (Sherman & Dominick, 1986). In a sample of MTV videos, females wore revealing clothing and initiated and received sexual advances more often than did males (Seidman, 1992). The lyrics and visual content used in videos vary widely depending on their genre (Tapper, Thorson, & Black, 1994). Rap music is particularly explicit about both sex and violence (Brown & Steele, 1995), and MTV frequently shows combinations of aggression, sex-role stereotypes, and sexual imagery. Country music videos (CMT) also use sexual images, but common themes include break-ups/divorce, dating, and romantic love.

Movies

Adolescents see movies in theaters, and the same movies are soon available on pay TV channels and video tape. Many of these movies are "R-rated" (i.e., restricted, under 17 requires accompanying parent or adult guardian), and they contain more frequent and more explicit portrayals of sexual behavior than broadcast TV — an average of 17.5 per film in one analysis (Greenberg et al., 1993). Like television, the most frequent sexual activity shown is unmarried sexual intercourse. Sex is often in the context of profanity, alcohol and drug use, and nudity.

Summary

Thus far, we have established that children and adolescents growing up in the United States today have numerous opportunities for exposure to sexual content in the media. In fact, a parent would be hard-pressed to protect a child from any such content. Moreover, children and young adolescents are often intensely curious about sex. They frequently seek information from both print and electronic media, and they use many forms of these media extensively. We turn now to our central question: How are young people affected by media sexual content?

Media effects

Many have argued that mass media are a particularly important resource for sexual information because parents provide little information and schools tend to emphasize a biological approach with little attention to romance and interpersonal relationships (Brown, Walsh-Childers, & Waszak, 1990; Strasburger, 1989; Strouse & Fabes, 1985). In one early investigation, family variables exerted no influence on an individual's sexual self-evaluation, but media and peers were significant influences (Courtright & Baran, 1980). We first provide a brief overview of the theories of media influence, then review the small body of empirical literature.

Theory

Sexual messages in the mass media can have both immediate and long-term effects. Viewing a television program may change a person's immediate state by inducing arousal, leading to inhibition of impulses, or activating thoughts or associations. It may also contribute to enduring learned patterns of behavior, cognitive schemas and scripts (organized representations of event sequences or expectations) about sexual interactions, attitudes, and beliefs about the real world.

Immediate effects are the focus of Zillmann's arousal theory. According to that theory, if television content produces emotional and physiological arousal, *some* type of behavior is likely to follow. Whether or not that behavior is "sexual" depends on both the personality of the viewer and the environmental circumstances. Because arousal is nonspecific, it can also lead to aggression, altruism, or other forms of behavior if the conditions are conducive to those behaviors.

Theories based on observational learning and information processing emphasize lasting effects of exposure to media content. Bandura's observational learning theory suggests that children will learn not only the mechanics of sexual behavior, but the contexts, motives and consequences portrayed. They will attend to and learn from models who are attractive, powerful, rewarded, and similar to themselves. Children do not usually act immediately on what they learn from television; instead, they store such knowledge to be used when their own circumstances elicit it.

Berkowitz's cognitive neoassociationist theory was proposed as a way of understanding effects of violent content, but it appears equally applicable to sexual content. Although similar to observational learning theory in many respects, the theory gives a central place to the viewer's emotional responses as the links between learned media content and later behavior. As emotional responses to sexual content are likely to be intense, this idea seems especially pertinent to "effects" of such content.

Huesmann argues that children learn social and sexual schemas and scripts for sexual interactions from exposure to television. This view implies that it is important to examine what is learned about the circumstances for sexual activity, communication, negotiation, and decision-making. Scripts and schemas learned in childhood have particular importance because children do not have well-developed ideas and understandings of sexuality. Content viewed later may modify such schemas or reinforce them, but will not have quite the "primacy" of what was initially learned. Cultivation theory (Signorielli & Morgan,

1990) also predicts that mass media convey images of socially normative behavior and that children absorb impressions and assumptions about who, when, how often, under what circumstances sexual interactions occur.

All of these theories recognize that media "effects" are not unidirectional. Children are not just recipients of media messages; they choose the content to which they are exposed, and they interpret the content within their own frames of reference. But, some theories give prime importance to the active nature of viewers in selecting and using media. From this viewpoint, "effects" result from availability of content to serve different functions and from understanding the viewer's interactions with the medium.

Cognitive developmental theory is especially important for the topic of sexuality because of the very large age differences in both comprehension and interest in sex. Collins' research on children's understanding of violent content has demonstrated that children interpret media content according to their level of cognitive development generally and their knowledge about the content more specifically. One would expect children in late childhood, early, and middle adolescence to interpret and react to media content very differently.

In the communications field, "uses and gratifications" theories emphasize that people use media to serve different functions. If we want to understand the "effects" of sexual content, we must know why a child or adolescent views it. Is that individual looking for information, for arousal (either alone or with a partner), for rebellion (forbidden fruit), or for something else?

Experimental studies

The ideal method for establishing a causal relationship of media exposure to child outcomes is the experiment. The few experimental studies measuring attitudes and knowledge in this area show some differences between adolescents exposed to media sex and a control group not shown the same fare. For example, boys and girls who were exposed to content portraying pre-, extra or non-marital sexual relations rated these portrayals as significantly less bad than did their peers who viewed either sexual relations between married partners or non-sexual relations between adults (Bryant & Rockwell, 1994). In another study, young adolescents who watched selected scenes from television programs containing sexual content learned the meaning of the language used to refer to sexual activities such as homosexuality and prostitution (Greenberg, Linsangan, & Soderman, 1993). Exposure to music videos led teenagers to state that premarital sex is more acceptable compared to those teens who were not exposed (Greeson & Williams, 1987). Students who were shown programs containing basic sex information (menstruation and reproduction) knew more factual information than students who were not shown the videos (Greenberg, Perry, & Covert, 1983).

While most of the sexual portrayals on prime time programs or in soap operas are not pornographic, many children and adolescents have access to explicitly erotic or pornographic materials. Experiments exposing individuals to pornography have not been conducted with adolescents for ethical reasons, but studies with young adults generally find that pornography that is combined with violence leads men to hold more callous attitudes about rape and sexual coercion (Zillman, 1982; Donnerstein & Linz, 1986). Whether sexual content without violence has these effects is less clear. Some find that massive experimental exposure to non-violent erotic material leads men (and to some extent women) to be more callous towards women's issues and sexuality (Zillmann & Bryant, 1982). Others have found a desensitization toward violence in general and sexual violence in particular only after viewing explicit sexual content containing violence. Participants exposed to explicit sexual content without accompanying violence did not become desensitized (Linz, Donnerstein, & Penrod, 1988; Linz, Donnerstein, & Adams, 1989).

Correlational studies

Correlational studies do not permit causal inference, but they do allow assessment of ways in which naturally occurring media use is related to sexual knowledge, attitudes, and behavior. Teenagers who chose TV diets containing a lot of sexual content were more likely than those who viewed a smaller proportion of sexual content on television to have engaged in sexual intercourse. Because of the cross-sectional nature of the study, it is unclear whether viewing sexy television contributed to a teen's decision to engage in intercourse (Brown & Newcomer, 1991). In a longitudinal design, Peterson, Moore, & Furstenberg (1991) found no evidence that amount or content of television viewing reported by early adolescents predicted early initiation of intercourse, but the measures of viewing were quite superficial. Strouse, Buerkel-Rothfuss, & Long (1995) found a positive correlation between music video exposure and attitudes about premarital sex, especially for females.

Television may also influence adolescents' beliefs about social context and the consequences of sexuality. For example, compared to those who do not watch soap operas, soap opera viewers believed that single mothers had relatively easy lives: they have good jobs, are educated and do not live in poverty. Viewers also were more likely than non-viewers to believe that a single mother's male friends will be important in their children's lives (Larson, 1996). If single motherhood is glorified, marriage is not. There is a positive relationship between viewing television and ambivalence towards happy marriage as a way of life (Signorielli, 1991).

Television and other media may also influence adolescents' sexual vulnerability indirectly by the messages concerning physical attractiveness and the ideal body. Women's bodies are frequently used in advertisements to sell a variety of products to both men and women (Henderson-King & Henderson-King, 1997). The media provide images of an unattainable "ideal" that may have a cumulative effect on individuals' satisfaction with their appearance. In several experiments, adolescents were shown slides of models who were thin, average, or large. Those who saw thin models had lower self-evaluations and body dissatisfaction than those shown models with other body types (Irving, 1990; McElroy, 1994; Stice et al. 1994 cited in Kalodner, 1997). Repeated exposure to such images may lead some adolescents to extremes of dieting and eating disorders. Although females are thought to be especially vulnerable to such media messages, males may be affected as well.

Factors moderating the effect of viewing sex

How sex on television affects young people's attitudes, knowledge and behavior may depend on age, gender, parental involvement, perceptions of reality, and reasons for media use, to name only a few possibilities. The appeal and characteristics of the media presentation are also likely to affect how it influences young viewers.

Age

There are developmental differences in understanding and interest in television portrayals of sexuality. For example, 14- and 16-year olds had a better understanding of televised sexual innuendoes than did 12-year olds (Silverman-Watkins & Sprafkin, 1983). However, in a focus group of 8-12 year olds who viewed various clips portraying sexual topics, most of the children (even the youngest ones) understood that the clips were sexual in nature. Most jokes and innuendos about sex were understood by 10-12 year olds, but the younger children (8-10 year olds) were often uncomfortable with portrayals of intimacy and sexuality in the clips (Kaiser Family Foundation & Children Now, 1996). In an ethnographic study of 11-15 year old girls, girls who were least interested in sexual content in the media were the least physically mature and were least likely to have had an intimate relationship with a boy (Brown, White, & Nikopoulou, 1993). The most physically mature girls had some experience with romance and were often critical of media sexual portrayals. In the middle was a group of girls who actively sought out media messages and were interested in teen characters and how they solved problems similar to ones that the teens themselves were experiencing.

Gender

There is some evidence that girls use the media to learn about interpersonal relationships more than do boys. Girls reflected about a video about teen pregnancy more than boys did (Thompson, Walsh-Childers, & Brown, 1993), and females were more likely to enjoy sexual content than boys (Greenberg, Linsangan, & Soderman, 1993).

Parent involvement

Parent involvement in adolescent television viewing could moderate the relationship between viewing and initiating intercourse. Adolescents who do not discuss television with their parents have higher rates of intercourse compared to those who do discuss television content with their parents (Peterson, Moore, & Furstenberg, 1991). Family communication patterns (concept-orientation versus socio-orientation) seem to influence the way adolescents make inferences and draw connections about sexual media (Thompson, Walsh-Childers, & Brown,

1993). Socio-orientation is defined as the extent to which deference and conformity is stressed in families, whereas concept-orientation is the extent to which questioning of ideas is stressed in families. Strouse, Buerkel-Rothfuss, & Long (1995) found that the relationship between music video exposure and premarital sexual permissiveness for females was much stronger in unsatisfactory home environments than for females in satisfactory home environments.

Perceived realism and use of media

Most theories predict that media messages will be most influential if children or adolescents perceive them as realistic and valuable guides to behavior. Adolescents do understand that television portrays romance and sexuality in ways that omit some of the real-life issues such as contraception. But, adolescents who use television to learn about social relationships believe that TV portrayals are more realistic than do other adolescents (Truglio, 1992). In cases where teenagers have little other knowledge about sexuality, media may create expectations. Teenagers were most likely to be dissatisfied with their first intercourse experience if they considered media messages to be accurate and if they perceived television characters to be their sexual superiors. On the other hand, teens who reported satisfaction with their initial coital experience reported that they perceived TV portrayals of sex as accurate (Baran, 1976a), and students who believed that media characters experienced high levels of sexual satisfaction reported being less satisfied with their own state of virginity (Baran, 1976b).

Appeal and quality

Messages that people perceive as high quality seem to have a greater impact on beliefs and attitudes than those they judge to be of low quality (Duck, Terry, & Hogg, 1995). The typical portrayals of non-marital sex may be more appealing than those of marital intercourse. For example, when shown a collection of clips, adolescents enjoyed married intercourse scenes the least and considered them least funny and least sexy while they thought unmarried intercourse scenes were the sexiest (Greenberg, Linsangan, & Soderman, 1993). In another study using sexual clips, young children said that their favorites were ones that gave prosocial messages such as using contraception and postponing sex until one is ready (KFF & Children Now, 1996).

A summary of research findings

There are good theoretical reasons to believe that television and other media can play an important role in educating children and adolescents about sexuality. Media portrayals surround children, and young people are intensely interested in sexuality, romance, and relationships. The few experimental studies show that television has the potential to change viewers' attitudes and knowledge. Correlational designs provide weak evidence that television viewing is linked with sexual behavior and beliefs, but the measures of viewing are crude at best. There is also some evidence that such personal factors as interest in sexual content, level of understanding, perceived reality, and parental mediation modify the influence of sexual messages. Much more empirical work is needed to substantiate the claim that naturally occurring sexual content in the media actually does cause changes in attitudes, beliefs and behaviors. What those changes are need to be examined as a function of what individuals are watching, the messages they are receiving, how they are interpreting them, and other factors that influence a young person's sexual personae.

Problems with conducting sexuality research

There are several inherent problems in doing research on children's and adolescents' knowledge, attitudes toward and behavior regarding sexual media content and sexuality, which may partially explain why research in this area is sparse. The broad outline of these issues can be subsumed under several general principles regarding: (1) use of human subjects concerns in the United States which have been articulated by the Department of Health and Human Services Belmont Report and how various institutional research boards (IRBs) interpret these general guidelines; and (2) the specific issue of gaining parental consent when adolescents are the subjects in a study.

Current federal regulations concerning research on adolescent health issues (under which sexuality research would fall) are outlined generally in the Belmont Report (National Commission for the Protection of Human Subjects of Biomedical and Behavioral Research, 1978). These regulations include a section outlining special considerations in conducting research with children and adolescents. For the purposes of federal guidelines, a child is anyone below the legal age of consent, age 18. Many issues, however, are not addressed directly in these guidelines and require individual IRBs to interpret the ethics of various research practices.

In general terms, the underlying principle guiding regulation of research practices is that the researchers show respect for the persons involved in the research. For children and adolescents, this means insuring protection of their rights and welfare. The second ethical principle is beneficence; that is, the researcher should do no harm to the subjects, and indeed the researcher should maximize the possible benefits and minimize possible harm to the subjects. The third ethical principle for conducting research on human subjects involves that of justice, or the requirement that individuals who are "vulnerable" receive special protections and "individuals who are vulnerable be protected from bearing the burdens of participation in research without appropriate justification; moreover, their access to the benefits of research are to be facilitated" (Levine, 1995).

The researcher who attempts experimental work in the domain of sexual content and sexual behavior cannot ethically devise an experimental manipulation that will cause a subject to actually engage in potentially risky behaviors. Furthermore, with underage subjects there is the question of the types of sexual materials that would be permissible for viewing. Thus, social science research could continually be subject to the criticism that it is impossible to investigate adequately the effects of sexual content because it (1) requires that the experimenter create exactly the kind of behavior that no researcher in a laboratory may seek to cause and (2) no real-world observer can hope to witness systematically.

Research on adolescent sexuality involves a range of ethical questions regarding the appropriateness of showing adolescents sexually-explicit stimuli, the use of language to elicit responses (colloquial or not, as well as the use of special ethnic or language minority terms), and providing subjects with appropriate debriefings or follow-up information after research participation. Again, the guidelines to insure respect for individuals, beneficence and justice should be considered. However, research practices may be influenced by individual IRBs' preferences for certain kinds of protections of children, the various local community (or school districts) concerns about dealing with sexual issues in schools, and the particular political climate of the community and state in which the research is being conducted.

Even if a research study involving media effects on sexuality is approved by an Institutional Review Board, there may be issues regarding parental consent. When respondents are children under age 18, consent must also be obtained from their legally authorized representative, who is usually the parent. If active parental consent is required, and it usually is when topics of sexuality are discussed, this may pose special constraints on conducting research on adolescents sexuality. It may be difficult to gain parental consent from families of high risk adolescents in particular.

Conclusions

There is need for an accumulated body of systematic studies using a variety of methods, interdisciplinary teams of investigators, and a variety of populations. Given the paucity of available studies and the need to develop a systematic research base, no one grand study will provide definitive answers. In the domain of media violence research, for example, our conclusions about effects rest on many studies using multiple methods and multiple populations, accumulated over many years. Similarly, the answers about sexual content in the media will not be obtained simply or quickly. Nonetheless, we must begin to accumulate a serious, systematic research base that could serve as a catalyst to stimulate further research and provide a solid foundation for understanding media sexual content effects.

Acknowledgment

This article is based on a report funded by and prepared with the help of the Henry J. Kaiser Family Foundation. We especially want to thank Vicky Rideout of Kaiser for her contributions to the conceptualization and preparation of the study.

References

Baran, S. J. (1976a). How TV and film portrayals affect sexual satisfaction in college students. *Journalism Quarterly, 53,* 468-473.

Baran, S.J. (1976b). Sex on TV and adolescent self-image. *Journal of Broadcasting, 20,* 61-8.

Baxter, R.L., De Riemer, C., Landini, A., Leslie, L., & Singletary, M.W. (1985). A content analysis of music videos. *Journal of Broadcasting and Electronic Media, 29,* 333-340.

Brown, J.D., Walsh-Childers, K., & Waszak, C.S. (1990). Television and adolescent sexuality. *Journal of Adolescent Health Care, 11,* 62-70.

Brown, J.D., & Newcomer, S.F. (1991). Television viewing and adolescents' sexual behavior. *Journal of Homosexuality, 21,* 77-91.

Brown, J.D., & Steele, J.R. (1995). *Sex and the mass media.* Menlo Park, CA: Kaiser Family Foundation.

Brown, J.D., White, A.B., & Nikopoulou, L. (1993). Disinterest, intrigue, resistance: Early adolescent girls' use of sexual media content. In B.S. Greenberg, J.D. Brown, & N.L. Buerkel-Rothfuss (Eds.). *Media, sex and the adolescent,* (pp. 177-195). New Jersey: Hampton Press.

Bryant, J., & Rockwell, S.R. (1994). Effects of massive exposure to sexually oriented prime-time television programming on adolescents' moral judgment. In D. Zillman, J. Bryant, & A.C. Huston (Eds.). *Media, children, and the family: Social scientific, psychodynamic, and clinical perspectives,* (pp.183-195). Hilldsale, NJ: Lawrence Erlbaum.

Comstock, G. (1991). *Television and the American child.* Orlando, FL: Academic Press.

Courtright, J.A., & Baran, S.J. (1980). The acquisition of sexual information by young people. *Journalism Quarterly, 1,* 107-114.

Donnerstein, E.I., & Linz, D.G. (1986). Mass media sexual violence and male viewers: Current theory and research. *American Behavioral Scientist, 29,* 601-618.

Duck, J.M., Terry, D.J., & Hogg, M.A. (1995). The perceived influence of AIDS advertising: Third-person effects in the context of positive media content. *Basic and Applied Social Psychology, 17,* 305-325.

Greenberg, B.S., & Busselle, R.W. (1996). Soap operas and sexual activity: A decade later. *Journal of Communication, 46,* 153-160.

Greenberg, B.S., Graef, D., Fernandez-Collado, C., Korzenny, F., & Atkin, C.K. (1980). Sexual intimacy on commercial TV during prime time. *Journalism Quarterly, 57,* 211-215.

Greenberg, B.S., Linsangan, R., & Soderman, A. (1993). Adolescents' reactions to television sex. In B.S Greenberg, J.D. Brown, & N.L. Buerkel-Rothfuss (Eds.). *Media, sex and the adolescent,* (pp. 196-224). New Jersey: Hampton Press.

Greenberg, B.S., Perry, K.L., & Covert, A.M. (1983). The body human: Sex education, politics, and television. *Family Relations, 32,* 419-425.

Greenberg, B.S., Siemicki, M., Dorfman, S., Heeter, C., Stanley, C., Soderman, A., & Linsangan, R. (1993). Sex content in R-rated films viewed by adolescents. In B.S. Greenberg, J.D. Brown, & N.L. Buerkel-Rothfuss (Eds.). *Media, sex and the adolescent,* (pp. 45-58). New Jersey: Hampton Press.

Greeson, L.E., & Williams, R.A. (1987). Social implications of music videos for youth: An analysis of the content and effects of MTV. *Youth & Society, 18,* 177-189.

Henderson-King, E. & Henderson-King, D. (1997). Media effects on women's body esteem: Social and individual difference factors. *Journal of Applied Social Psychology, 27,* 399-417.

Huston, A.C., Donnerstein, E., Fairchild, H., Feshbach, N., Katz, P., Murray, J., Rubinstein, E., Wilcox, B., & Zuckerman, D. (1992). *Big world, small screen: The role of television in American society.* Lincoln: University of Nebraska Press.

Irving, L.M. (1990). Mirror images: Effects of the standard of beauty on the self- and body-esteem of women exhibiting varying levels of bulimic symptoms. *Journal of Social & Clinical Psychology, 9,* 230-242.

Kaiser Family Foundation & Children Now (1996). *The family hour focus groups: Children's responses to sexual content on TV and their parents' reactions.* Menlo Park & Oakland: Authors.

Kalodner, C.R. (1997). Media influences on male and female non-eating-disordered college students: A significant issue. *Eating Disorders, 5,* 47-57.

Kunkel, D., Cope, K.M., & Colvin, C. (1996). *Sexual messages on family hour television: Content and context.* Oakland & Menlo Park, CA: Children Now & Kaiser Family Foundation.

Kunkel, D., Cope, K.M., & Farinola, W.J.M., Biely, E., Rollin, E., Donnerstein, E. (1999). *Sex on TV: content and context. A biennial report to the Kaiser Family Foundation.* Menlo Park, CA: Kaiser Family Foundation.

Larson, M.S. (1996). Sex roles and soap operas: What adolescents learn about single motherhood. *Sex Roles, 35*, 97-110.

Levine, R. J. (1995). Adolescents as research subjects without permission of their parents or guardians: Ethical considerations. *Journal of Adolescent Health, 17*, 288.

Linz, D., Donnerstein, E., & Adams, S.M. (1989). Physiological desensitization and judgements about female victims of violence. *Human Communication Research, 15*, 509-522.

Linz, D.G., Donnerstein, E.I., Penrod, S. (1988). Effects of long-term exposure to violent and sexually degrading depictions of women. *Journal of Personality & Social Psychology, 55*, 758-768.

Lowry, D.T., & Shidler, J.A. (1993). Prime time TV portrayals of sex, "safe sex" and AIDS: A longitudinal analysis. *Journalism Quarterly, 70*, 628-637.

Lowry, D.T., & Towles, D.E. (1989a). Prime time TV portrayals of sex, contraception, and venereal diseases. *Journalism Quarterly, 66*, 347-352.

Lowry, D.T., & Towles, D.E. (1989b). Soap opera portrayals of sex, contraception, and sexually transmitted diseases. *Journal of Communication, 39*, 76-83.

McElroy, E.S. (1994). *Cultivation of the thin ideal: The effects of media and self-perception on adolescent body satisfaction.* Unpublished masters thesis, University of Kansas.

National Commission for the Protection of Human Subjects of Biomedical and Behavioral Research. (1978). *The Belmont report: Ethical principles and guidelines for the protection of human subjects of research.* Washington, DC: US Government Printing Office, DHEW Publication No. (OS) 78-0012.

Peterson, J.L., Moore, K.A., & Furstenberg, F.F. (1991). Television viewing and early initiation of sexual intercourse: Is there a link? *Journal of Homosexuality, 21*, 93-119.

Sapolsky, B. (1982). Sexual acts and references on prime-time TV: A two-year look. *The Southern Speech Communication Journal, 47*, 212-226.

Sapolsky, B.S., & Taberlet, J.O. (1991). Sex in primetime television: 1979 versus 1989. *Journal of Broadcasting and Electronic Media, 35*, 505-516.

Seidman, S.A. (1992). An investigation of sex-role stereotyping in music videos. *Journal of Broadcasting & Electronic Media, 36*, 209-216.

Sherman, B.L., & Dominick, J.R. (1986). Violence and sex in music videos: TV and rock'n'roll. *Journal of Communication, 36*, 79-93.

Signorelli, N. (1991). Adolescents and ambivalence toward marriage: A cultivation analysis. *Youth and Society, 23*, 121-149.

Signorielli, N., & Morgan, M. (1990). *Cultivation analysis: New directions in media effects research.* Newbury Park, CA: Sage.

Silverman-Watkins, L.T., & Sprafkin, J.N. (1983). Adolescents' comprehension of televised sexual innuendos. *Journal of Applied Developmental Psychology, 4*, 359-369.

Sommers-Flanagan, R., Sommers-Flanagan, J., & Davis, B. (1993). What's happening on music television? A gender role content analysis. *Sex Roles, 28*, 745-753.

Strasburger, V.C. (1989). Adolescent sexuality and the media. *Adolescent Gynecology, 36*, 747-773.

Strouse, J., Buerkel-Rothfuss, N., & Long, E.C. (1995). Gender and family as moderators of the relationship between music video exposure and adolescent sexual permissiveness. *Adolescence, 30*, 505-521.

Strouse, J., & Fabes, R.A. (1985). Formal versus informal sources of sex education: Competing forces in the sexual socialization of adolescents. *Adolescence, 20*, 251-263.

Tapper, J., Thorson, E., & Black, D. (1994). Variations in music videos as a function of their musical genre. *Journal of Broadcasting and Electronic Media, 38*, 103-113.

Thompson, M., Walsh-Childers, K. & Brown, J.D. (1993). The influence of family communication patterns and sexual experience on processing of a movie video. In B.S. Greenberg, J.D. Brown, & N.L. Buerkel-Rothfuss (Eds.). *Media, sex and the adolescent*, (pp. 248-263). New Jersey: Hampton Press.

Truglio, R.T. (1992). *Adolescents' use of prime-time TV for sexual information: What are the risks?* Paper Presented at the Society for Research on Adolescence, Washington, D.C.

Ward, L.M. (1995). Talking about sex: Common themes about sexuality in the prime-time television programs children and adolescents view most. *Journal of Youth and Adolescence, 24*, 595-615.

Zillmann, D. (1982). Transfer of excitation in emotional behavior. In J.T. Cacioppo & R.E. Petty (Eds.), *Social psychophysiology*. New York: Guilford.

Zillmann, D., & Bryant, J. (1982). Pornography, sexual callousness, and the trivialization of rape. *Journal of Communication, 32,* 10-21.

Sexual Messages on Entertainment TV in the U.S.A.

Dale Kunkel, Kirstie Cope, Wendy Farinola, Erica Biely, Emma Rollin & Edward Donnerstein

It is well established that the stories children and adolescents watch on television can influence their lives in important ways. Heavy exposure to violent depictions can lead to a heightened risk of adopting aggressive attitudes and behaviors. Product purchase decisions are shaped significantly by TV advertising campaigns. Similarly, media portrayals involving sexuality can contribute to the sexual socialization of young people.

Many societal factors shape the socialization process by which young people develop their beliefs and attitudes about sex, and ultimately their patterns of sexual behavior. The role of parents and peers, among others, is certainly important, but influence from the media environment is also a factor. Media portrayals surround children and adolescents, and young people are naturally interested in learning about romance, relationships, and sexuality.

While many questions remain to be answered regarding the relative degree of influence from media as compared to other sources, we can be reasonably confident that television portrayals do exert an effect on adolescent sexual socialization. As adolescents are grappling with questions such as "When should I start having sex?" and "What will my friends think of me if I do or if I don't?", they inevitably encounter stories on television which speak to sexual issues. Identifying patterns in the portrayal of sex on television in the United States was the goal of the study reported in brief here.

In this research, a composite week of programming from the 1997-98 television season was sampled for each of ten of the most frequently viewed national broadcast and cable channels, yielding a total of 942 programs. These programs were evaluated for sexually-related talk and behavior using scientific content analysis techniques. Portrayals involving sexual themes were assessed on a range of contextual variables likely to shape the meaning of the depictions for viewers.

Results

The findings indicate that more than half (56%) of all programs examined contained some sexual content. Some of these shows included only minor references to sexual topics, but most of them (39% of all programs) contained one or more scenes with a substantial emphasis on sex. Across all of the programs that presented sexual material, there was an average of 3.2 scenes per hour involving sex. Clearly, sexual talk and behaviors are a common element in American television programming, and many programs that include sexual messages devote substantial attention to the topic.

Talk about sex is more common on television than the actual portrayal of any sexual behaviors. For example, programs were more than twice as likely to contain talk about sex (54% of all programs) than to contain sexual behavior (23% of all programs). In our sample of nearly 1,000 programs, we observed 1,719 scenes of talk about sex, compared to 420 scenes with sexual behavior. Most of the sexual behavior depicted tended to be precursory in nature (such as physical flirting and kissing), although intercourse was depicted or strongly implied in 7 percent of the programs in the sample. These programs rarely include explicit depictions in which nudity is shown, but nonetheless clearly convey that sexual intercourse is either imminent or actually occurring.

Figure 1 shows the percentage of programs within different genres that contain some sexual content.

One of the most important contextual factors likely to shape the socializing effects of sexual portrayals is the extent to which the risks and responsibilities associated with human sexual activity are included. In this study, we measured the presence of three possible types of themes concerning the risks or responsibilities of sexual behavior: (1) *sexual patience*: waiting until a relationship

Figure 1. Percentage of programs that contain sexual content, by genre

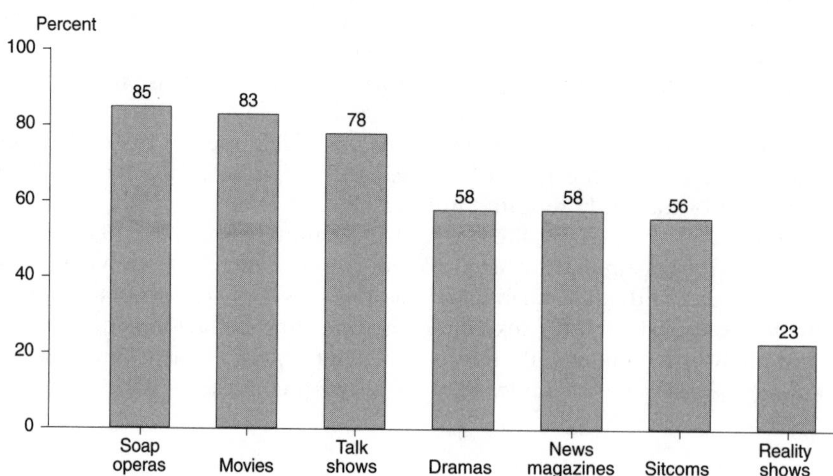

matures and both people are equally ready to engage in sex; (2) *sexual precaution*: pursuing efforts to prevent AIDS, STDs (sexually transmitted diseases), and/or unwanted pregnancy when sexually active; and (3) *depiction of risks and/or negative consequences* of irresponsible sexual behavior. Sexual encounters that are presented without any of these contextual elements certainly convey a much different message to the audience, and in particular to young viewers, than portrayals that include such elements.

In analyzing programs for this study, each scene involving any sexual content was evaluated for any mention or depiction of these themes. Only 4 percent of all scenes with sexual content incorporated any message about the risks or responsibilities of sexual activity. Of these cases, about half (or 2% overall) made such topics an important focus within a single scene. Of particular note is the finding that none of the 88 scenes that contained sexual intercourse included even a passing reference to sexual risks or responsibilities.

The study also evaluated whether each program considered as a whole placed *strong emphasis* on any theme about the possible risks or responsibilities of sexual behavior. This analysis indicates that programs with a primary emphasis on risk and responsibility themes were extremely rare, representing only 1 percent of all shows on television that contained any sexual content. As was the case with the scene-level data, the program-level analysis found that none of the 70 programs in the study that included portrayals of intercourse behavior featured a strong emphasis on risk and responsibility concerns throughout the show.

To summarize, risk and responsibility messages are not often presented in conjunction with the treatment of sexual topics on American television. When they are included, they do not tend to receive strong emphasis in a program overall. In addition, messages of risk and responsibility seem particularly lacking in those programs that portray intercourse behaviors, arguably the most salient context in which such messages might appear.

Conclusion

Sexual content is a common aspect of the overall television landscape in the United States. Portrayals of talk about sex, as well as sexually-related behaviors, are a potential source of socialization for most young viewers. Although most sexual behaviors shown on television are relatively modest, intercourse is frequently included. Collectively, these sexual messages provide an opportunity for the television industry to communicate an important and realistic view of the true risks associated with human sexual activity. Our research suggests that this opportunity has not yet been tapped very often by most segments of the industry. The pattern of sexual portrayals identified in this research raises concern that young viewers may be influenced to take sexual health precautions less seriously given their lack of consideration on television.

Note

The study reported here was supported by the Henry J. Kaiser Family Foundation of Menlo Park, CA. Full copies of the report are available from the foundation through its web site at www.kff.org

Does Pornography Influence Sexual Activities?

Margareta Forsberg

In 1971, Sweden became the second country in the world (only Denmark was earlier) to legalize pornography. However, it must be stressed that in 1978 child pornography was put under criminal code in Sweden, and a few years later the same occurred with media content presenting sexual violence and coercion.

Since the beginning of the 1970's, technological development has been very fast. In the middle of the 1980's, it was still necessary to walk into a video shop or cinema to be able to watch a pornographic movie. Today, porno films are available to anyone with access to the Internet or cable television.

This raises many questions. What influence does the access to pornography have on young people in the beginning of their adolescent or adult sexual life? *Does* it have an impact on them, or is this only a discussion influenced by moral panic among parents and other adults?

Research findings

Contemporary Swedish research in the field is still very limited, but some studies carried out in the 1990's give us a picture of connections between consumption of pornography and certain sexual activities. In this context it must be remembered that since the 1950's sexuality and relationships have been included in the Swedish school curriculum and, according to some studies, Swedish young people consider the school to be their prime source of information on these issues. There are indications that in other countries with access to pornography but without school education in sexuality/relationships, pornography plays a larger part as an information source for youth.

What the few Swedish research findings show is, firstly, that men, and especially younger men, consume pornography to a greater extent than women do. Despite this fact, we notice that young women have more experience in viewing pornography than do older men (Table 1).

Table 1. Men and women in different age groups who have seen pornographic film during the last year (1996) (%)

Ages	Men	Women
18–24 years (n = 412)	76	35
25–34 years (n = 626)	59	24
35–49 years (n = 819)	50	21
50–65 years (n = 605)	33	7
66–74 years (n = 192)	14	2

Source: Sex i Sverige [Sex in Sweden]. National Institute of Public Health, 1998.

In this study, *Sex i Sverige* (Sex in Sweden), published by the National Institute of Public Health, it is also stated that when women/girls look at pornography, it is often on the initiative and in the company of men/boys. Thus, 75 per cent of the women who in the study answered that they had seen a porno film during the last year had done so in the company of a man, and 25 per cent had done it alone. Matching numbers for the men were 50 per cent each. Sixty per cent of the men also agreed that "pornography can be very stimulating", while only 30 per cent of the women agreed.

Furthermore, the same study reveals connections between sexual activities, such as oral and anal sex, and pornography consumption (Tables 2 and 3).

Table 2. Share of men who have seen a porno film and who have experience of oral sex, vibrator sex (i.e., dildo) and anal sex, respectively (1996) (%)

	Have been "giving" oral sex		Have been "giving" vibrator sex		Have had anal sex	
Have seen porno film	No	Yes	No	Yes	No	Yes
No	68	32	99	1	99	1
Yes	18	82	81	19	77	23

Source: Sex i Sverige [Sex in Sweden]. National Institute of Public Health, 1998.

Table 3. Share of women who have seen a porno film and who have experience of oral sex, vibrator sex (i.e., dildo) and anal sex, respectively (1996) (%)

	Have been "giving" oral sex		Have been "giving" vibrator sex		Have had anal sex	
Have seen porno film	No	Yes	No	Yes	No	Yes
No	53	47	100	0	95	5
Yes	14	86	93	7	72	28

Source: Sex i Sverige [Sex in Sweden]. National Institute of Public Health, 1998.

The connection in itself does not necessarily mean that the activities mentioned in the tables are inspired only by watching pornography. It could also be that a group of highly experimental people is trying a large variety of sexually related activities, of which watching porno films is one and anal intercourse, for instance, is another. Furthermore, having experience with anal intercourse is not the same as having integrated anal intercourse as a frequent part of one's sex life. The experience reported in the investigation could also be a one-time experience.

Nevertheless, it is hard to ignore the connection between, for example, frequency of anal intercourse among people who have been watching porno, and the fact that anal intercourse is a very common act in pornographic movies.

According to another study on young Swedish women, 57 per cent of the women who had been watching porno thought that this had not influenced their sexual habits at all. Only 5 per cent thought it had had a large impact on their sex life.

On the other hand, the young women thought that "others" were more likely to get influenced by watching porno than themselves. According to the results, 22 per cent thought that "others" were influenced "to a large extent" and 56 per cent thought that "others" were "somewhat" influenced. When studying the results, it is obvious that when the young women are reflecting over the influence of pornography on "others", they are mainly thinking of *men* as "others".

Despite the fact that the young women don't believe pornography has an impact on their sexual activities, a connection between pornography consumption and oral and anal sex is obvious also in this study.

Taken together, results from different studies make it likely that consumption of pornography *does* have an influence on people's sexual activities, whether they are aware of it or not. Curiosity is also a central part of the nature of youth and it is not surprising that young people are receptive to new impressions and also want to experiment with them.

Illustrating this are the results from a recent study in a suburban area of Stockholm, where 30 per cent of the adolescent boys and 3 per cent of the adolescent girls were watching porno at least once a week. 42 per cent of the boys and 18 per cent of the girls had fantasized about trying acts that they had seen in pornographic movies. 30 per cent of the boys and 9 per cent of the girls had also put this into practice and actually tried some of the acts. Despite this, there is *not* the same connection between pornography consumption and anal intercourse in this study as in other studies.

Finally, we need many more results from a great deal of studies before we can be sure of the possible influences of pornography consumption on sexual activities. Questions that should be asked are, for instance: Do influences differ between different age groups? What are the differences between women and men? If there are influences, what do they look like? *If* pornography influences sexual *activities* (for example: trying anal intercourse), does this mean that it also influences long-term sexual *habits*?

What Is the Internet?

Basic Technology from the User's Perspective

Tor A. Evjen & Ragnhild T. Bjørnebekk

The Internet is a global high-speed network, consisting of a set of network computers. The network can be perceived as a collection of host and client or user computers. The explosion of Internet has occurred during the last decade. Twenty years ago, there were about 200 machines. According to recent figures, there are more than nine million server computers linking between 100 and 200 million users to the Internet.

The network communicates via a common language called Transmission Control Protocol/Internet Protocol (TCP/IP). The Internet Protocol contains information about the computer addressed to the sender-computer, and about the information sent. This is the base of Internet technology. The TCP/IP language can be used in all types of computers. What is unique, however, is that the information is not dependent on being routed to specific computers in order to reach the addressee. This was one of the US Forces' prerequisites for investing in the development of Internet technology in the early 60's. They wanted an amorphous communication system that would function even when vital communication agencies were unable to function.

Everyone who has invested in communication on the Internet owns a part of the Net. Persons or companies possessing a commercial network own this network. Those who own a server are free to close or limit access to it. Such a limitation affects cumulatively those connected to this network. The rest of the global network, however, is not affected by such limitations and functions as it did before.

The Internet has, as mentioned, been available since the early 60's, when it was developed and established to protect military communication from external interference. However, when a new generation of software – the World Wide Web (WWW) browsers – was presented in the beginning of the 90's, the Internet became widespread. This software offered a Graphical User Interface, and the WWW made it possible to navigate an endless number of web addresses: the Uniform Resources Locators (URL). Until the beginning of the 90's, the web browser was mostly an application used to move from one web page to another.

Today, the web browser includes most of the basic functions on the Internet. The functions have been integrated into the browser such that persons operating on the Net are scarcely aware of them. There are, however, three basic functions that are easy to separate from the others: the World Wide Web, electronic mail (e-mail) and news. These functions are crucial for understanding the accessibility and flexibility of the Internet.

World Wide Web

The World Wide Web (WWW) technology is one of the main reasons for the enormous interest in the Internet. The European Laboratory of Particle Physics in Switzerland developed the technology in 1990. Today, it is the most popular technology for exchanging information on the Net. Using a point-and-click hypertext system of control, it has made navigation on the Internet an easy task. It has also made possible the exchange of almost any kind of information by using a cursor, the mouse. The keyboard is the most common tool used to operate a computer. It is not, however, particularly important when surfing on the Internet. The keyboard is mainly used to address the groups and pages one wants to visit. When using a WWW browser, it is possible to send text, graphics, sound, animation and video directly on the Internet and to view it within the browser. The WWW browser is the application used to gain access to the WWW. A WWW browser has a Graphical User Interface and is available for all kinds of computers.

When using a web browser, one is automatically linked to a homepage. This page is the anchorage from which to navigate in highly flexible ways, towards other groups and pages belonging to other servers, all over the world. What makes this kind of web transfer possible is the pointer that indicates the next source of information. This pointer is what we previously referred to as Uniform Resource Locators (URL). "http://www.sintef.no/sintef.html" is such an address. "http://" tells the web browser to make a web linking. The address next read is "www.sintef.no". "no" is the name of the Internet covering Norway, and "sintef" is the characterisation of the research agency SINTEF in Norway, which has a server and where the homepage "sintef.html" has been created. "www" on the other hand, has no function other than showing that this is a web address.

Today, most of the web browsers are more than mere browsers. Increasingly, they are used as functional boxes. They are able to handle different Internet functions, such as e-mail, news, FTP and Gopher (see below) as well as streaming (whereby, e.g., a movie is transmitted directly onto the screen without prior downloading as a file), and they can function as editorial tools when creating new web pages.

E-mail

Electronic mail is one of the most popular functions on the Internet. Using this function one can send messages to anyone with access to the Internet and an e-mail address. A person may send a letter – an e-mail – to one or an unlimited number of persons with a mere click on the keyboard, or she may connect to discussion groups (mailing lists) and receive letters automatically. E-mail is a very fast and cheap way to communicate. Messages may be delivered to the other side of the world in just a few minutes.

In order to use the e-mail function, it is necessary to possess an e-mail address, ordered from one of the Internet service administrators. This address may look like "tom.zorro@westernbank.co.uk". The address has a logical structure. In this example "uk" is the name of the domain – the name given to the sphere of the United Kingdom. The computer belongs to a firm, indicated by "co" (= company). The computer, on the other hand, has the logical name "westernbank", which tells us that this is the server operating on the Net. It is registered with its own Internet address (IP number). The name of the employee with this address is "tom.zorro". The way the address is constructed tells us that his operations on the e-mail function are managed by the server "westernbank.co.uk".

When "tom.zorro" sends an e-mail, he must provide the name of the person (or persons) the e-mail is meant for, along with the message he wants to communicate. The recipient, then, receives a message telling her that there is mail in her mailbox. In addition, it indicates the name of the sender and the subject of his message. The message is easily brought to the recipient's screen by clicking on the message about mail.

News and newsgroups

News and newsgroups are services we have access to when we are linked to a news server on Usenet. Usenet is a common designation for the collection of all computers that exchange news globally. News is the characterisation of the service containing a collection of boards for presenting bulletins or messages. A news server is the computer that manages and distributes the bulletins or messages arriving at the news group.

Often news consists of messages published by a single person on a news server belonging to a newsgroup. Newsgroups, which are a kind of discussion forum, are usually topic-specific and identified by the title given. Everyone who has access to the newsgroup may download and read the messages on her own computer. News can be presented as text, a picture, "living" pictures like a movie, sound or a combination of all these formats.

A person wanting to publish a picture may easily do so from his e-mail software or web browser. The message may then be sent to a newsgroup that has a name. It is impossible to verify how many thousands of newsgroups and news titles exist in the world. No centralised service offers such a register.

A news server is placed on the Net to exchange information with the news server next to it. In this way, a message is gradually spread on the Net from one computer to the next, and so on.

A message will remain on a server during a certain period of time before it is removed. This period may vary from a few days to weeks. One reason for a short period is that a newsgroup may have a capacity shortage. Existing messages must, therefore, be removed in order to make room for more recent messages.

A news server offers a set of different newsgroups. Which newsgroups are offered depends on which filters the server uses. It also depends on the other news server it exchanges newsgroups with. The news server manager decides which filter is to be active. In this way, certain messages (e.g., illegal content) may not be admitted.[1]

When using the news, a person is at the starting point, linked to a news server on the server where she has her Internet connection. She is, however, free to link to other news servers, both nationally and abroad. This is easily done by changing the news server address in the news programme. Many large commercial news servers cover most of the newsgroups on the Internet without active censorship. Examples of such servers are American On-line, Compuserve, Netcome and Prodigy. There are also many non-commercial news servers, "the free public NNTP", still with admittance without active censorship, and where the customer does not have to pay for the services offered.

FTP, Gopher and Telnet

As mentioned earlier, several functions other than browsing, e-mail and news exist on the Internet and WWW. Several of them were developed before the WWW technology became dominant. FTP (File Transfer Protocol) and Gopher are functions especially suited to transferring files from one place to another. These functions are still accessible on most of the web browsers.

Telnet is a function that allows a person to take control of another computer from her own computer, if she has admittance as a user and a password. Telnet is text-based and line-oriented as computers were before the development of the Graphical User Interface.

BBS (Bulletin Board System)

BBS is another service the Internet user may call up using a modem and a computer. A modem is a tool for connecting the computer directly to the telephone network.

By calling the BBS telephone number, the user gains access to another computer that is connected to the telephone network by a modem. This technology is based on teletechnology, not on Internet technology. Messages can be posted on just about any topic. The function, however, usually involves smaller groups of users. The BBS is commonly tailored for a specific product, conference or geographic area.

Internet Relay Chat (IRC)

IRC is a "real time" communication system based on text messages. It implies that what one user writes from his keyboard shows up on the screens of every user taking part in the same channel or chat group. A "real time" communication system means that the messages – the "chats" – run simultaneously, in contrast to messages sent through the traditional e-mail system, managed by the e-mail service. Theoretically there is no limit on the number of users who can participate on one channel at the same time on the IRC. It is also possible to take part in different discussion groups at the same time. However, IRC allows private chats to be arranged and conducted between specific members. IRC is primarily a system for exchanging information and discussing.

When communicating on IRC, the users identify the particular IRC "room" – often referred to as "chat room" – to which they want to connect. It is identified by its title, which reflects the conversation subject matter.

Common across the Internet functions, such as News, IRC and BBS, are rules developed to govern on-line behaviour. These rules are referred to as "netiquette" and stress, among other things, that illegal behaviour is not allowed. The dynamics of the forums are extremely interesting for the police. Regulators fiercely monitor them. But there is constant use of Net alter egos and a high level of tolerance on the part of users. Some of the forums have moderators who control interaction in a passive or an active manner.

The search engines

An important source of information on the Internet is the search engines. Such an engine is a server that systematically searches for information on other Net servers and indexes the information into a local database. Indexing means that the information is categorised by its content or topic. Different search engines have developed their own specialities, depending on the methods used for searching and the profile of the service they offer. In many search engines, functions are developed that enable users to put in references to their own or other people's or organisations' web pages.

The search engine presents a page with one or more fields for inserting text that represents a cue or keyword or a logical criterion for reference during the desired search. Moreover, the search engine usually offers different kinds of information in the form of topic categories. The main categories are web page information and news information from Usenet.

The URL address, or information from a web page, constitutes the base of a keyword in the information to a search engine. This means that a search engine is the perfect tool for acquiring desired information. When the user clicks on a URL address on the list of search matches from the engine's index, she moves directly to the page.

When using the Usenet for a web page search in newsgroups without support from a local server, the user has to download the information indirectly. This means that she has to download it herself onto her own computer, save it, and transform the data to a readable format. Such indirect downloading is necessary when a target newsgroup handles text-based information, and not binary information such as certain pictures, sounds and movies. The possibility is not well known, but if the knowledge becomes more widespread, many persons will probably use this alternative method to download information that they have no access to from their local news servers.

There are many search engines available with different functionality and capacity. Common to them is that they use the search functions, "robots", to seek information on Net servers and then register the information in a server database. It is such a database the user has access to when searching. Some well-known search engines are Alta Vista, Excite, Infoseek, etc.

Digital Research Laboratories in Palo Alto develop Alta Vista. Both the number of pages indexed by the engine and the number of searches being carried out are extremely high. The engine is probably the fastest "spider" on the Internet. It has the capacity to index more than 3 million pages a day, and it indexes both web pages and newsgroups. Alta Vista news makes all the indexed newsgroups accessible for everyone using the engine. Through Alta Vista one can get information from newsgroups that are not accessible via many of the national local news servers.

There are also several private search engines accessible for a fee.

Anonymous remailers

Anonymity and remailing are important aspects of Internet for many of its users. A remailer is a Net server that offers senders of e-mails and news anonymity by removing their identity or replacing it with other addresses. Anonymity is mainly used to protect the senders' identity and reduce the pathways back to them to a minimum. There might be legitimate reasons for a sender to be anonymous on the Net. In autocracies where political and religious freedom of speech are repressed, remailing may give citizens an opportunity to take part in dialogues that they, according to human rights, are ensured to take part in. Remailing is, however, also a welcome opportunity for people who have reason to avoid being exposed for criminal and anti-social activities. Remailing gives them protection and minimises the risk of being discovered.

Anonymous exchanges may take the following form: In a newsgroup there is a message with the address "ano333 @anonym.server.no". This is probably an e-mail that has passed via a remailer with the address "ano@anonym.server". In this case, the sender's real address has been removed and replaced by "ano333@ anonym.server.no". When the e-mail replay is transferred to this sender, the remailer replaces the anonymous person's address "ano333" with the real e-mail address. Then the person who wants to remain anonymous may receive the e-mails without divulging her identity.

Principally, there are two kinds of remailers: "pseudo-anonymous remailers" and "anonymous remailers". The example given above is a "pseudo-anonymous remailer". The advantage of this kind of remailer is that it is easy to use. It is, however, not more secure than the persons handling the server. The "anonymous remailer" is far safer in the sense that it is more difficult to trace the sender. The disadvantage for someone seeking anonymity is that the latter remailer is difficult to handle. A common method to reduce the chances of tracing the sender further is to use two or more remailers.

Note

1. Most of the Norwegian news servers, for example, do not admit messages that contain pictures, sound or videos presenting sexual or violent content. Examples of newsgroups that are filtered out by The Norwegian University of Technology and Science's (NTNU) news server are: alt.binaries.erotica.*, alt.binaries.picture.erotica.*, alt.sex.*, alt.suicide, alt.pedophilia.

Sex on the Internet

Issues, Concerns and Implications

Mark Griffiths

The rapid growth of the Internet has led to the re-examination of many areas of behaviour. One such area concerns issues surrounding sexual behaviour and excessive Internet usage, particularly as some academics have alleged that social pathologies are beginning to surface in cyberspace. This article[1] examines the concept of "Internet addiction" in relation to excessive sexual behaviour and Internet pornography, as well as examining newer areas of Internet sexuality such as "online relationships" and sexually-related Internet crime (e.g., "cyberstalking").

Sexually-related uses of the Internet

Before examining the "addictiveness potential" of the Internet and its relationship with sexuality, it would appear wise to examine all the different ways that the Internet can be used for sexually-related purposes as it is probably the case that only some of these activities may be done to excess and/or be potentially addictive. The Internet can (and has) been used for a number of diverse activities surrounding sexually motivated behaviour. These include the use of the Internet for:

- seeking out sexually-related material for educational use. This includes those seeking information regarding (i) sexual health promotion (e.g., information about contraception, sexually transmitted diseases, etc.), (ii) self-help/diagnosis (e.g., advice about sexual dysfunctions, sexual diseases, etc.), and (iii) scientific research (e.g., reports of studies in the area of sexology, national reports on sexual behaviour, etc.). These may take the form of either stand-alone web pages or may be incorporated within Usenet discussion groups.

- buying or selling sexually-related goods for further use offline. This includes the buying or selling of goods for (i) educational purposes (e.g., books, videos, CD-ROMs, etc.), (ii) entertainment/masturbatory purposes (e.g., magazines, books, videos, CD-ROMs, etc.), and (iii) miscellaneous purposes (e.g., sex aids/toys, contraception, aphrodisiacs, etc.).
- visiting and/or purchasing goods in online virtual sex shops. Visiting a virtual sex shop may be done for either voyeuristic purposes ("window shopping") or for the sole intention of actually buying goods for use offline.
- seeking out material for entertainment/masturbatory purposes for use online. This can either be primarily image-based (e.g., pornographic web sites offering picture libraries, video clips, videos, etc., live online strip shows, live voyeuristic Web-Cam sites, etc.) or text-based (e.g., chat rooms, Usenet discussion groups, etc.).
- seeking out sex therapists. This may involve either individuals or couples seeking out an online sex therapist for advice about sex and/or relationship problems.
- seeking out sexual partners for an enduring relationship (i.e., a monogamous partner) via online dating agencies, personal advertisements/"lonely hearts" columns and/or chat rooms.
- seeking out sexual partners for a transitory relationship (i.e., escorts, prostitutes, swingers) via online personal advertisements/"lonely hearts" columns, escort agencies and/or chat rooms.
- seeking out individuals who then become victims of sexually-related Internet crime (online sexual harassment, cyberstalking, paedophilic "grooming" of children).
- engaging in and maintaining online relationships via e-mail and/or chat rooms.
- exploring gender and identity roles by swapping gender or creating other personas and forming online relationships.
- digitally manipulating images on the Internet for entertainment and/or masturbatory purposes (e.g., celebrity fake photographs where heads of famous people are superimposed onto someone else's naked body).

On first examination – and by evaluating the relatively sparse literature in this area – it would appear that excessive, addictive, obsessive and/or compulsive Internet use only applies to some of these behaviours. The most likely behaviours include the use of online pornography for masturbatory purposes, engaging in online relationships, and sexually-related Internet crime (e.g., cyberstalking). Before looking at these three areas in more detail, a brief overview of Internet addiction will follow.

Internet addiction

One area where Internet sexuality has been discussed academically is that of "Internet addiction". Despite opposition to the concept of behavioural (i.e., non-chemical) addictions, such as Internet addiction, there is a growing movement (e.g., Orford, 1985; Marks, 1990; Griffiths, 1996a) which views a number of diverse behaviours as potentially addictive, including gambling, overeating, sex, exercise, shopping, and computer game playing. Internet addiction is another such area since it has been alleged by some academics that social pathologies (i.e., technological addictions) may be beginning to surface in cyberspace (e.g., Griffiths, 1996b; 1998a; Brenner, 1997; Cooper, 1998; Scherer, 1997; Young, 1998a; 1998b).

Technological addictions are non-chemical (behavioural) addictions which involve excessive human-machine interaction. They can either be passive (e.g., television) or active (e.g., computer games) and usually contain inducing and reinforcing features which may contribute to the promotion of addictive tendencies (Griffiths, 1995a). They also feature the core components of addiction, including salience, mood modification, tolerance, withdrawal, conflict and relapse (Griffiths, 1996a; 1996c). It has been argued by Griffiths (1996c) that any behaviour (e.g., Internet use) which fulfils these criteria can be operationally defined as addictions. These core components are expanded upon below in relation to Internet sex of whatever type it happens to be (e.g., downloading pornography, cypersex relationships, etc.):

- Salience – This occurs when Internet sex becomes the most important activity in the person's life and dominates their thinking (preoccupations and cognitive distortions), feelings (cravings) and behaviour (deterioration of socialized behaviour). For instance, even if the person is not actually on their computer engaged in Internet sex they will be thinking about the next time they will be.
- Mood modification – This refers to the subjective experiences that people report as a consequence of engaging in Internet sex and can be seen as a coping strategy (i.e., they experience an arousing "buzz" or a "high" or paradoxically tranquilizing feel of "escape" or "numbing").
- Tolerance – This is the process whereby increasing amounts of Internet sex are required to achieve the former mood modificating effects. This basically means that for someone engaged in Internet sex, they gradually build up the amount of the time they spend in front of the computer engaged in the behaviour.
- Withdrawal symptoms – These are the unpleasant feeling states and/or physical effects which occur when Internet sex is discontinued or suddenly reduced, e.g., the shakes, moodiness, irritability, etc.
- Conflict – This refers to the conflicts between the Internet user and those around them (interpersonal conflict), conflicts with other activities (job,

social life, hobbies and interests) or from within the individual themselves (intrapsychic conflict and/or subjective feelings of loss of control) which are concerned with spending too much time engaged in Internet sex.

- Relapse – This is the tendency for repeated reversions to earlier patterns of Internet sex to recur and for even the most extreme patterns typical of the height of excessive Internet sex to be quickly restored after many years of abstinence or control.

Young (1999a) claims Internet addiction is a broad term which covers a wide variety of behaviours and impulse control problems. She claims it is further categorized by five specific subtypes:

- Cybersexual addiction: Compulsive use of adult web sites for cybersex and cyberporn.
- Cyber-relationship addiction: over-involvement in online relationships.
- Net compulsions: obsessive online gambling, shopping or day-trading.
- Information overload: compulsive web surfing or database searches.
- Computer addiction: obsessive computer game playing (e.g., *Doom*, *Myst*, *Solitaire*, etc.).

Only two of these specifically refer to potential sexually-based addictions (i.e., cybersexual addiction and cyber-relationship addiction) but Young's classification does raise the question of what people are actually addicted to? On a primary level, is it the sexually-related behaviour or is it the Internet? In reply to Young, Griffiths (1999a) has argued that many of these excessive users are not "Internet addicts" but just use the Internet excessively as a medium to fuel other addictions. Griffiths argues that a gambling addict or a computer game addict is not addicted to the Internet. The Internet is just the place where they engage in the behaviour. The same argument can be applied to Internet sex addicts. However, there are case study reports of individuals who appear to be addicted to the Internet itself. These are usually people who use Internet chat rooms or play fantasy role playing games – activities that they would not engage in except on the Internet itself (some of which are sex-related). These individuals to some extent are engaged in text-based virtual realities and take on other personas and social identities as a way of making themselves feel good about themselves.

In these cases, the Internet may provide an alternative reality to the user and allow them feelings of immersion and anonymity (which may lead to an altered state of consciousness). This in itself may be highly psychologically and/or physiologically rewarding. The anonymity of the Internet has been identified as a consistent factor underlying excessive use of the Internet (Young, 1998b; Griffiths, 1995b). This is perhaps particularly relevant to those using Internet pornography. There may be many people who are using the medium of the Internet because (a) it overcomes the embarrassment of going into shops to buy pornography over the shop counter, and (b) it is faster than waiting for other non-face-to-face commercial transactions (e.g., mail order). Anonymity may also encourage deviant, deceptive and criminal online acts such as the development of aggressive online personas or the viewing and downloading of illegal images (e.g., pornography) (Young, 1999).

There have been few studies of excessive Internet use which have found that a small proportion of users admitted using the Internet for sexual purposes (e.g., Morahan-Martin & Schumacher, 1997; Scherer, 1997; Young, 1998b). None of the surveys to date conclusively show that Internet addiction exists or that Internet sex addiction is problematic to anyone but a small minority. At best, they indicate that Internet addiction may be prevalent in a significant minority of individuals but that more research using validated survey instruments and other techniques (e.g., in-depth qualitative interviews) are required. Further to this, Griffiths (1999a) has also noted other problems with the criteria used in most of the surveys to date. They (i) have no measure of severity, (ii) have no temporal dimension, (iii) have a tendency to overestimate the prevalence of problems, and (iv) take no account of the context of Internet use. Case studies of excessive Internet users may provide better evidence of whether Internet sex addiction exists by the fact that the data collected are much more detailed. Even if just one case study can be located, it indicates that Internet sex addiction actually does exist – even if it is unrepresentative. Griffiths (1998a) has argued that excessive usage in a majority of cases appears to be purely symptomatic but that for what appears to be an exceedingly tiny minority, the Internet may be addictive.

Pornography on the Internet

From the earliest days of photography to the latest innovations in real-time, e.g., one-to-one video conferencing, sex has played a defining role in the development and advance of new communication technology (Sprenger, 1999). Although the pornography industry cannot be credited with inventing these new technologies, they were certainly the first to put them to profitable use. Pornographers have always been the first to exploit new publishing technologies (e.g., photography, videotape, Internet, etc.). It is estimated that the online pornography industry will reach $366 million by 2001 (Sprenger, 1999) though other estimates suggest it is already worth $1 billion (*The Guardian*, 1999). Further to this, the research company Datamonitor reported that over half of all spending on the Internet is related to sexual activity (*The Guardian*, 1999). This includes the conventional (e.g., Internet versions of widely available pornographic magazines like *Playboy*), the not so conventional (Internet versions of very hardcore pornographic magazines) and what can only be described as the bizarre (discussion groups on almost any sexual paraphilia). Further to this, there are also pornographic picture libraries (commercial and free-access), videos and video clips, live strip-shows, live sex shows and voyeuristic Web-Cam sites.

Research has also revealed that Internet surfing has many parallels with road traffic. There appear to be identical patterns of congestion and "solid block motion" where everyone is forced to advance at the same speed (Brooks, 1999). One web-traffic researcher, Bernardo Huberman (who works for Xerox Palo Alto Research Center) analyzed more than 500,000 visits to a major web portal and came to the conclusion that the Internet sex sites are the "undisputed kings" in selling advertizing space. Huberman noticed that Internet surfers typically click once or twice and then get out of a site. However, Huberman noted that some people were clicking up to 200 times and that nearly all of these instances were people accessing Internet sex sites. Further investigation revealed an amazingly sophisticated structure which led surfers deeper and deeper into the site (Brooks, 1999). The "click counts" data collected by Huberman suggests that there is an almost compulsive element in accessing online pornography and that some people are very heavy users of these services. Such research cannot show that Internet pornography addicts exist but is at the very least indicative of repetitive, habitual and/or pathological behaviour. Further to this, the Internet offers 24-hour constant access and has the potential to stimulate excessive use. In some cases this may become an addictive and/or compulsive activity.

One of the main reasons why the pornography industry has such a vested interest in this area is that in the online world the buying of most products is hassle-free and anonymous. However, buying pornography in the offline world may be embarrassing or stressful to the consumers particularly if they have to go to venues deemed to be "unsavoury". If pornography consumers are given the chance to circumvent this process, they invariably will. Pornography and its distribution are now widespread on the Internet – but how prevalent is Internet pornography? Academic researchers also claim that "sex" is the most searched for topic on the Internet (Cooper, Scherer, Boies & Gordon, 1999) and as many as one third of all Internet users visit some type of sexual site (Cooper, Delmonico & Burg, in press). In the UK, a survey carried out by University of Middlesex in 1995, and replicated in 1997, analysed a million word searches on an Internet search engine and reported that over half of them were aimed at locating pornography (Sparrow & Griffiths, 1997). However, these studies were carried out using word searches from only one search engine and the situation may have changed slightly in the last few years. Furthermore, the study reported that the pornography was more than just pictures of naked people but also included more worrying material. For instance, there was information for paedophiles on how to entrap and (in some instances) kill children.

Children and Internet pornography

One of the biggest fears among parents who are thinking of using the Internet is that their children will be exposed to pornography, particularly because over 17 million children are using the Internet world-wide (Thompson,1999). Issues surrounding censorship are high on the moral agenda but preventing access to such sites is difficult. A major US survey undertaken in 1998 by the Annenberg Public Policy Center (Lillington, 1999) reported that 75 per cent of parents were anxious about what their children might be exposed to on the Internet. To what extent is this fear justified? The media has certainly played a role in heightening parents' fears as two-thirds of all newspaper articles about the Internet highlight negative aspects and one in four mentioned child pornography (Lillington, 1999).

Internet pornography is not difficult to access – especially with the development of powerful yet easy-to-use search engines. In fact, a survey by the National Opinion Poll (NOP) in June 1999, found that a third of UK children had found content on the Internet that upset or embarrassed them – up from 20 per cent in the previous survey (Thompson, 1999; Lillington, 1999). Of this material, 58 per cent was described as being "rude". Given that the same NOP poll found that one in four UK children aged seven to sixteen years old (i.e., 3 million children) are regular Internet users with half of them doing it from home (Thompson, 1999), it therefore appears there may be widespread cause for alarm.

There are many steps a parent can take to prevent their child from accessing pornography including:

- reading guidelines for parents which run through issues and possible approaches for overseeing Internet use by children. These include those produced in offline versions (see Table 1) or those that can be found online. These include such sites as the Netparents resource collection (www.netparents.org/parentstips/resources.html), NCH Action for children site (www.nchafc.org.uk/internet/index.html) and Schoolzone's resources (www.schoolzone.co.uk/resources/safety_frame.htm).
- being with your children at all times when they access the Internet.
- joining an Internet service provider that prevents its users from accessing such things.
- installing one of the many different types of blocking package on the market that filter content in some way (Griffiths, 1997b; 1998b). These include those which use lists of key words that you can define (e.g., Net Nanny), software packages that can block certain areas of the Internet, such as Usenet groups, or which restrict access at certain times (e.g., Cyber Patrol), packages which have a built-in censor to certain categories as defined by the maker of the package (SurfWatch), or packages which block access to certain file types, like GIF and JPEG which are lot of pornographic images use. However, there may be a "technological generation gap" as the recent poll by NOP reported, that children knew more about filtering software than their parents (Thompson, 1999).

Table 1. Guidelines for children on how to be safe on the Internet

(1) Never tell anyone that you meet on the Internet your home address, telephone number or school's name unless you are given permission by a parent or carer.
(2) Never send anyone your picture, credit card or bank details (or anything else).
(3) Never give your password to anyone – even your best friend.
(4) Never arrange to meet anyone in person that you have met on the Internet without first agreeing it with your parent or carer.
(5) Never stay in a chat room or in a conference if someone says or writes something which makes you feel uncomfortable or worried. Always report it to your parent or carer.
(6) Never respond to nasty, suggestive or rude e-mails or postings in Usenet groups.
(7) If you see bad language or distasteful pictures while you are online, always tell your parent or carer.
(8) When you are online, always be yourself and do not pretend to be anyone or anything you are not.
(9) Always remember that if someone makes you an offer which seems to good to be true – then it probably is.

Source: NCH Action for Children: Children on the Internet. Opportunities and Hazards, 1998.

Despite packages like Surfwatch and Net Nanny which block access to pornographic sites, such packages can still be circumvented. There are also other packages like Babewatch which do the exact opposite (i.e., locate nothing but pornographic sites for the user) (Griffiths, 1997b; 1998b). It appears to be the case that parents are not as vigilant about their children's Internet use as they could be. For instance, a survey of 500 online households by the US-based National Center for Missing and Exploited Children found that 20 per cent of parents did not supervise their children's Internet use. It was also reported that 71 per cent of parents with children aged 14 or older said they had stopped monitoring their children's Internet use (Thompson, 1999).

Online relationships

Probably one of the most unexpected uses surrounding the growth of the Internet concerns the development of online relationships and their potentially addicting nature. It is hard to estimate the number of online relationships but in the UK it was reported in the media that there had been over one thousand weddings as a result of Internet meetings. Media commentators claim that cyberspace is becoming another singles bar as there are now numerous sites aimed at those who want romance and/or a sexual liaison. Some of these are aimed at single people (e.g., Widows, Thirtysomething UK, and Married with Kids) while others appear to encourage and facilitate virtual adultery (e.g., MarriedM4Affair, Cheating Wife or Lonely Husband).

Young, Griffin-Shelley, Cooper, O'Mara and Buchanan (in press) define an online relationship (a "cyberaffair") as a romantic and/or sexual relationship that is initiated via online contact and maintained predominantly through electronic conversations that occur through e-mail and in virtual communities, such as chat rooms, interactive games, or newsgroups. Young et al. report that what starts off as a simple e-mail exchange or an innocent chat room encounter can escalate into an intense and passionate cyberaffair and eventually into face-to-face sexual encounters. Further to this, those in online relationships often turn to mutual erotic dialogue (often referred to as "cybersex"). In this instance, cybersex involves online users swapping text-based sexual fantasies with each other. These text-based interactions may be accompanied by masturbation. Online chat rooms provide opportunities for online social gatherings to occur almost at the push of a button without even having to move from your desk. Online group participants can – if they so desire – develop one-to-one conversations at a later point either through the use of continuous e-mails or by instant messages from chat rooms. It could perhaps be argued that electronic communication is the easiest, most disinhibiting and most accessible way to meet potential new partners.

Infidelity online – how and why does it occur?

There are a number of factors that make online contacts potentially seductive and/or addictive. Such factors include the disinhibiting and anonymous nature of the Internet. This may be very exciting to those engaged in an online affair. Disinhibition is clearly one of the Internet's key appeals as there is little doubt that the Internet makes people less inhibited (Joinson, 1998). Online users appear to open up more quickly online and reveal themselves emotionally much faster than in the offline world. What might take months or years in an offline relationship may only take days or weeks online. As Cooper and Sportolari (1997) have pointed out, the perception of trust, intimacy and acceptance has the potential to encourage online users to use these relationships as a primary source of companionship and comfort.

Some researchers have made attempts to explain how and why infidelity occurs online. Cooper (1998) proposed the "Triple A Engine" (Access, Affordability, and Anonymity) which he claimed help to understand the power and attraction of the Internet for sexual pursuits. Young (1999) also claimed to have developed a variant of the "Triple A Engine" which she called the "ACE model" (Anonymity, Convenience, Escape). Neither of these are strictly models as neither explains the process of how online relationships develop. However, they do provide (in acronym form) the variables involved in the acquisition, development and maintenance of emotional and/or sexual relationships on the Internet (i.e., anonymity, access, convenience, affordability and escape). It would also appear that virtual environments have the potential to provide short-term comfort, excitement and/or distraction.

Types of online relationship

A number of researchers have forwarded typologies of the different kinds of Internet users in relation to sexual and/or relationship activity (Cooper, 1998;

Young, 1999; Griffiths, 1999b). Cooper, Putnam, Planchon and Boies (1999) suggest there are three types of cybersexual user (recreational, at risk, and compulsive) but this tells us little except about frequency of use. However, Griffiths (1999b) has outlined three basic types of online relationship in relation to actual online behaviour. The first one is purely virtual and involves two people who never actually meet. They engage in an online relationship which goes further than being pen-pals as the exchanges are usually very sexually explicit. Neither person wants to meet the other person and are engaged in the interaction purely for sexual kicks. It is not uncommon for these individuals to swap gender roles. The "relationships" may be very short-lived and the people involved will usually have real-life partners. These people prefer the distance, relative anonymity and control offered by the Internet and will prefer to confine the relationship to cyberspace. As far as these people are concerned, they do not feel they are being unfaithful.

The second type of online relationship involves people meeting online but eventually wanting the relationship to move from the virtual to the actual after becoming emotionally intimate with each other online. The shared emotional intimacy often leads to cybersex and/or a strong desire to communicate constantly with each other on the Internet. For many, the online relationship will progress after sending photographs of each other into secret phone calls, letters, and offline meetings. Once they have met up, and if they are geographically near each other, their Internet use will usually decrease considerably as they will spend far more time actually (rather than virtually) with each other.

The third type of relationship involves two people first meeting offline but then maintaining their relationship online for the majority of their relationship. This is usually because they are geographically distant and may even be living in separate countries. These people only meet up a few times a year but may spend vast amounts of time "talking" to their partners on the Internet most nights. As they are geographically distant, the relationship only continues for those who have the time, the budget and the travel opportunity to maintain the nominal physical contact. With regards to "addiction", it is only the first type outlined here that may be addicted to the Internet. The latter two types are more likely to be addicted to the person rather than the activity – particularly as their Internet usage stops almost completely when they meet up offline with their partner.

Although many people who have not engaged in an online relationship fail to understand the pull and attraction of such an activity, it quite clearly can have detrimental consequences for some people who do. An online relationship can lead to a loving and compassionate individuals to become uncaring towards their partner and/or family, evasive, and demanding privacy online. In an effort to help both couples and therapists, Young et al. (in press) produced a list of early warning signs in the detection of a suspected online relationship. These include (i) a change in sleep patterns, (ii) a demand for privacy, (iii) ignoring other responsibilities, (iv) evidence of lying, (v) personality changes, (vi) loss of interest in sex, and (vii) declining investment in the relationship.

Sexually-related Internet crime

Despite the seemingly marked absence of serious consideration, sexually-related Internet crime seems set to become increasingly important to all those involved in the administration of criminal justice. Sexually-related Internet crime is on the increase and some of the perpetrators may be addicted to the criminal activity in question and/or develop obsessions about their Internet victims. In the broadest possible sense, sexually-related Internet crime can be divided into two categories – (i) display, downloading and/or the distribution of illegal sexually-related material, and (ii) the use of the Internet to sexually procure and/or intimidate an individual in some way (e.g., online sexual harassment, cyberstalking, paedophilic grooming).

Charlesworth (1995) noted that criminal law and those who enforce it have taken time to come to terms with the implications of change with regards to Internet crime. Those in the criminal justice system continue to rely on their own familiar scheme of reference when attempting to comprehend the criminal behaviour. For the most part, they have some understanding of the mode of operation, likely benefits to the offender and costs to the victim of the criminal activity presented before them. However, the unfamiliarity of sexually-related Internet crime denies those in the criminal justice system all important access to their own scheme of understanding. The advancements in computer technology generally (and the increased availability of the Internet in particular) have provided for new innovations in, and an expansion of, the field of criminality (and more specifically in the area of sexually-related Internet crime) (Durkin, 1997; Durkin & Bryant, 1998; Griffiths, Rogers & Sparrow, 1998; Deirmenjian, 1999).

Most people's perceptions about sexually-related Internet crime are probably based on media reports. These usually concern:

- distribution of illegal pornography on the Internet.
- use of the Internet for paedophilic purposes (i.e., paedophiles distributing child pornography or pretending to be a child to make contact with children).
- high profile prosecutions of Internet pornographers (such as the recent imprisonment of the UK's largest pornography operator who was given an 18-month prison for designing web sites (e.g., Farmsex, Europerv and Schoolgirls-R-Us) featuring extreme pornography, bestiality, coprophilia and torture (Wilson, 1999).

However, one of the main problems with Internet pornography is that any country's attempt to interdict cross-border flows of pornography would be defeated by advances in communication technology – especially data transmission (Millar, 1996; Sprenger, 1999). The police crackdown on Internet pornography has been argued by some to be futile as it could drive it underground (Booth, 1996). Part of the Internet's appeal is its subversive nature, for it crosses frontiers, language barriers and is not policed by any one country.

Online harassment and cyberstalking

Stalking has been a high-profile crime in the 1990's leaving victims with a shattered sense of security and well-being. It now seems to be the case that stalkers are moving with the times and starting to harass and stalk in cyberspace. As a direct result of the increased accessibility of the Internet world-wide, the incidence of cyberstalking will almost certainly increase. Very recently the first prosecution case of cyberstalking or harassment by computer occurred in Los Angeles, when a 50-year old security guard was arrested for his online stalking activities (Gumbel, 1999).

In 1998, Novell (one of the world's leading providers of network software) began a UK study into "spamming" (i.e., the receiving of unwanted and unsolicited cyber junk mail). The focus of the study was to estimate the cost in business terms of time and money wasted. However, one of the unexpected findings of the research was that a large minority of women, 41 per cent of the regular Internet users, had been sent pornographic material or been harassed or stalked on the Internet (Gumbel, 1999). Three percent of these messages were highly personal and sexual, and 35 per cent of the messages were unsolicited pornography. Such unwarranted attention is intrusive and is a serious cause for concern.

CyberAngels (www.cyberangels.org) is a branch of the Guardian Angels and was set up in 1995. To date, it has dealt with over 200 cases of cyberstalking – two of which ended in the rape of the victims according to their Senior Director, Colin Gabriel Hatcher (Griffiths, Rogers & Sparrow, 1999). The organization claims that cyberstalking usually occurs with women who are stalked by men, or by children who are stalked by adult predators. Typically the victim is new online and therefore ignorant of "netiquette". In most cases, people just receive unsolicited junkmail but it can turn sinister. The risk of harassment intensifies if someone enters an Internet chat room. In most instances, the online harassment and stalking have eventually escalated offline (by tracing the victim's telephone number and address). Hatcher makes the point that cases such as these should not be trivialized as the paranoia of a small group of computer users (Griffiths, Rogers & Sparrow, 1998). In the US libel and defamation are taken very seriously but stalking is sometimes perceived as a crime related to women's hysteria.

One of the problems with Internet use is that there are always more novices than those experienced, so the novices are not being taught the ways that they can protect themselves from being exploited. At least with obscene phone calls there is a voice and with letters there is handwriting; with e-mails there is nothing to go on, no clue as to the personality of the person involved. To some this makes the whole thing creepier. What's more, these "new" criminals perhaps would never have interfered in other people's lives and committed such acts in a face-to-face scenario.

Cyberstalking: What can be done to combat the problem?

The development of computer technology is producing new categories of crimes in which the perpetrators believe they can hide behind the seemingly anonymous computer screen in an attempt to intimidate, threaten and spread hatred. These people appear to be naïve about exactly how anonymous they can be since specialists in this field can trace almost any electronic trail back to a computer. Every time a person visits a web site, they are leaving their e-mail address behind as a calling card. If that person takes part in any Internet discussions on a Usenet site, he or she is again leaving his/her identity. Where new crimes occur, new methods are used to combat it. For instance, a police officer was recently caught attempting to solicit minors over the Internet when a police officer pretended to be a 13-year old girl (Gumbel, 1999). This was a lot easier to do over the computer than it would have been in real life. The International Web Police (www.Web-Police.org) are well placed to fight this relatively new type of crime.

At present very few cases of cyberstalking have reached UK courts although UK law is adequately equipped to deal with such scenarios because of the recent 1997 Protection From Harassment Act. There is no specific mention of computers in the Act but the definition of harassment is based on the "reasonable man" test, i.e., any action which would reasonably be considered to be harassment are caught within the Act. This so-called "stalking act" sets out to create both criminal and civil sanctions for harassment, and in so doing, builds upon existing common law nuisance actions (Griffiths, Rogers & Sparrow, 1999). Criminal law and those who enforce it must come to terms with the implications of change with regards to computer crime. It could be argued that the technical complexity associated with cybercrime combined with the limited number of prosecutions has permitted criminal justice practitioners the luxury of ignorance. Sparrow and Griffiths (1997) have stated if computer-related crime is to occupy a position of increasing importance in the range of offending behaviour, then criminal justice practitioners must be willing to familiarize themselves with such activities in order to make judgements about the offender and the nature of their offending. In the future, cyberstalking may be viewed in the same way as other more "traditional" criminal acts are currently viewed.

Internet sexuality: Conclusions

One of the objectives of any future research should be to determine the object of the Internet sex addiction. If some people appear addicted to the Internet, what are they addicted to? Is it the medium of communication (i.e., the Internet itself)? Aspects of its specific style (e.g., anonymity, disinhibition, etc.)? The information that can be obtained (e.g., hard-core pornography)? Specific types of activity (gender-swapping, role-playing games, playing sex computer games, cyberstalking)? Talking/fantasizing to others (in chat rooms or on Internet Relay Chat)? Perhaps it could even be a complex interaction between more than one of these. It is most likely that the Internet provides a medium for the "addiction" to flow to its object of unhealthy attachment (i.e., a secondary addiction to more pervasive primary problems).

The Internet can easily be the focus of excessive, addictive, obsessive and/or compulsive behaviours. One thing that may intensify this focus are the vast resources on the Internet available to feed or fuel other addictions or compulsions. For example, to a sex addict or a stalker, the Internet could be a very dangerous medium to users and/or recipients. There is also the problem that the Internet consists of many different types of activity (e.g., e-mailing, information browsing, file transferring, socialising, role-game playing, etc.). It could be the case that some of these activities (like Internet Relay Chat or role-playing games) are potentially more addictive than some other Internet activities. It is also worth noting that there has been no research indicating that sexually-related Internet crimes such as cyberstalking are addictive. However, the small number of case studies that have emerged do appear to indicate that cyberstalkers display addictive tendencies at the very least (salience, mood modification, conflict, etc.) although further research is needed to ascertain whether these excessive behaviours could be classed as bona fide behavioural addictions.

With regard to online relationships and affairs, these behaviours present a new dimension in couple relationships. These sexually-related Internet behaviours appear as though they can be used from the healthy and normal through to the unhealthy and abnormal (i.e., use, abuse, and addiction) (Cooper, Putnam, et al., 1999). The Internet is anonymous, disinhibiting, easily accessible, convenient, affordable, and escape-friendly. These appear to be some of the main reasons for online infidelity. The detection of online affairs may be difficult but that does not mean it should not be given serious consideration in either an academic or practitioner context. These groups, along with those who engage in or who are on the receiving end of such behaviours, need to recognize that the Internet adds a new dimension to relationships. This has implications for assessment and treatment of couples who may, knowingly or unknowingly, undergo a relationship breakdown due to the impact of excessive online communication. However, as was noted earlier, text-based relationships can obviously be a positive and rewarding experience for many people. It is also an area in need of future research.

Interestingly, there is no clear evidence about the effects of pornography on users (Barak, Fisher, Belfry & Lashambe, 1999). However, Young et al. (2000) assert that future research is needed to more clearly delineate the identification and classification of problematic online sexual activities. Further to this Cooper, Putnam, et al. (1999) proposed a continuum of Internet sexual activities from life enhancing to pathological needs to be replicated and further refined. There are very few areas surrounding excessive Internet use and its relationship with sexuality that do not need further empirical research (e.g., online sexual addiction, Internet and computer addiction, and online relationship dependency and/or virtual affairs). More remains to be done in cyberspace to more clearly understand both the risks and benefits for Internet users, couples and society as a whole.

There is no doubt that Internet usage among the general population will continue to increase over the next few years. Social pathologies relating to Internet sexual behaviour do exist. This is certainly an area that should be of interest and concern not only to psychologists but to all those involved in clinical health issues. Excessive use of the Internet is not problematic in most cases, but the limited case study evidence available does suggest that for some individuals, excessive Internet usage is a real addiction and of genuine concern.

Note

1. A longer and more detailed version of this article will appear in an upcoming issue of *CyberPsychology and Behavior*.

References

Barak, A., Fisher, W.A., Belfry, S. & Lashambe, D.R. (1999). Sex, guys, and cyberspace: Effects of Internet pornography and individual differences on men's attitudes toward women. *Journal of Psychology & Human Sexuality, 11,* 63-91.

Booth, N. (1996). Clampdown can easily be beaten, say net experts. *The Times,* August 16, p.2.

Brenner, V. (1997). Psychology of computer use: XLVII. Parameters of Internet use, abuse and addiction: The first 90 days of the Internet usage survey. *Psychological Reports, 80,* 879-882.

Brooks, M. (1999). Sex site surfers teach traffic watchers. *The Guardian* (Online), September 30, p.3.

Charlesworth, A. (1995). Never having to say sorry. *The Times Higher Educational Supplement (Multimedia Section),* May 10, p.viii.

Cooper, A. (1998). Sexuality and the Internet: Surfing into the new millennium. *CyberPsychology and Behavior, 1,* 181-187.

Cooper, A., Delmonico, D. & Burg, R. (in press). Cybersex users, abusers, and compulsives: New findings and implications. *Sexual Addiction & Compulsivity: The Journal of Treatment and Prevention.*

Cooper, A., Putnam, D.E., Planchon, L.A. & Boies, S.C. (1999). Online sexual compulsivity: Getting tangled in the net. *Sexual Addiction & Compulsivity: The Journal of Treatment and Prevention, 6,* 79-104.

Cooper, A., Scherer, C., Boies, S.C. & Gordon, B. (1999). Sexuality on the Internet: From sexual exploration to pathological expression. *Professional Psychology: Research and Practice, 30,* 154-164.

Cooper, A. & Sportolari, L. (1997). Romance in Cyberspace: Understanding online attraction. *Journal of Sex Education and Therapy, 22,* 7-14.

Deirmenjian, J.M. (1999). Stalking in cyberspace. *Journal of the American Academy of Psychiatry and the Law, 27,* 407-413.

Durkin, K.F. (1997). Misuse of the Internet by pedophiles: Implications for law enforcement and probation practice. *Federal Probation, 61*(3), 14-18.

Durkin, K.F. & Bryant, C.D. (1998). Propagandizing pederasty: A thematic analysis of the on-line exculpatory accounts of unrepentant pedophiles. *Deviant Behavior, 20,* 103-127.

Griffiths, M.D. (1995a). Technological addictions. *Clinical Psychology Forum, 76,* 14-19.

Griffiths, M.D. (1995b). Netties anonymous. *Times Higher Educational Supplement,* April 7, p.18.

Griffiths, M.D. (1996a). Behavioural addictions: An issue for everybody? *Employee Counselling Today: The Journal of Workplace Learning, 8*(3), 19-25.

Griffiths, M.D. (1996b). Internet "addiction": An issue for clinical psychology? *Clinical Psychology Forum, 97,* 32-36.

Griffiths, M.D. (1996c). Nicotine, tobacco, and addiction. *Nature, 384,* 18.

Griffiths, M.D. (1997a, August). Technological addictions: Looking to the future. Paper presented at the 105th Annual Convention of the American Psychological Association, Chicago, Illinois.

Griffiths, M.D. (1997b). Children and the Internet. *Media Education Journal, 21,* 31-33.

Griffiths, M.D. (1998a). Internet addiction: Does it really exist? In J. Gackenbach (Ed.), *Psychology and the Internet: Intrapersonal, Interpersonal and Transpersonal Applications.* Pp.61-75. New York: Academic Press.

Griffiths, M.D. (1998b). Children and the Internet: Issues for parents and teachers. *Education and Health, 16,* 9-10.

Griffiths, M.D. (1999a). Internet addiction: Internet fuels other addictions. *Student British Medical Journal, 7,* 428-429.

Griffiths, M.D. (1999b). All but connected (Online relationships). *Psychology Post, 17,* 6-7.

Griffiths, M.D. (in press). Gambling technologies: Prospects for problem gambling. *Journal of Gambling Studies.*

Griffiths, M.D., Rogers, M.E. & Sparrow, P. (1998). Crime and IT (part II): 'Stalking the Net'. *Probation Journal, 45,* 138-141.

The Guardian (1999). Blue money. *The Guardian* (Online), May 27: p.5.

Gumbel, A. (1999). Techno detectives net cyber-stalkers. *Independent on Sunday,* January 31, p.17.

Joinson, A. (1998). Causes and implications of disinhibited behavior on the Internet. In J. Gackenback (Ed.), *Psychology and the Internet: Intrapersonal, Interpersonal, and Transpersonal Implications.* Pp.43-60. New York: Academic Press.

Lillington, K. (1999). Web life: Parenting. *The Guardian* (Online), September 9, p.5.

Marks, I. (1990). Non-chemical (behaviourial) addictions. *British Journal of Addiction, 85,* 1389-1394.

Millar, S. (1996). Police curb on Net porn 'impossible'. *The Guardian*, September 2, p.6.

Morahan-Martin, J.M. & Schumacher, P. (1997, August). Incidence and correlates of pathological Internet use. Paper presented at the 105th Annual Convention of the American Psychological Association, Chicago, Illinois.

Orford, J. (1985). *Excessive Appetites: A Psychological View of the Addictions.* Chichester: Wiley.

Scherer, K. (1997). College life online: Healthy and unhealthy Internet use. *Journal of College Development, 38,* 655-665.

Sparrow, P. & Griffiths, M.D. (1997). Crime and IT: Hacking and pornography on the Internet. *Probation Journal, 44,* 144-147.

Sprenger, P. (1999). The porn pioneers. *The Guardian* (Online), September 30, p.2-3.

Thompson, B. (1999). New kids on the net. *The Guardian* (Online), June 24, p.2-3.

Wilson, J. (1999). Net porn baron escapes jail. *The Guardian*, October 7, p.5.

Young, K. (1998a). Internet addiction: The emergence of a new clinical disorder. *CyberPsychology and Behavior, 1,* 237-244.

Young, K. (1998b). *Caught in the Net: How to Recognize the Signs of Internet Addiction and a Winning Strategy for Recovery.* New York: Wiley.

Young, K. (1999a). Internet addiction: Evaluation and treatment. *Student British Medical Journal, 7,* 351-352.

Young, K. (1999b, August). Cyber-disorders: The mental illness concern for the millennium. Paper presented at the 108th Annual Meeting of the American Psychological Association, Boston, MA.

Young, K.S., Griffin-Shelley, E., Cooper, A., O'Mara, J. & Buchanan, J. (in press). Online infidelity: A new dimension in couple relationships with implications for evaluation and treatment. *Sexual Addiction and Compulsivity: The Journal of Treatment and Prevention.*

Violent Pornography on the Internet

A Study of Accessibility and Prevalence

Ragnhild T. Bjørnebekk & Tor A. Evjen

Norway has traditionally been a quiet society with few social problems. During the last years, however, we have witnessed – as have other Western societies – an increase in violence perpetrated by very young people. Research shows that more children during the 90's have developed anti-social conduct disorders, and more are engaged in severe violent acts than previously (Bjørnebekk 1999). This is, of course, a problem for the child himself and his family, but it is also a serious problem for society. Violence and coercive actions challenge democracy and create fear and pain. What accounts for these trends? Violence results from a variety of factors. Some of them are more basic, anchored in the child's dispositions, upbringing and his or her primary relationships. Others are generated from the mainstream values and actions present in the culture. The media are, in interaction with other factors, important contributors to our ways of thinking and acting (e.g., Smith & Donnerstein 1998).

Several studies have shown that the violence profile in Scandinavian visual media has become more pronounced during the last decade (e.g., Cronström & Höijer 1996). It is also reasonable to believe that the liberal and worldwide character of the Internet offers new contributory dimensions of violence influencing youngsters' thoughts and actions.

"Violent Pornography on the Internet" is one study within a broader research project called "Violence Against the Eye – Relations between Violent Content in Visual Media and Youngsters at Risk". The study is a collaborative effort of the technological research management SINTEF and the research unit at The National Police Academy of Norway. The intention of the study is, first, to throw light on harmful and illegal content on the Internet, thereby making people who are involved with children and youth more aware of what children might discover when surfing the electronic highways. Second, we want to initiate discussions and actions regarding methods to prevent harmful contents, and to strengthen youngsters' resistance to undesirable influences.

Communicative processes

The technological development during the last decades has transformed the Internet into a hot, wide and fast highway of communication. New opportunities for relationships, interactions and learning are offered. The highway offers worldwide accessibility in the near absence of customs officers controlling the borders. Interactions between people may go on without the usual aspects of communicative signs and anchorage. During traditional communication a variety of signs, signals, and behaviour give meaning to the ongoing processes of interpretation. The participants are continually interpreting and reinterpreting each others' apparition and style: clothes, hair and make-up, voice, gestures, and visual as well as non-visual reflections of feelings and moods. In these processes, the persons involved cannot hide. They must confront their communication partners immediately, while the messages are being exchanged. Ordinary social and internal norms governing the communicative content are, therefore, continually at work.

This means that during ongoing communication – at least to a certain degree – people are also immediately confronted if they go beyond the bounds of privacy and cross the cultural and personal thresholds of what is acceptable, passing into the unacceptable, private and shameful. They are responsible for the communicative content and are forced to face others and their reactions to this content.

Communicative processes on the Internet differ from ordinary ones. On the Internet, persons may be actively communicating with or without any time delay. At the same time, they may be hidden and totally anonymous to each other. When this happens, the mechanisms regulating ordinary communication are out of function. This is certainly one of the reasons why persons with criminal, unacceptable or anti-social intentions may invade some of these lines of communication and use them to their own benefit, spreading unwanted and illegal content or getting in touch with others in order to influence them and/or attract them to a particular network (e.g., Feather 1999).

While surfing on the Internet, we made contact with open and hidden servers where Nazis, racists, Satanists and drug-users market their beliefs about and motives for violent actions or enjoying illegal drugs. We found newsgroups where recipes and formulae demonstrated how to produce bombs and chemical narcotic drugs. The same experience is frequently reported by other surfers, why these phenomena seem to be established and widespread both in chat groups and newsgroups.

Reports on Internet-related topics

Norway is a nation with widespread accessibility to the Internet, both in the public and the private sphere. When passing the millennium, 55 per cent of Norwegian females and 63 per cent of males above the age of 13 had access to Internet. About one million out of a total population of 4.4 million, reported being on-line on an ordinary day. During the last year, there has been a significant increase in the number of persons on-line, and the acceleration in Internet use is formidable. From February 1999 to February 2000, 36 per cent more people gained access to Internet (calculated from data given by Norsk Gallup 2000/InterTrack). Today, about 5,000 Norwegians also pay a fee for access to certain web pages. Most of these web pages present ordinary pornography. How much time the customers spend visiting the pages is unknown. The web master offering two of the most popular pornographic magazines reports, however, that there were 23 million clicks on his web pages during January 2000 (*VG-nett* 03.03.2000).

The pattern of diffusion of Internet use seems to follow the general pattern typical of a new medium spreading in society: Well-educated young males with high wages, students and youngsters are the innovators. The females and the elderly are the followers.

In terms of research, there are few, if any, systematic studies on how Internet is used by criminal groups. One report, carried out by the police (Feather 1999), is from a research project concerning Internet and child victimisation. Most knowledge, however, is based on unauthorised reports by professionals (e.g., the police) and organisations monitoring the Internet. The reports show that criminals form relationships and acquire knowledge in order to explore the new technology's possibilities as a tool for ordinary and new forms of criminal conduct (Feather 1999).

The latest reports on Norwegian criminal cases connected to Internet – cybercrime – show that six times as many cases were investigated in 1999 than 1998. The increase in criminal cases seems to be accelerating, and cases under investigation are judged to be just the tip of the iceberg. Most of the reported crimes are frauds connected to finance and business, credit cards, pirate copying of software, and different types of hacking (Årsrapport Økokrim 1999). Several of these categories might involve youngsters as offenders. Based on experiences related to criminal cases, the police claim that persons distributing child pornography on the Internet are responsible for recruiting child offenders (The Norwegian Bureau of Investigation 2000).

Specific categories of crimes are directly connected to or might involve children and youngsters as victims or targets of harmful and anti-social influence. These crimes include, among others, "hate speech", hate propaganda and racism, material marketing of or incitement to illegal acts, and communication of recipes for drugs and weaponry (Årsrapport Økokrim 1999).

Internet, from its very beginning as a public medium, has been used to distribute child pornography and illegal obscene material. During recent years, it appears that Internet has, to a lower or higher degree, even been a tool for child trafficking. Feather stresses that paedophiles are using the Internet to convey sexual fantasies about children, to recruit young children, to reinforce and legitimise sexual preferences. This occurs through associations and access support groups that facilitate networking. She emphasises that it is difficult to identify the exact relationship between child pornography and paedophile activity. Research indicates, however, that child pornography on the Internet is used by paedophiles as a means of desensitising children and normalising sexual activity between adults and children (Feather 1999).

Reports from several national Save the Children organisations tracking child pornography on the Internet indicate that Internet has become a distribution channel for commercial child pornography. Swedish Save the Children reports having obtained about 10 pieces of inside information on such activities daily during 1999. 20 percent of this information was about serious child pornography where adults perpetrated sexual acts on children (Åstrøm, Rädda Barnen 2000). Norwegian Save the Children has tracked child pornography on the Internet for several years. It claims that, last year, it was able for the first time to reveal Norwegian paedophiles engaged in "chicken hawking". "Chicken hawking" is a method used by certain persons to sneak up on unsuspecting children surfing the Net and to present themselves as someone else. The intention of "chicken hawking" is to make appointments with the child. Last year the organisation received more than 6,000 pieces of inside information about child pornography on the Internet, a small increase from the year before. Much information about child pornography is found in news- and discussion groups (Internet Relay Chat) (Årsrapport Redd Barna 1998,1999).

There are several factors that facilitate crime on the Internet. One of the key factors is the liberal and anarchistic tradition that has been established there and the transnational unwillingness to cope with the problems properly. Users' tolerance levels are extremely high. And the notion of Free Speech far overreaches that of being responsible for the messages one sends (Feather 1999). Other factors are, naturally, the global, transnational and anonymous character of the Net itself, all of which make it difficult to monitor and investigate.

Aims of our study and definition of violent pornography

The more precise aims of our study "Violent Pornography on the Internet" were to investigate the accessibility of violent pornography and to conduct systematic content analysis of its occurrences. Furthermore, we wanted to discuss how to prevent the injury such portrayals may inflict on children and youngsters. Here we will focus on the content analyses done during Autumn 1997 and early Summer 1998.

Violent pornography is a depiction of a violent act that occurs in an explicit sexual context. This makes it necessary to define a violent depiction. For this purpose we will use the definition given by the *National Television Violence Study* performed in the US:

Depicted violence is defined as…

> …overt depiction of a credible threat of physical force, or the actual use of such force intended to physically harm an animate being or group of beings. Violence also includes certain depictions of physically harmful consequences against

> an animate being or group that occur as a result of unseen violent means. Thus, there are three prime types of violent depictions: credible threats, behavioral acts, and harmful consequences. (Smith & Donnerstein 1998, p. 170).

Some additional elements need to be included to allow identification of a violent depiction in relation to a violent pornographic depiction. For this purpose we will add some distinctive characteristics to the definition:

Violent pornography is defined as...

...explicit sexual portrayals of acts that

- are valued and experienced as violent because of their grotesque, bizarre, disgusting or perverse appearance.
- in the process of production, involve – or look like they involve – physical or psychological injuries to individuals or creatures.
- are evaluated as involving a credible threat of physical force.
- involve actual use of credible force intended to physically harm an animate being or group of beings.
- lead to physically harmful consequences for an animate being or group that occur as a result of unseen violent means.

Thus, we focus on four prime types of violent depictions in our definition, instead of the three in the definition of violent depictions: credible threats, behavioural acts, harmful consequences, and the character of the depiction itself – all of which are placed into an explicit sexual context.

The *National Television Violence Study* includes intentional physical or mental injuries to individuals or creatures, portrayed as an ongoing process or as a consequence. We also include explicit sexual portrayals of acts that the onlooker experiences as violent because of their grotesque, bizarre, disgusting or perverse appearance.

The latter part is problematic, because it is normative. We find it, however, necessary to include this category, since it represents a distinctive part of what is presented on the Internet. The content of pictures presented in this category is deviant in the sense that it is experienced as a form of violence, e.g., the act implies actions that may result in the persons involved becoming ill or injured in more implicit ways.

One of the challenges of this study was to know where on the Internet to start the search, and how to localise the material. While ordinary pornography is very easy to find, gaining access to commercial web servers containing violent and illegal pornographic portrayals is not as easy. To accomplish this, we focused on commercial search engines and international newsgroups. The pornographic portrayals we then hit, represent a wide spectrum of genres and contain serious violence and perversities, many of them certainly illegal for distribution in Norway (§ 140: Incitement to criminal acts, § 211, the paragraph on fornication, and § 382: Portraying serious violent acts) as well as in many other countries. Some of the portrayals might not be evaluated as illegal, but they are probably of the kind that almost all societies would regard as unacceptable as a part of children's and youngsters' everyday lives.

The Internet – understandings of the channel

Deciding or settling questions about the accessibility of violent pornography on the Internet and understanding the logic connected to situational prevention methods both involve having knowledge of Internet technology. We have, therefore, briefly described some structures of its technology, and some of the main functions particular to accessibility – see a preceding article "What Is the Internet?" in this book. The description gives insights that can facilitate understanding of how we selected a sample for our content analysis.

Descriptions and understandings of the Internet vary among persons dealing with the medium. Some users, especially those with primary training in the humanities, understand the Internet metaphorically, as a world, a "space" for acting and interacting. When a person sits down to operate his mouse and keyboard, microphone or camera, he becomes a "Cybercitizen" – a citizen of the worldwide "space" that is offered on the Internet. In cyberspace, some create their own "homes" – their "sites" or "groups" or "pages" – where they welcome guests and offer them information, perhaps some services, and talks. The user who understands Internet in this way, "leaves" his physical local place when he sits down at the computer. He extends into the "Cyberspace", he is "driving on-line" on the highways, bridges and cities that constitute the "Cyberworld". In this space, the rules, norms and modes of interaction that dominate regular everyday communication are set aside. And the user accepts this. The user might surf from "place to place" looking at the views, selecting and fetching offered information as a tourist. If she wants to, she can meet with other "Cybercitizens". She may or may not interact with them. She might take part in or build superficial, flexible and hasty groups, or might prefer more rigid networks where she and the other "Cyber group members" present themselves openly or anonymously.

We do not believe such metaphors are fruitful. They create myths and images that might dramatise and exaggerate, or even minimalise, the influences of the Internet. They might generate irresponsibility and borderline-understandings. Most important, however, the metaphors are not sufficiently similar to the technology to make them fruitful as metaphors.

Our understanding of the Internet starts from the perspective of the technological sciences and that of educational psychology within media and communication science. Internet is understood as an effective and practical medium for transferring information from one place to another. These transfers offer opportunities for communication, for reading and interpretation. Internet is, in our opinion, to be understood as an extension and integration of the technology that the telephone, camera and computer media are based on. In this sense, the Internet is a multimedium, an amalgamation that consists of and integrates several media.

A medium is primarily a channel for the transmission of information. Information exchanged through "natural" media is propagated via waves. Media spread out or reproduce these waves. They must, however, be stimulated to action if communication of information is to occur. The electronic media have the same characteristics as "natural" media, and carry waves in the same manner. On the Internet, the stimulators are the operators of the mouse and the keyboard and the other technical equipment connected to the technology.

This means that the person acting and interacting on the Internet – the user – is a stimulator when she operates the mouse, keyboard and other Internet equipment. A user searches and sends electronic information, interacting with the electronic messages on the screen. The perception and interpretation processes activated when the person surfs the Internet are not different from those involved when the same person watches television or reads a book (e.g., Dallans Evans' discussions on brain functions during television viewing and other media activity, 1987). The learning processes, however, are different because of the flexibility and interactivity of the Internet technology. As a consequence, the mental results – the knowledge and images – may vary. From the searched electronic information occurring on the screen, the user creates mental representations based on how she experiences and interprets the information. Depending on how the perception process has proceeded, the representations become integrated into existing concepts, scripts, schemas and structures of what already constitutes the user's consciousness. The user's "real" experiences with the phenomenon, and her attitudes, values and norms, are crucial for how the electronic information contributes to her consciousness. This has importance for how the information may modify or develop earlier ways of thinking, or create new concepts and structures for thinking and acting (e.g., Schanck & Abelson 1977, Donaldson 1984, Bjørnebekk 1993).

With regard to violent pornographic content, the phenomenon portrayed is commonly one with which especially young users, but most often also older ones, have had very little or no experience, both in terms of "real" everyday life and the symbolic world. Therefore, young people have few established mental structures allowing them to competently handle such information. From portrayals of violent pornography, the users may create new mental structures to use in perception of the world. On the other hand, if the persons have had some experiences with actions of this sort, such content may legitimise and justify the phenomenon, causing the persons to perceive it as common and widespread.

Method and sampling

Our study deals primarily with searching the Internet in order to explore the accessibility and prevalence of violent pornography. Mapping the Internet without systematic knowledge of how it functions is an impossible task. It is not as easy to track violent pornography as it is to find ordinary pornography. This is why we have described the Internet technology, its functions and concepts, in the article "What Is the Internet?" in this book. The challenge is, among other things, knowing how and where to search for the target material. If one, for example, wants to use search engines such as Alta Vista and Excite to locate visual material, certain knowledge is necessary. One must, for instance, choose Usenet to search on Usenet groups, download by clicking on the link "b", and also know how to convert files into readable formats.

In order to study changes over time, we decided to perform our searches at two different occasions. The first was autumn 1997, from August to December, and the second early summer 1998, the last week of May.

Selection of function to study

For several reasons, news was selected as the function through which to sample the violent pornography. E-mail is impossible to study, because of its private and closed character. News, on the other hand, represents an open service, even when access is not given before paying a fee.

IRC has proved to be one of the channels of special interest to paedophiles when spreading their messages and constructing networks (e.g., Feather 1999, Årsrapport Redd Barna 1998, 1999). On the BBS, activity has also been registered that includes communication of violent pornography (e.g., Feather 1999). The IRC function, however, is hasty and transitional in character, making it more difficult to study. Moreover, anonymous use of IRC groups for research purposes is ethically questionable. Meeting ethical standards is easier if newsgroups are selected.

Newsgroup messages are usually stored for some time and offer, therefore, better opportunities for research. Most important, however, is that IRC is a text-based function, whereas newsgroups involve all kinds of formats. They are principally multimedia. Our primary intention has been to study visual portrayals, making newsgroups more convenient for our purpose.

Selection of search engines

Most foreign newsgroups do not subscribe to newsgroups aimed at Norwegians, thus using the Norwegian language. To access newsgroups with violent pornographic topics, it was necessary to use foreign web and news servers as well as high capacity search engines.

Alta Vista and Excite allow the user to locate web server material and news that are spread around the world. The capacity of these search engines made them particularly convenient for our study. Alta Vista offers an extensive index of web pages and a great selection of newsgroups. At the time we started our search, Alta Vista had indexed more than 30 million pages and more than 12,000 searches were carried out each day. It had a capacity to index more than 3 million pages daily. Moreover, it makes all newsgroups accessible to everyone, even to persons who would have been excluded from sections of them by their national servers. Excite is also a large search engine, indexing web pages and newsgroups that have been active during the last two weeks. At the time of our search, it had more than 50 million URL addresses in its database.

These search engines were our starting points. In addition, we included other commercial and "free" news servers in the search process when we found it necessary.

When we started our research, we found about 21,000 newsgroups on all kinds of topics. This number, however, continuously increases, and today it is certainly much higher.

Selection of actual newsgroups

To identify newsgroups with violent pornographic content that fit our definition (see the earlier section "Aims of our study and definition of violent pornography"), it was necessary to carry out several test searches. The results of these tests led to our decision to focus on three main newsgroups: "alt.binaries.picture.* ", "alt.binaries.picture.erotica.* " and "alt.sex.* ".

Upon entering the newsgroups, new references and links to other related sources were immediately offered. Addresses, telephone numbers and e-mail references were announced, as well as sales of magazines, videos, etc. We chose to follow a couple of these paths to see what was offered.

Searching on the free news servers was also done, but more sporadically. From this we learned that material in one group is relatively often duplicated on other more or less related newsgroups.

Besides the search engines, there are numerous web pages with explicit sex-related references to other servers. And most of the servers containing sex-oriented material also had references to other sex-servers.

Results

Access

Registration of web pages with violent pornographic material

Our main sources and starting points for surfing and downloading of web pages with violent pornographic content were the three central newsgroups mentioned above: "alt.binaries.picture.* ", "alt.binaries.picture.erotica.* " and "alt.sex.* ". From these groups, new web pages with related articles were identified.

An overview of the analysed groups is given in Table 1.

Table 1. Newsgroups analysed

Newsgroup	Activity
Alt.sex.bestiality Alt.binaries.pictures.erotica.bestiality	Themes connected to human sex with animals
Alt.sex.bondage Alt.binaries.pictures.erotica.bondage	Themes connected to sex with sado-masochistic acts and bondage
Alt.sex.watersports Alt.sex.fetish.watersports	Themes connected to sex with urination and defecation
Alt.sex.necrophilia	Themes connected to sex with dead bodies
Alt.sex.incest	Themes connected to illegal sexual relations between family members
Alt.sex.fetish.amputee	Themes connected to sex with injuring or injured body parts or mutilation
Alt.sex.pedophilia Alt.binaries.pictures.erotica.teen Alt.binaries.pictures.erotica.children Alt.sex.pre-teens	Themes connected to sexual relations between youngsters or to sexualising children
Alt.binaries.pictures.erotica.cartoons	Violent sexual themes connected to a variety of different content communicated in cartoon or drawing format
Alt.binaries.multimedia.erotica	Themes connected to a variety of content communicated by a variety of formats
Alt.binaries.sounds.erotica	A variety of sounds connected to sexual acts

Buying and selling services related to violent pornography

For most services on the Net, there is some limitation on admittance. Search engines seldom have any control over admittance; instead most web pages administer their own admittance control. Usually this means that one has to pay for an access code. By selling admittance codes, the editor, web master or owner can check to some degree a person's age and address. Admittance "rules" usually state that a person must be at least 18 or 21 years old in order to obtain an access code. The "age" of admittance seems to be related to the country from which the editor operates.

Payment is organised variously. The most common method is via credit card. The buyer must give his name, address and e-mail along with his credit card number and expiration date. The information is supplied in a questionnaire. Within a short time, the buyer receives his confirmation. If there is enough money on the credit card to buy the service, the buyer is given a user name and a personal password.

Control of the services is simple. A four-character word is usually enough to gain access to the "club". The services offered vary from ordinary pin-ups to bondage, sale of magazines, private videos and movies, procurement service, "live entertainment" directed by video conferences, and so on.

Pornopass, AdultPass, Adult Verification System (AVS) are examples of admittance systems for amateurs as well as professionals, offering services related to violent pornography. By using these systems, the seller is able to make more explicit announcements of illegal or shocking and indecent actions and material. The price of an admittance pass is usually about $10 for a period of three months. It allows access both to the web pages and to lists of members of hundreds of web servers that offer the same category of content.

Another payment system offered involves phoning a tele-market (usually a 900-number in the US). The call gives the customer an admittance code, a PIN-code allowing immediate access to the web pages. The fee is then charged to the telephone number used when calling.

When ordering a video conference, the fee is charged to the ordinary message unit used. Video conferences are services announced both on the Net and in Internet magazines. To access the service, the customer needs special software. This software is, however, offered free of charge from the Internet server hosting the service. It is just a matter of downloading it to a personal computer. The software is used as an integrated part of the web browser.

First Virtual Account is a payment agency with an Internet address. It seems to be one of the more serious agencies on the Net. Information about the credit card is not on the Net, and a combination of telephone and Internet is used when the service is provided. The user is given a fictive First Virtual Account name to use when buying a service. When using this agency, one must pay a quarterly fee for administration of the service ordered. The web master uses the First Virtual Account for payment transactions by referring the agency to his home page. The customer orders the service from First Virtual Account and not from the web master. When the agency has organised the transaction, the fee is registered on the web master's bank account, and the customer gains access to the service through the fictive First Virtual Account name.

We also registered "no payment" and free services that offered censored material on the so-called "public nntp sites". These news servers offer newsgroups belonging to a variety of categories. Most of them do not publish shocking or obscene content, but there were exceptions.

As mentioned earlier, the challenge when seeking violent pornographic content is to discover adequate addresses. In the beginning this was complicated, but some training and information made things easier. On the Net, services are offered that use "robots" to find "public" news servers that make lists of server addresses. We also identified persons or personal web pages offering similar services free of charge. Furthermore, it was possible to pay $10 to Alternative Internet Services to obtain specific guidance in how to "gain access to newsgroups you can't presently get – right now!".

An example of how to gain admittance to violent pornography

Admittance control varies depending on the intentions of the person or group offering the information. Several seem to have commercial intentions, and make no effort to protect children from accessing the material. Several may have more private motives, and as such protect themselves from groups or police monitoring the Net. On some web pages there is a three-step control of admittance. Each step guided the customer through some internal safety protection before permission was given to take part in the next circle. The first step is usually free. The visitor encounters a page that presents picture or video trailers marketing different sex topics. The visitor is informed that the topics will be available after paying a fee. The second step is to pay the fee, and then access is given to the second circle. Here a sample of sex topics is offered. Then new information is given. If the visitor wants access to, for example, child pornography, he has to take a third step. This step can be for the visitor to e-mail child pornographic pictures to the web master and to present himself using his real name and e-mail address. At this point, admittance will be given to the third circle.

As researchers we are, of course, not in a position to follow the instructions leading into the third circle. We have, therefore, no sure knowledge of what is being presented there. It would be mere speculation on our part to say that this circle represents a forum for building a network or that the security is just a strategy to hide and protect exchange of illegal material. However, an interview with a child porn collector, who is active on the Net, shows that there is extensive exchange of all kinds of severe child porn and active networking in an "inner circle" where he participates. His group seems to combine closed chat groups on IRC and newsgroups in their exchanges and communications (Bjørnevik & Johannessen 1997).

Our investigations on the Net revealed aggressive marketing of violent pornography. During the period we worked on the study, e-mails offering different services related to violent pornography were sent to our addresses. The only way these persons could have obtained the addresses is through lists of customers of and visitors to web pages containing violent pornography.

Prevalence

During the first period of the study, between 10 and 200 new articles were offered daily in each newsgroup. A total of 6,000 articles were registered as indexed in the groups. Our sample comprised two searches a week during a period of five months, i.e., about 40 searches.

This means that we registered an average of about 150 new bulletins each day of search. This number is, however, not well-founded methodologically, because the variations are not systematic. One person could suddenly send a large number of pictures or videos to several newsgroups and pages at the same time, and afterwards become passive. Thus, during one day, 300-500 new articles could suddenly be presented in the newsgroups, whereas the next day of search perhaps only 10 new bulletins would be registered.

The daily number of articles in the newsgroups or on the pages also varied depending on headline and topic. One rule of thumb is that the most grotesque, bizarre or repulsive topics received the fewest articles. There were, however, as we shall see, topics of severe violent character among the most popular topics, if popularity is evaluated in terms of the number of bulletins presented in the group or on the page.

Some material would not have been categorised as violent pornography if the content had been evaluated in isolation and out of context. Then it would have been just "violence". When placed in a sexual setting, the interpretation changes and the "violent" picture becomes a violent pornographic picture.

Our sample is classified and structured partly in the same way as the material is categorised on the Internet (genre of violence), and partly by its format (as picture, text, video, drawing, or sound). The format is used as the main category, and the genre of violent content as a subgroup.

Several of the downloaded files were videos. We decided, however not to include this medium. This is not because we think the format is unimportant. On the contrary, we find it is very important. Analysis of the kind of hypertext used in videos is, however, too complex to accomplish in this study. It requires a study of its own.

Most of the contents downloaded give a deep negative impression. The depictions are such that we decided not to use them as illustrations here. Most of them are indecent and probably illegal to publish in many countries. Instead of using visual illustrations, we will give a short written description of the mainstream content.

Pictures

The photograph is the most common format for communicating violent pornography. The reason is probably that such pictures are easy to scan from magazines and other media. It is also easy to transform them on the computer. They contain much information compared to the digital volume needed. Moreover, photos are relatively quickly downloaded and they are cheap to produce. The pictures registered during the first period of study derive from several sources, from amateur photos to professional ones, from freeze-frame video pictures to pictures generated from other media and digital constructions.

The content of the pictures can be divided into 11 groups:

1. Fisting and abuse of the genitalia

The pictures in this category focus on the genitalia, often presented as ultra close-ups. Extreme widening of genitalia using bottles, vegetables, tongs, etc. is presented. Big needles, clips, clamps and hooks are inserted into or fastened to the genitalia or nipples. Some of the pictures show heavy counterweights hanging from the penis, while others show injurious piercing of the genitalia or nipples.

This is a one of the largest subgroups studied.

2. Tied-up – torture

This category is the largest in the newsgroups studied. Most of the pictures show one or more victims, most often a female, tied to or held up by some kind of apparatus. Several are connected to the instruments and guillotines with handcuffs and footcuffs. Some are held up by metal sticks in their nose, arms or feet. Females are usually gagged, threatened and tortured in different ways.

The expression on their faces and eyes appears to be fright. Some are stabbed with knives, others with needles, hooks, sticks or different instruments constructed for torture.

The torture might be aimed at different parts of the body: the tongue, face, nipples or the genitalia. The acts are usually presented in a sexually explicit context, while the torture is going on. The females are usually almost nude. Belts and straps are twisted under and above their breasts and around the hips. Mostly, the torturer is a half-naked, disguised male, with a black hood covering his head and face. The appearance of some men gives associations to the Ku Klux Klan.

A specific subgroup involves strangling of a victim. Often several pictures are presented as a sequence showing the strangling process. Many portrayals in this group are presented as "real", as documentaries.

It seems almost as though there are no limits to the acts of tyranny that can be presented in pictures belonging to this category.

In connection to the web pages presenting this category, there are sometimes announcements for different instruments meant for sado-masochistic torture.

For the most part, pictures in this category are presented in newsgroups labelled ".bondage" – a kind of newsgroup with several subgroups presenting more specific forms of torture that we have categorised using other labels.

This is also one of the largest subgroups studied.

3. Plastic and strangling

This group consists of pictures where different plastic materials, bags and foils are used in a variety of ways for sexual satisfaction. Several pictures show a naked person, usually a male, standing in a room, wrapped in a big transparent plastic bag that covers the entire body. A vacuum cleaner, with the tube placed under the bag, creates a vacuum depleting the air supply. Whether the person has been strangled is, in several cases, impossible to determine. Other pictures show naked persons wrapped up with ropes around the neck and body and transparent foils around the head and face, while they gasp for air. The expression on their faces seems in several pictures to be one of despair.

One specific subgroup presents pictures focussed on strangling, without the use of the "plastic" or "vacuum" strategies. In one of the pictures, we see a male tied up in a rope that at one end is fastened around his neck. The other end is tied to a car. A centrifugal movement puts him into a position where he will either be almost strangled or, if he looses his control, strangled.

Several of the pictures presented are old black and whites, probably photos shot in relation to real cases in which the person involved died. The images seem to have received a kind of cult status. The number of pictures in this category presented in the newsgroups we studied is small compared to the previously mentioned categories.

4. Rape

Another large category of pictures presents a variety of rapes, most often portrayed as snuffers, i.e., as rapes that "really" have happened. Several seem to be amateur or "home-made" pictures. Some are "stolen" from identifiable movies, scanned and presented in a sequence of about 5-8 pictures. Most of the victims portrayed are female. Some of the pictures are close-ups, focusing on the encroachment, on painful facial expression or on different kinds of torture details, such as a knife cutting part of the body, the nipples or a breast.

The pictures occur in newsgroups with different labels. Many of them are, however, presented in subgroups systematised under the "bondage" variety of newsgroup.

5. Child pornography

The content of the child pornography pictures covers all kinds of sexual acts perpetrated on small and older children and on young people. The age of the smallest children we observed was about 5-6 years. Some pictures present nude children, some involve indecent exposure of the child, usually a male. Other pictures, however, represent a variety of intercourse acts, rapes and physical injuries towards both boys and girls. Most of the offenders are males. Some of them are presented as the child's grandparents or other family members.

The categorisation of pictures presenting child pornography is mostly based on highly specific factors, such as age spans of just a few years (4-5 years, and so on) and the children's gender.

6. Necrophilia and bestiality

Many pictures in this category depict suicide, murder or consequences of different accidents where the persons involved are dying or dead. Severely damaged, crushed or torn off body parts and wounds are shot in ultra close-ups. The focus is on the injuries. Many of the pictures seem to belong to archives from hospitals, pathologists, police, etc. Some of them are close-ups showing touching of corpses' genitalia or of blue and hideous marks on the neck after strangling. Labels and texts place the portrayals into a sexual context.

One subgroup contains bodies with dark blue death marks, showing processes of decay and torture of a corpse's body parts.

The pictures are presented both on specific web pages and on news servers.

This is a rather small group. During the period of the first study, however, the group was regularly supplied with new pictures.

7. Murder and dismemberment of bodies

Sequences of murder by dismemberment using a variety of tools are depicted through series of 4-8 pictures. The act is usually presented in detail.

This category also consists of very few pictures. During the period of the study, we registered only some new pictures on the page in question. They were similar to the ones first registered, presenting the same kind of sequences.

Access to these pictures was possible for a small fee. The page address was found in a newsgroup.

8. War-related accidents

Some pictures from wars are presented on pages with sex-related labels. One of them portrays two males executing a kneeling boy. The boy's body is still upright, though his head is cut off. In the background a crowd is watching the execution. Another young boy, also kneeling, with his arms behind his back, is gazing at what is happening. He is probably the next boy to be beheaded.

Another photo shows a group of young soldier-boys kneeling behind a bleeding, decapitated head. The head belongs to what seems to have been a young boy or girl. The text "Khmer Rouge" signals that this is a war photo.

Some of the pictures registered are identified as award winning photos from famous exhibitions. They are probably "stolen" and scanned from magazines or posters before being sent to a news server containing violent pornographic content.

This category is also rather small.

9. Animal pornography

Portrayals of sexual acts between animals and humans constitute quite a large category on the web servers and in the newsgroups investigated. A wide variety of animals are portrayed, and the human participants are both males and females, individuals as well as two or more people. The depictions cover intercourse, as well as a variety of close-ups of genitalia, and a general overview of the whole context.

The pictures are usually presented in groups labelled ".animal" and in subgroups that communicate what kind of animal is focused on, or the location where the acts take place. Often the labelling gives associations to "cowboy-culture", or to specific nations or places.

10. Defecation and urination

This category is usually presented in subgroups labelled "wet and messy". The pictures involve portrayals of defecation and urination, and eating and drinking of the excrements. There are depictions of people who smear the excrements over their bodies. Often there are close-ups focusing on the anus while a nude child or an adult male or female is defecating into another person's mouth or while he or she is "helped" by fisting. The process may be presented through picture sequences.

Pictures of different kinds of urination acts are also presented on ordinary commercial web servers offering pornography. Bulletins about defecation are, however, usually not communicated here.

11. Mutilated and dead infants and embryos

It is questionable whether this category should be included in violent pornography. The reason why we chose to include it is that, on the web servers and in the newsgroups we studied, this category is presented as a subgroup beside and along with violent pornography.

Several of the pictures seem to be illustrations from books about pregnancy and birth defects and injuries occurring during embryonic development. Some of them seem, however, to be photos from aborted embryos.

This theme is presented regularly in several newsgroups. Some of the pictures are identical to those presented in magazines published by satanic groups in Norway. It is impossible to say what the relations may be between these magazines and the web groups.

Drawings

The registered drawings are usually cartoon strips. This is the format most often found in newsgroups that present violent pornography bulletins. The different topics in the drawings and strips are nearly identical to what was found in the picture bulletins. We observed acts similar to those reported from the war category and from the "Tied-up and torture" group. Some details of the content are, however, even more grotesque and bizarre than in the photos. This is probably because a drawing allows the depiction of acts that are almost impossible to perform in real life. Usually the drawings are followed by a text presented in cartoon-bubbles (most often in English) or in a graphical symbolic language.

Several strips portray a person, usually a female, who is being impaled on a spit. The spit runs from her vagina to her mouth. Afterwards she is roasted on the spit and eaten by the audience watching what happened. Other strips focus on sexualised torturing of a woman before she is guillotined. She is cut off at her neck or waist. The end of the story might be a depiction of a man lifting the cut-off head by the hair, while another tied-up woman is waiting for the guillotine. Other cartoon stories concentrate on rape performed with different kinds of instruments and machines, while a group of men run the machines and watch what happens.

Several of the strips presented are identified as originating in French and Belgian cartoons. In Norway these cartoons are for sale in underground contexts.

Videos

In terms of computer technique, the video format is much more demanding to transmit and download than are pictures and cartoons. A movie consists of long sequences of pictures, thus requiring considerable storage and transmission capacity. Two different kinds of movie transformations are commonly used on the Internet. One is downloading of the sequence as a file, before it is possible to play the sequence. The other method is streaming, whereby the movie is transmitted directly onto the screen without prior storage. When the study was running, sound did not accompany the movies, probably because it dramatically decreases transmission speed.

The volume of movies presented in the newsgroups varied from one to ten megabytes for each sequence. Usually, every act consisted of several sequences.

The video sequences consist of similar, often identical, content to what was registered in the picture categories. Most of what was found belonged to the categories "Tied-up – torture", "Rape" and "Animal pornography". They were stored in newsgroups labelled ".multimedia", ".bondage" ".animal" and ".bestiality".

A large proportion of videos presented seems to be amateur shots. The sequences are very explicit in their sexual and violent expression. The reason is probably that, due to technical limitations, it is convenient to dense pack the story climaxes.

Sound

Two different kinds of sound were found in the sampled newsgroups: sound as an expression in a movie, and sound as an independent expression of information on a data file. There are no technical limitations when downloading sound from the Net. In order to record speech, however, it is necessary to possess a computer with the required technical equipment.

We registered no kind of sound that could be related to or associated with any category of violent pornography. Sounds of explicit sexual character were, however, registered in some of the newsgroups labelled "multimedia".

Thus, according to this study, sound seems to be of very little concern.

What has changed between the first and second period of study?

The technological development of Internet is rapid, especially in terms of the increased capacity and speed of the Net. At the same time, there has also been increased development of strategies to prevent illegal and harmful content. During the period between our downloadings, there was an explosion in the number of people with Internet access and in the number on-line. Are these changes reflected in what is communicated in the newsgroups presenting violent pornography?

As mentioned, we revisited the web servers, the newsgroups and web pages and did a second analysis during early summer 1998.

Accessibility

We found that the search engines had increased their capacity such that newsgroups had become more accessible for users with less computer knowledge and experience. Now, it was no longer necessary to decryptify or decode bulletins in order to interpret them. They were transformed directly on the screen when downloaded.

This means that, at the second study occasion, we had direct access to the messages in the free newsgroups, as well as in the closed ones, once the fee was paid. In several of the groups, however, there were files that had been "zipped". "Zipped" files have been compressed and need a program to decompress them. This indicates that there are still some limitations in accessibility for the less proficient user.

The admittance fee to several of the web pages had not changed. The visitors still had to pay about $10 to gain access.

The number

The number of bulletins had increased dramatically. From being about 150 a day, we registered about 600 bulletins in just one group on an average day. In the subgroup ".tasteless", the number registered during one night was more than 100, and in ".torture" slightly less than a hundred. On an ordinary Sunday (27.5.98), the number of bulletins that dropped down to the subgroup ".bondage" amounted to about 870.

The number of videos and movies had also increased substantially since the first downloading.

We are not certain that the increase is as large as it seems from the number registered. The number corresponding to the second period conceals many depictions that do not satisfy our definition of violent pornography. Even if the label and announcement promised hard core pornography for a fee, the bulletins could still present posing and ordinary pornography.

The content

We also registered a change in the labels used to characterise the subgroups. No longer were there groups labelled "child pornography" or "paedophilia". The analyses showed, however, that child pornography or paedophilia was not removed from the actual newsgroups and pages. They were categorised into other, more neutral labels, such as ".schoolgirl", "Japan.natural.art", ".latino", ".indian.girl" and ".teen". When visiting the group a warning was often presented: "This page may be *illegal* in your *country*. If this is so in your country, then please do not visit '8' " (from "geisha", 25.5.1998).

Whereas at the first study occasion the child pornography was highly specified, tied to categories of boys and girls and age, it was more differentiated and varied at the second. In the newsgroups studied, the most severe portrayals were removed. Pictures focusing on different kinds of posing had instead increased, as well as the total number of portrayals of children. The category ".teen", which consists of one main group and several subgroups, presented, for example, about 230 messages on an ordinary Wednesday during this second period of study.

Some of the groups with the most bizarre, grotesque and disgusting content, like "bestiality", had disappeared on the second occasion. A brief run through of a variety of pages showed, however, that the content had not been removed. The bulletins were presented under other labels that did not give associations to that kind of content.

In light of the critique against the distribution of violent pornography, this strategy of appearing to clean up the bulletins is probably an attempt to avoid unnecessarily provoking American server owners. Changing the labels of the news pages is also a strategy used to escape the Cyberangels, Save the Children, and other organisations that intentionally monitor the lines in order to stop illegal and harmful contents on the Internet.

Compared to the first period of study, one marked change was the increase in commercial groups announcing different products or services. The category of torture had, for example, got a new subgroup presenting a variety of products for sado-masochistic torture: masks made of leather, belts, hand-, feet- and neckpillories, police sticks, links and cuffs for different parts of the body, and metal rods for torturing the tongue. The assortment of products was surprisingly rich and as grotesque as the pages that depicted "acts" and stories related to violent sex. In our first study, the announcements were more sporadic, and the assortment much poorer.

Other groups announced exchanging of partners that were willing to participate in violent sexual acts. This was portrayed as a general commercial service. No such announcement was registered at the first study occasion. Then only "swapping" and procurement activity was registered. "Swapping" concerns girls who themselves announce their services.

"Necrophilia", which was an accessible group during the first period, was not in the same groups during the second period. The link "I prefer necrophilia" led us, however, to the necrophilia group and subgroups in the same genre. One message related, however, that there was no admittance to the actual group. We tried to link to another web group that announced necrophilia "totally free". But the web group did not seem to present any pictures belonging to the category. This probably means that the category is censored out of the news server.

Another group that had disappeared since the first study was "bestiality". The label "tasteless" seems, however, to have absorbed the "bestiality" genre as well as part of the necrophilia group. The new group presented pictures of a wide range of extreme and bizarre depictions of several of the more severe and grotesque genres. More than 350 bulletins were presented in the group during one week.

In the other categories, the results show smaller changes related to content.

A category that, at the first study occasion, contained so few pictures that it was not conceived of as a separate group, is digitally constructed or manipulated pictures. Quite new searches show, however, that today this represents a new distinctive expression. One reason why the group seems to be growing is that programs for creating pictures are offered. These three-dimensional modelling programs make it possible to create pictures and animation without real models, just virtual ones. Persons dealing with violent pornography use the programs for constructing anti-social depictions presented on the web pages studied.

Concluding discussion

When we started our study, some knowledge of Internet and searching methods was required in order to reach the web servers and web pages that communicate violent pornography. It was necessary to know how to decode the messages in order to transform them into pictures and texts. Today, the same knowledge is not required. Finding the web groups and pages with violent pornography is no longer as complicated. Access to violent pornography has become easier, and such content is voluminous on the Net.

One characteristic feature of the violent pornography portrayals across categories is that most of them are presented as "real" happenings or as documentaries. The depictions are characterised by their cruelty, extreme anti-sociality and sadism. Most of the pictures and movies portray events that are far-removed from what most people are able to think about. Presented are phenomena that exist neither in the mainstream culture nor in people's imaginations or consciousness. Access to violent pornography will therefore promote thoughts about new and anti-social phenomena.

Although some of the most extreme portrayals are no longer presented on the web servers investigated, other formats have been added. The number of representations of violent pornography in newsgroups and on web pages has, however, increased during the period of our analyses.

Today, inexpensive "human" modelling and animation programs (e.g., Poser from Metacreation) are available to Internet users. The programs allow the user to create "virtual" persons who can be visually manipulated and placed into different surroundings. The virtual portrayals may be presented as pictures or in an animated form as movies. The apparitions are realistic. This means that the creator of the pictures or animations is not dependent on real persons or physical models in his production of images that may almost look like documentaries. Part of the violent pornography we analysed, especially depictions belonging to the sado-masochistic genre presented in the newsgroups, consists today of virtual portrayals created by such programs.

We know relatively much about how violent pornography influences ordinary adult men. There are negative influences on men's attitudes towards woman. After reception of violent pornography, men become more positive to rape and evaluate women more callously. There are also results showing a relationship between consumption of violent pornography and aggressive behaviour in young males (Donnerstein, Linz & Penrod 1987). The studies focusing on influences of violent pornography are valid for adults. Few, if any, studies have focused on children. Today, extremely severe violent pornography is available to many children on the computer screen in their own home. We can only guess about the influences of this on children who already are aggressive and on children who are afraid of becoming subjected to crime.

Note

The Norwegian Government's Campaign on Combating Violence in the Visual Media contributed to the funding of this study.

References

Bjørnebekk R (1993): Reklame – Bevissthet – Kulturproduksjon [Advertising, Awareness, Cultural Production]. Paper to the XI. Nordic Conference on Mass Communication Research, Trondheim, 1993

Bjørnebekk R (1999): Gjenger, ran og vold – nittitallets kriminalitetstreenighet? [Gangs, Robbery, and Violence – the Criminal Trinity of the 90's?]. Sosiologi II, Pensumhefte PHS, Oslo

Bjørnevik H & Johannessen C (1997): Barnepornografi på internett [Child Pornography on the Internet]. Journalist- og mediestudiet, Merkantilt institutt

Cronström J & Höijer B (1996): *40 timmar våld i veckan* [40 Hours of TV Violence a Week]. Stockholm, Våldsskildringsrådet, nr 14

Dallans Evans T (1987): "De farliga bølgene [The Dangerous Waves]", in Andresen H (red): *Barn foran skjermen*. Oslo, Cap.

Donaldson M (1984): *Barns tankeverden* [Children's World of Thought]. Oslo, Cap.

Donnerstein E, Linz D & Penrod S (1987): *The Question of Pornography*. New York, The Free Press

Feather, M (1999): Internet and Child Victimization. Paper presented at the conference The Children and Crime: Victims and Offenders, Brisbane, June 1999

The Norwegian Bureau of Investigation: Police Chief Inspector Ole Petter Ekhaugen, *Aftenposten* 14.03.2000

Schanck R C & Abelson R (1977): *Scripts, Plans, Goals and Understanding*. Hillsdale, Lawrence Erlbaum

Smith S L & Donnerstein E (1998): "Media Violence", in Geen Russel G & Donnerstein E (eds.): *Human Aggression*. New York, Academic Press, pp. 167-202

Årsrapport 1999 [Yearly Report 1999], Redd Barna, Oslo

Årsrapport 1999 [Yearly Report 1999], Økokrim, Oslo

Paedophile Information Networks in Cyberspace

Rachel O'Connell

Two case studies within the COPINE[1] research project, University College, Cork, Ireland, are concerned with how individuals dedicated to child sex organise themselves on the Internet, and to the content of the pictures posted.[2] The studies focus on Usenet newsgroups. Newsgroups, a public form of virtual communication, are only one outlet for the expression of adult sexual interest in children on the Internet. It is likely that private e-mail, mailing lists, ICQ (I Seek You) and IRC (Internet Relay Chat) have a greater role than newsgroups in the dissemination of more direct sensitive information, 'private' photographs, contacts, etc. IRC also affords users the opportunity to communicate in 'real time', and the option to open a Direct Client-to-client Communication (DCC) between two users, which bypasses the need for a server and thereby raises the level of security.

The method used in the case studies involved subscribing to a newsreader that provided access to all newsgroups in which pictures were posted. The newsgroups that might be concerned with adult sexual interest in children were noted and accessed. References in these made to other similar newsgroups were also noted. Of the many thousands newsgroups identified, 0.07 per cent contained child erotica (children in stages of undress, but not sexually explicit) or child pornography. From an organisational perspective, restricting their activities to a limited number of newsgroups has obvious advantages for paedophiles. And few newsgroups do not restrict the large amount of picture trading that takes place in the groups.

Content of the pictures posted

Some results from the analysis of the pictures posted during one week in January and one week in April 1998 are the following:

Newsgroups that contained pictures of male and female children together were few. In total fifteen newsgroups were identified that contained female child erotica and pornographic pictures. The largest amount of picture posting took place in newsgroups with the words 'pre-teen' and 'children' in the title. The overall number of female child pictures during the first week amounted to 3,487, posted by 193 users. The number of pictures during the second week, when two of the newsgroups were no longer in existence but another group had become more active, amounted to 5,233, posted by 313 users. (However, posters may use more than one pseudonym when posting to different newsgroups).

In January, nine newsgroups were found where pictures of boys were posted. In general these newsgroups contained the world 'boy' in the title. The overall number of male pictures during the first week amounted to 2,546, posted by 126 posters. In April the number of pictures was 2,070 and the number of posters 100.

Two thirds of all pictures posted could be described as erotic in nature and many of these appeared to be relatively recent, featuring children of Asian extraction or including text indicating Japanese origins. Pornographic photographs (as distinct from erotic) were largely either European photographs more than 15-20 years old, or more recent ones featuring Asian children. It seems likely that most of the pictures have their origins either in scanned magazine photographs, or in video captures. New erotic (as opposed to pornographic) photographs were mainly scanned from Japanese magazines. There were also growing numbers of digitised video clips, derived from videotape originals.

The content analyses, as well as an analysis of paedophile fantasies discussed in IRC chatrooms, further suggest that there are clear indications of individuals' sexual preferences – an individual user's postings are specific and selective, defined in terms of factors including: sex of the child; stage of development of the child; ethnic origin of child; sexual interaction; use of force; adult involvement; sex of adult; number of adults; ethnic origin of adults; and sexual behaviour.

The posters

The pseudonyms of posters to one group who used the same pseudonym in January and April were noted. These pseudonyms represent some of the core set of posters to the group, which suggests that the individuals behind these pseudonyms are aware of each other, that there may be private communication between them, and that they gain recognition as the 'gurus' who seem to have access to large numbers of pictures and post regularly.

The structure and organisation of paedophile newsgroup activity are distinct. But the activity does not appear to operate in a strictly hierarchical fashion. Instead posters adopt a co-operative approach; the images are posted in a sympathetic environment that is supportive of the posters' rationalisations for child sex encounters.

Posters can be identified as having a variety of roles. The main 'promoting' roles are as follows:

Infrastructure advice co-ordinators act as a protective buffer zone orchestrating paedophile newsgroup activity and giving advice (e.g., about the group, how to download and decode articles and pictures, how to post anonymously and prevent discovery, suitable e-mail addresses and other newsgroups, how to respond to 'Flames', i.e., anti-paedophile reactionaries).

Literature reviewers give detailed information regarding paedophile related publications, how to become a member of paedophile organisations, etc.

Story/fantasy generators directly engage in the production and posting of stories.

Support people contribute to a supportive context in which sexual interest in children can develop. They detail positive aspects of adult child sexual interaction, claim to disagree with coerced sex between adult and child and fully support consensual sex between adult and child.

Posters and traders of child erotic and child pornographic pictures fall mainly into the following categories: child erotica only; child pornographic only; hard core child pornography only; mixed child erotica and child pornography; multi-sex deviants. A large amount of the activity consists of swapping pictures. Posts may ask for a certain picture to complete a particular series; there are posts containing 'prize pictures', recent pictures, offers of free CDs of series of photos, etc.

There are also 'detractors' posting material to the paedophile newsgroups, i.e., the *reactionaries* who aggressively react against the content of the newsgroup postings, and *paedophile register propagators* who post identification details of paedophiles.

Thus, the Internet provides a uniquely safe, easily accessible, and supportive context for posting, trading and collecting child pornography. This illegal material drives a market that is distinctive in that it typically, in the newsgroups, does *not* involve the exchange of money.

Justification to a wider audience

Not to forget, there are an unknown number of people engaged in the passive monitoring and downloading of images and information. All the evidence is that many people at least browse in this area, if not actively downloading. The easy accessibility and transnational distribution of child pornography and rationalisations for child sex has broader implications in the context of sexualising children to an audience who may not have any primary interest in child sex *per se*. The children depicted in child pornography pictures are engaged in sexual behaviour, and are directed by the photographer to behave in specific ways that serve to sexualise children, in order to gratify a whole range of fantasies. The result is that children engaged in sex acts are often smiling or have neutral expressions; very rarely do children in child pornographic pictures show signs of discomfort. These depictions appear to be designed to reinforce rationalisation and justification processes for adult sexual interest in children. To the wider audience the pictures depict children as 'willing sexual beings'.

Notes

1. Combating Paedophile Information Networks in Europe. For more information about the research project, see Rachel O'Connell's article "Child Sex Iconography" in this book.
2. This article is a summary of findings presented in a paper by Rachel O'Connell at the Expert Meeting at UNESCO, "Sexual Abuse of Children, Child Pornography and Paedophilia on the Internet", Paris, January 18-19, 1999.

Child Sex Iconography

Iconic Narratives of Child Sex Myths

Rachel O'Connell

This article seeks to explore the socio-historic origins of child sex myths transmitted via the iconic narratives of child sex iconography.[1] (The reasons for using the term 'child sex iconography' instead of 'child erotica' and 'child pornography' are given in note 1.) This approach marks a departure from a more typical discussion of child sex iconography within a narrow legal perspective. It is proposed that child sex iconography may be viewed as one of the media by which child sex myths and metaphors have been disseminated throughout the last century and a half. Furthermore, it is suggested that the template of these iconic child sex narratives may be situated in European turn of the century art.

This theoretical approach involves borrowing the methods of study of iconography, which Panojsky[2] described as the branch of art history, which concerns itself with subject matter or meaning, as opposed to form. This endeavor is important because, as Preziosi[3] points out, a picture is a discursive space in which it is possible to connect artistic motifs and combinations of artistic motifs, i.e., compositions with themes or concepts. Motifs are thus recognized as carriers of a secondary and conventional meaning and combinations of images can be described as stories. Images whose content are left unexamined continue to have hidden powers of persuasion, something which is of no great concern in images whose ideological messages are clearly understood. It would be very remiss to ignore the narrative content of child sex iconography which is continually disseminated worldwide, particularly in view of the facts that these narratives support and justify both child sex myths and actual child sexual abuse.

Three periods of child sex iconography

The three periods briefly explored in this article are characterised by proliferations of child sex iconography in the public domain.[4] Commencing this exploration around the middle of the last century seems appropriate, as it was around this time that a body of work became organised into a category referred to as pornography. Arguably, this began a process of both categorising material as pornographic and defining the meaning of pornography in terms of the 'forbidden'. With necessary selectivity, the article will explore the following media and periods in chronological order – the purpose is to briefly explicate the possible origins, embellishments and mutations of child sex myths over the last century and a half:

- works of art dating from the turn of the last century;
- photographs and videos from the period 1969–1979 when pornography was legalised in Denmark and subsequently disseminated worldwide;
- images, photographs and video clips disseminated via the Internet.

Tang[5] proposes that the history of pornography can be told in terms of technologies. A recurrent set of related issues arises in relation to child sex iconography at the turn of the last century, and permeate through to the present day. These issues can be outlined briefly in terms of the conjoining of a set of circumstances attendant to proliferations of child sex iconography – issues that will be addressed in greater depth throughout the article:

- increased technological sophistication;
- ease of accessibility of material;
- worldwide dissemination of child sex iconography;
- perceived lax, absent or difficult to enforce legal constraints.

The rationale for this historical approach is underpinned by the necessity to understand the meanings, myths and metaphors contained in child sex iconography. The approach facilitates the search for enduring commonalties, threads, and themes in these depictions. It is hoped that seeking to illuminate the unexplored meanings depicted in child sex iconography in a systematic manner may provide some valuable psychological insights into some of the seemingly implicit ideological assumptions made by adults with a sexual interest in children. Such an analysis would provide a means of eliciting useful discriminating variables that would assist theory building about sexual interest in children.

It seems reasonable to suggest that such a study may provide insights into how sexual behaviours with children are maintained. This process may ultimately assist in assessing the danger an individual may pose to the community. Equally, a systematic categorisation system of the child sex myths that an individual adheres to would be useful in a therapeutic setting, for the purposes of deconstructing those myths.

The COPINE project

The main body of research that informs this article stems from over three years of research investigating pedophile activity on the Internet as part of my doctoral thesis in psychology that commenced in 1996. In 1997, the Child Studies Unit, Department of Psychology, University College Cork, secured funding from the European Union for a European wide project called COPINE (Combating Paedophile Information Networks in Europe). The aims of this project were as follows:

- to promote an awareness and understanding of the issues involved;
- to facilitate the clear communication and development of contacts between law enforcement and other professionals in Europe;
- to identify areas for future operational co-ordination and co-operation.

The last three years have been spent working in close collaboration with the Irish Police, The Paedophile Unit, Scotland Yard, and the Belgian and Dutch Police to execute these aims.

Part of the research involved an analysis of the structure and social organisation of child sex related activities in cyberspace and its implications for investigative strategies.[6]

Research also involved the detailed analysis of over 1,000 child sex iconography images, in order to arrive at a systematic categorisation system of the content. The variables analysed centred on age, sex, and ethnic origin of the children, adolescents and adults depicted, along with the sex acts and sexual interactions featured.

A similar detailed analysis of over 100 child pornography videos was carried out again for the purposes of categorising the content of these videos.

And over twenty hours were spent in Internet Relay Chatrooms (IRC) dedicated to child sex gathering information about adult sexual interest in children.

Some broad findings of this research will be referred to later in this article.

Arising from the studies outlined above it became clear that a number of differing broad approaches can be employed when analysing the meaning, content, function and role of child sex iconography. By focusing on images defined as child pornography, the multifaceted layers of interpretation can be stated explicitly as follows:

- Child pornography images are the evidence of serious sexual assaults. As records of both the crime and the crime scene, these pictures are open to the techniques of crime scene analysis. This has important ramifications from a legal, law enforcement and child protection perspective.
- Research findings over the last four years suggest that adults with a sexual interest in children are highly selective in the kinds and content of the child sex iconography images they prefer. Therefore a forensic psychological perspective may be adopted when the collection of child pornography is viewed as a behaviour, rather than an intention or attitude. It therefore

constitutes a firm base on which to develop empirical analyses relating collecting behaviour to offending. Collecting choices are a behavioural expression of sexual interest, and as such therefore may provide objective and tangible insights in two senses:

i. by helping to identify the kind of pedophile interest that characterises the person concerned;

ii. by giving an objective and empirical basis to predictions of future risk and dangerousness, especially in circumstances where there is no history of offending on which to base predictions of dangerousness.

- Categorising the child sex iconic narratives that individuals subscribe to plays an important role in our understanding of adults with a sexual interest in children. This process would provide insights on a number of levels:

  i. Developing a categorisation of the various iconic narratives of child sex myths that individuals subscribe to will help to identify the kinds of child sex myths that characterise individuals.

  ii. Provide the opportunity to use sequential analyses to explore correspondences between the nature of myths that an individual subscribes to and the nature of the offences, if any, perpetrated.

  iii. Provide insights into the child sex myths and ideologies to which an individual subscribe. This has implications for treatment and predicting liability to offend.

Child sex myths are discursive products

Over the course of the last four years analyzing child sex iconography and text based accounts of alleged sexual abuse and fantasies recounted by adults with a sexual interest in children, I have encountered some frequently occurring myths surrounding child sex. These include notions such as 'children are sexual beings', 'children demand sexual gratification from adults', and 'sexual interaction between children and adults does not result in harm to children' – in fact it is often suggested that sexual interaction with children causes more harm to the adult than the child. How are we to interpret and understand these myths?

The approach taken here is a social constructionist one, which asks: How do culture, history and society shape and maintain child sex myths? The underlying premise of this argument is that people are embedded in conversations and we constantly make sense of the world through narratives and stories.[7] Child sex myths are discursive products, the roots of which can be situated in mainstream dominant narratives of our society. As such, these narratives and – of particular interest here – iconic narratives of child sex myths transmitted via child sex iconography are open to examination. They are located within, and defined by, the complexes of social activity. Nowhere is this more apparent than via computer-mediated communication which enables us to encounter many diverse people representing different ways of being in the world. Rom Harre[8] has argued that if there is one fundamental or most basic social psychological activity, then we would have to say that conversation and social interaction are the best candidates for this distinction.

This approach turns on its head the traditional methodology of looking at, e.g., cognitive distortions as ways of explaining the ideological assumptions about child sex. The cognitive approach tends to begin with attempts to locate the origins of child sex myths and ideologies within the individual. Murphy (1990, cited in Hollins and Howells[9]) and Segal and Stermac (1990, cited in Grubin[10]) have reviewed the role of cognition in sexual assault. They found that although clinical observations suggest that child molesters do have cognitive distortions that are related to their offences, it has been difficult to detect defective cognitions specific to child molesters in research.

This article tentatively situates the origins of child sex myths, as we know them today, within mainstream art at the turn of the century. As a part and parcel of mainstream art and popular culture the narrative discourse on child sex would have been incorporated into mainstream dominant narratives. The subsequent sub-cultural narratives that grew around these mainstream narratives are visible in the discussions that pedophiles engage in and the iconic narratives of the child sex iconography that they exchange in child sex related sites on the Internet. The sub-cultural narratives of adults with a sexual interest in children are accessible to research, something which will be discussed in greater depth later. The iconic narratives of child sex myths that encourage sexual offending are legitimate research targets, regardless of their causal status, because they may serve to maintain offending once it has begun. Child sex myths may be necessary, if insufficient, for child molestation.

In a discussion of myths and metaphors, Eliade Mircea[11] highlighted the central aspect of myths, i.e., the ambiguity that myths seek to create – an ambiguity that suggests that myths may be about the past but they may also be about the present, e.g., sexual interest in children has always existed. Using such a premise infers that sexual interest in children is something that stands outside of the realms of current social and legal sanctions and it is thereby granted enduring mythical and ideological status. Myths do not lose their relevance by virtue of being ancient, because they exist outside of ordinary time. In psychological terms the central figure of a myth corresponds to an archetype, which in this case refers to the 'forbidden fruit' or the 'sexually desirable child'. This archetype also exists outside of ordinary time and so is granted ideological status. The effects of such myths can be regarded as twofold. Firstly, for adults with a sexual interest in children these myths serve to provide an ideological and mythical basis for their sexual predilections. To society the citing of these myths in terms of the archetypal 'forbidden fruit' represents a circular argument which by the nature of its circularity is impossible to refute.

Furthermore, a reciprocal interaction between the child sex myths contained in the sub-cultural narratives, i.e., those of adults with a sexual interest in children, transact and shape the understanding that society in general has about child sex. Conversely, social and legal sanctions, media commentary, and reaction to child sex cases will have an effect on how adults with a sexual interest in children interpret child sex.

Iconic depictions of child sex myths in high art of the last century

Tracing the origins of child sex myths and metaphors depicted at the turn of the century is a difficult task, not least because this period is overshadowed by the impressionist movement and has received little attention in its own right from art historians. These facts are further confounded by the tendency to avoid child sex iconography as a subject for discussion. Speculating on the meaning of the material to viewers is fraught with even more difficulties, particularly as this exploration is carried out in retrospect. Exploring meanings and metaphors is further complicated by the differences in legal parameters surrounding child sex at the turn of the last century. In the United Kingdom prior to 1885, the age of consent for sexual relations was just twelve years of age. Until 1880, English courts held that if a female child consented to sexual intercourse no charges could be brought against the adult involved. Child prostitution was rife in certain parts of London at that time.

Bram Dijkstra[12] has provided an insightful and rare account of turn of the century art. From an art historian's perspective, he provides some illuminating insights into what he terms as the 'iconography of misogyny' from the middle up to the turn of the last century. Throughout this period the hegemony of the Darwinian creed prevailed, i.e., the well-proselytized 'scientific proof' that women were inferior to men and had minds that could at best be likened to a child's. Research findings such as these, made by the most eminent of scientists, offered license to artists and writers to depict women as child-like creatures. The 'woman-child analogy' became prevalent, and soon the parameters of that analogy saw some artists choose to focus exclusively on children. Turn of the century artists borrowed the symbolic motifs and iconic narratives that had traditionally been used to depict adult female sexuality and utilized the same motifs when depicting children. Hence, child sex iconography was born and in time it was further embellished with scripts and narratives of its own.

The audiences for these works of art consisted of a small elite of wealthy individuals who were well versed in the symbolic meanings of certain motifs and symbols. Toward the close of the century, gravure-assisted photographic reproductions printed in periodicals, books and magazines made the work of contemporary artists accessible to millions of viewers all over the world. This resulted in works of art being elevated to a position of international importance, which Dijkstra[13] describes as not unlike that occupied by television in our own time. It is important to point out that child sex iconography does not exist in a vacuum. Although it falls outside the scope of this article it seems reasonable to highlight that the child sex narratives and myths depicted in works of art were mirrored in the literature of that time.

The ideology and symbolism underlying the emergent child sex iconography has far-reaching relevance in terms of situating the origins and subsequent elaboration, mutations and dissemination of child sex myths. These issues will be returned to later in this article. The following paragraphs will briefly explore some of the motifs, myths and iconic narratives that surfaced in turn of the century depictions of children. All of the paintings mentioned were widely distributed in periodicals and magazines and thus were easily accessible to the general population at that time.

Iconic child sex myths and narratives

The search for the ideal of innocence

According to Dijkstra[14] there was an underlying quest in the art of this period for the contours of the adult woman's lost innocence in the features of the child. A curious crossing of boundaries began to take place where the sexual enticements of women were represented in the physical body of the child. For example, the female artist Susanne Daynes Grassot in her painting 'Child before a mirror' depicts a naked child approximately eight years old standing before a mirror. The child is depicted standing naked in an erotic pose and appears to be completely self-absorbed. Depictions such as this and many others serve to underpin the analogies between a nude little girl and the poses of vanity and sexual arousal given to adult females by turn of the century artists. The underlying scripts and narratives of these depictions were well understood by the turn of the century *viewer*.

Waiting and or pleading for carnal knowledge motif

Dijkstra describes the artist Paul Chabas as one of the most diligent artists in exploring the sexual implications of the woman-child analogy. He repeatedly painted scenes depicting adolescent girls posed naked and unprotected, surrounded by nature. The notion of therapeutic rape entered into the symbolic narratives of these depictions. There arose a veritable obsession with the certainty that these girls would come to have carnal knowledge. The motif at the time frequently used to depict children waiting for carnal knowledge was a naked girl, usually seated, eyes shut and seemingly waiting with an expectant air.

Promise of 'love without fear' motifs

As the century drew to a close, themes around the process of awakening the woman in the child became more prevalent. This was mirrored in literature where the notion of the young child unfettered by social convention, and as yet unaware of the wiles of womanhood, would embrace her sexual awakening into carnal knowledge by the *viewer* without fear. This process would be a natural conclusion to the child's plea for carnal knowledge. Dijkstra discusses Bruno Piglhein's use of a favorite artistic pose of a sexually sated woman and applied the same formulaic depiction to the pleasurable exhaustion of a toddler on 'Christmas Morning'. Simultaneously, in France Leon Perault made the erotic depictions of toddlers a specialty. In 1897, he painted a picture entitled 'Bacchus as a Child' in which he placed a naked infant in the characteristic pose of a nymph with broken back. This motif was frequently used in the depiction of naked adult women lying supine in sharp backward angles as if these women were in terminal backward spasms of uncontrollable sexual desire.[15] The position inferred that it was only natural to take these women by force and that they were in fact pleading for sexual gratification. That artists in the depiction of young children applied the same motif gives insight into just how close to pornographic the celebrated artist wished to take the eager viewers' imagination.

Anti-infantine sentiment

In 1900, Léon Frédéric painted 'The Stream' depicting the world of the child in what Dijkstra describes as a 'carnal orgy of infant flesh'. It seems that the turn of the century mind had reached the opposite end of the spectrum from where it had commenced. The artists had sought the ideal of innocence in female children which had quickly turned to viewing the child as somewhat precocious and self-obsessed. She was subsequently depicted as impatiently waiting for carnal knowledge. Her innocence in matters carnal represented to the turn of the century male the promise of yielding compliant love. At the close of the century, she was considered by the most eminent scientists to have criminal tendencies. Paul Adam, in an article 'On children' published in *La Revue Blanche* in 1895 (cited in Dijkstra[16]), warned that: "virtually all vices fester in the mind of the child".

These sentiments were echoed by numerous writers, scientists and philosophers and came to feature in the work of artists. The validity of Dijkstra's interpretations is open to debate, but his arguments are easily appreciated by looking at the artwork he refers to. Fortunately, turn of the century artists that he refers to adhered to the strict representational style that allows easy recognition of the handful of well used motifs and styles. This examination can be supplemented by examining the literature and scientific findings from this era – it is hard to dispute his findings. In any event that a debate should be initiated can only be a good thing, for if we do not scrutinize the messages and myths that are transmitted through iconic depictions, then in all probability they will continue to permeate throughout our culture.

Dissemination of the template of child sex iconic narratives

Towards the end of the last century, the template of child sex myths was disseminated throughout Europe and beyond. This dissemination was to be aided further by the then widespread use and accessibility of photography. It seems reasonable to suggest that photographers would have emulated and sought to reproduce the classical images of art. This is evidenced in the case of photographs of nude adult females, which the French Academy had initially accepted as works of art. With the advent of cheap mechanisms for producing negatives, an unlimited numbers of prints could be produced quite cheaply. The voyeurism facilitated by photography allowed viewers to look at real children while not being seen. At that time numerous obscene pictures were produced, traded and disseminated in and around Europe. A forging of distribution channels and trade links with this new photographic industry took place but the evidence of this has been obscured over time. The proliferation of child sex iconography came to the attention of legal structures that grappled with a number of issues. These issues can be outlined as follows:

- The reproducibility of the photograph and its relative cheapness created significant opportunities for wide-ranging public access to such materials.
- Transnational dimensions were added as porn dealers utilized the postal system as a means for disseminating pornographic images.
- Distinctive structured and socially organized group dynamics with porn dealers akin to drug dealers and those buying child sex iconography akin to users, were created and maintained.

Commercial child sex iconography magazines and videos – ten years of madness (1969–1979)

The second illustrative example explores the period 1969–1979 during which all forms of pornography were legalized in Denmark. This legalization was accompanied by the subsequent global dissemination of such material during the same ten years. This period witnessed a growth of commercial child pornography magazines and videos. Tate[17] provides the names of the fathers of commercial child pornography in the twentieth century. These men were two existing adult pornography producers, Peter Theander and Willy Strauss. Strauss launched a child pornography magazine entitled *Bambina Sex* in 1971. In the first issue he used pictures from a collection that a pedophile had given to him and printed, bound and sold these images in the form of a magazine. This method of soliciting pictures from readers became the standard method of acquiring photographs that were published in subsequent magazines.

According to Tate, Theander brought child sex iconography into the domain of the moving picture, applied the methods used in the filming of adult pornography and transposed them onto child pornography. Comparative analysis of the content of both adult pornography and child pornography videos produced during this period highlights the influence of filming methods applied in adult pornography, for example, the tendency to show angles that were normally hidden from view even of the participants. According to Tang[18] these explicit shots of penetration originated from early American stag movies; the recurrent motif was the low angle shot between the legs to reveal penetration in the missionary position. Films were subject to the demands of a mass market and this market was catered to in what appears to be a systematic manner. Just as in adult movies there were possible combinations of heterosexual, homosexual, and a mixture of both; sexual interaction between couples, or groups; vaginal, anal, oral, genital-digital penetration, etc. Similar methods were applied to child pornography movies. In these the number of children were alternated and the sexual interaction could be:

- child to self (e.g., self masturbating);
- child to child (children performing sex acts on other children);
- child to adult (child performing a sex act on an adult);
- adult to child (adult performing a sex act on a child);
- group of children and adults of either one or both sexes engaging in any number of sex acts.

Typically the children involved were Caucasian and appeared well fed and materially well cared for, which it seems reasonable to suggest further normalized the sexual abuse of children.

The child sex myths from the turn of the century were, thus, maintained in the cine-film and videos produced during the era (1969-1979) but also embellished further with motifs borrowed from adult pornography. The moving picture reinforced child sex myths with a dynamic real life quality that still pictures do not infuse. This increased the perceived veracity of child sex myths. These movie depictions became the new medium for the transmission of child sex myths.

The scenes were orchestrated and the children instructed to behave in ways which were designed to leave the viewer in no doubt about the 'truth' of the underlying child sex myths. The use and juxtaposition of the techniques applied to adult pornography in child pornography videos served to further blur boundaries and meaning of child pornography, i.e., serious sexual assaults. These aspects of child pornography were minimized, and myths about child sex maximized, using the following techniques:

- Children depicted in these films were generally smiling or had neutral expressions.
- They appeared to be well versed in their own and adult anatomy.
- They rarely showed hesitation in going through a series of sex acts, something which conceivably has the desired effect of normalizing and sanitizing child sex to viewers.

Through analysis of these films it was possible to discern a number of additions to the child sex myths from the turn of the century. These films typically depicted children as more than willing participants, and rarely contained evidence of harm having been done to the child. Between 1971 and 1978, Theander's company Colour Climax Corporation produced a series of at least thirty-six ten minute films, with titles such as *Sucking Daddy*, *Fucking Children* and *Little Girl Sex*. These shorts were marketed under the brand name 'Lolita' and were professionally made with titles, lighting and music.

This period also witnessed the dissemination of child sex iconography worldwide. The production of commercial film based child sex iconography utilized the most up-to-date and sophisticated technology available. As had happened at the turn of the century, the conjoining of lax or absent legal constraints, with increased technological sophistication, facilitated easy accessibility of this material, which was distributed worldwide. Tate[19] outlines that the subsequent re-instatement of the prohibition against child pornography simply resulted in cutting out the go-between. Pedophiles continued to exchange pictures of themselves abusing children amongst one another but without the commercial element to this trade.

Child sex related activities in cyberspace

Communication technologies such as the Internet facilitate the rapid dissemination of a virtual stream of child sex iconography that appears to cater to every sort of child sex fantasy. The global dissemination of iconic narratives of child sex myths has met the ultimate tool. Just as moving pictures had an impact on the nature and dimensions of child sex iconography, the Internet has impacted on the accessibility and worldwide distribution of a wide selection of images on an even greater scale. The interconnectivity and anonymity that the Internet affords, allows users to become increasingly engaged in child sex related activities. This has resulted in the facilitated formation of child sex related groups and the fostering of on-line relational development between adults with a sexual interest in children who engage in trading, collecting, disseminating, discussing and producing child sex iconography. These activities highlight the need to consider the following factors:

- The nature of on-line child sex related activities is illegal in most countries, so the forging of strong relationships based on a certain amount of trust would appear to be essential ingredients to underpin pedophile activity in cyberspace. How is this brought about in cyberspace amongst people whom in many cases have never met one another face-to-face? Research findings show how members of on-line child sex related groups appropriate identifiable sets of norms for behavior, or codes of on-line 'netiquette', which serves to protect group members in two ways. Firstly, any deviation by a user from a set of prescribed rules and norms of the group would serve to identify that group member as a potential risk to other members of the group. Alerted to possible danger group members can take steps to limit the damage that such a person may cause. Secondly, these rules serve to protect group members from detection, and social or legal sanction.

- Arguably pedophile activity in cyberspace has pushed child sex iconography from an offline covert 'closet' position into an on-line public position of prominence, which perhaps adds a new potency to the material. This may lead to a false sense of the acceptability and normality of these images and the underlying sexual abuse of children.
- Computer-mediated communication (CMC) provides an interactive medium that facilitates the on-line admixture of child sex myths. Users come on-line to discuss child sex related alleged experiences and fantasies, and to exchange masturbatory fantasies, by engaging in a form of cybersex which involves role-playing the abuse of a virtual child. These activities are often supplemented by the exchange of child sex iconographic images to illustrate individual preferences in terms of age, sex, ethnic origin, position of child (i.e., standing, sitting, straddling, kneeling, lying, bending over), and location (outdoors, indoors) of child. These images also depict the preferred sex act that the user likes to view children performing, and the direction of the sexual interaction (i.e., child to self, child to child, child to adult, adult to child, or group interactions). As these images are discussed users often record the conversations so a text and picture based record exists detailing the admixture of ideas, myths and metaphors of child sex. Admixtures may occur in a number of ways, i.e., interaction of both traditional and personal child sex myths with the child sex myths adhered to by others. Interactions such as these could conceivably result in the creation and appropriation of new or altered child sex myths. Researching the processes behind the creation of new or altered narratives of child sex myths may provide a measure of the social impact of adults with a sexual interest in children interacting in cyberspace.

Levels of publicly accessible on-line child sex iconography activity

In 1997, a study that involved monitoring activity in child sex related newsgroups on the Internet estimated that of the 30,000 newsgroups that were in operation at the time approximately 0.07 per cent (23 newsgroups) contained child erotica and child pornography (O'Connell).[20] In 1999, the number of newsgroups that contain child sex iconography fluctuates between 50 and 55 groups. This represents a doubling of the number of Internet newsgroups dedicated to child sex over the last two years. This figure has to be viewed with caution, as there is evidence that users migrate in a nomadic fashion from one newsgroup to another. So a newsgroup that contained a lot of child iconography activity may be perceived by users as under scrutiny from law enforcement officers. Users may move en-masse to a new newsgroup while activity may persist in the original group but at a far lower level, or may consist primarily of cross postings from adult pornography sites. Thus, the apparent increase in the number of groups is not necessarily an accurate reflection of an increase in pedophile groups in which child sex related activities take place.

Over the course of the last two years, the COPINE team has collected approximately 50,000 child erotica and child pornographic images. Approximately two thirds of this material consists of child erotica and the reminder consists of child pornography. Of the remaining one third consisting of child pornography, relatively much is comprised of old materials. Similarly, the number of pictures available at the publicly accessible layers of the Internet may not be an accurate representation of the number of images traded on more hidden layers of the Internet. Nor does that number represent an accurate picture of the number of images that may exist in any individual's private or personal collections. The figure 50,000 therefore must be viewed with caution. The key issue here has more to do with the fact that to sustain this activity it seems reasonable to assert that newness and novelty both play a crucial role this process.

Iconographic study of child sex iconography exchanged in cyberspace

A study of the content and meaning of the broad categories of child sex iconography available on the Internet will serve to highlight some of the myths that have persisted from the turn of the century to the present day. Many of the images valuable on the Internet originate from the period 1969-1979 and smaller percentages are more recent in origin.

Erotic child sex iconography

The first category 'Erotica' consists of images of children in various stages of undress, from fully dressed to depictions of children wearing only a panties or bikini bottom. Many of these images look like ones that could be found in any family photo album. Many of the children depicted seem to be unaware that a photograph of them was being recorded. Some of the photographs clearly involve sophisticated photographic equipment (e.g., zoom lenses). It is important to stress that these images – no matter how normal the content – are being exchanged in a virtual environment where children are regarded as sexual beings.

Within this category are images that I have subcategorized as 'Erotica 2'. These images depict girls in the latter stages of undress where the focus is again on panties either pulled to one side, half way on/off or removed completely. The girls are not in sexually explicit positions but are posed in a sexually suggestive manner. The subtext of these images is that these children are sexual beings. These poses are easily recognizable from adult pornography and are reminiscent of artistic depictions from the turn of the century. The underlying iconic narratives are suggestive of child sex myths that intimate that those children are sexual, precocious beings.

The iconic narratives of child sex myths that fall into these categories appear to be designed to be 'subtly suggestive of children's sexuality'. The broader impact of these images on the general public who may not realize that these pictures are orchestrated may assist in the propagation of sex myths.

The third category labeled 'Naked' consists of images of individual or groups of naked girls. The children depicted in these photographs are typically either toddlers (0-4 year old) or young children (5-8 year old) with far fewer preteens or pubescents. Within this category there exists further discrete subcategories of images that depict children in a natural state, i.e., not posed, and depictions of children in sexually suggestive poses which suggests an element of orchestration on the part of the photographer which serves to sexualize children.

Pornographic child sex iconography

The label for the fourth category 'Waiting' was taken from the heading of one of the images described by this category. It would appear that at this point images digress from the defining features of eroticism and move into the sphere of pornography. These images depict children in 'sexually prepared positions', i.e., lying or sitting with legs spread wide and genitals fully exposed, typically in the absence of an adult. The iconic narratives clearly suggest that these children are waiting for carnal knowledge. This motif of the lone child in a sexually prepared position typically on a bed suggests that these pictures represent a voyeuristic perspective on what children will do when left to there own devices. The iconic narratives serve to 'substantiate' iconic narratives laid down at the turn of the century that children are curious, precocious sexual beings that in their natural state crave sexual advances. The children's gaze may be directed at the camera suggestive of a plea to the *viewer*.

A subcategory consists of images that are close-up shots of children's genitalia which may cater to specific fantasies but also serve to educate those unsure about the capabilities of children's anatomy.

A further category labeled 'ready and inserting' show images of girls inserting sex objects in to their own genital orifices. The clear iconic narratives here again serve to reinforce the notion of children as curious sexual beings. Typically children are depicted alone and again the idea of a voyeuristic view of these activities is aided by the fact that children typically are not looking at the camera. The averted gaze motif that repeatedly recurs in images that fall into this category is designed to reinforce the pornographic voyeuristic element and child sex myths about the sex acts children engage in when they believe they are not being watched. The iconic narratives – that these kinds of activities do not harm children – are 'substantiated' by the orchestrated depiction of the children as smiling or with neutral expressions. Furthermore these images serve to minimize the sexual abuse of children by adults, by providing 'evidence' that young girls engage in means of penetration in lieu of sexual interactions with adult males.

The remaining categories depict children engaged in various sex acts from genital-digital penetration, cunnilingus, fellatio, masturbation, inserting sex aids and, less commonly, in sado-masochistic scenes, etc. The iconic narratives depict children as knowledgeable and with smiling or neutral expressions that are orchestrated to imply that these children are not averse to these activities. Part of the process of categorizing these images was recording a number of variables, including sex, age, and ethnic origin of children involved; the sex act(s) they were engaged in; the number, sex, and ethnic origin of adults involved; the sex act they were engaged in; and, most importantly, the direction of the sexual interaction, whether it was child to self, child to child, child to adult, adult to child or a group situation. This final factor is crucial to the development of subcategories of child sex iconography.

The most recent images show a new discursive child sex myth as series of pictures become available that depict children situated in domestic settings engaged in typical activities like watching television or playing with toys. As the series progresses the same children are depicted engaged in various sex acts either alone or with an adult, before they are pictured again engaged in normal everyday activities. The narratives of these child sex myths seem to be designed to engage the viewer in the discursive process of thinking about child sex as something which is a 'normal' part of everyday life.

These images engage the viewer in a discursive space where one is simultaneously engaged in a process of interpreting the narratives contained therein. The voyeuristic element maintained by motifs like the averted gaze serves to engage the viewer with the abuse that is being depicted. Confronted with such images the viewers' focus centers on the child. Typically, the child is smiling or has a neutral expression. The fact that this is an orchestrated image, designed to support child sex myths, is not readily observable and it is in this respect that the child sex iconography is a potent means of transmission of child sex myths.

The question then is: What effect will these activities have on child sex related activities?

- Is there a sense in which the child sex myths that an individual adheres to could provide useful discriminating variables? If the emphasis is shifted away from locating the locus of child sex ideologies or cognitive distortions from within an individual and situate them instead within society – are there ways in which the child sex myths that individuals subscribe to vary in degree along a continuum that could provide useful predictors of offence liability?

- Many social scientists have remarked upon how the social effects of immersion in cyberspace are potentially complex and only dimly understood. When adults with a sexual interest in children from different backgrounds come together, new ideas can arise from their conversations. Sometimes new ideas are built up incrementally from the fragments of different viewpoints. Ideas may be more robust when they have been bounced around, critiqued, polished, and repackaged by a group. Therefore any program designed to elucidate the process of pedophile activity in cyberspace must be cognizant of these potential effects and seek to record any changes or embellishments that occur to child sex myths.

Research investigating the appropriation of child sex myths in cyberspace

Central to elucidating the process of appropriation of child sex myths in cyberspace would be the arrival at a baseline taxonomy of child sex myths by analyzing the iconic narratives, motifs and symbols depicted in child sex iconography. These processes would be further enhanced by the use of discourse analysis of pedophile conversations to uncover the text based sub-cultural narratives of these myths, rationalizations and justifications of child sex. Designing a research program to investigate the appropriation of child sex myths in cyberspace would need to be cognizant of the effects of computer-mediated communication. Therefore research would be couched within the framework of existing computer-mediated communication (CMC) research.

A number of researchers have identified five broad factors that influence computer-mediated communication. These factors include: the external contexts in which the use of CMC is set; the temporal structure of the group; infrastructure of the computer system; the purposes for which CMC is used; and the characteristics of the group and its members (Contractor & Seibold, 1993; Hollingshead & McGrath, 1995; Seibold, Heller & Contractor, 1994; Steinfeld, 1986; cited in Jones[21]). I will address each of these issues in relation to pedophile activity in child sex related sites on the Internet.

External contexts

Users engaged on-line in exchanging, trading, collecting and disseminating child sex iconography, and in particular child pornography, are typically engaged in highly illegal activities. It seems reasonable to suggest that both legal and social sanctions may effect the extent individuals engage on-line in child sex related activities and these effects must be borne in mind. External contexts will also affect the likelihood of whether participants know each other or not, or if their physical locations mean that they can meet up. External contexts may play a role in on-line and offline networking amongst adults with a sexual interest in children.

Temporal structure

Walther (1996, cited in Jones[22]) has described the temporal structure of CMC activity in terms of synchronicity and asynchronisity. Research into pedophile activity in cyberspace suggests that the temporal structure of CMC activity lend itself to a further dichotomy, i.e., public or private and levels of activity:

1. Synchronistic activity involves a user being on-line and simultaneously engaged in reading and responding to computer-mediated communication. Synchronistic activity lends itself to more private levels of activity, which may also be affected by the level of technical sophistication of the user involved. Synchronistic activity can be situated in private and hidden layers of the Internet.

   1.1 Private or hidden layers of the Internet: For example, IRC[23] is one of a number of communication protocols, such as e-mail and ICQ,[24] that due to its ability to enable private communication has a role in the direct passage of sensitive information, as well as supporting the distribution of pornography. DCC (Direct Client-to-client Communication) is a feature of IRC that facilitates users connected on-line via a server the option to bypass the server and establish one-to-one contact. This increases the level of anonymity afforded to the user and it seems reasonable to suggest that these synchronistic, private layers of the Internet would be used in the transfer of sensitive information including recent child pornography images.

2. Asynchronistic temporal structure can be described as CMC that need not be on-line simultaneously. Users can read and respond at different times, e.g., in newsgroups and on mailing-lists. Because anyone can read or participate, all Usenet interactions is fundamentally multiparty and public.

   2.1 Public layer: An example of a public but potentially anonymous – i.e., users can strip the messages they post of any identity information – interface of the Internet would include Usenet newsgroups.[25] According to O'Connell[26] research into pedophile networking on the Internet indicates that child sex related newsgroups provide a passive supportive, virtual environment that facilitates the discussion of fantasies and alleged experiences of sexual offences against children in a context that sanitizes, routines and normalizes sexual contact with children. Asynchronistic public layer activity changes the relationship – places child sex iconography in a publicly accessible medium available to anybody who is interested. This serves to put law enforcement officers engaged in combating pedophile activity on the Internet in a position where they can watch these activities taking place.

The distinctions between public and private layers are closely related to system infrastructure.

System infrastructure

As the differences in possible temporal structures suggest, computer network interactions shape interaction in many ways. System infrastructure is important to users engaged in illegal activities. Seibold et al. (1994, cited in Jones[27]) argue that systems differ in three general ways:

- Physical configurations – includes such variables as how many computers there are and the speed of the system.
- Systems adaptability – includes such variables as the capacity for anonymous entries and systems programmability.
- Level of user friendliness – information about how to optimize system infrastructure for their own purposes is often exchanged amongst users along with detailed technical support. The fluidity of communication technologies allows technically sophisticated users to shape the technologies to their own uses that the rapid advances in sophistication allow for an infinite number of technical possibilities designed to support pedophile activity in cyberspace.

Similarly, the infrastructure of the systems available to law enforcement to combat pedophile activity will have an impact on interactions.

Group processes

McGrath[28] discusses group processes in terms of the tasks they need to complete. Tasks in child sex related groups include the transmission of technical and social information among members of the group and also the transmission of child sex myths. Research has indicated how these tasks are carried out in child sex related groups (O'Connell[29]). A brief summary of that research will highlight some relevant points:

The structure and social organization of pedophile networking activity on the Internet does not appear to operate in a strictly hierarchical fashion. Instead posters adopt a co-operative approach with an organizing executive, i.e., 'infrastructure advice coordinators' engaged in disseminating information about how to avoid detection and outlining the rules of 'netiquette'. These users also appear to have a role in orchestrating the en-masse migration of users to different newsgroups. Relational development amongst users seems to center around co-operative activities. A large amount of the activity on picture based child erotica and child pornography newsgroups is driven in a co-operative manner, around swapping pictures. Posts may ask for a certain picture to complete a particular series, posts containing what are described as 'prize pictures', 'recent pictures', and offers of free CDs of series of photos for all to access. A focus on completing series of pictures by filling in missing pictures, and the frequency with which recent looking pictures appear, gives an indication of the organized approach that these users adopt in relation to their child pornography collections and their appetite for newness. The development of behaviour norms and codes of 'netiquette' which are posted in the form of FAQ (Frequently Asked Questions texts) provide guidelines to users about how to behave both toward one another and to detractors while on-line. The overall sense is of a cohesive, well-organized set of group dynamics.

Participant characteristics

Group and member characteristics have been argued to affect outcomes of computer-mediated communication. Research undertaken by the COPINE project indicates that in cyberspace there are at least six not necessarily exclusive kinds of participant involvement with child sex iconography:

- The 'confirmed collector' pedophile, whose sexual preference is expressed in terms of a narrow and explicit range of material collected. Child sex iconography is a central aspect of the individual's sexual life. Examining the content, and underlying sex myths depicted in the material collected, may provide important information on the sexual fantasies of the individual.
- The confirmed 'active' pedophile, who not only has a sexual interest in children but also engages in the process of recording his sexual abuse of children and in so doing, produces child sex iconography. It is not clear whether there are distinct differences in the sexual interest expressed by the confirmed collector who does not engage in child sexual abuse and the active pedophile who does. It is not clear if they are different to some degree, or whether they are in some sense different.
- The sexually 'omnivorous' who collect a wide range of unusual sexual material, of which child sex iconography is simply one.
- The sexually 'curious'.
- The 'libertarian' who may be involved in trade for reasons that are not explicitly motivated by sexual interest in children but have more to do with striving to keep the Internet free from censorship. The libertarian is often highly technically sophisticated.
- The 'entrepreneur' who seeks to exploit a commercial opportunity by meeting the demand for child sex iconography. Such individuals may have previous experience on the fringe of the sex trade, and may have links with organized criminal activity. This may be combined with criminal activity or may be an opportunistic commercial activity.

Users' characteristics can be further categorized by using the criteria of level of engagement in child sex related activities on the Internet:

1. Passive involvement through lurking,[30] i.e., browsing through public layers of the Internet but not engaging with others. This level of activity is very difficult to detect and so there are an unknown number of people engaged in the passive monitoring and downloading of images and information. There is a sense in which these people constitute a passive market for child sex iconography and thereby add fuel to the process. Passive involvement may appeal to users for the following reasons:

- Users want to avoid detection, i.e., users are less likely to be detected if they confine their activities to lurking.
- Users' desire to engage in the collection of child sex iconography may not coincide with the desire to communicate with other adults with sexual interest in children.
- Engaging passively may be a precursor to engaging actively, or engaging passively may be the end stage of active involvement, i.e., may represent a diminishing involvement in the process.

Points of contact may exist between those who lurk on public levels but may engage with others at more private levels.

2. Active involvement in the process of producing or trading pictures, and stories or alleged experiences or fantasies. This kind of involvement may be engaged in at either public or private layers of the Internet. The persons actively involved in the process in many ways constitute the greater problem in that they keep the supply of images going. These individuals, by actively distributing illegal images, are in a position analogous to a drug dealer, as opposed to the drug user or passive user outlined above.

Conclusions

This theoretical article sought to explore the socio-historic origins of child sex myths transmitted via the iconic narratives of child sex iconography. The purpose of this endeavour was to highlight child sex iconography as a discursive medium in the transmission of iconic narratives of child sex myths. The premise in understanding child sex myths involves situating them along a continuum within the dominant narratives of our culture and the sub-cultural narratives of adults with a sexual interest in children. The necessity of such a perspective is highlighted by the advent of communication technologies such as the Internet, where the dynamic global discursive processes facilitate what Gergen[31] describes as 'social saturation' taking place. People appropriate new ways of interpreting child sex myths. It is hoped that this article will give rise to new avenues of research in the search for more discriminating variables with which to understand and ultimately combat adult sexual interest in children.

Notes

1. Child sex iconography: The definitions of pornography have changed over the last century and to avoid confusion the term child sex iconography will be used throughout this article. A second reason for using the term child sex iconography stems from the need to move away from the terms child erotica and child pornography which are often confused in readers' minds with

issues surrounding adult pornography and erotica. The term child pornography does not adequately highlight the fact that the mere existence of the product is the evidence of serious sexual assaults on children. Child erotica refers to images of children in various stages of undress, or naked but not sexually explicit. The definition of child pornography within legal parameters, and the exclusion of child erotica, seems to have resulted in a minimizing of the importance of child erotica in psychological terms. The term erotica is an unfortunate one because of its use in describing adult material. A perusal of the debates surrounding the distinction between adult pornography and erotica reveals the use of benign words to describe erotica, which are also applied to child erotica. Catherine Itzin, editor of *Pornography: Women, Violence and Civil Liberties* (1992), draws upon the arguments of the following authors to highlight some of the issues: Gloria Steinman (1992) draws what she describes as the 'clear and present difference between erotica and pornography'. 'Pornography', she wrote 'is about dominance, an imbalance of male-female power' while '*erotica is about mutuality*'. John Stolenberg (1992) defines erotica as 'materials premised on *equality, mutuality, reciprocity,* and so forth'. Diana Russell (1992) defined erotica as 'sexual representations *that are non-abusive and non-sexist*'. The language used here suggests that those depicted in erotica are engaged in consensual, mutual, and reciprocal activities. This prompts the question about how this language translates for child erotica. Indeed, mutuality and reciprocity may be exactly the ideas conveyed to adults with a sexual interest in children. Currently, there is a curious minimizing of issues related to child erotica premised on the idea that if the activities are not illegal then they do no warrant attention. From a psychological perspective such a blinkered view must be avoided and to that end I have coined the term child sex iconography in an attempt to attain a broader perspective of the issues. However, in instances where research has distinguished between child erotica and child pornography for purposes of clarity, these terms will be used.

2. Panojsky, E. (1995) *Meaning in Visual Art.* Penguin Books. Australia.
3. Preziosi, D. (1989) *Rethinking Art History: Meditations on a Coy Science.* Yale University Press. New Haven.
4. It is important to highlight that while this discussion largely focuses on proliferations of child sex iconography in the public domain, the author is cognizant that this is only one of the possible layers of activity. Hidden layers of child sex iconography activity include a 'private level' (activity between two or more individuals) and a 'personal level' (activity solely confined to personal use) that typically do not permeate into the public domain. The permeability of material between levels has probably helped child sex iconography activity survive during periods of strict social and legal sanction.
5. Tang, I. (1999) *Pornography: A Secret History of Civilization.* Macmillan Publishers. Oxford.
6. O'Connell, R. (in press) The structure and social organization of pedophile activity on the Internet: Implications for investigative strategies.
7. Sacks, H. (1992) *Lectures on Conversation.* Blackwell Publishers. Oxford.
8. Harre, R. (1993) *Linguistics and Philosophy: The Controversial Interface.* Pergamon. Oxford.
9. Hollins, C.R. and Howells, K. (1994) *Clinical Approaches to Sex Offenders and their Victims.* Wiley. New York.
10. Grubin, D. (1998). *Sex Offending Against Children: Understanding the Risk.* Home Office Research, Development and Statistics Directorate.
11. Eliade, M. (1954) *The Myth of the Eternal Return, or, Cosmos and History.* Pantheon. New York.
12. Dijkstra, B. (1986) *Idols of Perversity: Fantasies of Feminine Evil in Fin-de-Siècle Culture.* Oxford University Press. Oxford.
13. ibid.
14. ibid.
15. ibid.
16. ibid., p. 220.
17. Tate, T. (1990) *Child Pornography: An Investigation.* Methuen. London.
18. Tang, I. (1999) *Pornography: A Secret History of Civilization.* Macmillan Publishers. Oxford.
19. Tate, T. (1992) cited in Itzin, C. (ed.) *Pornography: Women, Violence and Civil Liberties.* Oxford University Press. Oxford.

20. O'Connell, R. (in press) The structure and social organization of pedophile activity on the Internet: Implications for investigative strategies.
21. Jones, S. (1998) (ed.) *Cybersociety: Revisiting Computer-Mediated Communication and Community*. Sage Publications. California.
22. ibid.
23. Internet Relay Chat is a feature that enables users to hold live keyboard chats with people worldwide.
24. ICQ (I seek you) is a feature that enables users to hold live keyboard conversations with people worldwide and operates like a paging system.
25. Newsgroups. News refers to a collection of articles carried by Usenet. These articles, or postings, are messages sent as contributions to public discussions. They are similar to e-mail messages but are transmitted on a separate system and are publicly accessible to anyone who wishes to read them.
26. O'Connell, R. (1998) Pedophilia, Networking and the Internet. First COPINE Conference Proceedings.
27. Jones, S. (1998) (ed.) *Cybersociety: Revisiting Computer-Mediated Communication and Community*. Sage Publications. California.
28. McGrath, J.E. (1984). *Groups: Interaction and Performance*. Routledge. Englewood Cliffs.
29. O'Connell, R. (in press) The structure and social organization of pedophile activity on the Internet: Implications for investigative strategies.
30. Lurking, i.e., reading postings without participating.
31. Gergen, K. (1980). *Social Exchange Advances in Theory and Research*. Plenum Press. London.

The Naked, Hairy Caveman

Child Abuse on the Internet

Carlos A. Arnaldo, UNESCO

Rado Brzoka, a Polish youngster, is an alert student adept in electronics, computers and media. He is also sensitive to deep human values. Speaking at the "Oslo Challenge" forum in November 1999 on the tenth anniversary of the United Nations Convention on the Rights of the Child, he attempted to portray his image of the future:

> It is a naked, hairy caveman, sitting in his dark cave. His whole body is hovering over something small and complicated. As we come closer, we see it is a modern cellular phone. You mean the cell phone is an old technology used by cavemen? No, I mean to say that technology is advancing to newer models of communication. But man risks going backwards to the cave!

In a very real sense this young man's vision portrays exactly what is happening today. Technology is advancing to newer and more complex forms of communication, such as the cell phone and the Internet. And yet some sectors of the human population are degenerating back to animal instincts and behaviour, even worse than animals for they seek the prey of young children! In war and conflict situations, some misuse their arms and their force to abduct children into prostitution. Others use the new communication media as an electronic net to catch their prey. In either case it is the same animal.

The Internet – as well as all future forms of electronic, global dissemination of information and knowledge – are indisputably powerful media, instantaneous and interactive. They offer gateways to education, culture and self-improvement. They can uplift individuals, they can empower whole societies, they can become hubs of business and profitable human enterprise. We should want our children to learn and master the Internet for their own education, their enlightenment, the social and civic upbringing.

But like any other communication technology the Internet is only a means, a carrier. The Internet can be the bearer of evil, as well. It can be the forum for hate speech, intolerance, racism and apartheid philosophies. It can present images of young children, boys and girls, tortured, sexually attacked, in various stages of suffering, and death. This is perhaps the worst violence that can happen to children anywhere in the world because they are violated twice, the first time when they are sexually abused, and the second time and many times over, when this criminal scene is portrayed in photos, film, video or digitised images on the Internet. And each time these mediatised images are shown, we know that the sexual crime has already happened in reality.

This is why UNESCO has been involved in this battle alongside the other specialised agencies of the United Nations system. The World Tourism Organisation fights the traffic of young children to serve as prostitutes and sexual tourism involving children. The International Labour Organisation seeks to protect children from unfair labour laws and working under hard labour conditions, and as prostitutes or sexual toys. UNICEF supports non-governmental organisations (NGOs) fighting the commercial and sexual exploitation of children. The UN Office of the High Commissioner for Human Rights works to enforce the UN Convention on the Rights of the Child and to strengthen it with a new international protocol. UNESCO and the other specialised agencies also work hand in hand with the many hundreds of NGOs working in these fields to save children, to protect children, to comfort them after the violence has been inflicted on them.

And hence, the UNESCO International Clearinghouse on Children and Violence on the Screen, hosted at Göteborg University, also fulfils its role as a principal partner providing the services of a clearinghouse on research and information concerning children and the many kinds of media violence they must face in the world. For while technology is advancing, the social culture of the human species seems to be regressing.

Concerning pornography and paedophilia in electronic forms, particularly as they occur on the Internet, the problem is often not known or not well enough understood. Some people are even so frightened of the subject that they do not want to know anything about it. But mature adults of this day and age must know, for their sakes and for their children or their children's children. We need to analyse what young people will find on the Internet and how they may overcome these problems. We will attempt to present this briefly in this article, though there are still many more aspects and details that should be studied and prepared for. For as we go deeper into analysing the Internet, it will be seen that not all problems are solvable within the scope of what parents or even parents and teachers together can do. The scope of the problem is much larger, as large as the Internet itself. When crimes cross frontiers, police enforcement and judicial processes must also be able to transcend borders; otherwise there is no sanction against cybercrimes. Child predators can look forward to a future of crime without punishment, such as they are enjoying now, because so far laws and enforcement are inadequate to keep up with crimes on the Internet.

We also need to draw a map of the Internet to show where the good forces are: child protection agencies, police and judicial services, Internet service providers, NGOs. For while the Internet is like a vast road map of broad highways and avenues, there are also dimly lit side streets and dark alleys where children should not venture. We should try to point out to them and their parents where the 'help' stations are. It is a vast task because while help is virtually all around, physically it may be only in some countries or in some cities or presented only in a few languages, and by far most sites operate in English. We will nonetheless point out the more available ones and show how others can be found.

The main concern of UNESCO are the young children of today. Children who are at the very crossroads of life where education and culture, tolerance and peace should beckon them to create their place in society, and not let them succumb to the traffic of prostitution and other forms of sexual abuse. These are the children who should be in the schools that UNESCO and its Member States seek to assist and for which the Organisation seeks to provide the latest resources and techniques in education, science and culture. The minds of children are the seeding grounds for the peace of the next generation.

"Who destroys children, destroys the future of society", said Ms Homayra Sellier, President of the World Citizens' Movement to Protect Innocence in Danger. She also said in Brussels last 17 March 2000 at the international forum "Fighting Paedophilia on the Internet" (organised by the Association Mondiale des Amis de l'Enfance in co-operation with the Movement): "A government that cannot protect its children has no right to govern its people." This should remind all of us, particularly governments, that they do have a serious obligation to study and fulfil the UN Convention on the Rights of the Child. A particular area where governments, specifically their parliaments and lawmaking bodies, can make a major contribution is to strengthen laws to protect children from harm in the media and on the Internet, and to sign agreements to make extraterritorial laws operable. Many countries still have weak outdated laws in this respect, some have no laws at all.

While seeking to protect children from the dangers of the Internet, it is also important to distinguish and punish the real criminals, and not destroy the tools, the new communication and information technologies, the creative environment which offers the means of transferring culture and education, as well as, unfortunately, child pornography and paedophilia. All too often, the temptation is merely to legislate against pornography and paedophilia on the Internet, in legal formulations that are difficult to separate from outright censorship. UNESCO has an ethical mandate to promote the free flow of ideas by word and image, a wider and better-balanced dissemination of information at international as well as national levels *without any obstacle to the freedom of expression*. The only way to cure the ills of freedom is to ensure more freedom, and the only way to cure the ills of democracy is to have more democracy. Censorship is not a solution.

This article will proceed to explain what are the real problems with the Internet as concerns young children, and attempt to review some of the solutions that have been operating for the last few years.

What is the real problem with the Internet?

Will children really find such pornographic images when surfing on the Internet for music to download or games to play? Are child predators waiting on every site to kidnap young children? What exactly is the danger?

The Belgian MAPI group (Movement Against Paedophiles on the Internet) does not confine the concept of child pornography to images alone. It defines child pornography as

> any material depicting children in explicitly sexual situations or inciting the sexual exploitation of children.

Interpol has established a very broad definition of child pornography:

> Child pornography is the consequence of exploitation or sexual abuse perpetrated on a child. It may be defined as any means of depicting or promoting the sexual exploitation of a child, including in written and/or audio form, centred on sexual acts committed by, or on the genital organs of, a child.

It is important to bear these concepts in mind, as there are several shades of pornography to be found on the Internet, some illegal, some not. Many offensive and vulgar, but not necessarily illegal.

Images of child pornography

Specialist psychology researcher Rachel O'Connell, University of Central Lancashire, UK, has studied pornographic and paedophile sites for several years. She presented a summary to UNESCO at the Expert Meeting on "Sexual Abuse of Children, Child Pornography and Paedophilia on the Internet" in Paris, 18-19 January 1999. To date, she has found no more than fifty sites (i.e., newsgroups) that really show or trade images of child pornography in the legally criminal sense of the word. Even supposing 100 per cent error, this means that there are probably no more than a hundred such sites around the world. These are accessed only by complicated codes and passwords, and thus normally accessible only by a small group of persons with whom the site owners or managers have cultivated a certain confidence and trust. This relationship is cultivated over several tradings or 'swaps' of photos usually increasing in daringness or illegality, such as images showing sado-masochism, torture and sometimes killing. As these sites are illegal and pursued by police from various countries, including Interpol, it is highly unlikely that a young child would fall accidentally upon one of these sites. For those who traffic these images commercially, the volume of business these few sources can transact go into several hundred gigabytes of digital storage.

Images of adult pornography and faked child pornography

One can, however, find many sites that offer images of adult pornography and what could be called 'pseudo child pornography'. It is called pseudo child pornography because the persons presented are not minors in the legal sense of the term, that is, they are not below the legal age of majority taken as 18 years in most, but not all, countries. But through make-up, hairstyle, kind of clothing and the background setting they are made to appear younger than they actually are.

A number of sites have also been reported that present nudity of young persons, boys and girls. These are usually photos of children and young teenagers taken at nudist camps. But at first sight, it is not always clear whether these images are illegal pornography or whether they merely portray nudity. When there is an undue emphasis on the sexual parts, or stances or poses which are usually not natural but contrived to 'entice', these may be said to go beyond just simple nudity. And hence the definition of pornography adhered to by MAPI is the more inclusive.

There is another form of 'pseudo pornography' using digital techniques, also called 'morphing'. Examples of morphing were shown in the well known film *Terminator* towards the end when the enemy cop's hand became a steel spike and struck through an elevator door, or when he appeared to emerge from the flat black and white harlequin tiled floor and take the form of a policeman in a black and white uniform. In the same manner some pornographers take unclothed bodies of girls or boys and attach the heads of younger boys and girls to make the person look like a child or to make innocent boys and girls look like sex perverts. In some cases it is not easy to apply the law since it is difficult to determine the involvement of the children in this kind of 'morphed' pornography where all the action stems from the image manipulator. Nor is it simple to tell whether the images are illegal pornography, unless one includes the aspect of the 'intention to entice'.

These images are almost always offensive, vulgar and can be harmful to young children, instilling in them at a young age a cheap outlook on human values, the worth of human beings and human sexuality, making another person's body equivalent to commercial merchandise. For these and many other reasons, there should be ways to limit young children's access to these images. Whether these images are also illegal or not, depends on the laws of the country where they are produced, where they are presented and where they are received. Some countries may outlaw adult pornography exhibiting persons of less than the legal age of majority, 18 in some countries, but 17 or even 16 in others; some may outlaw all kinds of pornography, that is, regardless of the age of the persons presented.

In countries where these images are illegal, they can be voluntarily removed from access by the Internet service provider (ISP) under request from the police, judiciary or the appointed authority, or sometimes on the advice of trustworthy and credible child protection agencies. As a matter of fact, most ISPs prefer to remove these sites voluntarily rather than have the whole server closed down or be labelled as having a questionable reputation because of these salacious sites. For such sites also affect their good business relations with other potential customers. When they are offensive and even harmful, but strictly not illegal, teachers, parents and family guardians have to resort to other means to prevent children from coming upon these sites.

One certain method is the parent's personal and continual (not nagging) advice, and seeking to learn and surf on the Net together with children, thus showing them good sites and helping them avoid bad sites. Since parents are not always home to render this service, but their children may have access to the computer in their absence, a help to ensuring safe surfing is the use of technical filters. A filter is an additional software that can be purchased, installed on the computer and programmed by the parent and child together. It is best to do this together so the child learns *why* he has agreed to block certain sites. For once a child understands how to programme a filter, he can also deprogramme the filter or turn it off in the parent's absence. Hence a co-operative approach to the use of filters is recommended.

Images attractive to paedophiles

Yet another set of images are those that are attractive to paedophiles, although they may appear otherwise completely normal to everyone else. Their main purpose is to inspire paedophiles or nourish their hopes of meeting young children, such as those in the photos. In these cases, children are usually clothed, or at least in shorts or a swimming trunks; they are usually young boys playing sports outdoors. Some are young movie actors that have faces and a physique attractive to paedophiles. But otherwise, there is nothing illegal in these images. You could find similar photos in a catalogue of children's clothing. While these images, found easily everywhere, are provocative for paedophiles, they are hardly illegal and impossible to outlaw. These kinds of images are shown on many of the 40,000 and more paedophile sites on the Internet.

Chat rooms

Another feature of the Internet, where child predators can meet children and seek to meet or kidnap them, is the chat room. In effect this is a large electronic bulletin board, where surfers may offer their name and start up a conversation with whomever wishes to respond. For obvious reasons, it is best for children to give only a nick name or a pen name to avoid their being traced by prospective predators or even by unwanted intruders. Some chat rooms are entirely free, that is, there is no moderator to give a topic or guide discussions. These can be very risky for young children, unless they have been well trained or are supervised at home or in school. A moderated chat room has a full time supervisor who, for example, monitors all the dialogue and may intervene to warn a surfer to use appropriate language, or may chase someone away who appears to be entering into salacious dialogue or seeking to set up a questionable rendezvous or meeting with a young surfer. It is here where child predators can easily put on the guise of a young person and seek to court a younger surfer to a meeting. A typical dialogue, culled by Parry Aftab of Cyberangels from several such dialogues and interviews with children, would go like this:

> On the Net they (child predators) can hide behind anonymity and pretend they are just another child, to lure children in ways that we are not yet prepared to teach them to avoid. Chat rooms, instant messages, ICRs (Internet Chat Relays) are like beeper messages that go right to our children. Anything that allows someone to speak in real time to our children on a one-on-one basis is dangerous.
>
> Children normally enter chat rooms. Paedophiles take note of this, they follow conversations and track children who are lonely. One child may send messages like: "My parents are getting divorced... I hate my mother, she never buys me the computer game I want... I don't like her boy friend either."
>
> The paedophile comes in and says: "My parents are getting divorced, too... I hate my mother... I can never get the game I want, until Uncle Timmy got it for me."
>
> "Oh yeah?" says the first child, trying to seek a companion in misery or possibly a solution.
>
> "Yeah", says the paedophile, "all you gotta do is go to the mall and meet Uncle Timmy."

Children require close supervision for work in chat rooms. Children should never give their real name online, nor their address nor the name of their school nor any information that may help in identifying where he or she lives. Of course, they should never give any information about the credit card of their parents!

Sites with stories, essays and other writings

The most subtle trap for children, and therefore the most risky because it is highly underestimated, are the several thousand seemingly innocent sites run by paedophiles to exhibit their stories, essays, real histories of themselves or the members of their association, photos of themselves or friends or even of celebrities who are attractive to paedophiles. Many paedophile sites aim precisely at proving that their deviant behaviour is normal or acceptable by the very fact that they are openly and prominently displayed on the Internet. Like water dripping relentlessly on a stone to crack it, repeated exposure to paedophile writings, essays and images can lead children and the general public to believe that there is nothing wrong with free sex for children of any age, that there is nothing illegal or harmful with the sexual abuse of children or in displaying such acts through pornography or paedophile web sites on the Internet.

Some 40,000 such sites have been identified by researchers and child protection groups. Their site names are simple and easy to fall into, and some are even attractive to children.

Drug abuse, trafficking of children, child prostitution and AIDS

The threat of sexual abuse of children should not be seen in isolation, for it is not an isolated phenomenon. It often happens that we see only that part of the crime concerning the child and not the entire organised crime behind it or other aspects. If there are over a million cases of child AIDS victims in South Asia last year, the mix of causes certainly includes child abuse and child prostitution among them, which is preceded by child abduction, kidnapping and child trafficking of many kinds. Drugs are involved as well, as a means to keep young victims manageable but also to lure them into habits difficult to break, thus forcing them to remain within the criminal ring. One vice thus easily leads to another. The difficulty is how to break in. Meanwhile, children's rights are being trampled upon and violated with impunity. Undoubtedly, more research is needed on these aspects where one social ill crosses into another.

Ways to cope

It is not easy to propose solutions. None is totally satisfactory. There is always one that could be left out. Nonetheless one has to make a start somewhere. This section attempts to review those organisations that have worked to protect children online by going online themselves and by using the technology of electronic databases and transmission. Inadvertently we trace a preliminary sketch of the evolution of these web sites over the last few years. Their shades of difference will also show how they developed differently in different regions and in response to different aspects of the problem. Their growth is exponential and there are today perhaps a hundred times more than there were even just five years ago. And there are many other sites that offer information or tips, like the Yellow Pages for Kids, Teen Tips, Tips for Kids, Safe Surfing by Disney Online. Indeed, this only shows that the study of these web sites is in itself a research worth undertaking. The main point in presenting the sites below is to show the comprehensive sites that combine information, reflection and action, and those that have been at the forefront.

Child protection agencies

Child protection agencies online have been established mainly in the United States of America and most have had a history of at least five to seven years. While most of these are per se non-commercial, some also have commercial aspects (like sale of books) to contribute to their sustenance. Others have a page for surfers to make donations online with tax rebates or other tax incentive measures. Protection groups – like Cyberangels and Safeguarding Our Children - United Mothers (SOC-UM) – are in many ways the pioneers of child safety on the Net and their experiences have been thoroughly grounded in legislation, Internet operations, and the various nuances of pornography, paedophilia and abuse of children through the Internet.

Cyberangels (http://www.cyberangels.org) seeks basically to educate parents, teachers and child Internet users on online safety. They also have teams of volunteers who search the Internet for child pornography and work with law enforcement agencies around the world to report paedophile luring activities online. They hold classes online to teach safety and have one of the most popular volunteer tiplines at the site to report cybercrimes against children. Parry Aftab manages the site and personally answers most if not all mail; her lawyer background provides further substance to the insights on her pages. She is also Head of the U.S. National Action Group of *Innocence in Danger*. Her first book, *A Parents' Guide to the Internet* (New York: SC Press, 1997), is a simple introduction to the pleasures and hazards of the web. Her second book, *The Parents' Guide to Protecting Your Children in Cyberspace* (New York: McGraw-Hill, 2000), culls from a longer experience and provides straight off the shoulder advice.

Safeguarding Our Children - United Mothers (SOC-UM) (http://www.soc-um.org) is similarly oriented to public awareness, education, and prevention of child abuse. Its web site serves as a resource to those who have been wounded by childhood abuse. It is highly informative, interactive, and provides access to information both for safety tips and for understanding the phenomena of child abuse and paedophilia. It is managed by Debbie Mahoney who is a fierce advocate for child protection.

In Europe and elsewhere, such helping agents are relatively rare. A number of sites went up following the "World Congress Against Commercial Sexual Exploitation of Children" which took place in Stockholm, Sweden, in 1996. Among these were, apart from the hotline *children@risk.sn.no*, the several sites of *Redd Barna* (Save The Children Norway) in English and various Scandinavian languages. The addresses of these web sites are for Norway: http://childhouse.uio.no/redd_barna, and for Sweden: http://www.rb.se/engindex.htm, which also contains material about the Stockholm World Congress.

ECPAT International (End Child Prostitution, Child Pornography and Trafficking of Children for Sexual Purposes) works today on political action, law-making and law enforcement, awareness-raising in the tourist industry, education and media coverage. ECPAT has national groups and affiliates in 50 countries. A clippings service is available on their web site: http://www.ecpat.net.

One of the more recent and dynamic ones is *Telefono Arcobaleno* (Rainbow Telephone) in Sicily, where a priest, Don Fortunato di Noto and his team of technicians, trace pornographers and traffickers of children in all parts of the globe, using technical tools and the Internet. Their web site (http://www.viesse.it/arcobaleno) is mainly in Italian but some texts are also available in English. They work closely with the state police as well as with researchers, particularly the CENSIS Foundation in Rome. Rainbow Telephone actively contributes to the defence and protection of the inviolable rights of children, by fighting against every form of abuse and maltreatment. The association monitors the entire Internet network against paedophilia, reporting games and programmes harmful to minors. As of last February 2000, the association identified and censured some 7,650 paedophile sites on the Internet. They further identified the countries where these servers are operating: 55 per cent are in the USA, 20 per cent in Asia, 13 per cent in Eastern Europe, 7 per cent in Western Europe and 5 per cent in the Mideast. Some 200,000 photos and 1,500 films were transacted. Last year, their efforts paid off when they sent a group of paedophiles in Brazil to police prosecution for operating a network for showing and distributing images of children chained and in obscene poses.

The Movement Against Paedophilia on the Internet (MAPI) is a research group working on paedophilia and child pornography on the Internet. Their objectives are to promote interdisciplinary research on the field, inform the users of the Internet and be available for the Internet providers concerning advice and recommendations. The site: http://www.info.fundp.ac.be/~mapi/plan.html will show the complete MAPI report on paedophilia on the Internet. But from being a purely research oriented group, MAPI has moved to being proactive with the recent publication of their brochure, *Internet and Child Pornography– how to deal with it?* (in French, located at: http://www.info.fundp.ac.be/~mapi/mapi-fr.html).

Casa Alianza, a non-governmental organisation (http://www.casa-alianza.org), is dedicated to the rehabilitation and defence of street children in Guatemala, Honduras, and Mexico. *Casa Alianza* monitors and cares for about 3,000 street children, most of whom have been orphaned by civil war, abused or rejected by their families, and who as a result are begging, stealing or selling themselves for a hot meal, a shower, a clean bed. The organisation has actively militated for justice even against threats to their own personnel. "Child prostitution exists in Costa Rica", said its Director Bruce Harris to the international forum in Brussels last 17 March 2000. "When you pay for sex, you convert the body of the other person into merchandise and you commit an aggression. Those of us who watch in silence are accomplices of this aggression." *Casa Alianza* has contributed to arranging for a two week inspection visit of the UN Special Rapporteur to Guatemala.

The PREDA Foundation (People's Recovery, Empowerment and Development Assistance Foundation) (http://www.preda.org) is a small but pro-active, charitable, not-for-profit organisation working on a national and international level for Human Rights, especially Women's and Children's Rights. It runs a residential therapeutic community for abused and exploited children, therapy and counselling techniques, and help for battling against discrimination and racism. PREDA campaigns against child labour, the sexual exploitation of children, and seeks to educate about AIDS. There is a full archive for documentation, information and news campaigns. PREDA has also been instrumental in new legislation concerning conviction of paedophiles and child abusers.

Childnet International (http://www.childnet-int.org) networks with child welfare and educational groups, governments and international agencies to provide information on how children can benefit from and be protected in using international communications systems like the Internet. "On this site you can find out how we are developing projects which promote the new media to children and widen access to those who are marginalized, as well as see how we are working at the strategic level on initiatives which protect children in the use of new technologies." Related to this is the *Internet Hotline Providers in Europe (INHOPE) Association*, a project initially funded under the European Commission Daphne programme to bring together the main hotlines/tiplines in Europe that deal with child pornography and other illegal material on the Internet. The Association is serviced by Childnet International – see site on: www.childnet-int.org/hotlines – but has a web site of its own: www.inhope.org.

While UNESCO is not per se a child protection agency, it has established a major web site called *Innocence in Danger* (www.unesco.org/webworld/innocence) to act as a gateway to fellow child protection organisations. After the welcome page which presents the *World Citizens' Movement to Protect Children Online*, including twenty national action groups, the site points to over 40 child protection agencies; furnishes papers from recent conferences; provides a calendar of coming events; and offers a news service to report on these conferences or other events. It is also planned to open a new site addressed directly to children and hosted by two puppets of Bululu Theatre, Agathe and Bartolo.

National police and Interpol

Many police services now have departments or services that handle crimes on the Internet, including pornography and paedophilia. In some countries, police agents are trained in informatics and some of them do searches for criminal sites. In France (as in Hong Kong for several years), recent laws have been enacted to require police handling such cases to turn the children over to certified medical doctors and psychologists for examination and care prior to police or judicial questioning. This ensures proper treatment of the child in these delicate circumstances and that his statements are not misconstrued or taken out of context. In other cases, care is taken to ensure the truthfulness of child witness and its usability in court.

Interpol is perhaps the most attuned to these problems because in almost every case, the use of the Internet has transformed what may have begun as a national police case to an international affair. Interpol has its own unit concerned with cybercrimes and hosts a web site providing information and contact numbers.

Because of the international dimension of crimes on the Internet, the International Bureau for Children's Rights, dealing with juridical process and extraterritorial legislation in response to the international dimension of child sexual exploitation, has become extremely active in recent years. The Bureau has held regular tribunals for children's cases in France (1997), Brazil (1998) and Sri Lanka (1999). The results of these tribunals and recommendations for more innovative legislative action is contained in their *Global Report: International Dimensions of the Sexual Exploitation of Children* (Montreal: International Bureau for Children's Rights, 2000). Their site is at: http://www.web.net/~tribunal.

These are but a few of the organisations, associations and agencies seeking to protect children from the dangers of media and the Internet, as well as all new forms of communication technology to come. It shows that there is a growing phalanx of troops ready and willing to fight this battle and that the walls of silence surrounding child abuse are quickly breaking down, whether this is through advocates who speak on these matters, or journalists who report them. The symbiosis is beginning to take place.

While technology advances and some of the human family regress to animal behaviour, there are some who see the moral and ethical implications and act to redress the balance. But it is a battle in which everyone has a role, where no work is too humble to be undertaken or too lowly to be acknowledged. The best contributions to this work have not been in the form of money, but in offering sincere help: students who work at documents in a conference, an artist who designs a cover, a trainee who photocopies until 4 in the morning.

But there is room for big contributions, too. Lots of room!

The UN Convention on the Rights of the Child

Article 34

States Parties undertake to protect the child from all forms of sexual exploitation and sexual abuse. For these purposes, States Parties shall in particular take all appropriate national, bilateral and multilateral measures to prevent:

(a) The inducement or coercion of a child to engage in any unlawful sexual activity;

(b) The exploitative use of children in prostitution or other unlawful sexual practises;

(c) The exploitative use of children in pornographic performances and materials.

Audience Perceptions of Violence and Sex in the Media

The Audience's Perception of Media Violence

Review of Research in the UK

Andrea Millwood Hargrave

This article presents a review of recent research findings in the United Kingdom on the audience's perception of violence on television, including the views of young people. Much of the work discussed here was commissioned by the Broadcasting Standards Commission (although not exclusively) and so has a British slant to it. This is an important point because the article will not cover, except in passing, studies which aim to prove that televisual violence can lead to actual violence. Little work of that nature has been conducted in the UK. Much British research has tested the active nature of the relationship between the audience and the screen, and allows the notion of 'influence' more easily than 'behavioural effects'. Hence the Commission's role in advising broadcasters about the care to be exercised in the depiction of violence, particularly in programmes aimed at the young who are felt to be more vulnerable to influence.

Certainly on-screen violence affects public perception. There are many stories in the media (especially the press) that seek to link behaviour with a televised programme or a film. The Commission has conducted tracking studies annually for seven years, asking questions of the public. Whether the answer is prompted or unprompted, violence remains the issue of most concern. In 1998, one-third of respondents said spontaneously that they had a concern about an issue on television; a third of these (32%) mentioned violence.[1] When prompted with a choice of issues, including violence, nearly three in five respondents (58%) now mentioned it. This has been a decreasing figure, however, and it will be interesting to see if the trend continues.

Young people (those aged between 16 and 24 years) were far less likely to mention that any issue was of concern to them (only 16 per cent mentioned they had a concern, unprompted). However, when prompted, they were more likely to mention violence (59%) than any of the other issues.

The tracking study has, in addition to this survey of public opinion, two other parts: a content analysis of incidents of violence, sexual activity and bad language across a sample of free-to-air and satellite programming, and an audience monitoring panel.

In line with the findings from the public opinion survey, these other data showed decreases in 1998, both in the number of violent incidents captured through content analysis and in reports of violent incidents on television (reports made by panels of viewers). Importantly, the viewer panels also noted a decrease in the amount of violence they thought editorially unjustified: less than a quarter of violent incidents (23%) were *not* thought to be appropriate within their editorial context. This has been a consistent finding, with violence far more likely to be thought justified within its programme context than either the use of bad language or the depiction of sexual activity.

This rather important point – the ability of the audience to see whether an incident was gratuitous or justified – is key to much of the research discussed below. It underlines again the view that television audiences are, by and large, sophisticated viewers who have developed critical skills that allow a significant interaction between themselves and the screen.

Definition of violence

The most recent work looking at audience attitudes towards violence came from an industry initiative, and was the result of a debate between broadcasters and regulators (including the Broadcasting Standards Commission). In 1995-96 the industry conducted an extensive content analysis of violent incidents. This analysis had shown that violence accounted for relatively little broadcast time (0.72% of all terrestrial broadcast time in 1995/96 could be defined as 'violence').[2] The then government asked the Commission to host a seminar which included a discussion of these findings. Programme makers at the seminar challenged the definition of violence used in these 'academic' analyses and it was agreed that a cross industry study should be undertaken looking at how *the audience* defined 'violence'. Concurrently the Commission, with the BBC (British Broadcasting Corporation) and the ITC (Independent Television Commission), set up a Joint Working Party on Violence with an independent Chairman,[3] which reported publicly in 1998.

The research by David Morrison et al. was published in 1999 and in the introduction, it is stated:

> The purpose of the research… was twofold. We, at the intellectual level, wanted to determine how violence was defined, and at the practical level to have information that would assist us in determining the perceived level of violence on television as opposed to the level as defined by some objective scoring… The research was not concerned with taste – that is, whether viewers enjoyed or disliked a particular scene of screen violence – but rather with how violence was determined or defined.[4]

The research was predominantly qualitative in nature. A total of 12 groups of eight respondents each were recruited according to their experience of and attitudes towards violence. Each group was played clips from programmes, most of which had already been transmitted on British television. Respondents were allowed to edit these clips but had to explain, at each stage, their decision for the edits they were making. In this process, they clarified how they defined violence.

Each group brought different attitudes towards the way in which televisual violence was defined. The research showed, as other work has done, that the audience was not homogenous, but was made up of people with many different mind-sets and levels of tolerance to material which could offend. The area that was least clear involved attitudes towards factual programming: here respondents seemed to concentrate their minds on violence that was interpersonal and, if they did not see the actual act of violence, were less likely to define it as such. By definition, this excluded much factual material. The following quotations regarding a news footage of the bombing of a marketplace in Sarajevo are illustrative examples:

> It's not violent. It's more upsetting.
>
> This is more people caring for each other after the violence. The violence is when it actually happens.
>
> (Females, aged 18-24, with experience of violence)

This would contradict other work conducted by the same research team for the Commission in 1993, to be discussed later.[5]

This research on definitions showed that most respondents graded the violence they saw. The researchers outlined three categories of violent scene:

I. *Playful violence* – Seen to be unreal. Recognised as being 'entertainment' and not graphic.

II. *Depicted violence* – Designed to be realistic and can be very graphic.

III. *Authentic violence* – This was violence set within an environment that was recognised by the viewer. Domestic violence fell within this category or, for this British sample of respondents, material showing violence in contemporary Britain. Importantly, the way in which the scene was filmed had a bearing on how violent the viewer considered it.

All respondents brought to their viewing of violence their view of violence in real life. The researchers summarised: *What constitutes violence is an act which breaks a recognised code of behaviour.* Crucial to this was a sense of what was 'fair' in a violent exchange. Within this concept of 'fairness' were matters such as the balance of power between protagonists, the extent to which protagonists were felt to be helpless, and whether or not the violence received was 'deserved'. The researchers called this desire for fairness a 'primary definer' of violence.

'Secondary definers' were those that affected the weight of violence in a scene, such as the use of bad language, or gore. The researchers contended that these definers were determined by what had been learnt by viewers from the screen – while the primary definer was linked back to knowledge of actual violence. So, as we shall see, the secondary definers for a young audience, raised on Tarantino-like realism, were different from those for an older audience, some of who had seen violence, and its consequences, in war.

Young people aged 18-24

In total, four groups of young people, aged 18-24, were interviewed. Two groups, one male and one female, were recruited because of their familiarity with violence in real life. Yet, even for these groups where violence was a fact of life, there was a baseline against which they would judge on-screen violence. For them, violence occurred in a world where there were certain rules to be followed, even for violent conduct. Fairness and the balance of power between protagonists were crucial to their attitudes. However, they also understood that real life violence rarely was as depicted cinematically and that production techniques were employed to increase dramatic effect. In so doing, the level of violence within a scene was often increased. As one respondent said:

> People who get hit actually fall over sometimes and don't get up. People can get shot 20 times on some films and then get up. (Male, aged 18-24, with experience of violence)

The male respondents in this group enjoyed violence, by and large, and – crucially – enjoyed graphic representations of violence. The setting of the violence was also important to the way in which they rated it. One of the clips shown, taken from the Ken Loach film *Ladybird, Ladybird*, was of domestic violence in which a male character beats up his female partner, swearing at her viciously, while the children are seen to look on. The young men recognised aspects of the violence to come, such as changes in the male character's breathing:

> You can tell he's going to lose it (control) by the way he's breathing but I wouldn't have thought he would have lost it that much. (Male, aged 18-24, with experience of violence)

What made this scene particularly violent to this group of young males was that their sense of fairness was transgressed. The female character so obviously could not defend herself against the physically stronger male. A respondent said the violence might have felt more balanced if she had lashed out first or if the male character had had better reason to be so violent.

Interestingly, an item on bear baiting (in factual material) was felt by these young males to be 'sick', but did not fall within their definition of 'violence'. It went against their sense of fairness. They noted the gross imbalance of power between the protagonists (the bear's claws had been blunted and its teeth pulled so that it could not defend itself against its attackers, dogs). But it was not an act of interpersonal violence and so was not rated as 'violence' in this context.

Sympathy for a character's weakness, then, could be important in a definition of violence. So too, could empathy with the victim, especially for the group of young women, recruited for their experience of violence. The researchers argued that the more the victim was known and liked, the more likely it was that they would define a scene involving that victim as 'violent', however inexplicit the action. This was demonstrated by this female group's reaction to a scene of domestic violence, which was not graphic, from a popular soap opera.[6] Nonetheless, for this group, as with the men, the violence had to be witnessed, not just alluded to. The exception to this was the use of serious bad language which could add to or act as violence in itself. The scene of domestic violence from the film *Ladybird, Ladybird* described above, clearly fell into the category of 'violence'. Crucial to this group's reading of it was the perceived viciousness of the attack, both physical and verbal, not just the imbalance of power.

These two groups of young people were counter-balanced by a group each of men and women aged 18-24, for whom violence was not potentially part of their everyday life. The researchers found that the men within this group, like their counterparts described above, enjoyed violence, and used production techniques, such as spurting blood, to help them rate a scene as violent. The equivalent group of women, however, did not show any pleasure in viewing violence; indeed for many, violence was upsetting. This group edited most of the clips of violence they were shown quite heavily. In particular, and in contrast to their 'equivalent' group of men, they took away many of the production techniques employed in scenes such as the use of slow motion or the sounds of violence. Unlike many of the other groups, this group of young women also questioned the moral value of the scenes they saw. As the researchers said, 'this group assessed violence as much by their emotional response to it as by analytical yardsticks'. For them, the violence had to be more than pure entertainment and was required to serve a purpose. As a result, this group accepted quite graphic violence in films or programmes, as long as they were based on real life events.

Other groups

The research went on to consider many other groups, including parents with children living at home. It was found that being a parent did not affect a general definition of violence, unless the violence depicted involved children. Then, mothers with children living at home[7] appeared to consider scenes within the framework of their own families, and with an awareness that their sons (if they had them) may be involved in violence. Also the depicted presence of children in scenes of violence, such as the scene of domestic violence in the film mentioned above, actually made it seem *more violent* to these women.

The males recruited because they had children at home[8] did not apply this particular frame of reference to their viewing, although they were sensitive to the 9 o'clock Watershed (the time before which programming should be suitable for all the family). This group reacted strongly to the scene of domestic violence, and edited the children's presence out of it. However, unlike the mothers but like most other groups, these men did not think the presence of the children made the scene more violent, just more upsetting.

This group also underlined the researchers' contention that verbal violence could constitute 'violence': Within the domestic violence scene 'the verbal assault became akin to physical assault, by delivering hurt in the form of fear. It threatened the imminence of real physical hurt'.

Crucially, however, the researchers argued, from the findings of these groups – where, for some, violence was a factor of life – that 'in general, a diet of screen violence does not seem to lessen the shock of violence in real life. The two types of violence are experienced entirely differently'. In summary, the reality of violence was well differentiated for all these respondents from the depictions of on-screen, fictional violence.

Fictional violence

The report reviewed above showed that the audience itself tended to define 'violence' as an interpersonal and witnessed act. The fact that the audience views fictional violence in different terms from factual violence has been well documented. One respondent interviewed as part of the Commission's research into factual television said:

> ...no matter how realistically any kind of acting is done, you always know it's fiction, there is always something that tells you that it's fictional and it acts as a kind of barrier. (Man, 40-50 years old)

Generally, other research has concluded that audiences found factual violence more upsetting than fictional violence, because they understood what they saw was 'real'. However, viewers could still be distressed by fictional violence and much of the research in this area shows that reactions to violence in fictional television were determined by matters of context. Indeed, it was this argument that the programme makers used when rejecting the definitions used in content analyses.

Unlike the British analyses, a content analysis undertaken by a research consortium of four American universities studying violence in the media, explored how the manipulation of contextual features in violent television portrayals could influence the audience's reactions to violence.[9] While this was based in a tradition of 'effects' research, it is interesting to note this attempt to understand how the audience interprets and perceives violent imagery. Indeed there were many similarities with the British work already discussed. The US study found that the way in which violence was presented in a programme could have different meanings to the viewer. The researchers went on to hypothesise that these meanings, in turn, could produce varied reactions in terms of personal aggression, fear and desensitisation. The contextual factors were broken down into categories:

- *Nature of the perpetrator* – violence carried out by a 'good guy' evoked a different reaction to that perpetrated by a 'bad guy'.
- *Nature of the target* – if the viewer could share the character's emotional experiences and perceived the character to be likeable, the level of fear of violence felt by the viewer increased.
- *Presence of weapons* – guns were seen as the most violent weapons.
- *Reason for violence* – unjustified violence was more likely to induce feelings of unease than socially sanctioned or altruistic violence. Therefore, violence used in self-defence was more likely to be seen as justified in a programme because the perpetrator of the violence was perceived as innocent and the victim was seen as guilty.
- *Extent and graphicness of violence* – the research reported that persistent close-ups of violence were interpreted as more violent than violence filmed from a distance.
- *Realism of violence* – the more realistic the nature of the violence, the more likely it was that viewers would be distressed.
- *Rewards and punishments* – the fears viewers expressed were reduced if the perpetrator of the violence was seen to receive the punishment he/she deserved.
- *Consequences of violence* – the research suggested that the audience judged scenes in which violence resulted in observable harm and pain to be more violent than scenes that did not show the results of violence.

This study, while a content analysis and a 'count' of violent incidents in programming, sought to recognise that viewers' interpretations of fictional violence were based on a complex set of values and judgements about the various different elements that made up any violent act.

The Broadcasting Standards Commission, which undertakes content analysis as part of its tracking study, has also sought to reflect these variables. It has attempted to measure incidents of violence against the 'definers' outlined by the British study and has incorporated the measures of 'consequence' from the US study. Results using these different measures are to be found in the Commission's Monitoring Report series.[10]

Years earlier, Barrie Gunter[11] had shown the complexities of response to perceptions of violence. He conducted twelve experimental studies in which respondents were shown clips from various fictional genres and asked how they felt about the violence portrayed in each. The programmes were British and American crime series, Westerns, science fiction and animation.

The results from these studies were broadly similar: British respondents rated violent acts in British crime series as more violent than violence in American crime drama series. Gunter suggests that viewer's responses to fictional violence were affected by the closeness to home of the violence portrayed. Violent behaviour in both the animation and science fiction programmes was not classed as 'violent' by the respondents because it was not seated in reality. Other factors such as the nature of the fictional characters who inflicted the violence, how the harm was inflicted and how much damage was done to the recipient also had a bearing on respondents' views.

Gunter's research showed, too, that the audience had clear opinions about the appropriateness of the level of violence used. This was especially true if the violence did not seem appropriate to the provocation. In crime genres, for example, the level of violence used to enforce the law should be appropriate to the crime committed – viewers would be particularly disturbed by a non-violent car thief being gunned down by a policeman.

Some forms of physical violence were perceived to be more violent than others. As with the US study – but preceding it by many years! – Gunter found that shootings were classed as more violent than stabbings, but were not found to be as disturbing. Fist fighting was the least distressing form of violent action. Gunter and his colleague, Adrian Furnham, proposed that because stabbings were rarer in British crime drama than shootings, viewers were more shocked by them. In contrast they had become accustomed, and thus desensitised, to shootings.[12] No evidence, however, was provided to support this reasoning. Gunter also found that, in general, viewers were more troubled by violence against, and by, women than such acts involving men. Violence involving women was especially distressing if it was featured in a scenario to which the viewer could readily relate, such as the domestic violence scene mentioned above, from the later work by Morrison et al.

The effect of contextual factors on perceptions of the suitability of violence was also discussed in a study undertaken by the Commission's predecessor body, the Broadcasting Standards Council.[13] A sample of viewers were sent video tapes of three full length fictional programmes and were asked how they would edit each programme before transmission.

The research showed respondents were widely accepting of the violence shown in an edition of the British crime drama serial, *The Bill*, broadcast on a mainstream channel. It depicted the killing, by police marksmen, of bank robbers who had held a gun to a cashier's head. An exceedingly small number of respondents either wanted to edit the programme or not show it at all.

The second programme was a drama about football hooliganism, *The Firm*, transmitted on a minority channel. It featured several violent scenes including a young black boy having his face slashed, an infant who put a blade in his mouth and various gang fights. Some respondents were so disgusted by the violence that they refused to watch the programme and sent back the tapes.

Out of the 54 respondents aged 35 or over, 57 per cent did not want the drama to be transmitted, whilst a significant number, 26 per cent, thought it could be shown in its entirety. Fewer of the viewers under 35 years of age (33%) did not want the drama to be broadcast and 50 per cent of this age group had no problem with showing it in full. The main concern of those who did not want to see *The Firm* transmitted at all was that they felt it glorified a certain type of violence, and they considered that it would encourage people to act in an irresponsible manner:

> I disliked everything about it. I think it encourages everything we want stamped out in this country and it helps to glorify mindless violence to those inclined. (Female, unskilled working class, over 35)

Importantly, those who were in support of showing the drama in full thought the violent imagery was necessary to convey effectively the programme's central message.

The third programme the respondents watched was the horror film *Nightmare on Elm Street* which includes particularly bloody special effects. The majority of respondents thought the film could be transmitted in its entirety so long as it was shown after the Watershed at 9.00 p.m. However, 25 per cent of the older respondents and 21 per cent of the younger ones did not think the film was suitable for transmission on television at all. They were disgusted by the violence, especially the special effects. Those respondents who thought the film could be broadcast, but only after editing, wanted to change the killing scenes, particularly the first murder.

In this study, the researcher drew on the concept of 'deep and shallow play', a concept originally developed by the anthropologist, Clifford Geertz. The suggestion was that viewers interpreted violent imagery in different ways according to the context of the violence shown. Viewers related directly to violence in 'deep play' fiction – *The Firm* was a drama about football hooligans and showed violence that was perceived to be indicative of British life. In contrast, violence in 'shallow play' fiction did not worry respondents because it was inflicted on a society they could not identify with. *Nightmare on Elm Street* was a horror film and, as such, the violence shown was socially, politically, and, for the most part, psychologically removed from society.

Factual violence

Reference has been made already to the perceived differences between fictional and factual violence – it has been suggested that respondents often found factual violence more upsetting than fictional violence, but they were also more accepting of it. Perhaps the most important recent work in this area was conducted by Morrison and his team in 1993, who also undertook the (later) work on audience views of the definition of violence, described above.

This team pioneered the editing group technique, which was used to considerable effect in this 1993 study of attitudes to factual television. Groups of men and women were recruited by age categories and shown a variety of factual material.[14] They were allowed to edit the material they were shown to make it more 'acceptable' to them, but had to explain the reasons for their edits.

Importantly, many of the criteria that affected audience perceptions of fiction seem to apply to perceptions of actual violence. Different items created different reactions. In response to a local news item about a bar fight, which showed graphic shots of the victim's wound and was accompanied by a detailed description of the fight, each respondent group made different comments. Most agreed the report had over-sensationalised the event – it was clear that viewers did not want the news to dramatise events or create sensation. They regarded the news as the purest form of factual programme and objected to the dramatic words of the voice-over. Some of the young female respondents felt they did not need to know the level of detail that the item provided. Some, notably the 24-35 aged group of men, made a judgement about the men involved in the reported brawl, saying they would be the 'type' of persons used to such violence. This group of men would have been more shocked and, indeed, more sympathetic if the victim was seen to be someone not used to being caught up in such violence. This link between audience reaction and sympathy or empathy with the victim was noted in other factual material, and had also been found in research into fictional representations.

Footage from the Vietnam war was shown, including a scene showing the shooting of a 'Vietcong' suspect. Most of the groups had seen it at least once before and all of them were shocked by the scenes. Once again, however, sympathy and, by extension, emotional upset as a response to the scene was dependent on the perceived and accorded status of the victim. A woman who had felt strongly for the 'Vietcong' man changed her views after she was told that he was suspected of several murders.

Despite the distress caused to them by this footage, most respondents felt it was necessary and acceptable to show the pictures. Most groups expressed a desire for the material to be shown after the Watershed; others suggested a less graphic pre-Watershed version whilst others suggested a warning. One group, the 40-55 year old women, suggested that if the footage were from a current war, there would be more justification in broadcasting it as news at any time. Since the material featured in a documentary, it should be transmitted later. What appears to be operating is the principle of 'need to know' or 'duty to be informed' about current events, a principle that did not apply so clearly to past events.

This difference between the news and documentaries was highlighted again when groups had to consider the suitability of other footage they were shown. Respondents thought that documentaries should elaborate on the basic information provided by the news. The nature of a documentary, describing past events, also made it easier to accept difficult content, since viewers could expect to know beforehand the type of scenes that might be transmitted.

What the research findings also show is that violence in war reports was perceived differently from violence in civilian circumstances. War is war and it was expected to be violent. In a study of the audience's opinions about television and the Gulf war, the majority of respondents (70%) felt it was right to show all the footage they were presented with.[15] However, over half the sample (57%) felt that footage showing captured coalition pilots should not be shown on British television. Many respondents thought these pictures were too upsetting to be shown; this opinion was voiced specifically because of concern for the pilots' relatives.

In the same study, focus groups were used to test responses to different levels of coverage of the bombing of the Amiriya bunker. Reports of the bombing had been transmitted by the BBC and ITN (British news agencies), and WTN (a Canadian/American agency). The BBC and ITN films used edited footage of the human devastation caused by the strike, whilst the WTN film showed more explicit material, including charred bodies. The BBC and ITN material was accepted by most of the groups despite its distressing nature, because it was held to have a clear purpose. In contrast, the WTN footage was deemed to go far beyond what was necessary to explain the event that had occurred. As with the research into violence in factual television, the differences between such material being used for news as opposed to documentary purposes was highlighted – respondents agreed that more graphic material could be shown in documentaries, as the viewer could expect, and therefore be mentally prepared for, violent images in a documentary about war.

Similar findings were reported in an earlier survey of public response to footage of the Falklands war.[16] Respondents were asked whether all or only part of the material available should be shown. The research found that respondents placed limits on what they wanted to see, and they were only marginally less sensitive about seeing explicit coverage of dying or wounded Argentinean soldiers. However, the message was quite clear – greater consideration needed to be given to the sensibilities of the British audience if injury and death involved British nationals.

As shown, documentaries were allowed greater licence to use more violent imagery than news by respondents, as long as the Watershed was applied and warnings were given. However, it had to be used to make a valid point – gratuitous use of violence was not tolerated in this genre.

One documentary used in the research was a programme which investigated the psychological make up of serial killers.[17] It was generally felt that the programme did not have a justifiable purpose and that the interview with a murderer was misjudged. This man expressed his view strongly:

> The public had not been served anything from that. Absolutely nothing wrong in producing that for experts, pathologists, if it's an insight into them sort of persons, but what the hell is me, or the public, getting from that, I just don't know. (Male satellite viewer)

This view echoes the argument about news footage – respondents considered the showing of violent scenes justifiable only if the display of violence lent purpose to the story. Another concern about this particular documentary was for the relatives of the victims. Respondents thought such a programme with such explicit descriptions of the violence inflicted on victims would be likely to cause extreme distress to any friends or family that might be watching. It is also worth noting that several viewers who had seen the programme when it was broadcast, said that they had been disturbed by it, and the memory of it had stayed with them for longer than any fictional violence they had ever seen.

Another documentary shown to the groups featured a dramatic reconstruction of a kidnapping, using the stylistic techniques of slow motion, soft focus shots and sound effects. Most of the groups said the use of dramatic techniques made it more like a drama than a documentary, and they felt these over-sensationalised a factual story.

The researchers hypothesised four main factors which they considered had an influence on viewer perceptions and reactions to violence in factual television:

- *The Factor of Closeness* – The more distance, in terms of geography, time and other relationships, between the violence and the viewer, the less disturbing it was found to be.
- *The Factor of Certainty* – Viewers were less likely to be shocked either if they knew the outcome of a violent scene or if they fully understood what was happening in it.
- *The Factor of Status* – Viewers were likely to tolerate a higher degree of violence if the victim is regarded to have lower claim to justice. The victim's perceived innocence was an important factor in how much violence was accepted and how disturbing it was likely to be.
- *The Factor of Minimalism* – Violent imagery, whether real or reconstructed, should not use greater detail in factual programmes than was needed to illustrate the point being made. Dramatic techniques were not thought appropriate to this type of material.

Children's perceptions of violence on television

Much of the concern about the effects of the media on behaviour has concentrated on children and their propensity for imitative responses to what they watch, read or hear.[18] Yet it is interesting that studies find that concern amongst parents that children might become violent as a result of watching media violence was almost always voiced with reference to 'other people's' children.[19] The parent's fears about the possible negative impacts of violence on television for their own children lay with a concern that their children might become frightened or traumatised by on-screen violence.

In research commissioned by the Broadcasting Standards Council, investigating the attitudes of young people (aged 6-17) to the media, the views of parents concerning the effect of television were also considered. The dominant view held by parents was that there was too much violence on television. The research also showed that parents did not believe that such violence adversely affected *their* children.[20] When they said they wished to restrict the amount of violence their children viewed on television, the reason for doing so was usually that they were worried that the children might be frightened by what they saw, rather than because they thought the children might be encouraged to behave violently.

> I don't like it, but it doesn't harm him in what he does – has quite a mind of his own. (Father of 14 year old boy)

When asked in what areas of programming they restricted their children's viewing, parents predominantly mentioned those programmes that contained sex.

When children themselves were asked if they were concerned about the possible effects of television, they did not consider themselves to be at risk. Some children did say, however, that they thought that younger children, who might not be able to tell the difference between fiction and reality, might be affected by violence on television. Again, it is the case of 'the other' being affected and not the respondents themselves.

Children, and indeed adults, were shown to be able to differentiate between various forms of violence. Even children of a pre-school age have been noted to respond differently to different forms of media violence as evidenced in the changes in their facial expressions.[21] These children were shown: schematic violence, realistic violence in which the suffering of the victim was also shown, cartoon violence, verbal violence, and a non-violent scene. They were found to watch both the schematic and the cartoon violence with joy and understanding, showing no signs of distress or fear. The realistic physical violence troubled the children most and produced facial expressions of seriousness, tenseness, and anger in the children.

Other research has shown that pre-adolescent viewers could distinguish between real violence and fantasy violence.[22] Children were noted to perceive real violence as sickening rather than frightening, and they preferred to see violence in a 'make believe' and play context which they could enjoy and subsequently forget.

In 1996, the Commission (then the Broadcasting Standards Council) asked David Buckingham to conduct a study which looked at how children reacted to and coped with difficult images. His research began with an extensive literature search.[23] Buckingham then conducted a series of focussed interviews with small groups of children aged between six and sixteen, and interviews with the families of some of these children.[24]

Buckingham found that negative emotional responses were recalled by most of his sample of children, but there was little predictability in the content that could create such a response. The programming that could lead to upset ran from horror films to the news. In the horror film, as in many programmes of fiction, the negative response was often counterbalanced by positive responses such as excitement or enjoyment. In factual programmes, children themselves often felt that their negative emotions were part of a learning process. Generally, these had a positive outcome therefore – except for the news at times. Many of the young respondents said that the scenes they saw on the news evoked a sense of helplessness in them, a powerful emotion:

> I try and turn over the channel and try and watch a little cartoon and try and block it out of my mind. But it's always there, like wars and things and bombing, and you see all the Ethiopians. Like at Christmas, they always put them on, and you're sitting there and you're like having tons of chocolates and things... You can't exactly get a doggie bag and send it off. But we donate money and stuff... I just feel like that's unfair, I just think there must be some way, some way. It could just like give them tons of food and fix it, but I don't know, it's just impossible. (12 year old girl)

The children described a variety of strategies they adopted to cope with possible distress. They included avoiding the material (turning away from it, leaving the room), distracting themselves, and actively reinterpreting the text (as in fiction, or providing alternative endings for themselves!).

Summary

This review of recent research could look in greater detail at all the issues discussed here. Gender differences have been largely ignored and one of the Commission's most valuable pieces of work considered the responses of survivors to media coverage of the events they had lived through.[25] All these studies deserve the reader's full attention. What this review has sought to do is to establish the underlying similarities in response found in British research, regardless of the type or place of violence. Encouragingly, many of these baselines are found in other work – an American example is given here – and it is to be hoped that a time will come when comparative research can be extended to look at the viewing of violence, particularly as programmes increasingly cross national frontiers.

The Joint Working Party on Violence in the UK reported in 1998. It said:

> To seek to stop broadcasting from telling and retelling hard truths about the world would be a substantial disservice both to democracy and to our understanding of the human condition. The portrayal of violence has played a major part in popular storytelling throughout human history, and continues to have a place in the civilising process of which broadcasting is a part... At the same time there are anxieties among sections of the viewing audience about why, how and when violence is shown on television... Broadcasters accordingly have a responsibility to the public to ensure that a property balance is struck between freedom of expression and protection of the vulnerable.[26]

This is where much of the research effort has been focussed.

Notes

1. *Monitoring Report 7.* Broadcasting Standards Commission, 1999.
2. *Violence on Television in Britain: A Content Analysis 1995-96.* London: Independent Television Commission.
3. Charles Denton, a former current affairs programme maker.
4. Morrison D.E. et al: *Defining Violence: The Search for Understanding.* University of Luton Press, 1999.
5. Millwood Hargrave, A.: *Violence in Factual Television.* Broadcasting Standards Council, 1993.
6. The soap opera was *Brookside.*
7. These were mothers aged 25-45, recruited so that the eldest child was aged between 5 and 11.
8. These were fathers aged 25-45, recruited so that the eldest child was aged between 12 and 16.
9. *National Television Violence Study – Scientific Papers 1994-1995.* Four studies by University of California, Santa Barbara; University of North Carolina, Chapel Hill; University of Texas, Austin; and University of Wisconsin, Madison. Published by Media Scope, Inc.
10. *Monitoring Report 7.* Broadcasting Standards Commission, 1999.
11. Gunter, B.: Perceptions of television violence: Effects of programmes genre and the physical form of violence, 1988, p.33; Gunter, B. and Furnham, A.: *British Journal of Social Psychology Vol.23,* 1984, p.155-184.
12. Gunter, B.: Perceptions of television violence: Effects of programmes genre and the physical form of violence, 1988, p.33; Gunter, B. and Furnham, A.: *British Journal of Social Psychology Vol.23,* 1984, p.155-184.
13. Docherty, D: *Violence in Television Fiction.* Broadcasting Standards Council, 1990.
14. Millwood Hargrave, A.: *Violence in Factual Television.* Broadcasting Standards Council, 1993.
15. Morrison, D.E.: *Television and the Gulf War.* University of Luton Press, 1992.
16. Gunter B. and Wober M.: *Violence on Television: What the Viewers Think.* John Libbey & Company Ltd, 1988.
17. Millwood Hargrave, A.: *Violence in Factual Television.* Broadcasting Standards Council, 1993.
18. For an overview of the literature, see Gauntlett, D.: *Moving Experiences: Understanding Television's Influences and Effects.* John Libbey & Company Ltd, 1995.
19. Buckingham, D.: *Moving Images: Understanding Children's Emotional Responses to Television.* Manchester University Press, 1996.
20. Millwood Hargrave, A., Halloran, J.D. and Gray, P: *Young People and the Media.* Broadcasting Standards Council, 1996.
21. Lagerspetz et al. (1978) in article by Gunter, B. 'Television Violence and Entertainment Value', *Bulletin of the British Psychological Society,* March 1979, Vol. 32.
22. Snow et al. (1974) in article by Gunter, B. 'Television Violence and Entertainment Value', *Bulletin of the British Psychological Society,* March 1979, Vol. 32.
23. Buckingham, D. and Allerton, M.: *A Review of Research on Children's 'Negative' Emotional Responses to TV.* Broadcasting Standards Council, 1996.
24. Buckingham, D.: *Moving Images: Understanding Children's Emotional Responses to Television.* Manchester University Press, 1996.
25. Shearer, A.: *Survivors and the Media.* Broadcasting Standards Council, 1991.
26. Violence and the Viewer. Report of the Joint Working Party on Violence on Television, BBC, BSC, ITC, 1998.

Violence on Chilean Television and Audience Perception

Veronica Silva & Maria Dolores Souza

This article is a summary of the main findings of a research program conducted by the Consejo Nacional de Television (CNTV) in Chile (Chilean National Television Council)[1] and comprising five studies about violence on television.[2]

After an introduction describing the penetration and output of television in Chile, we summarize the findings of the research program in three sections. The first section includes opinions of the adult audience about violence on television, the second section contains children's opinions, and the third deals with a content analysis of television programs shown before 10 p.m., especially cartoons. Finally, we suggest elements to be addressed in the debate around these issues.

Status of television in Chile

In Chile, television is a product of mass consumption. Urban households have an average of almost two television sets, and this average rises to three in high-income segments. The characteristics of television sets have improved tremendously over the past few years. Almost 94 percent of the households have color sets, 79 percent have remote controls and 14 percent have black and white television sets.[3]

Open television reaches Chile's thirteen regions, leaving only small communities without coverage.[4] It offers eight free channels, which together provide about 60,000 hours per year of television programs. All the channels have general programming, which means that their output contains television genres targeted at different kinds of public. Sixteen percent of programs are aimed at children. Sixty percent of the total offer is made up of national programs.

On the other hand, 21 percent – or almost one of every four Chilean households – has cable television. It is present in most high and middle-income segments and is rapidly penetrating the lower-income segment.[5]

Over 70 cities throughout Chile have access to cable television; it is available in practically all cities with over 50,000 inhabitants. There is a clear national trend toward market concentration between two big operators, which together account for almost 95 percent of the total market.[6]

These operators offer over 1,200,000 hours of television programs per year, 61.5 percent of which are broadcast on theme channels and 38.5 percent on general channels. Programs are made up of different television genres, with a high proportion of mixed programs, video clips and movies. Of the contents on the 180 cable TV channels, approximately 63.4 percent are foreign and about 36.6 percent local. It is worth noting, however, that almost 75 percent of the programs on these channels are in Spanish, most of which originate in Latin America.[7]

The irruption and expansion of cable television, especially in provinces, has brought about an unprecedented phenomenon, namely the emergence of local television channels including programs aimed at informing about the local reality.

Also satellite television, offered by two companies, has a rising penetration rate in Chile. Both companies include audio-only channels – which are divided into different musical genres – and audiovisual channels of the general and theme type. Subscribers are concentrated in the high and middle-high income segments.

Statistics indicate that Chileans spend approximately three hours per day in front of the television set and that children are the greatest television consumers.[8] This has brought about many debates and discussions, among which violence on television is an issue of greatest concern.

Several studies periodically conducted by the CNTV have clearly indicated that the audience's priority concern regarding television programs is that of violence, especially in programs for children and other programs shown before 10 p.m., which is considered a time period for all kinds of viewers. These results are consistent with those of research in other countries such as the United States and England.[9]

However, although the Chilean government and people are concerned about violence on television, and some studies and seminars have been conducted, extensive debate has not taken place. Therefore, the CNTV decided to conduct a research program about violence on television and present its findings to the public in order to stimulate an informed debate on the issue.

The research program comprised five studies, carried out during 1996 and 1997. It focused on two major topics not dealt with before: the amount, nature and distribution of violence shown on Chilean television, and the public's opinion and perception in that regard, giving special emphasis to children. The idea was to deal with the issue using a multi-methodological approach and considering various aspects, in order to have a broad view and, thus, to provide new elements for a more thorough debate.

Public opinion about violence on television

In this section we include the findings of two studies, one quantitative and one qualitative, of the research program. They deal with the adult audience's opinion on the amount and type of violence shown on television, how the viewers define it, their perception of individual and social effects, and their demands for regulation of violent content.

One of the studies is a survey conducted in Santiago with 800 people between 16 and 65 years of age.[10] The other consists of focus groups, performed in two stages, with 41 groups of people over the age of 18.[11]

General opinion on violence

According to the opinions expressed in the surveys and the focus groups, we can state that violence on television is the issue that disturbs viewers most. When asked "what aspects shown on television bother you most?", 42 percent of respondents spontaneously mention elements related to violence on television.[12] Other aspects are, for example, commercials, censorship/politics, and sex, but these aspects are mentioned by less than ten percent each.

When asked the comparative question with fixed-choice items, "what bothers you most on television: violence or sex?", the number of answers stating that violence bothers them most rises to 54 percent (Figure 1).

Figure 1. What bothers you most on television: violence or sex? (%)

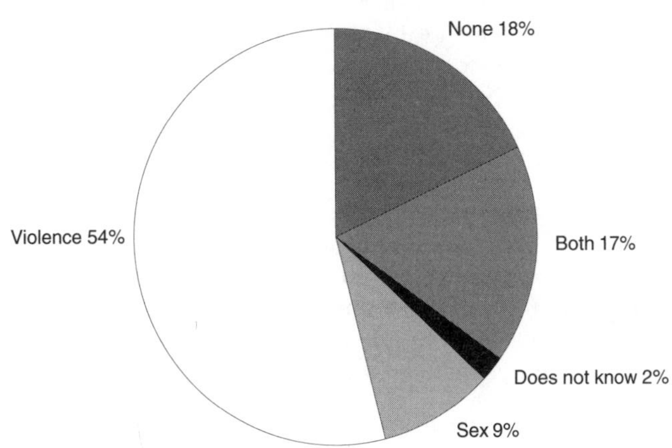

n = 800 (total sample)

However, the opinions about violent content on television are complex.[13] Violence is considered unnecessary and not contributory to the value of entertainment. Moreover, it is thought to be harmful for the social well-being. At the same time many believe that violence reflects real life (Figure 2).

Figure 2. Level of agreement with statements about violence on television (%)

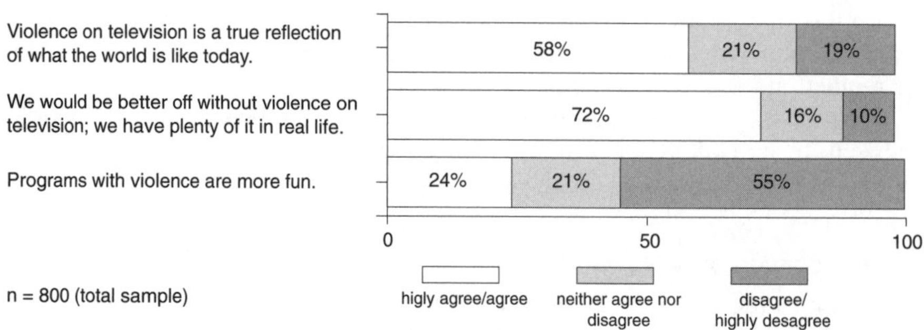

Moreover, a large majority of people (71%) consider that violence on television has increased over the past five years. The audience perceives that not only have the number of violent scenes increased, but also expresses its concern about the images showing violence and that these become more and more graphic.

Further, respondents give reasons why they expect an increase in violence on television in the future. Some of these reasons are that (i) the industry increasingly associates more violence with entertainment, e.g., the U.S. movie industry; (ii) a large majority likes violence; and (iii) the industry seeks to cause an impact on the viewer both in fiction and non-fiction, involving him/her emotionally through images of destruction and violence.

In general, the negative evaluation of violence on television is related to its potential impact. Firstly, respondents express their concern about the values delivered. Violence is a bad example for people because of the behaviors themselves and the underlying values. Secondly, respondents consider that violence on television can cause harmful effects on the audience, particularly children:

- One of the principal effects is the learning and imitation of violent, nonconforming, and antisocial behaviors. For example, with regard to watching cartoons, people perceive imitation and aggressive behaviors in children under 10 years old. These phenomena are attributed to children's identification with their favorite characters. Movies and documentaries are also mentioned as genres that can teach youngsters or groups at risk about the use of violence.

- A second effect of violence on television perceived by viewers is the desensitization to social violence. On one hand, they express their concern that television may legitimize violent behaviors as a way of achieving certain objectives, such as fighting against evil and obtaining justice. On the other hand, viewers manifest their apprehension that the viewer may become accustomed to watching violent scenes and, therefore, certain social values, such as non-violence and respect for physical integrity and life, may be trivialized.

- A third impact is related to the fear, pain and confusion that may be generated in the viewer by violence on television. Children and adolescents are of special concern because they are not sufficiently mature to understand some of the problems depicted in movies, news broadcasts and documentaries.

Finally, it is worth noting that opinions regarding behavioral effects of violence on the screen differ among the respondents. For example, although most of them acknowledge that there is an imitation effect on children, this opinion varies according to the respondent's educational level. The higher the education level, the less people agree with the hypothesis of direct effects on behavior and vice versa.[14] People surveyed also tend to agree more about the impact of violence when it occurs to others, but there is little awareness of the effects on one's own conduct.

Identification of violent content according to program genres

As already mentioned, the notion of violence on television is complex and depends to a large extent on three factors: (i) the television genre; (ii) the program's general context; and (iii) the characteristics of the different audience segments. These factors are treated below.

In general, the programs considered most violent are cartoons, movies, documentaries and news broadcasts.

Cartoons

A large majority of respondents express their great concern about cartoons. This apprehension has grown over the past few years because there is the perception that the television industry is producing and showing cartoons with increasingly violent contents. At the same time, cartoons are children's favorite programs from an early age.

The people surveyed declare that violence in this genre is expressed in scenes that show physical aggression – fights, torture – and the consequences of that aggression – injuries, blood, destruction and death. They also mention psychological aggression like threats and humiliation, as well as their emotional effect. This refers especially to fear and moral suffering, typical of certain series such as Japanese cartoons.

Another characteristic that makes people consider this genre excessively violent is the realism of some programs. Realism is associated with the type of characters shown in cartoons. People tend to consider aggressive actions by characters that represent human beings more harmful. Respondents also mention that depiction of pain and the effects of physical aggression make violent scenes cruder and more realistic.

Respondents mention, too, that violence is present in the theme itself of some cartoon series. The most severe violence is perceived in the confrontational scripts of some series where the roles of "good" and "bad" characters are not clear or defined.

Movies

Respondents mentioned different types of violent content in movies, depending on the sub-genres of the films. Detective movies, suspense movies and thrillers – occasionally including martial arts and science fiction films – are considered typical examples of violent movies, showing scenes of death and destruction and special effects to intensify the impact of violence.

Within this context, scenes where physical aggression has an excessively destructive power on people are considered extremely violent. This characteristic, plus the following five, were specified:

- Realism of scenes.
- Showing the effects of aggression.
- Foreground or middle ground images.
- Scenes where violence seems unjustified or unnecessary.
- Scenes where the victim appears weak or defenseless.

Images of blood, dismemberment, physical disintegration and excessive suffering of victims are understood as the effects of aggression. Within this context, death in itself is not considered particularly violent, but the way it is shown.

Scenes of sexual aggression are also considered extremely violent, especially if the scenes are long and portray the victim's suffering in a very realistic manner.

Violence in the drama genre tends to have a greater impact on the audience because the content is generally associated with events and situations of real life. Physical and psychological aggression that cause intense human suffering are violent contents perceived both in drama scripts and scenes. These contents are identified especially in family dramas and historical events, where suffering in extreme situations of tremendous psychological stress is portrayed.

However, the opinions of this drama genre are not necessarily negative. On the contrary, many respondents state that although this kind of content may have a great impact on the audience, it may also sensitize viewers about certain human problems and situations, thereby teaching a lesson.

Non-fiction, news broadcasts and documentaries

Opinions on programs about real and current events are less severe than for drama.

Although real-life violence shown in documentaries and news broadcasts is considered to have a great impact on the audience because it shows real people and events, its presentation is accepted due to its informative content aimed at the public's right to know.

Coverage of events that imply intentional and involuntary aggression, both by people and by natural forces or accidents, is perceived as violence in *news broadcasts*. Violence is associated with physical and material loss that causes suffering to human beings.

The greatest concerns are related to values and ethical standards presented by editorial lines in television news broadcasts. Therefore, although people feel that news broadcasts do not exaggerate the amount of violence in the country, particularly violent contents are identified in certain scenes that depict actions of voluntary and involuntary aggression.

Especially worrisome is the treatment of certain events in which sensationalism is perceived as common practice. An example would be scenes with more than necessary detail to inform the public as a means to attract a greater audience. Another concern is journalistic intrusiveness, which is perceived as a form of violence toward the victims or the relatives of victims of criminal actions, tragedies and/or diseases. This refers mainly to interviews and questions asked by journalists, aimed at deepening human suffering and giving emphasis to affliction.

Respondents also say that news broadcasts tend to emphasize negative news, which is considered a kind of violence toward the audience. This is an ethical concern, but viewers fear that the major, most pervasive effect of this kind of violence is increasing people's feeling of insecurity, vulnerability and fear of society.

Opinions about *real life documentaries* differ depending on the type of program and its social interest and relevance. Current events and scientific and technological documentaries are highly valued.

However, police-related documentaries, particularly the *reality shows*, which recreate criminal actions and dramas – homicides, maltreatment, and cases of severe abnormality – are more controversial, and opinions tend to be divided depending on the socioeconomic background of the viewer.[15] Some audiences, especially the upper income segment, perceive that there is violence not only in the scenes themselves but also in the selection of the themes. These programs are attributed the power of teaching non-conforming and antisocial behaviors. On the contrary, other audiences, especially the lower income segments, consider that these contents contribute to the prevention of crime and educate the public. Moreover, they feel that these types of programs reflect their lives.

Characteristics of the audience and perception of violence on television

The characteristics of the audiences also determine their assessment of violence on television. The five principal characteristics are: education level, age, sex, level of television use, and the level of fear of violence in society.

Only the opinion on children programming is universal and, consequently, it is here more difficult to find any differences among the groups.

- Considering *education*, people with a higher education level tend to rate violence on television poorly. This is determined chiefly by their values and not because of its impact. In fact, this group perceives the lowest impact of violence on children. This group is also the one that demands less regulation from the State or television channels, giving greater importance to the parent's role and rules for children's television viewing.
- Regarding *age*, young people give less importance to violence on the screen. They consider it a minor source of annoyance and feel it will have little impact on the public – with the exception of violence in children's programs. Young people are not in favor of a legal framework to regulate television, and fear such regulation could result in censorship. On the contrary, adults express the greatest concern about violence and believe it could have a greater effect on people; therefore, they demand more regulation.
- With respect to *sex*, the survey's findings indicate that women tend to perceive more violent content in television programming and have a lower tolerance for it.
- Regarding *levels of television use*, people that spend more time in front of the set place less importance on violence. They consider it is just another element of programs that appears to be the least disturbing and most acceptable. They also say that violence has little influence on people. On the contrary, people that spend less time in front of the screen express greater annoyance and concern about violence shown in television programs, and demand greater regulation. They tend to believe that violence has significant effects on the audience and allege that there is excessive violence on the screen. Annoyance about violence on television is also greater among people who have cable television in their homes.
- Finally, the proportion of the audience expressing greater *fear of social violence* tends to be more critical about violence on television and believe that television has a great potential to influence people's behavior, as compared to those who have less fear. The more fearful people are the ones that demand more regulation of violence on television.

Demands regarding violence on television

Television viewers tend to support a regulatory system with the involvement of the State, broadcasters, and the family in general.

A great majority – with the exception of youngsters – supports the enactment of a law regulating the presentation of violent programs, and expresses the need for parents of children and adolescents to assume an active role in the control of their children's television use.

Within a legal framework, regulating the hours during which programs with violence can be shown is the system preferred for open television. Opinions are quite divided for cable television, with similar levels of support for the alternative of regulating the hours during which the programs can be shown, and for the option of self-regulation of the service operators.

At the same time, specific demands are made for the different television genres. For example, in the specific case of *cartoons*, a great majority of respondents agree that cartoons should not have violent themes or scenes. They believe programs aimed at young children should definitely not contain any violence and demand that such violent programs should be eliminated altogether.

Further, respondents request the diversification of *movies* shown. They perceive that television programming – especially that on open television – gives priority to movies with violent content.

In the case of *news broadcasts and documentaries*, demands from respondents focus on the ethical aspect. People demand greater respect on the part of journalists and cameramen for the victims, especially with regard to their privacy and feelings. However, respondents tend to attribute information value to coverage of events that show the consequences of different types of aggression and destruction. In this regard, it is difficult to draw the line between what must and must not be shown on television. A significant proportion of respondents agree that there should be standards for scenes of violence, avoiding foreground images of dismembered and dead people.

At the same time, respondents request that television channels not show previews of programs containing scenes or informing about subjects inappropriate for minors before 9 p.m.

Respondents also express the need for parents to take measures at home when they watch violent scenes with the children present. Among these measures are explaining or criticizing what is being shown. In this same line, and in order to support the parents' rules, there is wide adhesion to the existence of warnings about violence contained in programs, especially those appearing on the screen before and during the program.

Children's opinions about violence on television

We will now present the findings of a qualitative study aimed at investigating the opinions of children about violence on television. Twenty-three groups of children of different ages, 4-5, 8-9, 11-13 and 14-15 years, were consulted using group dynamics and focus group methods. The children lived in the metropolitan area.

Perceptions and rating of violence

Children's evaluation of violence on the screen differs. Girls of different age groups and younger boys – pre-school and approximately up to eight years old – express the greatest rejection and displeasure toward violence both in fiction and reality.

On the other hand, boys from an early age (4-5 years) express their preference to watch struggles and fights in certain fiction programs, asserting that they find it entertaining, especially in the cases of cartoons and action and terror movies.

Adolescents of both sexes rate the violent content of true-to-life programs favorably when they show the real world around them. They say it is a way of warning them to prevent some risky situations.

Although children express a certain concern for violence on television, this is not an important issue among children over 10 years of age; they are more concerned with television censorship or movies being cut, excess of commercials during programs, lack of program variety and program repetition.

It is worth noting that some boys – especially the younger ones – spontaneously say that when they play, they imitate violent behaviors they watch on television without giving it an aggressive intention.

From a broader standpoint, violence is one of the television contents that causes a great impression and produces a tremendous emotional impact on children of all ages. Many children acknowledge being terribly affected when watching painful situations on television, especially of real life, like death, accidents, rape or maltreatment. With few exceptions, these contents are present in programs aimed at an adult audience and not in programs for children.

According to the children, the television genres that have a greater impact on them are those that show or represent situations of real life, like news broadcasts, documentaries – mainly the reality show sub-genre – and movies of the drama genre. It should be noted that especially among pre-school children and primary school children, terror films are also mentioned to have an impact due to the many dismemberment and blood scenes.

Programs with the greatest impact are, according to the children, those that generate mainly negative emotions. Fear and sadness are emotions frequently associated with this kind of program. Older children also attribute a sensitization value to certain contents with greater impact, when they are shown in real life documentaries or news broadcasts.

Television content identified as violent

In general, children identify violence with physical aggression like fights, abuse, including effects like pain, wounds, blood and death. Adolescents also understand psychological aggression as violence, including threats, offense and insults, that generates hatred and resentment.

The children studied say that the most violent television genres are *cartoons*[16] and *movies* – especially terror films, followed by *news broadcasts, documentaries* on real life and *reality shows*. They consider soap operas less violent.

Children 10 years old and over say that the *intensity of violence* in television programs depends on a combination of characteristics that somehow determine their impact, like (i) the extent of the harm and the effect caused by the aggression; (ii) the way the physical injuries and suffering caused by the aggression are presented audio-visually; (iii) the closeness to reality of the television content; (iv) the consistency of values in the context of the aggression; and (v) the presence or absence of humor.

Children's perception of parental rules

Small children – pre-school children and children approximately under 10 years of age – are the ones most frequently mentioning that their parents try to control screen time. Older children say that they have practically no restrictions, except for very specific programs. Children of the higher income segment – regardless of age – state that they are subject to greater television regulations by their parents at home.

Children say that their parents try to set up rules regarding the amount of television they may watch. They say that rules are set at home, but they generally result in turning off the television set for an hour at night, especially on weekdays, because they must do their homework. They assert that the rules are usually not applied on weekends.

Children say that their parents forbid or try to regulate certain television content, particularly sex and violence. According to them, the parents' behavior varies according to the children's ages. They express that violence ceases to be a major concern for parents of pre-adolescents and adolescents, but sex continues to be the television content that parents try to restrict until a more advanced age.

In relation to the television genres that are subject to greater parental control, child viewers mention movies, especially terror films (often characterized by showing violence and sex) and violent cartoons. In the upper- and middle-income segments, parents also try to restrict other programs they consider inappropriate from the point of view of values, and which might set a poor example. In this context, they say that the most restricted genre is the Latin-American soap opera.

The large majority of the groups state that they try to avoid asking for permission or being subject to any kind of rules set by their parents. This behavior is more frequent among children over ten years old and among those who have a television set in their bedroom.

Presence of violence in television programming

In this section, the results of two content analyses of the amount and kind of violence shown on television are presented.

The first study is an analysis of those programs that generate greater concern among the public because of the violence they show, namely movies, news broadcasts and cartoons shown before 10 p.m.[17] The second study is a detailed analysis of the characteristics of violence in cartoons, which contain the largest amount of violence compared to movies and news broadcasts within the same schedule.[18]

Violence in three genres before 10 p.m.

The findings of these studies indicate that 78.6 percent of movies, news broadcasts and cartoons shown before 10 p.m. contain at least one act of physical violence. The time during which violence is presented is quite relevant: 9.1 percent of the total time of the programs in the sample studied was devoted exclusively to violent content. One fourth of the programs with violence devote 20 percent of their time to violent scenes.

In other words, many of the programs shown between 6 a.m. and 10 p.m. contain some elements of violence, and the violent content accounts for a significant share of total program time.

In the specific case of cartoons, we can state that during the schedule before 10 p.m. 80 percent of cartoons contain some action of violence. In addition, the cartoons analyzed devote an average of 11.4 percent of transmission time to violent content. Over 25 percent of cartoons with violence dedicate at least one fifth of total program time to violent images.

Violent acts, however, must not be considered identical but must be analyzed within their context and evaluated in that regard.

The criteria and variables of this study that make it possible to analyze and distinguish violence on television are:

- nature of the violent acts
- realism
- elements of production
- justification of violence

Nature of the violent acts: Although 81 percent of the violent acts recorded were aggressive behaviors of direct physical violence against a victim, a relatively small number could be classified as having a high degree of violence. This is due to the fact that the weapons used were generally of low destruction power (bombs or heavy weapons were used in less than 10 percent of the actions) and, generally, the victims' injuries were not shown (55.7% of the acts), or they were minor injuries (19.2%). However, it should be noted that 28.6 percent of the actions used conventional weapons (guns, knives or rifles).

In *cartoons*, 88 percent of the actions recorded were aggressive behaviors with direct physical violence against a victim, but a relatively small number of them could be classified as very violent. Less than 8 percent of the cases used bombs or heavy weapons, and 57.2 percent did not show the harm suffered by the victim. 26.6 percent were minor injuries. However, it must be pointed out that almost 28 percent of the violent actions recorded in cartoons used conventional weapons like guns and knives.

Realism: Violence seems to be greater or to cause more impact when it is real or appears genuine. Many violent actions occur between human beings, which contributes to increased realism and the intensity of the violence shown.

Elements of production: The way of showing violence in the programs and the use of certain production methods also determine the intensity of the impact of the violence and how it affects the audience. In the sample analyzed, violent acts were frequently accompanied by music in order to increase the tension. At the same time, in connection with more than 40 percent of violent actions, foregrounds were used to magnify the scene's intensity. In the actions recorded, however, blood was practically never used to add drama to the scenes.

Justification of violence: Whether violence is justified is evaluated differently depending on the program genre and the reasons explaining the aggressive behaviors. In this regard, it may be stated that in the sample studied there are seldom reasons to justify violence, and violence tends to be greater in cartoons.

Four classes of cartoons

In the more detailed analysis of violence in cartoons, we may distinguish four classes of cartoons according to their degree of violence, ordered from a lower to a greater degree.

This can be evidenced mainly by the analysis results of four variables applied to the sample:

- the means or weapons used in violent actions;
- the production elements that accompany the incidents;
- the presence or absence of humor; and
- characters' immediate intention with aggression.

The *weapons* used in violent actions in cartoons are increasingly heavier through the four classes.

There is a steady increase of *production elements* as violence increases. In the first class production elements are not used, whereas in the fourth class, the scenes are complemented with music, foregrounds, moans and suspense to increase the tension of the moment of violence.

There is a marked reduction in the use of *humor* from the first class to the fourth class (with the highest level of violence), where it practically disappears.

Regarding the *immediate intentions* of the characters in cartoons for using violence, these range from the wish to weaken the enemy in the first class, to the intention of killing him in the fourth.

The increase in intensity of the violent incidents is strongly related to the *relevance* of violence in the stories narrated in the different cartoons. Thus, in cartoons where violence is more intense, its relevance within the plot is more significant. On the contrary, in cartoons with a lower level of violence, it is irrelevant to the story.

Cartoons with more intense violence, where it is more relevant to the story, add another characteristic: They generally take place in a fantastic future and sometimes violence is good, depending on the plot of the story. Most of the time, the issue at stake is saving or destroying the planet, where we can see confrontations between the good and bad characters. We can also view internal struggles between members of the same group.

Epilogue

As this article shows, when examining the statements of respondents about violence on television, we found complex opinions that tend to evaluate violence from a multiple perspective.

People do not demand the elimination of violence on television because they consider that it has always been part of human history. Rather, they demand paying attention to the way violence is shown and considering the specific characteristics of the program's genre and the schedule in which it is broadcast.

These audience concerns seem to be well grounded in relation to the content analyses of Chilean television programs. According to the characteristics of programs offered on the programming grid before 10 p.m. and which has a significant audience of children, there is a large number of programs that contain at least one act of physical violence. Cartoons are more notorious in this regard than news broadcasts or documentaries, whereas movies fall in-between.

An aggravating factor is that people perceive that over the past few years there is a trend in the television industry to increase the amount and crudeness of violence. This may be true, not least in the case of cartoons, because we see that some of them (i) give greater emphasis to aggression and harm; (ii) are more realistic; (iii) include violence that seems less justified; and (iv) use technical methods to intensify the impact.

At the same time, in real-life genres, the "show time" character of news events, perceived as journalistic sensationalism and intrusiveness, are also considered violent. Within this context, the greater the gratuity of violence and the greater the effort to present it in an attractive way, the less legitimate it appears.

Therefore, beyond the academic debate on the effects of violence on television, there is an ethical imperative applied to programs for children and the way violence must be shown in other television genres. This must be publicly debated by all the social players involved in the mass consumption of television.

Notes

1. Consejo Nacional de Television is a State agency, which according to the Television Law, is responsible for the correct operation of television services. It has the authority to grant and take away licenses and supervise television programming.
2. Original title: Consejo Nacional de Television, *Cinco Estudios Sobre Violencia en Chile* [Five Studies on Violence in Chile]. Santiago, 1998. See: www.cntv.cl

3. Establishment Survey. Time Ibope, Santiago, 1998.
4. Consejo Nacional de Television, 1999.
5. Consejo Nacional de Television, *Informe de Television por Cable* [Report on Cable Television]. Santiago, 1998.
6. The remaining 5 percent is divided into 25 operators. See: Consejo Nacional de Television, *Informe de Television por Cable* [Report on Cable Television]. Santiago, 1998.
7. Consejo Nacional de Television, *Informe de Television por Cable* [Report on Cable Television]. Santiago, 1998.
8. Telereport. Time Ibope, Santiago, August, Septembre and October, 1997.
9. Gunter, B. and Wober, M., *Violence on Television. What the Viewers Think.* London, John Libbey, 1988.
10. This study was carried out in conjunction with Market & Opinion Research International (MORI).
11. A total of 24 groups was studied in the first stage. An audio-visual CD with scenes of programs with violent content was shown to 12 groups. The programs belonged to six television genres containing some kind of physical and/or verbal violence: movies and series, video clips, cartoons, soap operas, news broadcasts and documentaries. A total of 17 groups was studied in the second stage. Television-related subjects were dealt with, in addition to violence, in order to confirm the results previously obtained.
12. Among others, "violent movies; violence in news broadcasts; and movies with crimes".
13. Gunter, B., *Acerca de la Violencia de los Medios* [On Media Violence], in Bryant, J. and Zillman, D. (eds.), *Los Efectos de los Medios de Comunicacion* [The Effects of the Media]. Barcelona, Paidos, 1996.
14. The lower the education level of the audience, the greater perception of direct effects of television on children's behavior.
15. This is closely related to the education level of the people.
16. They mention especially cartoons of Japanese origin.
17. The study was made on a one-week random sample of approximately 145 hours of transmission. The data were processed with SPSS.PC statistics software.
18. The study was developed in two stages: the first stage provided an overview of the amount and kind of violence shown in cartoons, reviewing 325 cartoon programs shown before 10 p.m. In the second stage, the cartoons were classified according to the characteristics of the violence presented. A total of 37 cartoons were reviewed applying a partially structured analysis model, of which the results were processed through multiple match factorial analysis of the SPAD-N program.

Censorship and the Third-Person Effect

A Study of Perception of Television Influence in Singapore

Albert C. Gunther & Peng Hwa Ang

This article[1] presents a study on public opinion about television censorship in the island nation of Singapore. More specifically, we tested the third-person effect hypothesis, which suggests that people expect media content to have more negative influence on others than on themselves, and that some support for censorship is based on that perceptual bias. Data for the study came from interviews with adult Singaporeans who evaluated ten categories of "sensitive" television content – among them sex and violence.

It is commonly assumed that control of mass media and other sources of information is exercised by an authoritarian government and imposed on an unwilling public. The scenario of a repressed public is certainly accurate at times, but an important question that follows is to what extent, and why, a nation's populace may itself support constraints on the content of mass media. People in a developing nation may oppose official constraints on information for widely understood reasons, such as the political and social importance of a well-informed populace, or a concern for individual liberty. But citizens in such nations may also support censorship for good reasons: They may do so because of concerns about the stability of the economy, or concerns about maintaining harmony among racial or ethnic groups. They may also favor censorship of mass media because of concern over negative effects on a society's moral structure, or the potential erosion of traditional values.

Many of these attitudes reflect people's concerns about others, and such concerns relate to a more specific hypothesis in this study. A great deal of research has shown that people commonly demonstrate a curious discrepancy when they consider the effects of mass communication on themselves and on society in general. The phenomenon, called the "third-person effect", has two components. First, people tend to estimate that media content will influence others more than themselves. This is a perceptual bias. Second, and more importantly, people may react in some way according to this estimate of larger effects on others. In other words, people support censorship because they consider others to be more vulnerable to perceived harmful influences of mass media (see, e.g., Davison, 1983; Cohen et al., 1988; Mutz, 1989; Lasorsa, 1989; Gunther, 1995). Thus, censorship of mass media content is often justified in the public mind by the perception that a message will have undesirable effects on society, though not on the self.

Previous research and theoretical rationales

Research on the third-person effect has documented the first component, the perceptual bias – there is much empirical evidence of the tendency to perceive greater media influence on others than on the self (for a review, see Perloff, 1993).

The importance of this perceptual bias in the third-person hypothesis depends crucially on its consequences. However, little research has demonstrated solid evidence of a connection between the perceptual bias, on one hand, and attitudes or behaviors, on the other. One study, about the perceived influence of X-rated media content, found that as the discrepancy between perceived negative influence on self and others increased, sentiment favoring censorship also increased (Gunther, 1995). Although behavioral outcomes like censorship are central to the ultimate significance of the third-person effect, few other studies have attempted to document this second component, and those that have, produced mixed or ambiguous results (Mutz, 1989; Rucinski & Salmon, 1990; Gunther, 1991). So another major goal of the study presented here was to explore further evidence of the second component, for any relationship between the perceptual bias and public opinion redefines the third-person perception; rather than an intriguing curiosity it becomes a psychological factor with real social consequences.

Several theoretical rationales might explain the third-person perception. Most appear related in some respect to optimistic bias – the idea that, to maintain a positive sense of self, people will see themselves as less likely to experience negative or harmful events than others (Weinstein, 1989). In support of this explanation, experimental research has demonstrated that people perceive more influence on others only in the case of media content with apparently harmful potential (see, e.g., Gunther & Mundy, 1993).

Theories underlying this second component of the third-person hypothesis may involve distinctly different processes. People may react to perceived negative effects on others because of simple altruism – the act of putting social concerns ahead of personal interests. Or they may react out of ultimate self-interest – the belief that what is good for society, in the end, makes society a better place for the self.

This entire body of self- and social-level conceptualization, however, is subject to a caveat. It is argued that social psychology has taken a mono-cultural approach to construals of the self and others. The Western view of the self is of a unique and bounded individual who seeks to maintain independence from others (Markus & Kitayama, 1991). Research on cultural differences suggests that Asian conceptions of the self and others are significantly more integrated, that they center on "the fundamental relatedness of individuals to each other" (Markus & Kitayama, 1991, p. 224; see also Triandis, 1989) and that Asian cultures emphasize belonging and fitting in, rather than individual uniqueness.

Typical research on the third-person effect, conducted almost exclusively in the U.S. cultural context, envisions each individual's conception of self as distinct from others. A natural consequence of this distinction is to see others affected differently by societal institutions like mass media. And the theoretical justification for this phenomenon, as noted above, is based on an optimistic bias, the ego-reinforcing motivation for people to see themselves as smarter or better off than others. However, the alternative conception of self and others as interdependent would suggest, for Asian cultures, that the optimistic bias is less likely to operate, and therefore that people are less likely to see themselves as different from others and less likely to consider others more vulnerable to mass media influences.[2]

Hypotheses in the Singaporean context

The island nation of Singapore, one of Asia's celebrated "little tigers", provides an ideal context for this study. It is a prosperous and cosmopolitan city-state with a sophisticated media infrastructure. It is a model nation in many respects – clean, orderly, nearly crime free, with negligible corruption and many democratic economic and social policies (Sesser, 1992; Crossette, 1995). But Singapore has been criticized for some authoritarian practices and institutions, prominent among them mass media unapologetically controlled by government (Hachten, 1993; Kamm, 1995), and it is not clear to what extent people support this official censorship. Also notable is that Singapore has taken the lead in promoting a philosophical array of "Asian values", with emphasis on core beliefs like the importance placed on society vs. the unique individual (Koh, 1993; Emmerson, 1995).

Thus, this research was designed to put the third-person hypothesis to the test in a number of challenging circumstances: (1) a political climate where the mass media are firmly under government control, (2) a cultural context in which a more socially integrated view of the self may not incline people to separate perceptions about themselves and others, and (3) a broader range of types of media content than just one type of media content or issue coverage tested before. In addition, the range of ten content categories provided us with a field manipulation suitable for testing the optimistic bias explanation. If people perceive less potential harm in some types of television content, the optimistic bias model would predict less third-person perception for those categories. Also, we intended to look for further documentation of the "behavioral" component of the third-person effect. Hypotheses (H) took the following form:

H1. Respondents will perceive more negative influence from "sensitive" media content on the average Singaporean than on themselves.

H2. As the perceived negative influence of content categories decreases, the perceived difference between self and others will also decrease.

H3. To the extent that respondents perceive greater influence of media content on others relative to themselves, they will express greater support for censorship of such content.

Method

Data for this study were gathered in face-to-face interviews with 506 adult (18 years of age and older) Singaporeans from May through August, 1994. We employed a stratified random sampling scheme to select respondents. Most Singapore residents live in compact complexes of public, high-rise apartment blocks, which are congenial to representative sampling. We first randomly selected complexes and blocks, and then followed a systematic procedure for the selection of floor, flat and household member. A similar randomization scheme was followed in private housing estates and residential areas. If interviewers encountered no answer or a refusal they went to adjacent flats or residences, following an established pattern, until an interview was completed. Statistics from the sample closely matched demographic parameters in 1994 Singapore – including gender, race, age, housing-type and marital status, although respondents tended to be somewhat higher in education and income.

Interviewers were upper-level students at the National University of Singapore trained in interviewing techniques. The interview took 20-25 minutes and was conducted in the respondents' language of choice. They answered questions about their use of mass media, their opinions about the effects of television content and censorship of such content, and various demographic measures. Early in the survey, interviewers introduced a block of 10 questions on "sensitive topics you can see on television these days – like sex and violence". Respondents were asked about their perceptions of the influence of television portrayals of violence, extramarital sex and adultery, homosexuality and lesbianism, foreign television programs, programs with religious themes, foul language, men with long hair, premarital sex, women who choose to have children without being married, and nudity or partial nudity. Respondents were asked to rate the influence of such content on "themselves personally", and they were also asked to rate influence on "the average Singaporean". Interviewers asked them to respond to each question using the following response scale (displayed on a printed card): (1) large negative influence, (2) small negative influence, (3) no influence, (4) small positive influence, (5) large positive influence.

Asking people to rate influences on both themselves and others may introduce the potential for biased responses, as answers to the second question may be altered by answers to the first. To provide a check on this possible order effect, we randomly assigned people to one of two versions of the questionnaire – asking either about self first, or about the average Singaporean first.

To measure support for censorship, respondents were asked about their opinions on the regulation of TV content. For all of the above topics (again using a printed response card), people were asked: "Do you personally think censorship of [TV violence/other topics] (1) should be a lot more strict, (2) should be a bit more strict, (3) is about right as it is, (4) should be a bit more liberal, (5) should be a lot more liberal?".

Results

Perceived influence on self and others

Our first hypothesis proposed that people would perceive more negative influence from "sensitive" TV content on the average Singaporean than on themselves. The data confirmed this notion in every case. A majority of Singaporeans thought there would be some negative effect on themselves, but more negative effect on others.

Not every person saw more negative influence on others, but that was the perception of a substantial majority. For example, in the case of TV violence, 60 percent of respondents thought there would be more negative influence on other Singaporeans, 27 percent perceived no difference, and only 12 percent reported more negative influence on self. Though for other content areas the differences were less extreme, they generally followed the same pattern.

Only for portrayals of men with long hair, foreign programs, and religious programs did the "more negative influence on others" category fall below 50 percent, and in every case they remained substantially larger than in the "more negative influence on self" group. With two exceptions, discussed further below, the percentage of people who reported more negative effect on self was small and stable – between 9 and 12 percent.

However, the reliability of these perceptions is important to verify. The major question is whether respondents give accurate answers once they know they are being asked to compare themselves to others. To answer this question, the interview was, as noted above, designed so that one half of the respondents, chosen at random, received the block of questions about influence on self first, followed by the block about influence on others. The other half received the same question blocks, but in reverse order. If the third-person perception is merely an artifact of question order, one would expect to see respondents adjusting their second answer.

Analysis of this test, however, revealed no sign of order effect. There was no significant change in respondents' second set of answers, which is good evidence that the differences in perceptions they reported were genuine, and not a result of the way the questions were asked.

Another way to test the third-person perception hypothesis is to compare the average estimate of influence on self to influence on others. For example, the mean respondent rating for perceived influence of TV violence on self was 2.75, while influence on the average Singaporean was rated at 2.12 (a lower score represents more negative influence). Table 1 displays the mean estimates of influence on both self and others, along with t-tests. Differences were significant in all 10 cases, lending further support to hypothesis 1.

Table 1. Mean estimates of perceived effect of television content on self and others

Topic	Effect on self	Effect on others	Difference	t-value
Violence	2.75	2.12	.63	12.2***
Premarital sex	2.66	2.03	.63	12.6***
Extramarital sex	2.68	2.08	.60	12.5***
Foul language	2.60	2.02	.58	11.8***
Unwed mothers	2.67	2.12	.55	10.9***
Homosexuality	2.60	2.04	.55	11.6***
Nudity	2.61	2.01	.53	11.3***
Foreign programs	3.26	2.91	.35	6.8***
Men with long hair	2.80	2.49	.31	7.6***
Religious programs	3.34	3.17	.17	3.9***

Note: Effect items were coded so that 1 = large negative effect, 2 = small negative effect, 3 = no effect, 4 = small positive effect, 5 = large positive effect. Significance levels were calculated using paired t-tests. Asterisks indicate whether there are significant differences between effect on self and on others. *** = p<.001 (the chance that the difference is not significant is 1 out of 1000).

A graphic representation of these differences is displayed in Figures 1 and 2.

Figure 1. Perceived effects of sex-related TV content on self and others
Negative values indicate perceived negative influence and vice versa.

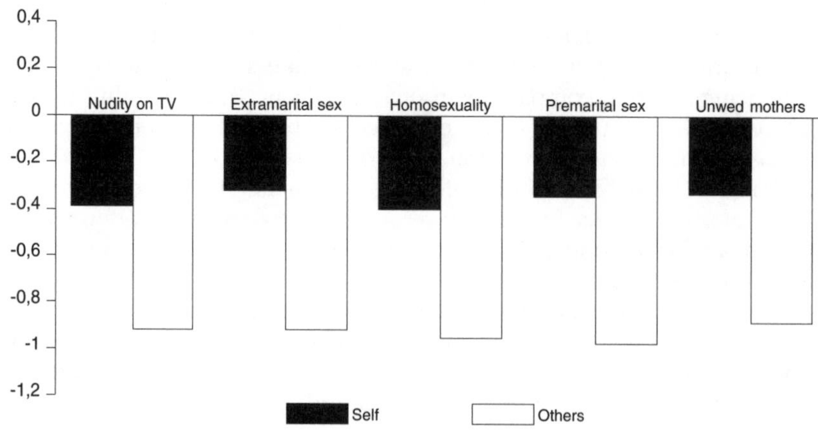

Figure 2. Perceived effects of other TV content on self and others
Negative values indicate perceived negative influence and vice versa.

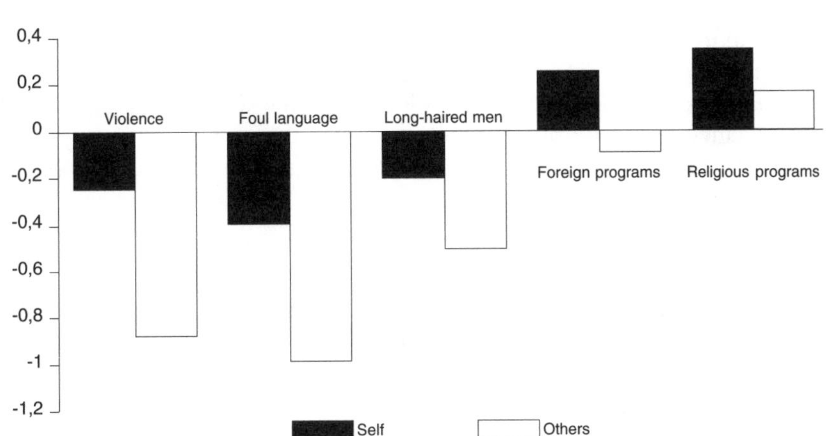

Optimistic bias?

As a test of the optimistic bias, hypothesis 2 predicted that as the perceived negative influence of content categories decreased, the perceived difference between self and others would also decrease. The difference column in Table 1 illustrates the pattern predicted in this hypothesis. However, Figure 2 reveals that for the final two content categories perceived influence does not simply decrease, it actually reverses.

Categories in Figure 1 deal with sex-related content, and show a consistent contrast in perceptions. Figure 2 pictures the five additional content categories, and shows a more varied result. For foreign and religious programs, people perceived on average a positive influence, rather than a negative one. More specifically, for foreign TV programs respondents in the aggregate reported a positive influence on themselves, but a small negative influence on other Singaporeans. In other words, people seem to feel foreign programs are actually good for them personally, but not good for other people. In the case of religious programming, people went further in the positive direction, estimating that religious programming would have positive influences on both themselves and others. However, they reported a fairly strong positive influence on the self, and a significantly less strong, but still positive, influence on the average Singaporean. This result is particularly persuasive in support of the optimistic bias explanation.

These two special cases illustrate what has sometimes been called the "first-person" effect. In these cases people actually perceive *more* effect on themselves than on others. However, the greater perceived personal-level effect is a positive one. While perceived positive influence for these two categories goes in a direction opposite to the norm, the pattern of results for the positive and negative programs is the same. That is, for the positive categories there is greater positive influence on the self and less (or none) for others. In the negative categories – the five sex-related contents, as well as violence, foul language and men with long hair – there is less negative influence on the self and more negative influence on others.

In summary, the data show that Singaporeans in general believe sensitive content like sex and violence in television programs will have a significantly greater negative influence on other Singaporeans than on themselves personally. The two partial exceptions occur for programming that is seen as having positive influences.

For or against censorship?

An important descriptive question addressed in this study is to what extent Singaporeans favor or oppose censorship. Public support for censorship appeared to be strong. For half of the "sensitive" categories – extramarital sex, homosexuality, premarital sex, nudity, foul language – a majority of Singaporeans said they felt censorship should be more strict. In these categories another 30 to 40 percent said they felt current levels of censorship were appropriate. Ten percent or fewer thought censorship should be relaxed. Support for censorship of unwed mothers, and portrayals of violence was also strong. For men with long hair support was less dramatic but still more persons were for than against.

Opinions about foreign TV programs appeared more divided: 21 percent felt censorship should be more strict, while 31 percent said it should be more liberal. Religious programming also received a mixed result, although 63 percent felt the current level of restriction was about right. Only in these two categories did the mean response fall on the "more liberal" side of the scale. (Table 2 illustrates these results.)

Table 2. Opinion distribution (%) and mean scores concerning censorship in Singapore

Topic	Censorship should be more strict	Censorship is about right as is	Censorship should be more liberal	Mean
Violence	43	38	19	2.6
Premarital sex	59	34	7	2.2
Extramarital sex	53	40	8	2.3
Foul language	56	38	6	2.4
Unwed mothers	49	42	10	2.4
Homosexuality	61	32	7	2.2
Nudity	52	38	10	2.3
Men with long hair	27	63	10	2.8
Foreign programs	21	48	31	3.2
Religious programs	15	63	22	3.1

Note: Support for censorship was measured on a 5-point scale where 1 = should be a lot more strict, 2 = should be a bit more strict, 3 = is about right as it is, 4 = should be a bit more liberal, 5 = should be a lot more liberal. Values 1 and 2, and 4 and 5, respectively, were collapsed for display in this table.
Rows may not add to 100% because of rounding.

The third-person effect

The central focus of this research, however, is not opinion about censorship *per se*, but rather its *relationship* to the difference between perceived influence on self and others. To test the hypothesis, that the third-person perception leads to support for censorship of television content, we analyzed the relationship between opinion about censorship and an array of factors that might influence such opinions. Respondents' age or gender, for example, may affect their support for censorship. People with more education might oppose strict censorship, while people with children might be expected to support it. We also included income, religion (vs. no religion or "free thinkers"), marital status and exposure to entertainment television in the analysis. We added these characteristics in blocks, so as to examine their cumulative effect in predicting opinion about censorship.

In two final steps, we first added respondents' estimations of influence of the content categories on themselves, and finally the difference between estimates of effect on self and other Singaporeans (the third-person perception).

Adding factors in steps or blocks serves a number of purposes: 1) it allows us to examine the effects of multiple factors simultaneously – a more realistic picture of the actual process, 2) it tells us how much each additional factor adds in explaining the outcome of interest, and 3) it provides the most conservative test of the explanation. It is the most cautious test because it examines the influence of the third-person perception on opinion regarding censorship only after the effects of the many other potential predictors are factored in. Most importantly, the test allows us to pit the two most salient causes – effect on self and the self-other difference – against one another. The self-other difference is the variable of most interest, and so we entered it in the equation last.

Since respondents evaluated 10 television content areas, this detailed analysis results in 10 equations, each predicting support for censorship of one category – violence, premarital sex, long hair, and so on. To give a global picture, Table 3 reports standardized regression coefficients for all 10 categories. Asterisks indicate the level of significance for each factor, and these significance levels reveal that the two variables of primary interest in this study – perceived effect on self, and the perceived additional negative effect on others – play the strongest role in shaping opinion regarding censorship.

Among the other variables, income was the only one to make a consistently meaningful difference. People with higher incomes were less likely to favor stricter censorship. This was true for all categories except portrayals of men with long hair, and religious programs.

Other factors showed only an occasional association with the outcome variable. Women were significantly more likely to favor stricter censorship of violence; men were somewhat more likely to favor stricter censorship of religious programming. Age played no significant role in all categories except violence, and portrayals of men with long hair; in both cases, as one might expect, older people tended to support more censorship. Education and children in the household appeared to have no role in shaping attitudes toward censorship,

Table 3. Standardized regression coefficients showing effect of demographic and perceptual factors on attitudes toward censorship of television content

	Violence	Pre-marital sex	Extra-marital sex	Foul language	Unwed mothers	Homo-sexuality	Nudity	Foreign programs	Men with long hair	Religious programs
Age	-.17**	.03	-.05	-.06	-.05	.02	-.06	-.08	-.21**	-.01
Sex	-.19***	.00	.00	-.09	.05	.04	-.07	-.06	-.04	.10*
Income	.13*	.21***	.27***	.19***	.19***	.15*	.20***	.12*	.06	.00
Education	-.04	.08	.04	.08	.09	.11	.08	.09	.10	.03
Religion	.05	.00	-.01	-.09*	.00	.02	-.02	.04	.06	-.01
Married	-.07	-.15*	-.13	-.18*	-.13	-.18*	-.01	.02	.06	.02
Children	.07	.04	.02	-.02	-.05	-.08	.07	.06	.08	.06
Television entertainment	.08	.09*	.06	-.03	.02	.07	.07	.02	.10*	-.05
Effect on self	.26***	.36***	.37***	.23***	.45***	.42***	.45***	.33***	.33***	.37***
Self/other difference	.24***	.23***	.30***	.16**	.32***	.35***	.30***	.20***	.26***	.21***

Note: Lower score on the dependent variable (support for censorship) indicates support for stricter censorship. Demographic and perceptual variables were coded as follows: Sex (1 = male, 2 = female); Religion (1 = any religious affiliation, 2 = no religious affiliation); Married (1 = married, 2 = not married); Children in household (1 = yes, 2 = no); TV entertainment (1 = low, x = high); Effect on self (1 = large negative effect, 3 = no effect, 5 = large positive effect); Self-other difference (-4 = more negative effect on others, 0 = no difference, 4 = more negative effect on self).

Asterisks indicate whether values are significant: * $p < .05$, ** $p < .01$, *** $p < .001$ (= the chance that the difference is not significant is 5 out of 100, 1 out of 100, and 1 out of 1000, respectively).

Increment to R^2 values were not included in this table in the interest of parsimony, and because they parallel the results described here.

and religion mattered only in the case of foul language, where, surprisingly, people without any stated religious affiliation were slightly more likely to support censorship. Married respondents were significantly more likely to favor censorship in the categories of premarital sex, foul language and homosexuality. Exposure to entertainment television made little difference, although in a few cases higher exposure was related to more liberal attitudes toward censorship.

To further condense the results, and put a spotlight on the factors of most interest, Table 4 gives a summary picture of the relative effect of the two variables with the strongest influence on censorship opinions. For each content category, it shows the percent of variance in the dependent variable – support for censorship – explained by the two independent variables – perceived influence on self, and the perceived self-other difference.

Table 4. Increment to R^2 for "effect on self" and "self-other difference" in predicting support for censorship of TV content by 10 content categories

	Full sample		Respondents showing third-person perception	
Topic	Effect on self	Self-other difference	Effect on self	Self-other difference
Unwed mothers	.07 ***	.07 ***	.00	.10 ***
Premarital sex	.06 ***	.04 ***	.00	.08 ***
Nudity	.09 ***	.06 ***	.03 **	.06 ***
Extramarital sex	.05 ***	.07 ***	.03 **	.05 ***
Homosexuality	.06 ***	.08 ***	.00	.04 **
Foul language	.02 **	.02 ***	.00	.02 *
Violence	.02 **	.04 ***	.00	.05 ***
Men with long hair	.04 ***	.05 ***	.03 *	.04 **
Foreign programs	.07 ***	.04 ***	.06 ***	.04 **
Religious programs	.08 ***	.04 ***	.05 ***	.02

Note: Asterisks indicate whether values are significant: * $p < .05$, ** $p < .01$, *** $p < .001$ (= the chance that the difference is not significant is 5 out of 100, 1 out of 100, and 1 out of 1000, respectively).

Results from the full sample of 500+ Singaporeans are listed in the first two columns. In general, a person's estimate of influence on him- or herself has a significant effect on support for censorship. The more negative that influence is seen to be, the more that person supports stricter constraints on television content. However, even after controlling for effect on self, the third-person perception shows a strong relationship with support for censorship. This result suggests that peoples' assessments of media influence on themselves affects their attitudes about censorship, but that the third-person perception has an additional and independent effect that is equally important.

There is another way to examine the central idea in the third-person effect, and that is by focusing only on those respondents who perceive more negative influence on others than on themselves. In almost all cases these are the majority, but they are also the people most likely to be overestimating negative influence on others. Results of this analysis are shown in the third and fourth columns of Table 4. With this sub-sample one can see more dramatic evidence of the third-person effect. Support for stricter censorship is strongly related to the self-other difference, but shows relatively less connection to perceptions of effect on self.

The reader will note at the bottom of Table 4 two exceptions. In the cases of religious programs and foreign programs – those that most people consider to have more positive influences – the pattern is reversed. Support for censorship is more strongly related to perceived influence on self. Its relationship with the less positive, or more negative, influence seen on others is sharply reduced.

Conclusions

Perceptual bias

Singaporeans did find the influence of the "sensitive" television content categories primarily harmful, but substantially more harmful to others than to themselves. Their estimates of harmful influence were consistent regarding the sex-related categories, and for TV portrayals of violence and foul language. Portrayals of men with long hair were seen as less harmful, but still negative in effect. Religious programming was the one clear-cut exception; in this case most respondents reported positive influences. Estimated influence was most ambiguous for foreign programming. In general, respondents reported that foreign programs would have positive influences on themselves, but a negative effect on the average Singaporean. This finding suggests that people see the potential for both kinds of influences in foreign programs, and that most think they are personally able to derive benefits from the positive side of such programs, but that others will be vulnerable to the negative elements.

Optimistic bias

The above-mentioned difference in perceived effects of foreign programs perhaps best exemplifies a plausible explanation for the third-person perception. We believe that an important underlying reason for this perceptual bias is the tendency for people to see others as more vulnerable to undesirable experiences or influences than themselves – a mechanism to maintain self-esteem. These data, based on repeated measures of perceived influence across 10 content areas, give some persuasive support to the optimistic bias explanation. When the influence of media content appears harmful, respondents perceive more of that influence on others, but when the influence is seen as positive, they expect to experience more influence themselves. It is probable that, unlike the negative categories of sex and violence, people find foreign TV programs and programs with religious themes to have more beneficial than harmful elements – at least to an intelligent and discerning viewer. Therefore, respondents attribute greater influence to themselves. This outcome, an interesting twist on the classic third-person perception, is also consistent with the optimistic bias.

These findings are additionally persuasive because, while previous tests of the optimistic bias were experimental, with university students as subjects, these survey data document the third-person perception in a large population. A useful question for further research would be to determine whether the optimistic bias is a character trait, or a response to the situation. Self-other differences across the 10 issues in this study produced fairly high reliability,[3] favoring a personality explanation. But ratings of religious and foreign programs were more mixed,[4] suggesting that situation may matter as well.

Order effect

It is an important element of this study that respondents appear to be giving genuine answers to the questions about their perceptions of media influence.

Without the order-effect test, we could not be confident that the differences were not simply a result of the way questions were asked.

The cultural factor

There was no cultural difference in the results. People in this study exhibited the perceptual bias just as strongly and consistently as their counterparts in Western cultures. Most of the people surveyed were very much inclined to separate their conceptions of self from that of others in questions of media influence. The Asian conception of a self more integrated with society may be quite real in Singapore, but it does not seem to interfere with the third-person perception.

Opinion about censorship

Singaporeans represented in this survey were concerned about many facets of television content, and, generally, to be heartily in favor of censorship. Given the heavy degree of existing government censorship, this may not seem surprising. But these respondents did not simply support the status quo. They voiced highly variable opinions. In the "sensitive" or "harmful" categories – such as sex and violence – those approving of current censorship levels ranged from 32 to 42 percent. But interestingly, in every case they were outnumbered by those saying censorship should be more strict – often a lot more strict. Only in the case of religious programs and men with long hair did a majority say censorship is about right as it is. And foreign programs received the most sympathy, 31 percent saying censorship should be more liberal.

The portrayals of violence category also presents an unusual case. While it rated among the categories highest in perceived harmful influence, 20 percent of respondents nevertheless said it should be liberalized. In the other "harmful" categories, opinion favoring more liberal censorship never rose above 10 percent. This difference suggests that violence may be a special case – a type of content that is perceived as harmful, but nevertheless meets with less objection.

A question of reliability comes naturally to mind when one considers the censorship responses. It is possible that the survey respondents were giving "politically correct" answers to the censorship questions. That is, they may have been concerned about their anonymity, or other issues, and may have given answers which they felt would meet with official approval. If that were the case, however, one would expect most people to choose the option saying censorship is "about right as it is", an affirmation of existing policy. The fact that many respondents said censorship should be even stricter argues that they are voicing opinions that are truly conservative, but also genuine.

Third-person effect

While official censorship of mass media in Singapore makes an easy target for critics of the government, these data indicate that there is strong public support for censorship as well. Why censorship receives such popular support is the central question in this study. One answer is clearly related to income; low income groups, perhaps those holding more traditional values, seem to have more conservative views, while Singaporeans in the higher income levels favor more liberal censorship policies. Also, as expected, the degree of harmful influence that people perceive, both influence on themselves and influence on others, plays a major role in how much they think sensitive television content should be censored. But most interesting of all, among those who think others are more negatively influenced than themselves (the majority in all cases), it is the perceived *additional* influence on others that primarily predicts support for censorship.[5] In other words, the opinions of people prone to the third-person perception stem largely from their perception of a differential effect on others, rather than any effect on themselves.

While these findings focus on public opinion favoring censorship, sound theoretical reasons exist to suggest that politicians and policy makers may be even more prone to the third-person effect than are ordinary citizens (Schoenbach & Becker, 1995). And to compound the irony, while restrictions on content may be based on false perceptions of influence on others, they may increase the personal appeal of that very same restricted content, a phenomenon known as the "forbidden fruit syndrome". "Almost invariably, our response to banned information is to want to receive that information to a greater extent and to become more favorable toward it..." (Cialdini, 1988, p. 239).

It is important to note here that some related research has shown that people are more likely to overestimate the harmful effects on others, rather than underestimating harmful effects on themselves (see Cohen, et al., 1989; Gunther, 1991; Perloff, 1993). Thus, in exhibiting the third-person perception, people are probably about right in estimating modest influences on themselves, but in error when they think others are more seriously affected.

This overestimation is important, for, to the extent that people are basing their opinions about censorship on their estimates of effects on others, their opinions are based on a false perception. Public opinion, so strongly in favor of television censorship in Singapore, may be inflated by the tendency toward a bias in the perceived difference between oneself and others – a bias that appears to be pervasive across media, across content areas, and across cultures.

Notes

1. An earlier version of this article was published in the *International Journal of Public Opinion Research, Vol. 8* (1996), No. 3. The current version is printed with permission of the publishers of the journal, Oxford University Press, UK, in association with The World Association for Public Opinion Research.
   Funding for the study presented in the article was provided in part by grants from the University of Wisconsin-Madison Graduate School Research Committee and the Television Corporation of Singapore. The authors would like to acknowledge the assistance of Ka Hwie Chan, Ben Lee and Shelly Strom. Please address questions or correspondence to the first author.
2. The non-Western conception of self, however, puts an additional twist on explanations for the third-person effect. While it may reduce the likelihood that people will see themselves as

different from others, it may increase the likelihood that people will react to perceived influences on others.
3. alpha=.79
4. Item-total correlations were .13 and .26 respectively.
5. The possibility that respondents in this survey may have been inclined to give 'politically correct' answers more in line with official censorship policies, while a potential problem in gauging actual opinion about censorship, is a lesser threat to the validity of the third-person effect relationship. Such response bias is likely to be more-or-less systematic; that is, people will adjust their answers (if they do so at all) in a similarly conservative direction. While such a pattern might bias the censorship responses themselves, it would not affect the relationship between perceived influence and opinions about censorship.

References

Cialdini, R. B. (1988) *Influence. Science and Practice*. New York: Harper Collins.
Cohen, J., Mutz, D., Price, V. & Gunther, A. (1988). Perceived impact of defamation: An experiment in third-person effects. *Public Opinion Quarterly, 52*, 161-173.
Crossette, B. "New watchdog group ranks nations in 'corruption index'." *New York Times*, p. 8Y (August 13, 1995).
Davison, W. P. (1983). The third-person effect in communication. *Public Opinion Quarterly, 47,* 1-15.
Emmerson, D. K. (1995) Singapore and the "Asian values" debate. *Journal of Democracy, 6,* 95-105.
Gunther, A. C. (1991). What we think others think: Cause and consequence in the third-person effect. *Communication Research, 18,* 355-372.
Gunther, A. C. (1995). Overrating the X-rating. The third-person perception and support for censorship of pornography. *Journal of Communication, 45,* 27-38.
Gunther, A. C. & Mundy, P. (1993). Biased optimism and the third-person effect. *Journalism Quarterly, 70,* 58-67.
Hachten, W. (1993) *The growth of media in the third world*. Ames: Iowa State University Press.
Kamm, H. "In prosperous Singapore, even the elites are nervous about speaking out." *New York Times,* p. 6Y (August 13, 1995).
Koh, T. "The ten values that undergird East Asian strength and success." *International Herald Tribune,* p. 6 (December 11-12, 1993).
Lasorsa, D. L. (1989). Real and perceived effects of "Amerika". *Journalism Quarterly, 66,* 373-378.
Markus, H. R. & Kitayama, S. (1991). Culture and the self: Implications for cognition, emotion and motivation. *Psychological Review, 98,* 224-253.
Mutz, D. C. (1989). The influence of perceptions of media influence: Third person effects and the public expression of opinions. *International Journal of Public Opinion Research, 1,* 1-21.
Perloff, R. (1993). Third-person effect research 1983-1992: A review and synthesis. *International Journal of Public Opinion Research, 5,* 167-184.
Rucinski, D. & Salmon, C. T. (1990). The 'other' as the vulnerable voter: A study of the third-person effect in the 1988 campaign. *International Journal of Public Opinion Research, 2,* 345-368.
Schoenbach, K. & Becker, L. B. (1995) "Origins and consequences of mediated public opinion", in T. L. Glasser and C. T. Salmon (eds.) *Public Opinion and the Communication of Consent*, p. 323-347. New York: Guilford.
Sesser, S. "A nation of contradictions." *The New Yorker Magazine,* p. 37-68 (January 1992).
Triandis, H. C. (1989). The self and social behavior in differing cultural contexts. *Psychological Review, 96,* 506-520.
Weinstein, N. D. (1989). Optimistic biases about personal risks. *Science,* p. 1232-1233 (December 8).

Attitudes to Television Content in Australia

Margaret Cupitt

The Australian Broadcasting Authority (ABA) has conducted five research studies since 1994 to determine the attitudes of Australians to program content broadcast on free-to-air television services. The studies addressed a range of issues that were relevant to research priorities at the time when each study took place. Some questions were also replicated to track trends over time. The trends presented in this article cover the level of community concern and the issues of concern about television content. The article focuses on the results from the fifth study that was conducted in 1999. The fifth study targeted community attitudes to news and current affairs programs on free-to-air television, and movies classified M (mature audience)[1] and MA (mature adult audience)[2] on commercial television. It also measured community awareness of, and experience with, the complaints process identified in industry codes of practice.

The study findings contribute to periodic reviews of codes of practice to determine whether they are in accordance with prevailing community standards. For instance, the 1999 survey results will provide a benchmark to assess the effectiveness of the revised Commercial Television Industry Code of Practice which came into effect in April 1999 with a new AV classification (adult violence).[3] The results also assist the ABA to investigate unresolved complaints and to complement the information about complaints received from broadcasters.

The fifth survey occurred in all states and territories of Australia covering a representative sample of households. Telephone interviews were conducted with 1,203 people (693 females and 510 males) aged 15 years and over between 21 April 1999 and 2 May 1999. The survey was commissioned from Keys Young Pty Ltd in Sydney. Prior to the fieldwork for the national survey, in February and March 1999, staff from the ABA facilitated seven focus group discussions in three states (New South Wales, Queensland and Tasmania). Fifty-three people aged 15 years and over took part in the discussions. Some of the comments made by focus group participants are reproduced in this article.

Background

The free-to-air television industry in Australia comprises five main television services. Three of these services are the metropolitan commercial networks (the Seven, Nine and Ten networks) that are affiliated with various regional stations, and two national public networks known as the Australian Broadcasting Corporation (ABC) and the Special Broadcasting Service (SBS).

The commercial television industry, the ABC and the SBS each have a code of practice that identifies their obligations relating to the complaints handling process and the content of programs. The codes govern all aspects of program content, including program classifications and content advisories, program promotions, accuracy and fairness in news and current affairs programs, warnings before potentially distressing news material, discrimination, privacy, and the timing and placement of advertising where relevant.

Codes of practice generally incorporate a system of time zoning where programs with certain classifications can only be shown at particular times of the day. For instance, the M, MA and AV classifications commence at 8.30 p.m., 9.00 p.m. and 9.30 p.m., respectively. The classification symbols and time zones provide tools for adults to select programs for themselves and for children in their care. ABA research has shown that the classifications are important to the Australian community, and that some groups such as carers of children are reliant on them. The classification system in Australia has been operating in one form or another for about 40 years. Specific content advisories about sex, violence and language were implemented in Australia in 1993.

The Commercial Television Industry Code of Practice requires that program classifications be visually and orally announced on-air at the start of a program, after each advertising break, and in program promotions. Content advisories are mandatory for M, MA and AV programs where visual and oral advice is broadcast at the start of programs and visual advice is given after each advertising break. Classification symbols and content advisories must also accompany press advertising of programs and program listings in program guides.

Codes of practice are part of a co-regulatory framework whereby the industry sectors develop their respective codes, consult the public, and then register them with, or notify them to, the Australian Broadcasting Authority.[4] Complaints about matters covered by the codes of practice must be made to the television stations in the first instance. They can then be directed to the ABA for investigation if the complainant is either dissatisfied with the station's response or the station does not answer the complaint within 60 days.

The use of television, pay TV and the Internet in Australia

To provide some context about television use in Australia, people watched an average of three hours and 14 minutes each day in 1998 with about 98 per cent of households owning at least one television and 59 per cent owning two or more sets.[5] Pay TV was introduced to Australia in 1995 and had a penetration level of 12 per cent in 1998[6] comprising just over seven per cent of total television viewing.[7]

Internet access in the home has risen from 9 per cent in February 1998[8] to 22 per cent in May 1999.[9] A study conducted in June 1999[10] found that most Australians (76%) believed there were risks to Internet use. The top five risks were: unsuitable content for children, pornographic material, risks associated with financial transactions, data protection and privacy issues, and illegal content. A substantial number of people said they would like to block certain material if it were technically feasible. Such material included racist messages (60%), pornography and sex scenes (53%), depictions of violence (41%), obscene language (38%) and nudity (26%).

Australia has recently established a co-regulatory scheme for Internet content that is similar to the scheme that is in place for television. It is based on the development of industry codes of practice, the investigation of complaints by the ABA, and the establishment of a complaints hotline. The ABA is currently working with the Internet industry and the community to implement the scheme from 1 January 2000.

Major trends – attitudes to television content

There has been a substantial and relatively consistent level of concern about television content between 1995 and 1999. Thirty-eight per cent of people surveyed said they either disliked or were concerned about something seen on television in 1995, 1996 and 1997, and 33 per cent said they were either concerned or offended by something seen on television in 1999.

News and current affairs programs, violent content, sex and nudity, and advertising have each appeared in the top five issues of concern that were mentioned spontaneously by survey respondents. The data appears to fluctuate depending on current events and the particular programs shown during the survey periods. The following points reflect the main trends.

- News and current affairs programs have been the top concern between 1994 and 1997. These programs were the second concern in 1999 as expressed by 11 per cent of the sample.
- The portrayal of violence on television was the top concern in 1999 as mentioned by 12 per cent of the sample. This represents an increase from six per cent in 1997. Violent content was the second issue of concern behind news and current affairs between 1994 and 1997.
- Concern about sex scenes and nudity reached a peak at nine per cent of the survey sample in 1996, probably due to the broadcast of lifestyle programs, such as *Sex/Life*, at that time. The level of concern fluctuated between four and six per cent for the years either side of 1996.

- Concern about advertising has remained relatively constant between 1994 and 1999, ranging from a low three per cent to a high six per cent of the sample.
- Coarse language was the fifth highest concern mentioned in 1997 and 1999. The level of concern about coarse language increased from one per cent in 1994, 1995 and 1996 to five per cent in 1999.

Level and issues of concern about television content in 1999

In 1999, survey respondents were asked three questions to measure the level of concern about television content in the three months prior to the survey. The results showed that:

- 33 per cent of survey respondents were concerned or offended by something seen on free-to-air television;
- 30 per cent were concerned or offended by the way news and current affairs programs were presented on free-to-air television; and
- 16 per cent had seen something in a movie on commercial television that should have been broadcast at a later time (12%) or not shown at all (4%).

When the responses to these three questions were considered, a total 52 per cent of survey respondents indicated concern about some aspect of television content. A smaller proportion of survey respondents (35%) agreed they had seen something on television that had bothered them enough to make a complaint. However, most of these people did not actually complain.

More females and people in the older age groups were concerned about television content than males and younger people. They were also more likely to have seen something on television that bothered them enough to make a complaint.

Violent television content and the way material is shown in news and current affairs programs were the top two issues that were mentioned spontaneously by respondents who were concerned or offended by something seen on free-to-air television. Those concerns were followed by sex scenes and nudity, advertising and coarse language, with each of these being mentioned by five per cent of survey respondents (Table 1). Concern about the portrayal of violence related to movies, drama programs, real life police shows, and news and current affairs programs.

Table 1. Issues of offence or concern about content on free-to-air television, 1999

Issues of concern or offence	Number of people	% people	% concerned people
Violence	141	12	36
News and current affairs	129	11	33
Sex scenes or nudity	65	5	17
Advertising	62	5	16
Coarse language	55	5	14
Programming	35	3	9
Sexist, racist stereotyping	21	2	5
Content that provides bad role models for children	19	2	5
Promotion of adult programs during children's viewing times	17	1	4
Content that promotes antisocial/immoral values	15	1	4
Drug use	4	<1	1
Depictions of suicide	2	<1	1
Other	23	2	6
n =		1,203	391

Note: News and current affairs include: bias/unfair (5% of the survey sample); unnecessary graphic images of accidents, death, violence, war (5%); intrusive reporting, e.g., grieving relatives, distressed victims (1%); sensationalist, exaggerated, 'hyped up' (1%); and all news is depressing (<1%).
Advertising includes: too many ads (4%); increased volume (1%); and content of ads (1%).
Programming includes: poor quality programs (2%); too many US programs (1%); and not enough variety (1%).

In focus groups, desensitisation to violence was a common theme discussed. Many participants felt strongly they were being bombarded by too much violent material and were concerned that some of the unusual activities depicted on television (e.g., certain violent acts, drug use) could become normalised or accepted by society. These concerns were made alongside the beliefs that: television is a powerful medium, there is an increasing amount of violent material being shown across many program types, and there are potential long-term influences of television content. While some people believed that such material would affect people, many were uncertain about the nature of that impact in the future. A small number of people were reluctant to believe that television influences could be isolated from other influences, such as exposure to other media and difficult life circumstances. Some of the comments made by focus group participants are given below.

> It would desensitise me if I watched it for long enough. Anything desensitises – people who live in a war zone lose their sense of horror about war. It's just part of their life... but it wouldn't program me to go out and do it because it's entirely and absolutely against what I think is right. But, having said that, if someone's brought up on a diet of that, where they're constantly exposed to it, it becomes normal to them. (Male over 55 years)

> I just wonder how much of what children see... how much they tend to think it may be... a reasonably acceptable situation what's happening, and how much it does get into their brains, and I think... we don't know really until they start to grow up and see what they do. But I just think that sometimes they get the impression that it's not evil or whatever, that it's okay to be happening. (Male 40-54 years)

> So if people are constantly bombarded by this, you do get immune to it after a while... Your children I'm sure become desensitised... Yes, children and a lot of adults. Because it is so constant, there is so much of it that we're seeing on TV... And I know my kids become bored, "Oh, no, not the news again Mum", and I'm sure they do it to a certain extent because there's also a lot of violence in a lot of movies and things like that and they must become desensitised to a lot of the violence that's going on in reality – in the real world. (Female 40-54 years)

> I'm not sure where TV goes. Well, is it a reflection of our culture or is it pushing our culture? (Female parent)

There was a similar but slightly higher level of concern about what is shown in televised movies (38% of the survey sample) than the way things are shown in news and current affairs programs (30%). Almost one-quarter (24%) said they were equally concerned about movies and current affairs, and the remainder said they were not concerned about either.

News and current affairs programs

Above it was reported that 11 per cent of the sample spontaneously mentioned news and current affairs as an issue of concern. When all survey respondents were asked directly about the way news and current affairs programs are presented on free-to-air television, 30 per cent said they had seen something in the last three months that offended or concerned them. Over two-thirds of the total sample (68%) had not seen anything of concern and 2 per cent were not sure.

Concern about news and current affairs programs tended to be expressed more by people aged over 30 years, where the proportion of concerned people peaked at the 35 to 39 year age group (38%) and the 55 to 59 year age group (40%). A higher number of people with post-graduate qualifications also said they were concerned (40%) compared to people educated to secondary school level (21%).

An equal proportion of people surveyed mentioned concerns about classification aspects of news and current affairs programs (14% of the sample) and the treatment given to individual stories (14%). Classification aspects comprised unnecessary graphic images of death, dead bodies, and people in distress (10%), and excessive violent content. Concerns about the treatment of individual stories included biased content, intrusive reporting techniques or lack of respect for people's privacy, and sensationalised or exaggerated content (Table 2).

Table 2. Issues of offence or concern about news and current affairs programs on free-to-air television, 1999

Issues of concern	Number of people	% people	% concerned people
Classification issues	**166**	**14**	**46**
Unnecessary graphic images of death, dead bodies & war	94	8	26
Unnecessary graphic images – other, e.g., people in distress	39	3	11
Excessive violent content, e.g., brawls, riots, assaults, violent arrests	33	3	9
Material not suitable for children	26	2	7
Drug use, condoning drug use	5	<1	1
Nudity or sexual references	4	<1	1
Treatment of individual stories	**165**	**14**	**46**
Biased/judgemental content, one-sided or narrow views	56	5	16
Intrusive reporting techniques, no respect for people's privacy, not sensitive to victims	55	5	15
Sensationalised, exaggerated, melodramatic	33	3	9
Untrue, inaccurate factual material reported	14	1	4
'Manufactured' news stories	12	<1	3
Discrimination, misrepresentation, patronisation of minorities	10	<1	3
Glorification/legitimisation of violence	8	<1	2
Scheduling of stories	**30**	**3**	**8**
Other	**28**	**2**	**8**
Not sure/ no clear answer	**43**	**4**	**12**
n =		1,179	357

Note: The "other" category contains issues that were individually mentioned by fewer than four people. The issues include: trial by media; irresponsible reporting; inadequate warnings; kids being interviewed or shown; self interest on the part of media outlets; too real or close to home; stories designed to 'brainwash' or mould opinion; over-simplification of issues; or can give people ideas (e.g., Colorado school shooting).
The "scheduling of stories" category includes repetition of news items, too much bad news, inadequate treatment given to important news stories.

Unnecessary graphic images

When asked directly about graphic images, over half the survey respondents (58%) either strongly agreed (29%) or somewhat agreed (29%) that news and current affairs programs tend to show unnecessary graphic images of accidents and tragedies. Focus group participants expressed the need to know about news events but many questioned the benefit in showing images that are too graphic and repeated throughout the day and evening. Some suggested that graphic footage be delayed until late in the evening, while others thought it should not be shown and were in favour of hearing about it instead.

> When you are actually seeing it [violence] on the news in those sort of time slots it's just horrifying. You don't want to see real things like that. I don't anyway... It's okay to hear about it... I don't even think it's something that

> should be shown later at night you know... I just think it's something that shouldn't be shown in general. (Female 25-39 years)

> I mean okay we need to know as a society that's fine, but [do we need to]... have something that graphic thrust in front of us when we are just to sit down before our evening meals? (Male 40-54 years)

On the other hand, some participants were positive about news coverage and accepted the need to confront ugly events.

> I think that TV [news] presents life as it is. It doesn't embellish it, it doesn't necessarily dramatise it. It doesn't overlay any editorial comment on it. The news is just – these are the pictures, this is the story – and it does because of the sheer volume of it... throw a lot more pressure on you to try and explain it and put it into some sort of perspective to your kids. You have to take the time to sit and say well, look I know all these things are happening, but they're not happening here... right this minute. ... And I think that's the effect it is having on kids in the general sense. They grow up with a bit of a negative point of view of the world at large. They think disaster is about to befall them any minute. You talk to pre-teens or teenagers and they have not confidence in the fact that the world is going to continue on as it has done. They think it's about to come to an end one way or another. (Male 40-54 years)

Some people commented that violent or graphic material seen on news and current affairs programs is worse than seeing similar images in fictional programs such as movies and drama programs. This was because news events were actually happening somewhere in the world.

Intrusive reporting techniques

When asked specifically about interviews with grieving relatives, there was equal division in the community about reporting techniques. Almost half the survey sample (47%) held the view that news and current affairs programs usually lacked sensitivity to people involved in traumatic incidents. The same number held the opposite view. While the sample was evenly split, almost one-quarter strongly agreed that news and current affairs programs lacked such sensitivity. Older age groups were more likely than younger people to believe the reporting techniques were insensitive.

> Some of the reports I think can be quite intrusive on the families and things like that. I mean they're grieving, they've lost loved ones and things like that. And you sort of think, come on reporters, give them a heart, you know you wouldn't like it if it was one of your own family and you've got somebody with a microphone stuck up under your face. I do think that's sort of a little bit hard for the media to do that to people. And to actually show that on TV. (Female 40-54 years)

> That's probably one thing that annoys me a bit about the media, they do that sort of thing and they justify doing it because they think that I have a right to know. Well I as a member of the public I don't need to see a reporter being that intrusive... So they can't justify it in the sense of what I should be seeing or hearing or knowing. So I'm not really certain as to why they do it at all. Is it a cynical, commercial thing, you know, the more blood and gore you have the more viewers you get... (Male 40-54 years)

Sensationalism

In the focus groups there was a widespread view that some reports and footage on news and current affairs programs are broadcast to entertain audiences, compete with other news programs and gain high audience ratings, particularly with regard to the commercial television stations. Criticism of sensationalism was made in relation to unnecessary and repetitive graphic images, biased or one-sided reports, intrusive reporting techniques, and stories that were seen as irrelevant.

About half (51%) the survey sample agreed that news and current affairs programs put unnecessary emphasis on personal characteristics such as ethnic background, sexuality or disability. Some focus group participants described certain stories as "gossip news" which included material about con-artists, battlers, cockroach-infested or dirty houses, and negative stories about youth unemployment.

> They downgrade us, I reckon, all the time... It's like every young person is a dole bludger. (Female 18-24 years)

> They focus on exceptional cases... that are really out of the ordinary, as opposed to showing what the average young person is going through, trying to get a job. (Male 18-24 years)

Accuracy

A considerable number of people in the survey believed that news and current affairs stories were accurate. Fifty-four per cent either strongly agreed (13%) or somewhat agreed (41%) that news and current affairs programs are accurate in the facts they present to the audience. Forty per cent disagreed with the statement. The accuracy of news and current affairs stories was not discussed as a specific issue in focus groups.

Depiction of drug use

Some focus group participants commented on the depiction of drug use in news reports. They referred to some of these as being like documentaries on how to use drugs.

> Everyone knows it's [drug use] such a widespread problem. Like, they don't need to show it in such detail... Like, you know, they are showing you how to shoot up a needle. Why do they do it? (Female 18-24 years)

> That thing that was on tellie a little while ago it was on the news about them giving... heroin out to children. You actually see them injecting. I don't think we need to see that. (Female parent)

Measures to address concerns

Almost a quarter of survey respondents said their concerns about news and current affairs would be addressed by presenting the item in a different way (23%), providing warnings or better warnings before certain stories (15%), not showing the news item at all (8%), or showing the news item at a later time (8%).

Presenting news items differently and not showing news items at all were seen as the main ways to reduce concerns about issues such as bias, intrusive reporting and sensationalised reports. The use of warnings and showing news items at a later time in the evening were seen as the most likely ways to deal with classification issues such as unnecessary graphic images and violent news content. More parents said that certain news items should be shown at a later time than non-parents.

There was strong evidence that the warnings currently used to prepare viewers for potentially distressing images are appropriate. A majority of people (83%) either strongly agreed (42%) or somewhat agreed (41%) that appropriate warnings are given before potentially offensive or distressing material is shown.

Movies classified M and MA on commercial television

There was certain material in M and MA classified movies broadcast from 8.30 p.m. on commercial television that some people believed should either have been broadcast at a later time (12 % of the survey sample) or not shown at all (4%). The proportion of people who were concerned was much the same across the sample with no particular demographic group holding greater concern. The reasons for concern are identified in Table 3 with violence topping the list.

When asked specifically about a range of classification issues associated with M and MA movies, the results confirmed that violent content was least acceptable compared to other issues (Table 4). A considerable number of people (45% of the sample) said the amount and kind of violence broadcast in movies was not acceptable. After violent content, the depiction of drug use was least accepted (43%), followed by coarse language (38%), the portrayal of suicide (32%), sex scenes (24%) and nudity (21%). It was widely believed by focus group participants that the use of coarse language in movies had increased over time. Views varied about whether the (sexually explicit) F word should be cut completely from movies, used infrequently, or only appear in movies broadcast after 9.00 p.m. or 9.30 p.m.

Table 3. Reasons for M and MA movies to be shown at a later time or not at all

Reason	Number of people	% commercial TV viewers	% concerned people
Violence (total)	107	9	58
Sex scenes or nudity	50	4	27
Coarse language, swearing	33	3	18
Not appropriate for children	30	3	16
Content that provides bad role models for children	12	1	7
Depictions of same sex relationships	4	<1	2
Depictions of drug use	4	<1	2
Immoral or antisocial messages	4	<1	2
Other	16	1	9
Not sure/ no clear answer	23	2	13
n =		1,145	184

Note: The "violence (total)" category includes: violent content that is excessive, too frequent or sustained; violence that was/is graphic, explicit, realistic, brutal or cruel; too gory, bloody or horrific; murder/killing; guns, knives, bombs, weapons shown or made to look attractive; violence unnecessary in the context of the movie; and violence made to seem attractive or acceptable/ glorified.

Table 4. Acceptability among commercial TV viewers of the amount and kind of violence, depictions of drug use, coarse language, suicide, sex and nudity (%)

	Violence	Drug use	Swearing and bad language	Suicide	Sex scenes	Nudity
Totally acceptable	11	11	14	9	19	20
Mostly acceptable	39	34	44	27	49	50
Not very acceptable	28	21	21	15	15	13
Not at all acceptable	17	22	17	17	9	8
Never seen	3	11	4	30	6	7
Not sure	1	2	1	3	2	2
n = 1,145						

Confirming the relative importance of violence as an issue of concern in movies, 78 per cent of the sample said they would not be comfortable with more violence being shown in movies. A smaller proportion (65%) said they would not be comfortable with more sex scenes and nudity.

People in the younger age groups were considerably more accepting of violent content in movies than older people. Eighty-two per cent of 15 to 24 year olds said violent content was totally or mostly acceptable compared to 26 per cent of those aged 55 years and over. Males (58%) were also more likely to say that violent content was totally or mostly acceptable than females (44%). People who described themselves as having strong religious beliefs said that violent content was less acceptable than people with some or no particular religious beliefs.

A similar demographic pattern was evident for coarse language, the portrayal of suicide, sex scenes and nudity where each was found to be less accepted by the older age groups in particular, but also by females and people with very strong religious beliefs. These groups were also the least comfortable with having more violent or sexual content. Coarse language, sex scenes and nudity were more acceptable to parents than non-parents. Parents, however, were more likely to say they would not be comfortable with more violence being shown in movies than non-parents.

Contextual aspects of movies

The lack of realism, the high degree of realism, and the narrative context of violent portrayals were important considerations when assessing violent material. Fifty-nine per cent of survey respondents agreed they had seen violence that was presented in a way that did not show its true consequences. Almost the same number (57%) agreed that some portrayals of violence were too close to what can happen in real life. About half (52%) had seen violent content that was unnecessary in the context of the movie, and 45 per cent said some violence was presented in a way that made it appear attractive. Fewer people agreed that the violence they had seen in the last three months was too graphic or explicit (37%) or too frequent (36%).

There is an apparent contradiction between concern about the lack of realism on the one hand and realistic violence on the other hand. One parent of a primary school aged child explained the difficulty he had in dealing with each form of violent content.

> We watch television and we see all these shows and people get beaten up and punched and kicked… they just bounce back up and have another go. But the reality of this is you get hit by a baseball bat and you die… And the kids don't see that… It's violence but it's not true violence… Now I'm not saying that that's bad because after seeing the reaction of my daughter to real violence it's probably good… I wouldn't like to be having all the gore and the real true violence paraded all the time. It may be misleading, but it's better than seeing the real thing.

Narrative context was also a prominent consideration with regard to sex scenes and nudity in movies. Thirty-eight per cent of survey respondents said they had seen nudity or sex scenes that were unnecessary in the context of movies. Twenty-eight per cent said such material was demeaning to women or men, 19 per cent said they were too graphic or explicit, and 18 per cent said they were too frequent.

Appropriateness of the M and MA classification and time zones

The Commercial Television Industry Code of Practice specifies that MA (mature audience) classified movies should not commence before 9.00 p.m. The new AV (adult violence) classification for television requires that movies with strong levels of violence should not start until 9.30 p.m. The AV classification was introduced with the revised code of practice in April 1999 when this survey was conducted. The survey and focus group findings provide evidence that this change is in line with community standards.

A clear majority of people in the survey (76%) believed that MA movies on commercial television should be shown only after a certain time in the evening. Just less than one-third (31%) identified 9.00 p.m. as the earliest time and almost the same proportion (29%) said MA movies should start at 9.30 p.m. Sixteen per cent specified a later start time and 19 per cent said earlier than 9.00 p.m. or anytime during the day (Table 5).

Table 5. The earliest time in the evening to show MA movies on commercial television (%)

Time	Total	Female	Male
Earlier than 9 p.m./ anytime	19	16	23
9.00 p.m.	31	28	34
9.30 p.m.	29	31	26
10.00 p.m.	11	13	8
10.30 p.m.	3	4	2
Later than 10.30 p.m.	2	2	2
Should not be shown at all	2	2	1
Don't care	1	<1	2
Not sure	2	<1	1
n =	1,145	662	483

Males tended to nominate 9.00 p.m. or earlier/anytime as a start time for movies compared to females who were more likely to nominate later times. People with post-graduate qualifications said 9.30 p.m. more than any other group, while 10.00 p.m. was nominated by more people with very strong religious beliefs. A substantial number of young people aged 15 to 24 years (40%) said that MA movies could be shown earlier than 9.00 p.m. or anytime, compared to 11 per cent of people aged over 55 years.

Many parents and some non-parents in focus groups suggested that certain M classified movies shown on television at 8.30 p.m. had not been appropriately classified. They included *The Professional*, *Bad Boys* and the telemovie *Killer Net*. The times 9.00 p.m. and 9.30 p.m. were frequently mentioned as the threshold for adult movies to more accurately reflect children's bedtimes. Other people believed that parents should take the responsibility for checking the classification and determining whether children should be allowed to watch certain movies.

Most people in the survey (about two-thirds) believed that the content of M and MA movies and the times they were shown were always or usually classified appropriately. Twenty per cent said that M classified movies were only sometimes or never appropriately classified, and 17 per cent said this about MA classified movies (Table 6). Many comments made in focus groups implied considerable reliance on the television classifications and associated time zones.

Table 6. Appropriateness of the classifications for M and MA movies (%)

Level of appropriateness	M classification	MA classification
Always appropriate	20	21
Usually appropriate	49	45
Only sometimes appropriate	17	13
Never appropriate	3	4
Not sure	5	6
Had not seen any M or MA movies	5	10
n =	1,145	1,145

Complaints handling process

Codes of practice identify the television industry's obligations with regard to the content of programs they broadcast. They also set out the process for the community to complain about television content. Complaints about matters covered by the codes of practice must be made to the broadcaster in the first instance. Such complaints can then be directed to the ABA if the complainant is either dissatisfied with the station's response or the station does not answer the complaint within 60 days. The codes of practice normally require complaints to be made in writing to the television station.

Most survey respondents (67%) said they took some form of action in the last three months after seeing something on television that caused them offence or concern. Almost four out of every ten said they had discussed the matter with someone else or had changed the television channel. Just less than one-third said they had prevented a child from viewing certain material at some stage (Table 7).

Parents and females were more likely than non-parents and males to take some form of action about their concerns. Sixty-eight per cent of all the parents who took part in the survey said they had prevented a child from watching television at some stage in the last three months.

Only one per cent of respondents (16 people) said they took their concerns out of their immediate home or social environment by making a formal complaint.

Table 7. Action taken after seeing something of concern on television in the last three months (%)

Action taken	Total	Males	Females	Parents/ guardians	Nonparents
Discussed the matter with someone else	39	33	43	44	37
Changed the channel	38	31	43	40	37
Prevented a child from watching	30	24	34	68	14
Turned off the TV	25	20	29	28	24
Covered your eyes or looked away	23	9	33	24	23
Left the room	19	14	22	21	18
Made a formal complaint	1	1	1	1	1
n =	1,203	510	693	359	844

A larger proportion of six per cent (or 77 people) recalled *ever* making a complaint. It is likely that survey respondents who said they complained were referring to complaints made by phone in addition to formal written complaints. Most of the complainants were not satisfied with the way their complaint was handled (50 people or 65% of those who complained). Nineteen people (25% of the complainants) were satisfied and eight people (10%) were not sure. Lack of satisfaction was either because no action had been taken, the person contacted was not interested or was rude, no reply was received, or there was no one to take the complaint. The small group of complainants tended to be older and have post-graduate qualifications.

Reasons for not complaining

Notably, the majority of people surveyed (58%) believed that making a formal complaint would not change the kind of things shown on television, and 50 per cent said they would not know who to complain to if they wanted to. Most people also said they had not seen information about how to complain on television in the last year (57%).

With 52 per cent of survey respondents expressing concern or offence about content issues and 35 per cent indicating they were bothered enough by something on television to make a complaint, the research suggests possible reasons why only six per cent had actually complained in the previous year. Of the 35 per cent of potential complainants, 63 per cent said they had not seen information on television about how to complain, 54 per cent lacked confidence in the complaints process, and 51 per cent said they would not know who to approach with a complaint. Having enough time to complain was given as an explanation by 26 per cent of potential complainants.

The focus group discussions indicated very low awareness and understanding about the industry codes of practice, including the complaints handling process. The following quotes illustrate the nature of that lack of understanding in association with a general lack of confidence in obtaining a satisfactory outcome from making a complaint.

> It all depends on the ratings doesn't it? They are not going to change it if they get good ratings, for anyone. (Male over 55 years)

> I did ring up the TV station and complain about it [a report about the child support system]... Nothing [happened]. I just wanted to speak to the woman that had edited – created this show. She said watch tonight and hung up on me. (Female parent)

> That particular evening I was watching a movie which went on pretty late and I timed it and there were literally 35 minutes of ads to the hour and I rang the station just to make that point and complain about it... I said... why do you do that and who should I complain to about it and they said well complain to these people, complain to those people. They didn't explain or apologise or even acknowledge that it happened... They didn't give me names and addresses or anything of that nature. They were not the least bit interested in what I had to say... [I didn't take it any further because] I felt that since it had been done and it had passed and I had no evidence or proof that it happened that it would have been extraordinarily picky and pedantic of me to pursue it. If I'd taped it or something like that and had hard evidence... Without evidence they would have dismissed it. Just somebody whingeing. (Male 40-54 years)

> But most people that do complain... think it's inappropriate at the time or whatever, but you just don't worry about it... I mean, you probably think "well, what's my saying going to do?" (Female 18-24 years)

Epilogue

It should be noted that while this research focused on program content that concerned or offended Australian television viewers, many viewers said they had no concerns (48%) and most said nothing had bothered them enough to make a complaint (65%). Focus group participants commented positively about certain programs, having access to live sporting events, keeping up-to-date with news and current affairs, and the variety and choice of programs and channels. They liked viewing television because the experience was entertaining, informative or relaxing, and it allowed some people to keep their minds off other things.

From the ABA's perspective, the historical trends and recent data show there are a substantial proportion of people who continue to be concerned about the presentation of news and current affairs programs, about the portrayal of violence in movies, and about some other programs. The recently introduced AV (adult violence) classification would appear to address community concern about violence content in movies. The concerns about news and current affairs programs as they relate to unnecessary graphic images, bias or one-sided reports, and intrusive reporting or privacy are potential areas for further tightening of the codes of practice. These issues were problematic because they were perceived as techniques that sensationalise the news and create entertainment in order to achieve higher audience ratings. The research will be made available for television broadcasters to consider when they next review their codes of practice.

In a co-regulatory environment where the industry is responsible for developing its own codes of practice, the results that show a considerable lack of understanding and confidence in the complaint process are significant. The commercial television industry is now required to provide regular information about the code of practice and its complaints procedures. Three hundred and sixty on-air spots must be broadcast each calendar year across all viewing zones. A reasonable proportion of the on-air information must also explain how viewers can obtain a copy of the code of practice. The effectiveness of this action will be assessed by future studies.

Notes

1. Material classified M is recommended for viewing only by persons aged 15 years or over because of the matter it contains (violence, sex and nudity, language, drugs, suicide, adult themes), or the way the matter is treated.
2. Material classified MA is suitable for viewing only by persons aged 15 years or over because of the intensity and/or frequency of sexual depictions, or coarse language, adult themes or drug use.
3. Material classified AV is suitable for viewing only by persons aged 15 years or over. It is unsuitable for MA classification because of the intensity and/or frequency of violence, or because violence is central to the theme. In other respects, the classification's requirements are identical to the MA classification.
4. The Commercial Television Industry Code of Practice is registered by the ABA once it meets certain criteria. The codes of practice for the ABC and SBS are not assessed by the ABA but are notified to the ABA.
5. *ACNielsen Metro Television Facts* 1999.
6. ACNielsen TV Trends 1999, *B&T Weekly*.
7. Meade, A and McKenzie, A 1999 'TV chiefs disagree on parallel universes', *The Australian,* 3 August 1999, p.3.
8. Australian Bureau of Statistics 1999 'Continued growth in home Internet use', *Media Release 78/99*, 30 June 1999.
9. Australian Bureau of Statistics 1999 *Use of the Internet by householders,* 6 September 1999.
10. Australian Broadcasting Authority 1999 'International research on attitudes to the Internet', *News Release 71/1999*, 24 August 1999. *Editors' remark:* See also the article "Opinions in Australia, Germany and the U.S. on Control of Misuse on the Internet" by Jens Waltermann and Marcel Machill in this book.

Contents in Context

A Study on Canadian Family Discourse about Media Practices in the Home

André H. Caron & Letizia Caronia[1]

Historically, the study of television use and consumption has dealt largely with genres, semiotic characteristics of programs and their effects on the audience, and the encoding and decoding processes that characterize the relation between the text and its audience. Since Lull's studies (Lull, 1980; 1987; 1991), a number of authors have, however, emphasized the need to understand the relation between audience and television in the complex, finely shaded context of daily life. The natural setting for viewing – the home – has thus become increasingly central and research has focused on understanding viewing as a situated activity.

Instead of audience preferences for certain programs, the activity itself has become the focus of study (Morley, 1992). The hypothesis underlying this perspective is that television viewing is a complex activity that is integrated into domestic life and invested with different meanings by family members. Reactions to television messages thus depend on the meaning assigned to this technology and on the role and purposes attributed to viewing as an everyday activity (Morley, Silverstone, 1991). They also depend on the psycho-social place given to television by the various social actors and on the relation television has to other activities in daily life.

Television consumption must therefore be understood as a situated activity that structures and is structured by the social organization of people's everyday activities. It is a part of everyday life and plays a role in it that needs to be investigated.

How does television viewing structure the range of everyday practices that characterizes family life? Inversely, how do they structure it? How does it participate in the dynamics of family relations? How do parents mediate the more sensitive contents (sex and violence)? The programs that television offers to its audience join a background of specific everyday habits, understanding and mediating practices by which they acquire their meaning.

The very concept of "viewing" then becomes nothing more than a covering term for a multitude of practices, in and through which family members construct their relation to this medium. The process of decoding – to which a certain research tradition had reduced the notion of reception – then becomes one aspect of a more complex activity (viewing) that, in turn, belongs to a larger context of practices.

At present, studies on family relation dynamics with respect to television provide us with a conceptual framework and research perspective that could be described as a *contextualist approach to television viewing in the network of family interactions*. In sum, this perspective conceptualizes viewing as an activity situated among family practices and texts as discourses among others. The incorporation of television into daily life is conceived as a process that produces and is produced by family interactions. This technology, its uses and the content it offers then become objects or mediators of these social interactions. The question is thus how the specific culture and social organization of a family is defined by this technology and – reflexively – how the latter is appropriated and incorporated by the social dynamics of the family environment and the cultural worlds of its members (Caron, Meunier, 1995).

According to several authors, grasping and understanding the phenomenon defined in this way requires a qualitative approach targeting the microcosm of daily interactions and the members' discourses about their own media experiences (Lindlof, Mayer, 1987; Morely, 1989; Morely, Silverstone, 1991; Casetti, 1995; Proulx, Maillet, 1998). It is on this level and through these dynamics that the members of a family constantly construct what, for them, watching television means. By the way of such interactions, they assign this practice a meaning (a certain meaning), which integrates the content into their own culture, and establish their daily routines in relation to television.

Two methodological approaches (that are not mutually exclusive) can be identified in this tradition of qualitative studies in mass communication: one is especially based on (more or less participatory) observation in the *natural setting* of viewing, the other focuses more on triggering *discourse* through in-depth interviews (Proulx, Maillet, 1998). In the first case, attention is focused mainly on the communicative behavior produced in response to the screen and the informal conversations that occur between family members on various occasions in their daily life (Lemish, 1987; Brice, 1987; Casetti, 1995; Mancini, 1993). In the second case it is mainly a question of grasping the reconstruction of the media experience produced by users in specific declarative situations: individual or group interviews (Morley, 1992; Bianchi, 1990; Casetti et al., 1985, 1986).

These approaches target and reveal two different levels of the media experience as a subject of study: the process level of the situated action, of the actual behavior, and the declarative level of the reconstructed action, of the said behavior, organized in discourse and by discourse. These approaches thus offer us two different types of qualitative data, two distinct views of television's integration into daily family life – one focused more on the performance of practices, the other on the meanings attributed to the practices.

The study we are proposing continues in this tradition of qualitative research. It adopts a contextualist perspective on television viewing as an activity embedded in a range of everyday practices and takes into account a specific phenomenon: *the sense making activity accomplished through family discourse on television viewing in the home.*

Sex and violence and other contents as discourse topics: a phenomenological research approach

The study involved eight families in Canada. They were recruited for a study on television use in the home that had both quantitative and qualitative aspects and involved elementary school children aged 10 to 11 (Grade 5). The socio-economic level (revenue, employment and education) and media consumption habits of these families closely match the features generally identified with members of what is considered the middle class.

Each family was made up of two adults and 1 to 3 children. Since we were also interested in contrasting the different accounts of the parents and 10- to 11-year olds in the same families, we interviewed the children and adults separately.

Semi-directed interviews were adopted as methodological tools. These interviews lasted on average one hour and took place in each home. A series of propositions was introduced by the researcher in order to give rise to a discourse on family practices concerning television. The 24 interviews were transcribed verbatim and then used as a corpus for an in-depth analysis of the accounts through which family members reconstructed media practices in the home.

The exploratory nature of the study and the choice of a qualitative analysis of the discourse explain the limited sample. The study's intention was not to gather representative data but to explore a form of analysis and establish a point of departure for the individualization of a phenomenology of family television experiences.

The purpose of such in-depth individual interviews was to trigger discourse on family practices with respect to television. The aim of analyzing this discourse was to show how television contents, whatever they are, should always be considered texts-in-context. They belong to a particular practice – television viewing – which in turn is embedded into a complex range of other daily practices. Each one of these practices may have different significance for different people and whatever the contents are, their meaning ultimately depends on the phenomenological context in which they are experienced.

Television contents in general but also more sensitive contents, such as sex and violence, acquire their meaning and have different impacts according to the multilevel concentric context in which they occur. Different members of different families thus integrate in different ways television viewing during their life and have different representations of what "television viewing" or "being exposed to certain contents" can mean for them or their children.

The analysis we undertook focused specifically on family members' discourse on contents that are often considered today as "sensitive" for children and parents. We looked at the interpretative and active work parents and children make of these texts and the multiple ways they integrate them into crucial dimensions of their day-to-day family life.

This approach allows us to better comprehend how "being exposed to such contents" are situated activities and need to be considered and investigated as such. In so doing we propose a phenomenological oriented analysis that goes beyond the traditional impact of content on children paradigm and considers what parents and children actively do with the contents.

Choosing violent or sentimental contents: an identity making strategy

The young people interviewed saw television mainly as a source of entertainment. Boys enjoyed adventure shows or those that are exciting. Films considered "sentimental" or resembling everyday experiences seemed to be much less appealing to them. However, this sort of show seemed to be highly appreciated by girls for the opposite reason: they were attracted by the realism of situations depicted.

> *What do you watch on television?*
> The boy: I watch films, like *Alien, the Resurrection*. My Mom and Dad didn't want me to see it...
> *But you watched it anyway?*
> Yes... it was great. There was lots of blood... as if it were for 18 and over, but it was for 13 and over...[2]
> *And you're not quite 13?*
> No, but *Jurassic Park* and *Batman and Robin* are for 13 and over...
> *And you watch them?*
> Yeah! *Batman and Robin* doesn't even have a single drop of blood. It's for 13 and over...
> *Did it scare you?*
> No, it's a good film. It's not like a love story... That's pretty boring... a real-life film is boring. It's like you're watching your life. Your own life. When you watch a real-life film it's boring... It's like *Titanic*, every one is crazy about it now... (10 years old, family No. 1)

> *What do you watch on television?*
> The girl: Cartoons, shows like *Watatatow* (dramatic series for young people), etc. I watch that...
> *What do you like about those shows?*

The adventures and things that happen...
Why are they your favorite shows?
Because they're funny, there's lots of jokes. And *Watatatow* seems like it's really true... (11 years old, family No. 2)

The above examples suggest the degree to which the use of television in a family can be a complex, multipurpose practice. Even at the level of preferences (what they say) and television choices (what they do), it can be seen that it is also a question of the strategies by which members establish certain aspects of their family life, such as their identities, roles and the reciprocal relations binding them together (Casetti, 1995).

These preferences and choices are indicators of classifications performed by various family members with respect to the television content to which they are exposed. As we will see here, young people themselves reclassify content in two ways: with respect to their suitability for children or adults, and with respect to the gender for which the content is intended. In this way they position themselves with respect to the adult/child and girl/boy oppositions.

Regarding the presentation of a film (*Alien, the Resurrection*), the young boy adds: "my Mom and Dad didn't want me to watch it". Thus, speaking about one's own television preferences becomes an opportunity to represent oneself as a grown-up. Watching television, and especially choosing what to watch, is an activity that can include a number of important stakes: asserting one's independence from one's parents (through opposition) and one's own desire to become an adult and be considered as such. In other words, television preferences become a symbolic practice through which young people gain access to ways to define identity.

This example shows how watching television and choosing violent contents can be used by young people as a symbolic practice. It is used to say something else. In this case, watching a film with "lots of blood" becomes a way of portraying oneself as an adult. In a symbolic sense, young people also use the content coding system for programs.[3] Not only do they watch films for "13 and over" even when they are underage, they re-code the content of such films ("the film could have been for 18 and over"). A number of elements transform the fact of watching television into an activity with a value and a symbolic function: the criteria that guide preferences, the transgressive use of the code and the interpretation of content intended more for adults. Thus, this activity becomes a strategy for self-definition. In the case cited, it was a matter of portraying oneself as a "grown-up", though this is not the only symbolic aspect.

In this respect, it is interesting to note the opposition that the boy points out between television genres: a blood and gore film *versus* a love story (understood as a realistic story about life and thus boring). Television preferences would thus be a way to symbolically mark one's own gender identity. The masculine identity of these young people is built and nurtured through a different choice of television offerings. Thus we can validate the preceding hypothesis: television, like other situations, presents texts that become pretexts used by children to assert "who they are". The child is grown up and a man because he watches films for grown-ups and prefers films presenting violent contents instead of love stories. If we compare the boy's statements to those of the girl, we find another element supporting this hypothesis: the girl prefers dramatic series for young people, those that seem "real".

The construction of gender identity is nurtured by distinctive features and oppositions. Young people seem to use what is offered by television as a pool of identity making resources: what they like to watch, and what they do not, become choices that define their systems of values. This does not mean that television exerts unconditional influence on them. Rather, it offers a range of symbolic contents used by young people to develop their roles and identity, through classification and choices.

Another element in the construction of the identity of young people is expressed in the following statements:

> *When you watch television with your father, sister or mother, who chooses the show?*
>
> A girl: Usually it's me or my sister Émilie.
>
> *How do you choose?*
>
> Well, we ask our parents "do you feel like watching teenager stuff like *Melrose Place*, things like that, or *Beverly Hills 90210*?", then we watch it. (10 years old, family No. 3)

As we saw with respect to films with "lots of blood", an expression like "teenager stuff" (for example, *Beverly Hills*) expresses a classification process for television genres that is based on criterias belonging to the cultural world of young television viewers. Through classifying television offerings, young people impose their own order and place specific meaning and value on what they watch. As we have seen, this sometimes takes the form of simple signs of personal identity, but this classification by children can also play another role in the identity making process. The texts that are interpreted in this way by young people are transformed into symbolic instruments *to emphasize the distinctive features of their own culture* and to establish how it differs from that of adults.

Yet what is more important on the level of family dynamics is what is at stake in this process of interpreting television genres: once the text is redefined, *negotiations about choosing which programs* to watch become symbolic strategies for identifying and proposing to parents a specific universe of reference that is different from that of adults. Producing a classification of reality (as is done, in this case, in the discourse on television shows) using it in interactive situations (by negotiating who watches what) are among the most important means for members of a group to express and construct their own culture. Watching television can create this sort of social dynamic: the negotiation of preferences operates as one of the means (but certainly not the only one) of progressively producing the relative identities and cultures of the age groups of family members (Casetti, 1995; Morley, Silverstone, 1991).

Thus it seems that young people use specific criteria to choose their shows. They also make television watching a meaningful experience in an active sense. Watching television may be an opportunity to defy parental authority – or at least to ignore it – to develop and construct one's own identity to ritually mark the various periods of one's own daily life and the passage of the growing up process.

Violence in television programs does not occur in a social or cultural vacuum. On the contrary it fits in a context made of other media contents and discourses, parental mediation, permissions and prohibitions, children's representations of what is typical for a girl or a boy, for a child or an adult, and family dynamics such as children's transgression of parental rules. A component of the world around, violence in television works as a text that waits for an interpretative work which depends of all these components.

Between contents and children. The role of parents' representations in mediating and regulating children's exposure to television

In most of the families interviewed, it was noted that the parents intervene in one way or another to define the relation between their children and television. This is done in different ways, either by granting permission, watching together, or applying restrictions on the overall amount of time devoted to such viewing (to promote exchanges during meals, ensure that school work gets done, etc.) or on content considered unsuitable.

The analysis of the discourses that we have collected shows, however, that this *proactive or restrictive mediation* (Caron, Meunier, 1998) seems to be based on different underlying interpretations of the medium. The examples we will present reveal a certain degree of consistency between the various perceptions of the medium and its content, and the behavior proposed by parents.

Television as a simulation of reality

There are a number of ways to see television as a medium, *depending on the programs* to which one refers (the different television genres), and also on the way one conceives of the relation between the content and its addressee. In this relation, children may be seen by parents as a simple "sponge" that absorb all content, or as people who play an interpretative role and set up their own frameworks of understanding and prior knowledge.

> The mother: When we watch together it's always family shows. As for films… a little more… for 13 and over, we've started letting Mélanie (their 10-year-old daughter) watch. She knows the difference between right and wrong, and she knows it's fake. …Mélanie asks lots of questions during that show, *Virginie* (adult drama), because she sees adolescence coming. She wonders a lot. I think it's good. Maybe it's eye-opening sometimes (meaning perhaps it is a

> little explicit). But I think it's a little like preparing them for reality, that life is like that too. (Family No. 2)

In this statement, the mother perceives certain television programs as presenting a context that simulates reality, such as adolescence and its problems. In her discourse, reality and television fiction are thus separated to produce an *interpretation of the television text considered as a "simulation of reality"*. From this mother's point of view, television allows her daughter to learn, in a non-threatening manner, about experiences that concern her. The realistic text is seen as a framework or sheltered domain that allows access to this experience in a mediated form (Bianchi, 1990). It also allows reality to be anticipated and the foundations of mental frameworks to be established, which could be useful to the adolescent if she were to experience something similar in daily life.

Just as listening to stories allows children to experiment with emotions and situations within a context in which anything can happen but nothing really happens, television shows are perceived as a mediated, simulated experience through which children can develop certain abilities that are useful and necessary in real life. This interpretation of television as a "simulation of reality" allows its viewing to be seen as a protected context for learning. The daughter, in this case, is perceived as capable of wondering about what she sees, as someone who knows how to tell right from wrong and who grasps the basic elements of the media language to differentiate between reality and media illusions.[4]

The content of certain shows can be the *subject of discussion* within the family, either with respect to aspects of reality or to situations experienced by the characters (e.g., teenage pregnancy). The events are then transposed into the potential reactions of members of the family.

> The mother: Well, yes, actually, my oldest daughter already did. One time there was a character who was pregnant and in the story her mother kicked her out, and my daughter asked me, "Mom, would you do that to me?", so I said "...I say I wouldn't do it to you, but you never know, maybe... I don't see why I'd kick you out, it wouldn't solve your problem, and it wouldn't solve mine. You're my daughter, you'll always be my daughter...". I thought it was fun to talk about it. (Family No. 4)

The analogies perceived between what happens on television and what happens (or could happen) in real life allow to consider viewing as belonging to a field of development of self- and other-referential hypotheses. Television provides models for interpreting or anticipating the world of action. Analogies can be made and differences identified between textual situations and behavior, and life. This all takes place on the level of comparison of the fictional dimension (television) with the real (daily life). Here, television plays a role similar to that of other media (books, narratives, stories), which are often representations of possible worlds, as models for interpreting the real world and in consequence as "fields for envisaging and evaluating" one's own actions and those of others on the imaginary level.

Television also allows parents to focus on their role of "good parents" and to reflect on their way of acting in that context. In support of this view, as can be observed in the statement below this role is assumed and recognized by parents, when they *choose to watch a show with their children*. If they fear that the content could upset the child, they prefer to be present. Such supervised viewing can, however, become a source of shared entertainment.

> *Do you watch shows with her?*
> The mother: Yes… *Goosebumps*… before I used to watch it with her because she was scared, now I like it too, mysterious things… (Family No. 7)

Here we see a way of interpreting the role of parents with respect to television viewing: *watching together*. In this example, mother-child relationship is anchored in shared consumption ("before I used to watch it with her because she was scared") and television becomes the focus of this joint activity. At first the parent played the role of a mediator between the text and the child. Then the television text became the mediator between the parent and the child. This evolutionary view of the television-parent-child triad illustrates one of the roles television can play in the family: *the role of "assigning parents their roles"*, in other words, placing parents in the roles they are supposed to play.

Most of the work of parents lies in introducing their children to their environment by trying to bring reality within their grasp and gradually sharing their experience. This work is related to parents' skill in regulating their own presence and progressively reducing the support provided, to leave a greater degree of independence to the young person.

The perception of television as a text waiting for interpretation by the child can thus lead parents to wonder about the interpretation and, if so, intervene between the two. This strategy is different from that adopted, as we will see, by parents who see television as pure entertainment and by those who see it as a source of disturbance for children.

Television as pure entertainment

> The mother: They're fun, cartoons… and they laugh, too! It makes people happy, even! You forget something… Sometimes you come home tired, then you watch something funny on TV, you forget your problems… And children, even though they don't have any problems, after a hard day at school, they're tired… It relaxes them too!… Because it's funny. Most of the shows on Teletoon are funny. (Family No. 4)

For some parents, the notion of entertainment associated with television is thought of as a positive element, not a detriment to school or other activities considered important.

> The father's spouse: Homework has always come first.
> The father: Yes, yes, yes, homework comes before TV. She comes home from school, she does some on her own, I arrive, we continue… we take a break for

> *101 Dalmatians*, then we continue until suppertime. Sometimes we do homework after supper. (Family No. 8)

For other parents the discourse is once again built around an opposition: school and homework *versus* television and leisure. This opposition signals *a certain interpretation of television consumption: television viewing is perceived as pure entertainment*. This interpretation becomes a premise that leads to the automatic exclusion of the hypothesis that viewing could encourage the development of certain cognitive abilities or be a simple healthy "escape". The logic of the argument could be summarized as follows: if television is nothing more than pure entertainment (a definition reinforced by the opposition with homework and school), then watching it involves little effort and provides nothing of merit.

> The father: One thing I have to criticize about television is that it takes a lot of time away from children that they could spend on other things... Because they're hooked by it. It's something that uses up a lot of their time, and it takes no effort... Like us, I remember when I was young, there weren't many shows for children, so we went and played outside, made things, visited our friends, found games. But now... the child just says "I don't feel like doing anything else", and sits down in front of the TV. It uses up all their time. (Family No. 2)

One possible consequence of this play of ideas is that parents could seem to remove the learning potential from this activity and, in doing so, any mediation role parents could play. Indeed, in order to want to intervene, it is necessary to consider it useful to do so. When parents adopt this sort of interpretation of their children's television viewing, they perhaps do not expect that their child could be faced with content beyond his or her cognitive and emotional abilities, or with texts that are difficult to understand even though they are amusing.[5]

However the opposition between homework and television also plays a structuring role. As we saw with respect to ritual times in family life, the contrast between television viewing and school work places importance on the latter, according to the parents. The importance of school in their children's lives is underlined and a hierarchy of values is assigned to daily activities when they are placed in opposition, as in the case of family meals, with something else: television.

When parents perceive television as a pleasure requiring no effort, its consumption is withdrawn from their sphere of action. Taken to an extreme, this view emphasizes minimizing the loss of time and insisting on children spending time on activities considered more meaningful.

> The mother: You have to set limits. My 15-year-old daughter... she likes TV, but she does other things... Francis, he watches TV a *lot*. You really have to tell him, "that's enough, now you go outside". (Family No. 5)

Parents intervene in their children's activities when they consider the children are spending too much time in front of the television. They invite them to find another form of entertainment. In families with many children, parents may have to intervene in the case of only one of the children, since the level of consumption varies from one to the next and, also, the level of intellectual effort required depending on the age of the child.

Television as a source of disturbance for children

Generally, the parents we met felt uneasy with respect to the sexually explicit content to which young people are exposed during programs broadcast during prime time (8 p.m. to 9 p.m.). With respect to this type of content, parental action remains more sensitive in comparison, for example, with the comments they may make to their children about differences in the language used in shows and family practices.

> The father: Yes! There are rules...
> The father: Between 8 and 9 they still show some things that are pretty... hot and spicy (risqué)...!
> The mother: Sometimes we supervise the content... Like we do with the Internet...
> The father: Anything with sexual connotations...
> The mother: There are things they don't need to know right away. They're still innocent, and it's nice that they are...
> The father: When it's the language you can tell them: "Okay, those people, they don't speak well, they speak poorly, try not to imitate them..." But when there's sexual connotations, it's more visual... it's more difficult I think. I think they can wait, he can wait until he's 10. He might know what making love is, but between that... and seeing it...! (Family No. 4)

As can be seen here, parents worry about content, especially when it is represented pictorially; pictures are most problematic for them. Visual saturation with sexual content seems to lend itself less to certain types of parental mediation, such as indirect mediation. It is more difficult to help a child interpret a picture than language, for example. The only mediation seen as possible in cases of sexually explicit content is *restrictive mediation* (Caron, Meunier, 1998), i.e., parents censure the type of content that makes them feel powerless.

Some parents also avoid programs and films with content that could frighten their children. For example, they may avoid scenarios where there is a lot of death or dramatic features (e.g., hurricanes) that could have effects on their children, including feelings of fear, which are often manifested by sleep disturbances.

> The mother: Me anyway, I find that on television there is a lot of violence in films. And it begins at 7:00. It's too early. When the children are still up. My daughter is watching TV and she stops when that comes on. Of course, they warn us that it's for 13 and over, but at 7:00 a 7-year old isn't in bed yet...

> The mother: Pierre-Luc is pretty sensitive, when he sees something like a dead person, it stays in his head… It bothers him, then before going to bed he talks to me about it… this is why I'd rather he watch real-life stories and dramas as little as possible… Light entertainment is better. One time I was watching a film about a hurricane and he asked me "is that going to happen here?". I said, "No, no…" It was a realistic film, everything concerning death or disasters affects him, and in the evening, at bedtime, he doesn't like it very much. (Family No. 1)

This case illustrates a strategy different from that of other parents who use programs as situations of protected experience where they act as mediators. Aside from a few occasions, this mother does not seem to want to play the role of a "recipient for fears", or to think about the possibility that the content (even though it is disturbing for her child) could be tamed and made acceptable through her mediation: she prefers to distance the television text. This strategy demonstrates a way of viewing the role of parents in relation to television media and the resulting behavior.

It should be noted that some young people are also able to self-regulate, to judge television content and anticipate negative consequences for themselves.

> *What do you say, that you are not allowed to watch, why?*
> Oldest daughter: Because sometimes, it's violent. (10 years old, Family No. 3)
> Youngest daughter (Émilie's younger sister): It's 13 and over. Because maybe I'll have bad dreams. (7 years old, Family No. 3)

Children sometimes answer by repeating their parents' arguments. The normative discourse (in other words, the regulation of viewing) very often produces the need to provide explanations. Through this system (rules imposed and reasons why) one produces an interpretation of the regulated event. In this case, it is *an interpretation of television as something violent that can be frightening*.

Thus, television can play different roles in family dynamics. Television can be seen simply as a source of entertainment, and so parents feel they must mainly limit the overall time children spend on it. Television can also be perceived as a potential source of upsetting content, so parents act by censoring certain programs. Another possibility is that television is seen as sometimes offering realistic representations of true life, in which case parents emphasize mediation and viewing television with their children. What is, however, significant is that the more or less considered or accepted interpretations of television seem to be expressed and passed on from one generation to the next through (among other things) the mechanism of family regulation and the discourse accompanying it.

Summary and conclusion

First, it should be noted that not only does the television experience vary from one family to the next, but each member's behavior with respect to television is also distinct. While we do not claim these interviews are representative of all families, they still *bring out the diversity of television experiences in the family setting*. In particular, they illustrate the various ways that family members organize and give meaning to their own media experience. The very notion of "television viewing" includes and distinguishes between various forms of behavior: the use of this media is a "practice that is not only varied but also mediated, negotiated and ritualized" (Casetti, 1995:30).

In this sense we should remain prudent when dealing with statistical and quantitative data offering a general view of trends. To the contrary, the qualitative data presented here provide a glimpse of the fact that, beyond the numbers, the day-to-day reality of families and television media is composed of many shades of meaning, negotiations, questions and even doubts, on the part of both parents and young people.

In this subtly shaped panorama of behavior related to television – and structured by it – it is still possible to envisage obtaining general data from interviews.

First of all, discourse analysis reveals to what extent television content, even the more sensitive ones, are embedded in the context of family members' day-to-day life. A number of variables intervene in defining how exposure to television will influence a child, whether it be parents' perceptions of the role television plays in their children's lives, their cultural models of childhood and parenthood, rules governing viewing, the way television is used within the family, parents' and children's interpretative work on texts or the symbolic functions accomplished by their consumption.

Television texts, and among them violent, sexual and other sensitive contents, are experienced and have to be considered as discourses among others. Their significance or their impact does not depend just on the content. On the contrary it appears to be the result of a more complex and situated process in which a fundamental role is played by a network of interactions and discourses in and through which television contents are experienced and integrated into the family culture and social organization.

Our analysis showed that, beyond content, the dynamics that accompany viewing itself (negotiations, agreements, preferences, regulation of consumption) become practices for defining identities and roles in the family.

Television activity puts the emphasis on the role of parents, among other things, and reveals parents' perception of television. Their perception may be that of a reality that can be mediated or that of one from which the young person must be sheltered. Depending on the degree of cognitive or emotional investment granted to the experience, television viewing is compared to other activities and made subject to certain regulations. For young people, television also becomes a medium for asserting their values and their own culture in relation to others (boy *versus* girl, young person *versus* adult). Television is also an area where power is exercised in the play of "who controls viewing". One after the other, the triad – television, parents, children – thus takes on different configurations.

Programs and contents enter in family daily conversations and produce new interactions (choices and preferences, permissions, prohibitions and related reasons, etc.) through which family members assert, defy or negotiate relations with the other family members, identify different spheres of culture, construct an ordered set of priorities and impose a hierarchy of values in the family.

What is really interesting is not that this occurs in itself (indeed, these are dynamics proper to the developing structure of a family) but that (among other things) it occurs *by using television and its contents* as a concrete point of reference for these symbolic processes. Television's appropriation by the family and its integration into everyday life are indicative of the fact that family members treat it as a "medium" (in the etymological sense of the word) for expressing and producing what a family is.

A second result of our analysis refers to the role television seems to play in the family: the role of *assigning parents their roles*. In other words it places parents in the roles they are supposed to play with their children. For most of the parents interviewed television consumption is something that reveals their responsibilities as parents. Television seems to take on the role of a "magnifying glass": it forces parents to focus their attention on their presence or on the reasons for their absence in the daily life of their children.

When confronted with contents perceived as "sensitive", this role is even more assumed with parents who tend to mediate or regulate their children's exposure to these kind of contents. The rules imposed on television viewing, and the ways it is used, are the subjects of subtle negotiations that must adapt to changes in the age and viewing habits of young people. The parents' criteria for suitable contents and the reasons why they are suitable or not also play a role in this play of negotiations. This set of family discourses and interactions about television contents becomes a way to socialize children to certain representations of what television is, and what is good or wrong for them.

In a very recursive way and depending on the age of children, parents' ideas about television and its contents can become a platform for new dynamics and new negotiations: accepting parents' rules and reasons and avoiding unsuitable programs, or transgressing parents rules and watching forbidden contents, are ways through which children reach different developmental levels in their growing up process.

Another finding that is revealed by our analysis is the *level of consistency between ideas and behavior in relation to television*. Consumption practices (including parental regulation) and the behavior of the parents interviewed seem to reveal (among other things) interpretations they have of television and its effect on their children. The relation between the various interpretations of the media and parental behavior could be summarized as follows:

1) When television is perceived as nothing but pure entertainment, its potential effect on children is generally underestimated: on this view, television would provide children only with occasions to relax and have fun. This view, in parental discourse, often goes along with reduced responsibility with respect to social television-viewing expectations. Their responsibility is to limit the time children spend in front of the screen to place more emphasis on other activities seen as more meaningful.

2) When a relation is perceived between television content and the child's abilities, mediation behavior is adopted to watch programs with children. Television is used this way by parents as a context for protected learning. Parents place themselves between the media and the child to explain content or make it acceptable, while the television text places itself between family members to become a subject of discourse and source of conversation.

3) When television is personified and seen as the direct cause of certain undesirable effects on children, parents are led to censure dangerous content. Parental action with respect to the child is limited to that alone and the parental role seems to be conceived of less as a possible mediator for the same content.

From the data gathered, we can conclude that parental behavior and roles change depending on the different ways the medium is viewed. However, regardless of this and no matter what the underlying interpretation, television seems to make the role of parents visible. Whether it is a question of limiting the number of hours devoted to television, of censuring content or of watching together, when it comes to television, parents feel they are brought into play as parents.

Family television viewing thus seems to be a phenomenon characterized by two levels of meaning. It is experienced and conceived of as an event taken for granted, a habit that even makes up part of daily life. However, almost paradoxically, it can also call upon parents to wonder about television's potential effect on the development of their children. This call-for-role effect is sometimes overplayed in the case of violence or other sensitive contents. Because of this, parents find themselves forced to reflect on their own role with respect to television itself, and with respect to the relation they have with their children and television.

The results of our analysis about television viewing and contents show how important it is to investigate the impact of television contents within the whole range of family dynamics and practices. Rather than looking at the impact of television contents solely with a two-dimensional model (text-children), the phenomenological oriented framework we have proposed enlightens us to the role of a third component: the sense making activity accomplished by family members, their active use of the medium, the interpretation brought to these texts and the symbolic levels of viewing. All these dimensions reveal their constitutive role in defining the significance of television contents, even the more sensitive ones, in the life of children. Far from occurring in a social or cultural *vacuum*, violence and sex on television as all other media contents are experienced and have to be analyzed as contents-in-context.

Acknowledgements and notes

1. We are very grateful to Marysol Charbonneau for assisting us in the collection of the data some of which are reported in her Master's thesis. We would also like to thank Line Grenier, Diane Raymond and Stéphanie Barker for having made valuable comments on this article, for which we alone are, however, responsible. Finally we would like to express our most sincere gratitude to Mary Baker for her excellent work in translating our material.
2. Note that, in Canada, a newly introduced classification code for television shows identifies the intended age group for programs and films. It is interesting to note that though the classification code presented at the beginning of each show is posted only briefly and for information purposes (in the form of a small icon) it is mentioned as frequently by young people as by adults in the interviews. Young people seem to be very aware of this code and relatively proud to transgress it from time to time.
3. In its report, *Respecting Children: A Canadian Approach to Helping Families Deal With Television Violence* (1996), the Canadian Radio-television and Telecommunications Commission set out the broad lines of its policy regarding television violence and required that broadcasters develop a classification system for programs. Broadcasters have adopted a voluntary code (Caron, Jolicoeur, 1996).
4. A child's ability to grasp the various levels of realism of a television picture and to distinguish between (programs as belonging to) the genres of *fiction* and *reality* is one of the most frequent concerns of parents and also one of the aspects regarding which they most often play a mediating role (Messaris, 1987; Weintraub Austin, Roberts, Nass, 1990).
5. Much research has emphasized the difficulties children have in understanding television texts because of specific syntaxes or two registers of communication (verbal and visual), even in cases of programs such as cartoons, which are supposedly designed for children. Regarding the processes of comprehension and incomprehension, see Bagett (1979); Meringoff (1980); Beagles-Roos, Gat (1983); Cardarello (1986); Bertolini, Manini (1988); Lumbelli (1994); Caronia, Gherardi (1991); Caronia (1997).

Bibliography

Bagett, P. (1979). "Structurally Equivalent Stories in Movie and Text and the Effects of the Medium on the Recall". In *Journal of Verbal Learning and Verbal Behaviour*, 18: 333-356.

Beagles-Roos, J., Gat, I. (1983). "Specific Impact of Radio and Television on Children's Story Comprehension". In *Journal of Educational Psychology*, 75(1): 128-137.

Bertolini, P., Manini, M., Eds. (1988). *I figli della TV*. Florence: La Nuova Italia.

Bianchi, J. (1990). "La promesse du feuilleton". In *Réseaux*, 39: 7-18.

Brice, J. (1987). "Family Time and Television Use". In T.R. Lindlof, Ed. *Natural Audience: Qualitative Research of Media Uses and Effects*. Norwood: Ablex.

Cardarello, R. (1986). "Incomprensioni di un cartone animato alla TV: itinerari delle informazioni perdute". In *Ikon-Ricerche sulla comunicazione*, 13: 35-68.

Caron, A.H., Jolicoeur, A.E. (1996). *Systemized Summary of Canadian Regulations Concerning Children and the Audiovisual Industry*. Montreal: Centre for Research and Development Policies.

Caron, A.H., Meunier, D. (1995). "L'enfant et l'environnement familial captifs des médias? L'expérience canadienne". In *Recherches Sociologiques*, 26(1): 55-72.

Caron, A.H., Meunier, D. (1998). "Dynamiques familiales et habitudes techno-médiatiques: une question de médiation". In *Revue québécoise de psychologie*, 19(1): 151-169.

Caronia, L. (1997). *Costruire la conoscenza. Interazione e interpretazione nella ricerca in campo educativo*. Florence: La Nuova Italia.

Caronia, L., Gherardi, V. (1991). *La pagina e lo schermo*. Florence: La Nuova Italia.

Casetti, F., Ed. (1995). *L'ospte fisso. Televisione e mass media nelle famiglie italiane*. Torino: San Paolo.

Casetti, F., Lasorsa, M., Pezzini, I. (1985). "Per una microstoria del consumo dell'audiovisivo". In *Ikon. Ricerche sulla comunicazione*, 11: 69-210.

Casetti, F., Lasorsa, M., Pezzini, I. (1986). "Per una microstoria del consumo dell'audiovisivo". In *Ikon. Ricerche sulla comunicazione*, 12: 129-205.

Lemish, D. (1987). "Viewers in Diapers: The Early Development of Television Viewing". In T.R. Lindlof, Ed. *Natural Audience: Qualitative Research of Media Uses and Effects*. Norwood: Ablex.

Lindlof, T.R., Mayer, T.P. (1987). "Mediated Communication as Ways of Seeing, Acting, and Constructing Culture: The Tools and Foundations of Qualitative Research". In T.R. Lindlof, Ed. *Natural Audience: Qualitative Research of Media Uses and Effects*. Norwood: Ablex.

Lull, J. (1980). "The Social Use of Television". In *Human Communication Research*, 6: 197-209.

Lull, J. (1987). "Audience, Text and Context". In *Critical Studies on Mass Communication*, 4: 318-322.

Lull, J. (1991). *Inside Family Viewing. Ethnographic Research on Television Audience*. London: Routledge.

Lumbelli, L. (1994). "Catturare I processi di compensione di testi televisivi". In *Ikon. Ricerche sulla comunicazione*, 28: 41-93.

Mancini, P. (1993). *Guardando il telegiornale. Per una etnografia del consumo televisio*. Torino: Nuova Eri.

Meringoff, L. (1980). "Influence of the Medium on Children's Story Apprehension". In *Journal of Educational Psychology*, 72(2): 240-249.

Messaris, P. (1987). "Mothers' Comments to Their Children about the Relationship between Television and Reality". In T.R. Lindlof, Ed. *Natural Audience: Qualitative Research of Media Uses and Effects*. Norwood: Ablex.

Morley, D. (1989). "Changing Paradigms in Audience Studies". In E. Seiter, H. Borchers, G. Kreutzner, E. Warth, Eds. *Remote Control: Television Audience and Cultural Power*. London: Routledge.

Morley, D. (1992). *Television, Audiences and Cultural Studies*. London: Routledge.

Morley, D., Silverstone, R. (1991). "Communication and Context: Ethnographic Perspectives on the Media Audience". In K. Bruhn Jensen, N.W. Jankowski, Eds. *A Handbook of Qualitative Methodologies for Mass Communication*. London, New York: Routledge.

Proulx, S., Maillet, D. (1998). "La construction ethnographique des publics de télévision". In S. Proulx, Ed. *Accusé de réception. Le téléspectateur construit par les sciences sociales*. Sainte-Foy: Presses de L'Université Laval.

Weintraub Austin, E., Roberts, D.F., Nass, C.I. (1990). "Influences of Family Communication on Children's Interpretation Processes". In *Communication Research*, 17(4): 545-564.

The Internet and the Family

The View of U.S. Parents

Joseph Turow with Lilach Nir

The Internet has been spreading rapidly to U.S. households, but researchers have barely begun to understand its spread, use and consequences in the home. The Annenberg School for Communication has embarked on a number of studies on this topic. This article presents findings from our national telephone survey on the Internet and the family, the first of its kind in the United States. Through the survey, we sought to

- delve deeper than previous research into parents' attitudes and beliefs about the Internet and the potential impact this new phenomenon is having on their children and the entire family unit;
- understand how parents who have the Internet at home are coping with the potential uses and abuses of this new technology that is rapidly becoming a fixture in people's lives; and
- begin identifying factors that contribute to, and even predict, why parents in some computer households subscribe to an online service and others do not. By limiting the research to families with computers, our analysis could look beyond the number one obstacle to being online: having the discretionary income necessary to have a computer.

The Roper Starch Worldwide research organization conducted the interviews, based on a set of questions prepared at the Annenberg School for Communication. 1,102 parents in households with at least one working computer and at least one child between ages 8 and 17 were interviewed by phone between November 12th and December 20th, 1998.[1]

Our findings reveal that the rush to connect the Web to American homes is happening despite parents' substantial insecurity. In certain ways, the fears parents have revealed to us are similar to the fears parents have expressed during introduction of the movies, broadcast television, and cable TV. But the concerns are not merely repeats of past litanies.

For example, over 75 percent of parents in computer households are "strongly" or "somewhat" concerned that their children might give away personal information on the Internet, and an equal percentage fear children might view sexually explicit material. Nearly two thirds of parents believe the Internet can cause their children to become isolated.

Meanwhile, parents also believe that the Internet is an essential tool with positive potential. For instance, 75 percent say the Internet is a place for children to discover fascinating, useful things, 72 percent say the Internet helps their children with their schoolwork, and more than half of the parents feel children without Internet access are at a disadvantage compared to their peers.

We found that parents are particularly nervous about two features of Web programming they haven't seen in broadcast or cable television: its wide-open nature and its interactivity. Parents fear the Web for its unprecedented openness – the easy access by anybody to sexuality, bad values, and commercialism. They also fear the Web for its unprecedented interactive nature – the potential for invading a family's privacy and for adults taking advantage of children. These fears are heightened among many parents because they don't believe they understand the technology well enough to make the best use of it. Yet they believe their children need it. The following pages present these and other findings of the study in some detail.

The study and the population

Table 1 presents basic demographic characteristics of our population of 1,102 parents. As mentioned, all have computers and children aged 8-17. In the table, the population is divided into those whose households are and aren't online. The main difference between the two groups relates with respect to online households' higher income. Another difference is that parents in online households have higher education.

While income and education differences between the two are noteworthy, they don't seem to be big or consistent enough to explain why some computer households are online and others are not. Considering that 12 percent of the online parents and 8 percent of those not online at home refused to reveal their income bracket, the differences between the two groups may not even be as large as their answers suggest. Later we will see that parents' income and education are not, in fact, major predictors of whether or not a computer household is online. Before doing that, however, we will examine what both groups of parents say and do about themselves, their kids and the online world.

Table 1. Parents with children aged 8-17 and computers at home (%)

		Online at home	Not online
Sex	Male	47	46
	Female	53	54
Age	20-29	4	3
	30-44	60	66
	45-59	33	28
	60 or older	1	2
Race	White	86	81
	African American	5	8
	White Hispanic	5	6
	Black Hispanic	1	1
	Asian	1	1
	Native American	1	1
	Other	2	2
Married		86	84
Employed		88	87
Number of children, aged 8-17	One	47	43
	Two	37	36
	Three	11	15*
	Four or more	5	6
Last education degree	Grade school or less	–	1*
	Some high school	4	7
	High school graduate	25	34*
	Some college	27	29
	College graduate	26	19*
	Post graduate	18	10*
Yearly income	Less than $30,000	8	14*
	$30,000 - $49,999	23	29*
	$50,000 - $74,999	25	31*
	$75,000 or more	32	18*
	No answer	12	8
n =		676	426

Note: * indicates that the row difference is statistically significant. When numbers add up to more than 100%, it is because of rounding error. The margin of error is +/- 4%.

Parents and the online world

An overwhelming majority of "online" and "offline" parents have used computers. The difference between the two groups is much greater when it comes to the ability to navigate the Web. While 96 percent of the online parents said they had "ever gone online", only a bit over half of the offline parents said that. And while only 27 percent of the online parents called themselves beginners, 42 percent of the offline parents *who have gone online at all* dubbed themselves beginners. This means that 68 percent of all the offline parents have either never used the Web or consider themselves neophytes with the Internet.

On average, online parents have had the Web at home 1.8 years. They are likely to use the Web at home fairly frequently. 23 percent said they use it every day, with 30 percent saying they use it every other day or every few days. Their use of the Web outside the home tends to revolve around work. Offline parents' relative dearth of Web experience shows up not only in their inability to access it at home but also in their comparatively low use of the Web at work or elsewhere outside the home. Only 32 percent used the Web at work "during the past month", and only 16 percent said they used it anywhere else.

Despite their major differences in uses of the Web, there were remarkable similarities between online and offline parents in their attitudes about the Web and in their supervision of children regarding the Web. In fact, each group of online parents has a corresponding group of offline parents that is more similar to it than the other online groups. To see how this works, we look at the views of parents in each segment.

The views of parents from online homes

All the parents in our survey were presented 21 statements about the Internet and children with a Likert type 5-point scale ranging from "agree strongly" to "disagree strongly". The statements included 8 favorable assertions about the Web, 8 unfavorable assertions about the Web and 5 opinions about the Internet's practical utility for their households. We used cluster analysis to discover if all *online* parents fit one profile in their answers to these statements or if there is diversity among them regarding their attitudes toward the Web. The mean of replies to the scale was calculated for each question. Positive deviations from the mean reply indicate group agreement to the statement.

As Figure 1 shows, we found three groups of online parents with startling differences in the six statements that deviate most from the mean. We label the groups "online worriers", "disenchanted" and "gung-ho parents". Table 2 notes their agreement to the statements in terms of percentages. Here are their major characteristics:

Online worriers (39% of online parents)

These parents are more concerned than those in the other two groups about the effects that the Internet might have on their children and their families. "Online worriers" show above average agreement with the statements that deal with issues of values and social isolation. 72 percent agree that children's exposure to the Internet may interfere with family values and beliefs. 88 percent agree that going online might lead to the child's isolation. Two thirds (66%) agree it could lead to anti-social behavior by the child.

Figure 1. Groups of *online* parents based on their views of the Web

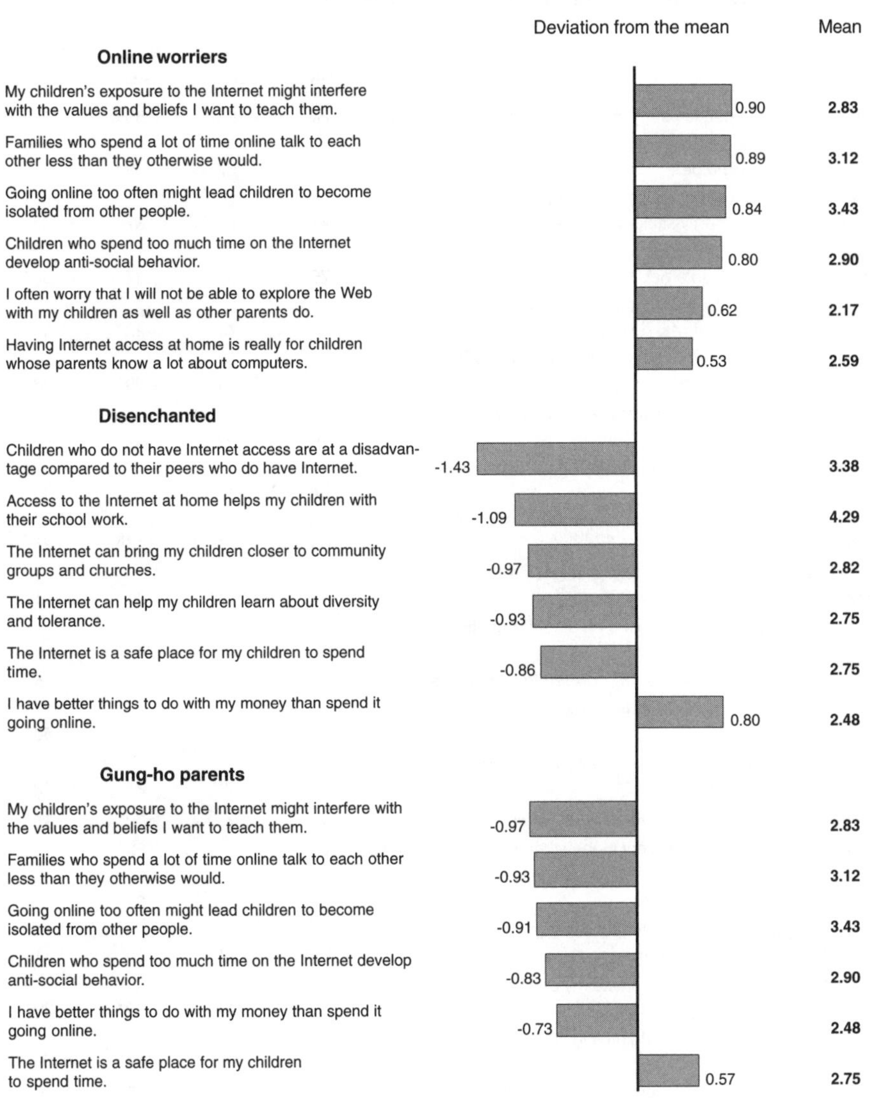

Table 2. Percentage of *online* parents who agree "strongly" or "somewhat" with statements about the Internet (%)

	Total	Online worrier	Disen-chanted	Gung-ho
Access to the Internet helps my children with their schoolwork.	84	92	53*	93
Online, my children discover fascinating useful things they never heard of before.	81	87	58*	88
I am concerned that children give out personal information about themselves when visiting web sites or chat rooms.	77	88	87	60*
I am concerned that my child/children might view sexually explicit images on the Internet.	76	86	87	59*
Children who do not have Internet access are at a disadvantage compared to their peers who do have Internet access.	68	79	22*	83
Going online to often might lead children to become isolated from other people.	60	88*	60*	33*
The Internet can help my children learn about diversity and tolerance.	60	65	28*	72
People worry too much that adults will take advantage of children on the Internet.	57	56	56	59
Families who spend a lot of time online talk to each other less than they otherwise would.	48	77*	47*	21*
My children's exposure to the Internet might interfere with the values and beliefs I want to teach them.	42	72*	44*	11*
Children who spend too much time on the Internet develop anti-social behavior.	40	66*	37*	16*
The Internet is a safe place for my children to spend time.	40	39*	13*	56*
The Internet can bring my children closer to community groups and churches.	37	39*	9*	50*
Having Internet access at home is really for children whose parents know a lot about computers.	34	49*	27	22
It is expensive to subscribe to an Internet service.	29	37	36	17*
I have better things to do with my money than spend it going online.	28	34*	52*	8*
My family can get access to the Internet from other places so we do not really need it at home.	23	30*	32	6*
I often worry that I won't be able to explore the web with my children as well as other parents do.	21	37*	10	11
I do not mind when advertisers invite my children to web sites to tell them about their products.	21	20*	9*	29*
My children are not interested in having an Internet connection at home.	15	18*	27*	6
My computer is not powerful enough to handle the Internet well.	15	20*	13	10
n =	676			

Note: * means that the percentage difference is statistically significant from the percentages of the two other parent groups in the row.

But these concerns are balanced by a belief in the benefits of connecting to an online service. These people – a majority of whom have had an Internet connection at home for a year or more – are also convinced that there is real value for their kids having access from home: Nearly eight in ten (79%) agree that children without Internet access are disadvantaged. More than nine in ten (92%) agree access helps children with their homework.

Disenchanted (22% of online parents)
While "online worriers" are convinced of both the happy and scary elements of the Web, "disenchanted parents" are not at all sure of the Internet's value for their kids. Unlike the other two groups with Web experience, "disenchanted parents" reject the common wisdom that access to the World Wide Web is a near-necessity for students to succeed today. "Disenchanted parents" are much more likely than other online parents to reject the notion that kids learn useful and fascinating things on the Internet. In addition, unlike the others, these parents disagree that the Internet helps with bringing children closer to community groups or that it can help children learn about diversity and tolerance. "Disenchanted parents" are even more despairing than the "online worriers" when it comes to seeing the World Wide Web as a safe haven for exploration. 77 percent disagree somewhat or strongly that the Internet is a safe place for kids.

Clearly this group is not sold on the inherent value of the Internet experience for their children. The pattern of answers suggests that disenchanted parents keep the Web more because they think it has become a requirement for up-to-date families in the late twentieth century than because they think it will bring great benefit.

Gung-ho parents (39% of online parents)
"Online worriers" and "disenchanted parents" together comprise 61 percent of those with Web connections at home. "Gung-ho parents", who are highly positive about the Web, comprise the other 39 percent. What places these people in a separate group is not their strong belief in the Internet's positive effects; "online worriers" respond that way, too. Rather, "gung-ho parents" stand out because in large numbers they reject nearly all statements about the Internet's alleged negative effects. 78 percent disagree that their children's exposure to the Internet might interfere with the values and beliefs they want to teach their kids. That contrasts with 18 percent of the "worriers" and 46 percent of the "disenchanted parents" who disagree.

"Gung-ho parents" have had an online connection longer than other online parents. (51 percent have been connected from home for two years or more, compared to only a third of either of the other two groups.) They are more likely themselves to go online every day from work, and somewhat more likely to rate themselves as advanced or expert users. These parents seem to have assimilated the Internet into their homes as a benign, beneficial new technology.

Parent supervision regarding the Internet

We found that the three different parent groups' beliefs about the Internet's influence associated with statistically significant differences in their actions. "Online worriers" were consistently more likely than the others to supervise their children – and to exercise the strictest supervision. "Disenchanted parents" were next, with "gung-ho parents" coming last.

In devising the survey, we recognized that parents' approaches to their children regarding the Web might depend on the age and/or sex of a particular child. As it turns out, the child's sex does not play a statistically significant role in parents' answers. Age (range 8-17, median = 12, mean = 13.2) sometimes does. In parents' reports, younger and older children differed statistically when it came to whether or not they *ever* went online; 93 percent of the older children have done it, while a smaller (but still very large) 81 percent of the younger ones have gone on the Web. Looking at parents' reports of the children who did go *online from home*, there were no age-related statistical differences in usage.

As for going online *out of home*, 36 percent of the parents of younger children said their kids had done it "during the past month", while 48 percent of the parents of older children reported that they had used the Web outside the home. Table 3 indicates that school was the most popular location, with friends' houses second and the public library third. Doing homework and e-mail were the most common task for the older kids, while playing games came first for younger ones, with homework second – see Table 4.

Table 3. From where has the child (with the most recent birthday) gone online outside of home? (%)

Asked of parents with online connections at home who say that the child has gone online outside of home in the past month.

	Age 8-12	Age 13-17
School	76	83
Public library	14	12
At a job	1	3
A friend's/relative's house	20	28
Local college/college libraries/community services/museum	2	–
Church	–	–
Other mentions	2	–
Don't remember	1	1
n =	115	173

Note: None of the row differences is statistically significant. Numbers don't add to 100% because multiple answers were acceptable.

Table 4. What two activities does the child (with the most recent birthday) most do online? (%)

Asked of parents with online connections at home who say the child goes online at home.

	Age 8-12	Age 13-17
Do homework	27	38*
Conduct research	26	22
Send and receive e-mail	18	28
Play games or puzzles	32	14
Participate in chat rooms	11	25*
Surf to discover things he/she never heard of before	12	12
Read online magazines or newspapers	6	5
Create a web site about her/himself or hobby	5	4
Listen to music	2	6*
Visiting museums or cultural sites	2	2
Buy things	1	3
Participate in community or religious groups	–	1
Conduct business	–	–
Other mentions	6	3
Don't know	7	3
n =	259	332

Note: * indicates that the row difference is statistically significant. Numbers don't add to 100% because multiple answers were acceptable.

Most parents are quite sure they keep up with their children's Web activities, both in and out of home. As Table 5 shows, the percentage of confident parents did change with the child's age and whether the online computer was at home or out of home. Both groups of parents were more likely to feel confident of their knowledge if the Web activities were in- rather than out- of the home. And parents of the younger children were more likely than parents of older ones to believe they know where their kids go in the virtual world.

But, as Table 5 also indicates, the sense by most parents that they understand their children goes beyond their assertions about their Web habits. Most parents also state that they talk to their children frequently or sometimes about their online activities, and most say they trust their kids to do the right thing on the Web. What's more, when asked whether they argue with their child about their Internet use, a huge percentage said no.

Table 5. Parents' confidence in, trust in and discussions with children about being online (%)
Asked of online parents regarding the child with most recent birthday.

	Age 8-12	Age 13-17
Confidence about child's online activities out of home		
Very confident	75	55*
Somewhat confident	19	33*
Confidence about child's online activities at home		
Very confident	86	69*
Somewhat confident	8	26*
Child talks to parent about online activities		
Frequently	54	46*
Sometimes	23	37*
Trust in child's online behavior		
Complete	58	61
Some	31	34
n =	319	357

Note: * indicates that the row difference is statistically significant.

An obvious question arises: If so many of these parents are knowledgeable, trusting, communicative and non-combative with their kids, why are so many of them worried about the Web and their children? The answer seems to be that while parents trust their children, they do not trust the Web. Perhaps from discussions with other parents, perhaps from personal experience, they have come to believe that a substantial part of the Internet has the potential of invading children's privacy while preying on them sexually and commercially.

Table 6 indicates the extent to which the parents set rules for their specific child's navigation of cyberspace. A consistently higher percentage of parents noted rules for younger children than older ones. Most parents of both younger and older children said they have rules regarding particular sites to visit, the time of day for going online, the amount of time spent online, and what the child can do online. Parents of the young children are more likely than parents of the older kids to require the child to have an adult around when going online. Going online only for schoolwork is a rule that the great majority of parents of both age groups reject, perhaps because they consider it too constraining for their children.

Table 6. Types of rules parents set for a child when the child goes online (%)
Asked of online parents regarding the child with most recent birthday who goes online at home.

	Age 8-12	Age 13-17
The sites (child) visits online	84	71*
The time of day or night he/she is allowed to go online	84	68*
The kind of activities the child performs online	78	70*
The amount of time spent online	63	55
Going online only with an adult, be it from home or outside of home	73	29*
Being online only at home	49	35*
Only going online if it is relevant for schoolwork	30	21*
n =	259	332

Note: * indicates that the row difference is statistically significant. Numbers don't add to 100% because multiple answers were allowed.

Table 7 indicates the extent to which the parents use certain methods "to protect their children from negative influences of the Internet". We asked the respondents to think of all their children when they gave answers, so the age of the specific child that some questions asked about does not apply here. Overwhelmingly, parents told us that they do set rules and that they "keep an eye on what the child is doing" when he/she is online. We found, however, that parents are much less likely to say they get involved in restrictive regulations that require direct intervention in their kids' Internet use. Perhaps because of ignorance, they are also unlikely to use computer technology to control their children's Web-surfing behavior. Still, a substantial minority of the online parents – 31 percent – did say they use a Net Nanny-type program that guards children's access to sites.

Table 7. Methods parents in online households use to protect their children from negative influences on the Internet (%)
Asked of online parents.

	Age 8-12	Age 13-17
Set rules that the child needs to follow when being online	86	80
Keep an eye on what that child is doing when he/she is online.	88	73
Do not allow the child to go online except with a parent present	67	29*
Use protective software such as Net Nanny that guards children's access to sites	35	27*
Deny children online access at home	24	17
n =	319	357

Note: * indicates that the row difference is significant. Numbers don't add to 100% because multiple answers were allowed.

The views of parents from homes not online

Parents from computer households without the Web worry about their kids' use of the Web outside the home. 43 percent of parents of younger children said their children go to the Web outside the home. This is the same percentage as online parents. When it came to older youngsters (ages 13-17), the percentage of offline parents saying their kids use the Net outside home is actually higher than the reports by online parents – 61 percent to 48 percent.

The reports by parents of where their children go online are quite similar. We did not ask parents without the Web what their children most like to do online. That is unfortunate because offline parents are similar to online parents in their confidence that they know what their children are doing on the Net outside the home. Most offline parents also state that they talk to their children frequently or sometimes about their online activities, and most say they trust their kids to do the right thing on the Web.

We asked parents without a Web link at home whether they think the child with the most recent birthday would be likely to use a home connection if the household had one. 88 percent answered yes, and only 6 percent said they would prohibit the child from doing so. We then asked the other 94 percent about rules they might have for those children. Their answers very much parallel those of parents with the Web at home. That is, the offline parents would embrace rules that limit the time kids spend online, the times of day they go online and the kinds of activities they do online.

The beliefs of parents without home connections

When it comes to expressed beliefs about the Web, a higher percentage of parents without the Web at home are pessimistic compared to those with the Web at home. Offline parents are also less likely to agree strongly (as opposed to agreeing "somewhat") regarding the good points of the Web, and they are more likely to disagree strongly (as opposed to disagreeing "somewhat") regarding the bad aspects of the Web. However, as with the online parents, our cluster analysis found three dramatically different groups among the offline parents – see Figure 2. As a comparison between Figures 1 and 2 shows, each group has a corresponding group of online parents that is similar in beliefs about the Internet and the family. Here are the offline groups and their major characteristics:

Offline worriers (41% of offline parents)

Comparing Figures 1 and 2, and Tables 2 and 8, we find that "online" and "offline worriers" share four of the six statements that most signal the personality of their groups. The statements reflect concerns about the Web. 88 percent of the "offline worriers" (and 72 percent of the "online worriers") agree that children's exposure to the Internet might negatively impact family values and beliefs. 79 percent of the "offline worriers" (and 77 percent of the "online worriers") agree the Internet will steal family time. More than 91 percent of the

Figure 2. Groups of parents *not online* based on their views of the Web

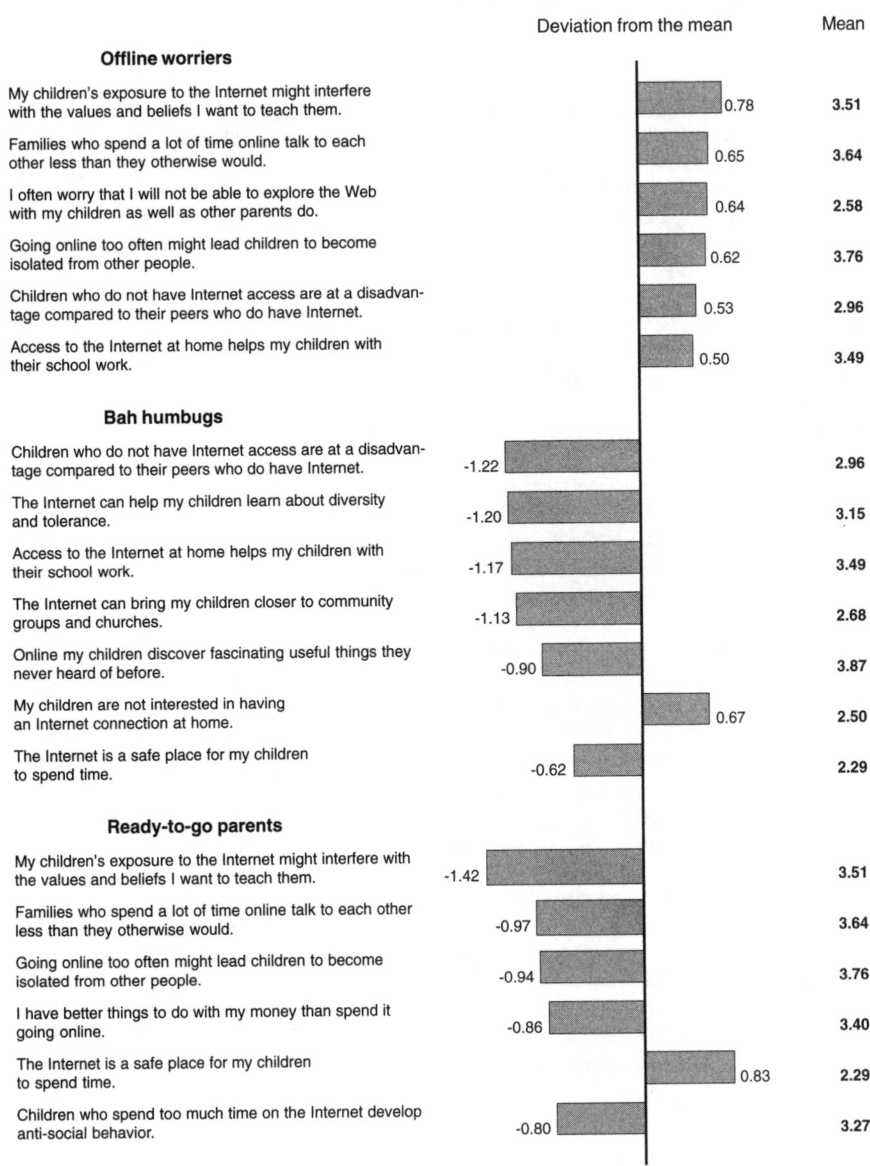

Table 8. Percentage of *offline* parents who agree "strongly" or "somewhat" with statements about the Internet

	Total	Offline worrier	Bah humbug	Ready-to-go
I am concerned that my child/children might view sexually explicit images on the Internet.	82	**95** *	83 *	63 *
I am concerned that children give out personal information about themselves when visiting web sites or chat rooms.	81	92 *	79 *	**71** *
Going online too often might lead children to become isolated from other people.	70	**91** *	68 *	44 *
Online, my children discover fascinating, useful things they never heard of before.	65	**76**	**39** *	**79**
My children's exposure to the Internet might interfere with the values and beliefs I want to teach them.	60	**88** *	**68** *	13 *
People worry too much that adults will take advantage of children on the Internet.	59	**66**	51 *	60
Families who spend a lot of time online talk to each other less than they otherwise would.	59	79 *	60 *	**30** *
My family can get access to the Internet from other places so we do not really need it at home.	58	**55**	**71** *	**49**
I have better things to do with my money than spend it going online.	54	**64**	**65**	**30** *
Access to the Internet helps my children with their schoolwork.	53	**65**	**22** *	68
The Internet can help my children to learn about diversity and tolerance.	47	58	**13** *	68
Children who spend too much time on the Internet develop anti-social behavior.	45	59 *	46 *	24 *
Children who do not have Internet access are at a disadvantage compared to their peers who do have Internet access.	43	**60**	**7** *	56 *
It is expensive to subscribe to an Internet service.	39	43	44	**29** *
Having Internet access at home is really for children whose parents know a lot about computers.	38	55 *	31 *	21 *
The Internet can bring my children closer to community groups and churches.	32	37 *	4 *	54 *
My children are not interested in having an Internet connection at home.	31	**30** *	45 *	**19** *
My computer is not powerful enough to handle the Internet well.	29	31	22	34
I often worry that I won't be able to explore the web with my children as well as other parents do.	29	**49** *	11 *	19 *
The Internet is a safe place for my children to spend time.	26	**21** *	9 *	50 *
I do not mind when advertisers invite my children to Web sites to tell them about their products.	19	21	10 *	27
n =	426			

Note: * means that the percentage difference is statistically significant from the percentages of the two other parent segments in the row. Bold numbers signify that the difference is statistically significant from the percentage of the corresponding segment of *online* parents in Table 2.

"offline worriers" (88 percent of the "online" ones) agree that the Web might isolate a child.

The percentage of "offline worriers" who acknowledged anxiety about the Web was consistently higher than their "online" counterparts. "Online worriers", however, revealed a higher *level* of anxiety. On the statements of concern (agree or disagree "strongly") the "*online* worriers" had a greater deviation from the mean than did their "offline" counterparts.

Bah humbugs (30% of offline parents)

Like the online "disenchanted parents", the second group of offline parents labeled "bah humbugs", does not accept the hype about the wonders of the Web. "Bah humbugs" reject both that the Net is a necessary tool for school and the idea that people coming together online is going to make this a better world.

63 percent of the "bah humbugs" (and 50 percent of their online "disenchanted" counterparts) disagree that the Net is a tool for teaching about diversity and tolerance – while disagreement of the other offline and online clusters is closer to 20 percent and 10 percent, respectively. Only 22 percent of the "bah humbugs" accept the notion that "access to the Internet helps my children with their school work", compared to about 66 percent of other groups of offline parents.

Ready-to-go parents (29% of offline parents)

We named the third segment of offline parents "ready-to-gos" because the beliefs they expressed reflect a strong favorable attitude toward having the Web in the home. In fact, the statements that most distinguished this group from the two other offline groups create a profile that is uncannily similar to the "gung-ho" group of online parents.

A comparison between Figures 1 and 2 shows that the "gung-hos" and ready-to-gos" share every one of the six top-ranked statements, and in almost the same order. Like the "gung-ho" group, "ready-to-go parents" don't accept the common wisdom that the Internet might hurt their kids or families, and they don't begrudge the money it costs to subscribe. Only 11 percent of "ready-to-go parents" (and only 13 percent of "gung-ho parents") agree that exposure to the Internet might interfere with their family values and beliefs.

Nevertheless, the similarity in attitudes between the "gung-ho" and "ready-to-go parents" is remarkable, and it begs asking why many of these people (at least the aforementioned 61 percent) aren't connected already. In fact, the similarities between the other two online and offline groups also lead one to wonder what factors drive some parents in computer households to connect their families to cyberspace while others do not.

Factors predicting whether households with computers have the Internet

We did not find their household income, education, computer ability, their spouse's education or any other demographic variables to be major predictors of online connections when the family already has a computer. Instead, a discriminant analysis found that the best predictors were five variables that describe the parent's experience with the Web outside the home and reflect their beliefs about the practical necessity of the Web in the home. Together, the following variables predict 38 percent of the variance – a substantial amount with these sorts of data – see Table 9.

- Factor 1: "Have you [the parent] personally ever gone online?"

The online and offline groups tended to give very different answers to this question. 96 percent of the parents with online connections at home told us that they have gone online somewhere. By contrast, only 54 percent of the parents with no online connections at home said they have ever used the Internet. This variable is the highest predictor of the set. It suggests that parents' lack of experience with the Web *outside* the home is the most important single factor differentiating a computer household without the Web from one with it.

The next four key predictors of online and offline households relate squarely to the way online and offline parents weigh the Internet pragmatically in their families' lives.

- Factor 2: "My family can get access to the Internet from other places so we do not really need it at home."

58 percent of parents in offline households agree strongly or agree with this statement. Only 23 percent of online parents do. What we have here are fundamentally different perspectives about the practical necessity of bringing the Web into the home.

- Factor 3: "I have better things to do with my money than go online."

54 percent of offline parents say they have better things to do with their money than spend it going online. That's versus 60 percent of online parents who disagree that there are better uses for those online subscription fees. This response adds a second practical dimension to the calculus of decisions that online and offline parents make. The issue here does not seem to be one of basic affordability. The key phrase here is "better things". In the scheme of things, the Internet simply does not seem worth the price for offline parents.

- Factor 4: "Access to the Internet at home helps children with their school work."
- Factor 5: "Children who do not have Internet access are at a disadvantage compared to their peers who do have Internet access."

These two final factors highlight an additional part of the Internet equation that many offline and online parents consider – the specific utility for their children. Like the third factor, these stand out not so much because offline parents overwhelmingly disagreed with them. Rather, they popped up as predictors because online parents seemed so overwhelmingly to accept them while offline parents were much less united.

Table 9. Variables correlating most with having an online connection at home

Variable	Correlation*
Have you ever personally gone online, that is, used the Internet, the World Wide Web, and/or e-mail.	.697
My family can get access to the Internet from other places so we do not really need it at home.	-.593
I have better things to do with my money than spend it going online.	-.436
Access to the Internet at home helps children with their school work.	.347
Children who do not have Internet access are at a disadvantage compared to their peers who do not have Internet access.	.325

Note: * These are pooled within-groups (online, not online) correlations between discriminating variables and standardized canonical discriminant functions. Variables are ordered by absolute size of correlation with function.

In the face of concerns about the Web and kids, parents conduct a cost benefit analysis that weighs the benefits they perceive against their assessment of what their families would lose by not having it. Our data begin to suggest that it is the parent's lack of experience using the Internet outside the home that may make them more likely to downplay its utility in the face of worries about children and the Internet. By contrast, worried parents who *have* had repeated Web experience at work, in friends' homes or at public libraries may decide that despite their fears an online connection is on balance useful for their family.

But why do "disenchanted parents" continue their home links? It may be that they see the technology as a new kind of social leveler. That is, they may feel that while it isn't what it's cracked up to be, the Internet nevertheless is necessary if they and their children are to keep up with The Joneses.

Concluding remarks

Our findings raise a number of policy issues. Here it may be useful to bring up three research directions that we are pursuing in order to fill holes in our understanding of ways families deal with the new Internet realities.

Parents' experiences with the Web

The present study highlights the importance of experience and pragmatic assessments by parents regarding the utility of the Web. In view of this finding, we are trying to learn more about parents' experiences around the Web outside the home. Is it the case, as we expect, that people whose households are online tend to have experience with the Web at work before getting it at home? How much of the decision to get the Web at home relates to *parents'* needs as opposed to those of their children? And why do "disenchanted parents" keep the online connection at home?

What children do and say

One of the startling findings of this study is how confident parents are that they know what their kids are doing online, at home and out. Well, is their confidence justified? What do youngsters tell us about their Web habits, and how does that compare to what their parents tell us? Compared to "online worriers" and "disenchanted parents", are "gung-ho parents" more or less likely to predict what their kids say? What do the similarities and differences tell us about tensions and misunderstandings between the generations – and about trends in Internet usage? Are children with off-line parents likely to go to sites that are different from children whose parents are "gung-ho" about the Web – and are the kids likely to get less enjoyment out of it?

The Web and family lifestyles

How does the Web fit into the entire intricate pattern of family activities? Do family members see it as leisure, work, or a combination of the two? How are the rules that parents said they are setting down actually being implemented? Do parents with different beliefs about the Web's consequences act differently when it comes to laying down and enforcing rules? Do the children of "gung-ho", "online worrier" and "disenchanted parents" adopt their parents' perspectives on the Web? Do they act differently toward the Web as a result of it?

There is much to puzzle out, and the answers are likely to change over time. We look forward to expanding on this research in the months to come.

Note

1. At that time, 60 percent of U.S. households with children aged 8 to 17 had computers. Of those 61 percent were connected to the Internet.

U.S. Adults and Kids on New Media Technology

National Public Radio, the Henry J. Kaiser Family Foundation, and Harvard University's John F. Kennedy School of Government made two national surveys on U.S. adults' and kids' perceptions of new media technology. The surveys were conducted through telephone surveys during November-December 1999 by International Communications Research. The first survey interviewed 1,506 adults 18 years or older, the second 625 children 10-17 years of age (both including an over-sample of African-Americans). The results are weighted to reflect the actual distribution in the nation.

Findings

The first findings were released on February 29, 2000. Here is a small selection:[1]

- African-American kids (44%) and kids from lower income households (41%) are considerably less likely to use a computer at home than white kids (76%) or kids from higher income families (83%). However, virtually the same percent of all kids have used a computer at school (55% of white kids, 60% of African-American kids, 56% of high-income kids, and 59% of low-income kids).
- Compared with adults (38%), more kids have trust in the information on the Internet (56%), and fewer kids than adults think that violent games is a problem with computers or the Internet (39% for kids, 56% for adults).
- More than half of adults (58%) say computers have led people to spend less time with their families and friends. The corresponding figure for children is 39 percent; instead, half of the kids (50%) say that computers hasn't made much difference in this respect. However, a majority of kids (61%) believe that the use of computers has led kids to spend less time outdoors, and 63 percent say they know kids who are addicted to video or computer games.
- About one third (31%) of kids aged 10-17 with computers at home say they have seen a pornographic web site, even by accident. This is truer for older

users: 45 percent of those 14-17 years old compared with 15 percent of those 10-13 years old.

- About three-quarters of parents (76%) say they have rules about what their kids can do on the computer; however, fewer of their own children (57%) mean that their parents have such rules.
- Slightly more than half of kids (53%) say their parents know "a lot" about the things they do and the sites they visit, but this is more true for younger kids (67% of 10-13 year-olds) than for older kids (38% of 14-17 year-olds).

Note

1. Printed with the permission of National Public Radio. More results from the on-going project are available at: http://www.npr.org/programs/specials/polls/technology

Kids Discuss Safety on the Internet

Children's Express[1]
Editors: Katie Niepoth, 15 & Jennifer Vallier, 14
Reporters: Jessica Bess, 12, Anna Johnson, 13 & Brittany Martin, 13

Whether kids are surfing the Net, chatting or just plain e-mailing, some people worry about the risks, including computer viruses, dangerous online conversations and exposure to pornography. Others stress that if you use the Internet right you can have fun, get help with your homework, and get information on just about anything you can imagine.

A Children's Express team from the Marquette, Michigan, US bureau talked to a group of teen Internet users about their experiences. A similar discussion was held in the Washington, D.C., bureau:

Mariya McCormick, 14, Michigan:
I use the Internet just to have fun and keep in touch with my friends and my family.

Lars Larson, 13, Michigan:
I use the Internet for research for school, e-mail and just looking around at stuff.

Chris Grondine, 14, Michigan:
I go in the (chat) rooms right after school. There's not many people and most of my friends are on there. Maybe around 9 or 10 o'clock there's a lot of different people, kind of strange people. There's never a time that I'm using it that my parents aren't watching me so I don't go in any perverted rooms.

Brittany Martin, 13, D.C.:
I've been online since '94. A lot of the stuff you have to actually be looking for to find it. If you're gonna find porn, it's probably because you went into Alta Vista and entered "sex + pictures".

Jerry Wourenmaa, 14, Michigan:
My mom doesn't really know about all the stuff that the Internet holds, so there's no reason for her to be worried about it. I usually get to use it alone.

Lars:
My parents aren't usually looking unless they just walk by and see what I'm doing.

Mariya:
No one's ever around when I use the Internet. Around 10 or 11 it gets really freaky. The people get really sick and perverted. It's actually very scary.

Brittany:
You should just know not to send out your address to people. I think parents should take some responsibility for the children at a young age, when they start getting on the Net, and say, "Don't do that. If someone is sending you their address, just move on." In a lot of cases, if you don't ask for people to meet you it's not gonna happen. If you're careful, it's gonna be OK.

Chris:
One time, a guy – he was a lot older than I was, by about 20 years – kept following me around in the chat rooms. That was kind of scary for me because he wouldn't leave me alone.

Mariya:
This one kid kept asking me what I was wearing and was being really sick. One time when I was on there some 50 year-old guy was hitting on me.

Jerry:
It's kind of unsafe – all of the pornographic e-mail you get all the time. Almost all the e-mail you get is usually porno. That's pretty bad, because it's so easy to visit one of those sites.

Brittany:
Sometimes you just need to say, "Yeah, there are freaks who are gonna abuse this privilege, but it's an important privilege." We do [in the United States] have a First Amendment to the Constitution that says people have a right to freedom of speech. As soon as you start getting into censorship then you start getting into a terrible society where we aren't allowed to go around saying things.

Chris:
When adults set up the computer so kids can't get into those porn sites, they limit you from a lot of other things that aren't like that for school research.

Mariya:
If you can get on the master account you can alter the parental controls yourself.

Brittany:
There are softwares that you can buy that do block certain web sites. Some come with lists pre-made. Those are bad because they block out lots of stuff that's actually useful. Like the National Organization for Women is blocked out on about three different software pieces because they think it deals too much with mature topics like rape, violence against women, things like that.

Note

1. This article is an excerpt from a 1998 story by Children's Express, originally published through the New York Times News Service.

Children's Express (CE) (www.cenews.org) is an international news service produced by reporters (ages 8 to 13) and editors (ages 14 to 18) for adult print, broadcast, and online media. Operating from working news bureaus or on travelling news teams, the approximately 650 CE journalists develop the angles and follow stories from inception through amplification. Headquartered in Washington, D.C., CE operates US bureaus in New York City, New York; Washington, D.C.; and Marquette, Michigan. CE in the UK operates bureaus in London, Newcastle, Sheffield, and Birmingham. Bureaus are opening in Belfast, Northern Ireland, in fall 2000 and in Tokyo, Japan, in early 2001. Plans are underway to bring Children's Express to many other spots in the world, including Germany, South Africa, Vietnam, and California.

Opinions in Australia, Germany and the U.S. on Control of Misuse on the Internet

Jens Waltermann & Marcel Machill

On behalf of the Bertelsmann Foundation in Gütersloh, Germany, and in cooperation with the Australian Broadcasting Authority in Sydney, Australia, the Institut für Demoskopie Allensbach completed a study in June, 1999, ascertaining the current views of the populations in Australia, Germany and the United States with regard to possible risks associated with the Internet and practical ways of selecting and controlling Internet content.

The representative survey was conducted with 1,200 phone interviews in Australia, 1,423 subjects in Germany, and 1,003 subjects in the U.S. among the general population over 18 years of age. Due to the fact that fewer persons have Internet access in Germany (see below), the sample was disproportionally structured through an over-sampling of online users, why the study also can base its results on the judgement of similar proportions of subjects with Internet access – in the United States 698 subjects, in Australia 718 subjects and in Germany 605 subjects.

This article summarises a few of the main findings.[1]

Access to the Internet

- Nine per cent of Germans aged 18 and over have access to the Internet at home (June 1999), as compared to 46 per cent of the adult population in the U.S. and 29 per cent in Australia. If direct access to the Internet means in their home, workplace or through other means, the figure is 14 per cent of Germans aged 18 and over, 70 per cent of the Americans and 60 per cent of the Australians. In all three countries, private Internet access is most common.
- The possibilities for children under 18 to access the Internet also differ considerably. 61 per cent of American parents and 55 per cent of Australian

parents say that their children have Internet access at home, in school or elsewhere, whereas 18 per cent of the German parents make this claim.

- Despite the highly varied levels of personal experience among the general population, respondents in all three countries often display an amazing degree of consensus when it comes to their attitudes towards the Internet and ideas as to how to deal with problematic content.

Risks

- In all three countries, the great majority of the population – and of Internet users – is convinced that while the Internet may entail many advantages, it also has a number of inherent risks.
- The issue of protecting children and young people is emphasised much more greatly by the populations in Australia and the United States than in Germany, where the threat of "data privacy and the 'Big Brother' syndrome" is the predominantly perceived risk. Due to their lack of personal experience, many Germans have yet to form an opinion on the threats posed to children and young people by the Internet. When respondents do have personal experience with the Internet, their perception of the risks involved largely resembles that of respondents in the other two countries.
- As regards personal experience, one-fourth of the Internet users in Australia, one-fourth of the users in Germany and 35 per cent of the users in the U.S. have encountered inappropriate content at some point during their Internet sessions. Most of these persons have encountered pornography, followed, with some distance, by depictions of violence, and political propaganda. With respect to political propaganda, reports thus far are exclusively about radical right-wing content.
- The American and German populations agree that many of the things being shown both on television and the Internet nowadays are problematic. In addition, more than half of the Americans and Germans think this trend is going in a very disturbing direction. (These two questions were not posed in Australia.)
- At the same time, the majority of the population in all three countries is convinced that they are not helpless in the face of these new developments in the traditional as well as the new media but that they can protect themselves from unwanted content. A majority also believes that there are ways for parents to prevent their children from viewing inappropriate contents or sites on the Internet.

Supervision

- There is a widespread desire to counter problematic content on the Internet.
- The overwhelming majority does not question that the legal authorities should increasingly interfere in cases where clearly illegal contents, such as child pornography, are concerned, and appeals for a clear expansion of police controls of illegal content on the Internet and prosecution of those responsible. However, given the global access to Internet content, many doubt whether the police would be able to effectively combat misuse.
- The assessment of who can best control misuse of the Internet displays strikingly different national perspectives. Internet users in the U.S. have greatest confidence in self-regulation, whereas Germans and Australians have comparatively great faith in the major online providers, while also, for example, citing web site producers and the courts to a greater degree than the Americans do. A high percentage of Australians also have confidence in government and independent agencies (Graph 1).

Graph 1. Supervision of Internet content (%)

Place the highest confidence in supervision by:

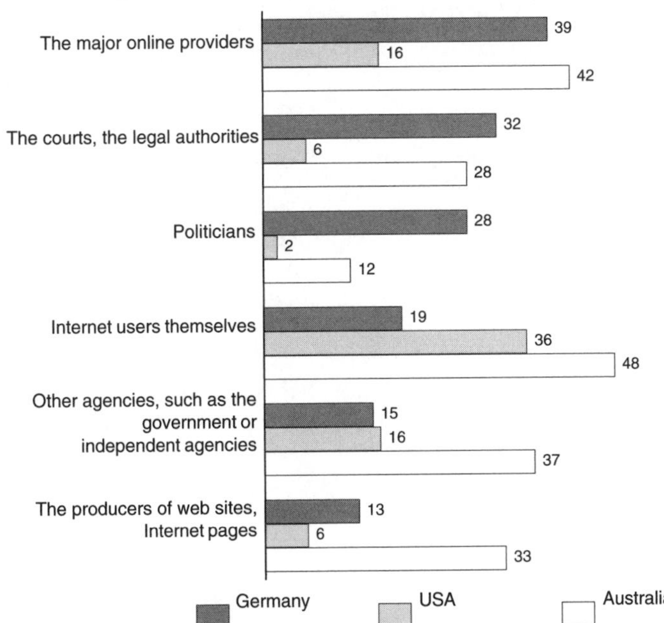

Question: "Who do you think would be most able to ensure the supervision and selection of Internet content, in whom would you have the most confidence?"

Basis: Germany, USA, Australia – population 18 years and older.

Rating and filtering

- Large majorities of the populations in all three countries think it would be good if undesirable messages could be filtered out automatically. About 90 per cent of all Internet users assess a proposed rating system, allowing users to filter out unacceptable web sites, as good and useful. The proposed system is one where the providers have to develop criteria for the classification of content that are then accepted by the users.[2]
- The great importance which Internet users attach to filtering systems is particularly evidenced by the finding that about one out of two users say that an important criterion when choosing a suitable Internet provider is whether the provider offers such a filtering system or not.
- Large majorities of the populations in all three countries would also appreciate ratings that take children's age into consideration, ratings comparable to those used for movies. Among parents the proportion that embraces this idea is even higher.
- In all of the countries studied, there is considerable consensus – albeit with certain subtle distinctions – as to which content should be filtered out or blocked. Racist messages, and pornography and sex scenes, are most frequently cited as types of content that should be blocked by all means. Obscene language is also mentioned fairly frequently. Germans reject the glorification of violence, and right- and left-wing propaganda, to a much greater extent than Australians and Americans do, who for their part object more strongly to being confronted with nudity (Graph 2).
- Women and older people in all three countries would filter Internet content more rigorously than men and particularly young people would.
- The critical attitude towards depictions of violence, pornography and nudity does not present an appeal for a rigorous censorship of all media content. Most are absolutely aware of the fact that a general ban on depictions of, for example, violence is hardly in line with the principles of a free society and would massively curtail the free flow of information. The majority wants to differentiate between violence that is shown in an informative programme, such as political news or sports reports, and violence in the context of entertainment.

Monitoring chat rooms, hotlines

- The Germans – given their lack of personal experience of Internet – have little awareness thus far of the problems which children and young people may encounter in chat rooms. Germans who have experience with chat rooms support monitoring chat rooms to the same degree as Americans do

Graph 2. Internet content that would be blocked by all means (%)

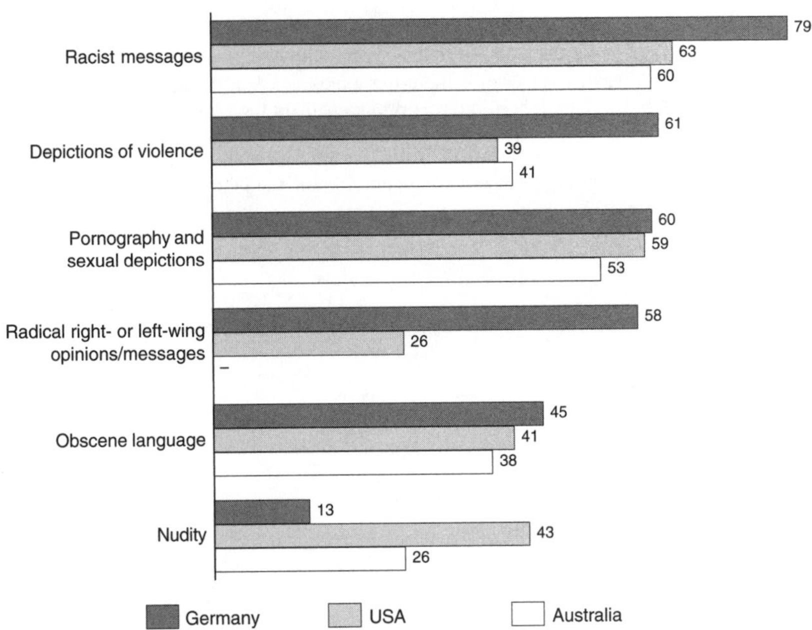

Question: "There are also things on the Internet which are not actually illegal, but which some people consider unsuitable for themselves or their children and would like to black out or block access to. Other people don't think these things are unsuitable and would like to view them. If it were up to you, which contents would you personally block by all means, if it were technically possible, which would you only block under certain circumstances, and which wouldn't you block at all?"

Basis: Germany, USA, Australia – population 18 years and older.

(i.e., about 80 per cent of the American Internet users with children younger than 18).

- About two thirds of the populations in Australia and the United States, and about 80 per cent of the German population, think that hotlines which users could contact to report what they believe is dangerous Internet content, would be helpful. Many expect Internet service providers to set up hotlines of this kind. In addition, many Germans and Australians think governmental hotlines would be good, whereas Americans set more store by private initiatives.

Notes

1. A fuller report of the survey is included in a chapter in Jens Waltermann & Marcel Machill (Eds.): *Protecting Our Children on the Internet. Towards a New Culture of Responsibility.* Gütersloh: Bertelsmann Foundation Publishers, 2000.
2. This system was concretely presented to the polled individuals as follows: "A system has now been developed that enables users to filter the Internet sites and pages they have access to in their homes. It works like this: all Internet providers mark their pages with symbols indicating whether the page contains depictions of violence, sex or other such things. All Internet users can then set their computers at home so that certain topics and depictions are automatically blacked out. Do you think this is a useful system on the whole or don't you think so?"

The Protection of Minors in the Public Opinion

An Austrian Perspective

Ingrid Geretschlaeger

Communication is a means of transmitting information and developing culture. The mass media, and especially the electronic media, are channels through which our society communicates to an ever-growing extent. Thus, our introduction to the world and our experiences are increasingly obtained by watching television, going to the movies, listening to the radio, cassettes, discs or tapes, consuming advertisements in various settings, reading newspapers, using the Internet, etc.

During recent years, Europe has seen an extensive discussion about legislation on the protection of minors, especially with regard to depictions of violence and sex in the electronic media and on the Internet. This prompted an intensive focus on, among other things, rating and filtering of media contents. Criteria must be developed for classifying audio-visual and other media products in member states of the European Union (EU).

The bases for these discussions are:

- the United Nations Convention on the Rights of the Child (celebrating its tenth year of existence in November 1999), including at least three articles of special concern for communication and the media: Articles 3, 13 and 17.
- the EU directive Television Without Frontiers (adopted in 1989 and amended in 1997), asking broadcasters to take measures to ensure that no programme might seriously impair the physical, mental and moral development of minors, and demanding support to parents and guardians in their task of controlling children's TV viewing.
- the EU Recommendation on the Protection of Minors and Human Dignity in Audiovisual and Information Services (1998), covering all electronic media and asking television and Internet service providers to try new methods of parental control (such as codes of conduct, filtering software, etc.) in addi-

tion to existing regulations, and also asking member states to promote the awareness of media issues among minors, parents, educators and teachers.

- the EU Green Paper on the Convergence of the Telecommunications, Media and Information Technology Sectors, and the Implications for Regulation (launched in 1997 and adopted in 1999), mainly being concerned with ways to ensure self-regulation and responsibility among the providers of products in the electronic media sector.
- the EU Action Plan on Promoting Safer Use of the Internet (1998), dealing with fostering awareness programmes, initiating hot-lines, supporting self-regulation and developing rating and filtering systems in connection with the Internet.

Let us ask a few questions about the intentions underlying the protection of minors. The answers will be derived from the above-mentioned documents and discussions in various European countries, and illustrated using results from a representative survey in Austria.[1] This study is focussed on opinions held by the adult population (15 years and over) concerning the protection of minors from various media contents. It was conducted via 1,000 face-to-face interviews in February and March 1999, and commissioned by the Alliance for Media Competence and the Austrian Board of Film Classification at the Austrian Ministry of Education and Culture. The results shown in the following graphs stem from this survey unless otherwise stated.

Who is in charge of protecting our minors?

In each of the documents mentioned above, the protection of minors is seen as the responsibility of parents and guardians alike. But they need to be supported. Governments must supply the legislative basis that, in turn, must force the media to take their share of society's responsibility for minors. Support systems may include independent structures to issue classification guidelines, to monitor classification systems and self-regulation measures, etc. But also any concerned citizen might be active and ready to take on responsibility.

Figure 1 shows that the majority (64%) of the Austrian population is convinced that protective measures with regard to the media are "necessary in all cases". Thus, almost two-thirds are strongly in favour of such measures. An additional 28 per cent think they are "rather necessary". Altogether, 92 percent are in favour of measures to protect minors.

Looking at the results more closely (Figure 2), one finds that it is especially women (71%), elderly people (74%) and people living in households with children younger than 6 years of age (75%) who see the greatest need for protective measures. But even 61 per cent of people with no children share the same concern. Younger people tend to see such measures as less important, but still more than half of the 15- to 29-year-olds state that they are "necessary in all cases" and 34 per cent think they are "rather necessary".

Figure 1. Austrians' perceived necessity of measures to protect minors with regard to the media (%)

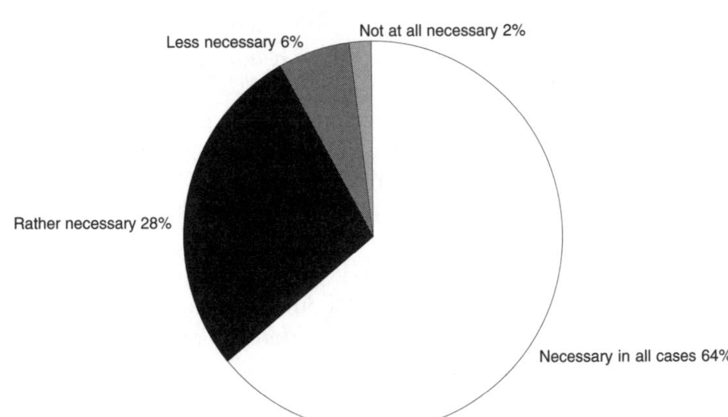

Figure 2. Austrians' perceived necessity of measures to protect minors with regard to the media, by gender, age, and type of household (%)

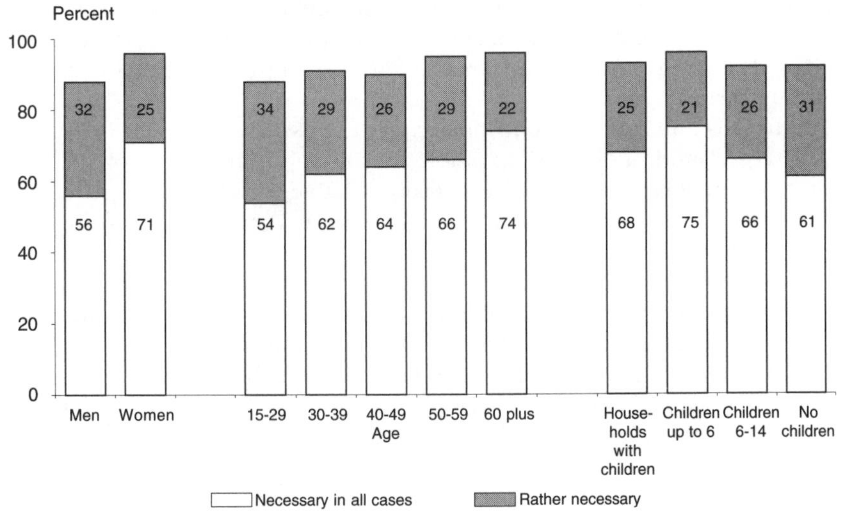

What measures are being considered?

There are various measures to ensure protection. Prohibition of access is the most oppressive measure. Offering material only in encoded or enclosed environments is also a very protective measure, and the same could be said of certain kinds of scheduling. More transparent is age classification as predominantly applied at movies in cinemas, video cassettes and computer games – measures intended to prevent children under certain ages from being exposed to certain media products. This measure not only requires classification of the product in question, but also a set of criteria for what is considered as harmful. These criteria depend on the sensitivity of each country's classification body and on something more complicated: publicly held values. Another measure is warnings. In Europe, warnings concerning television programmes are usually presented in TV guides or on the television screen, accompanied by acoustic and/or visual signs. (However, apart from in France, visual warnings are almost exclusively related to films.) More comprehensive descriptive labelling is sometimes used for video cassettes and CD-ROMs. Such descriptive information can include information about, for example, violence, sex, obscene or bad language and, occasionally, discrimination. It could take into consideration prerequisites for viewing that are specific to the content and target groups of a media content. This sort of consumer advice should work like food labelling, thus enabling the consumers to make individual decisions based on the information provided. On the other hand, it could also be misused as advertisements when produced by the industry itself.

The V-chip as a technical device has been rejected in Europe. It is not considered technically feasible and, in a digital age, other models are preferred, such as ratings and more emphasis on media literacy education.[2] Even if Europeans choose not to introduce the V-chip, the demand still exists for a harmonised classification or rating system, either for transborder viewing or for Internet services. The main problem appears to be agreement upon criteria acceptable to all European citizens.

In the Austrian survey, the respondents were asked about their opinions as regards age classification, e.g., "possible for minors from the age of 10", more explicit recommendations, e.g., "especially suitable for children aged 6 plus", and content description for labelling of harmful material (Figure 3). Seventy-four per cent of the Austrians surveyed are positive to age classification. Furthermore, 49 per cent agree that it is sensible to use more explicit recommendations. Particularly parents with children under the age of 6 (61%) would like to see such recommendations. Preferences for recommendations are closely followed by preferences for more comprehensive content descriptions – 46 per-cent like that idea. Content description seems to be slightly more favoured by the 60+ age group (52%) than by other groups.

Whom are we going to protect?

Thus, we have legal documents indicating the people in charge, and we have opinions on suitable measures. But whom are we going to protect from certain media outputs?

In the given international and European contexts, children or minors are defined differently. In some countries, they can be up to the age of 12, 14, 15 or

Figure 3. Austrians' opinions about how to label harmful material (%)

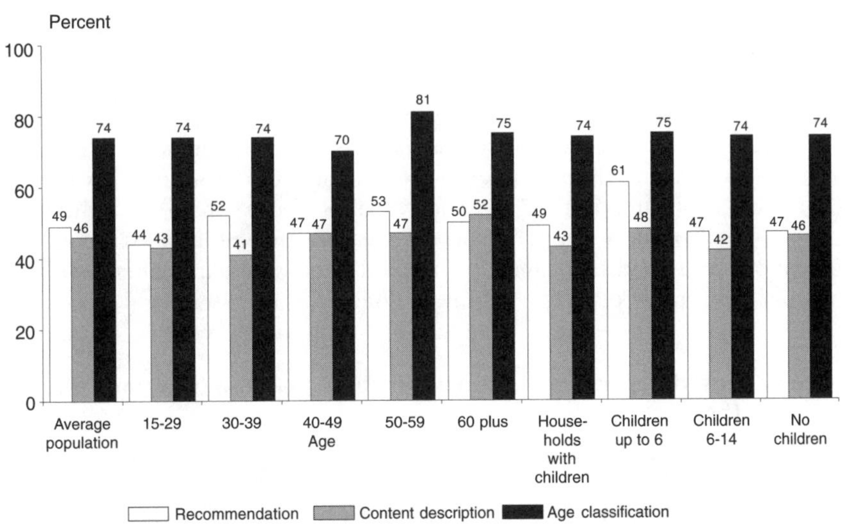

16, and in others up to 18. In some countries, protective media measures for minors are related to various age groups – but when parents are accompanying them, the age limit becomes irrelevant. In these cases, society only interferes when parental responsibility is lacking. Research often indicates the need for protection of children in problem situations, or stresses the fact that children in harmonious and supportive family environments are not endangered by media contents sometimes considered harmful.

In Austria, we have an important age limit at 16 years (valid for presence in public, at cinemas and, since January 1999, also for television, with 10 p.m. being the watershed, the time before which everybody should be allowed to watch programmes). There is no exception from the age restrictions at cinemas when an adult is accompanying the minor. The age groups applied by the Austrian Board of Film Classification are "all ages", "6+", "10+", "12+", "14+" and "16". In the cinema context, Austrians prefer to be told what age group is allowed access and, therefore, what group would not generally risk any harm.

What are we protecting minors from?

The most obvious fear expressed in European societies seems to be about the effects watching harmful media violence might have on actual behaviour. Children should be protected from aggressive acts, as well as other injurious material, that might negatively affect their well-being. Other concerns expressed are, for example, about media's discrimination (in terms of, e.g., gender, race or nationality), commercial exploitation, and about viewers' desensitisation to violent acts and subsequent lack of sympathy for victims of any mistreatment.[3] Desensitisation could also be a consequence of bad language (including humiliation, cynicism, clichés, and stereotyping). Indecency and impeded emotional development as expressed in the need to be "cool" are also emerging as topics of recent studies.[4]

Figure 4 shows that most Austrians express concern and want information about media's portrayals of "violent acts/brutality" (85%) – and "sexual acts" (79%), "drug consumption" (73%) and "alcohol abuse" (68%).[5] Furthermore, more than half of the respondents in the survey want information about "discrimination" and "bad language" in the media, of which the latter issue is of particular concern to parents of younger children.

Figure 4. Austrians' desired information about potentially harmful material (%)

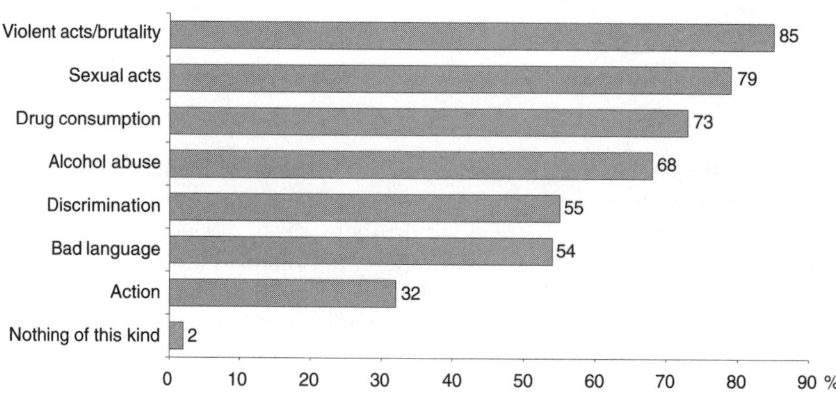

Why protect children from these elements?

Why do we want to protect children from these media contents? First of all, there is definitely the overall idea of having to protect children in an (unjust and competitive) adult society. It seems as if today's childhood does not correspond to what we would like childhood to be. "Childhood is the period of time in each person's life which society allocates for the process of training to become the kind of member that the society wants him/her to be. During this period different agencies of society are expected to ensure that the child will be transformed into an adult in accordance with the adult-image acceptable in that society."[6] Childhood is the period in which individuals are subject to a set of rules and regulations that are unique to them, that do not apply to members of other social categories. Children are neither expected nor allowed to fully participate in social life. Adults have the responsibility for children's welfare, but at the same time the right to control and supervise them. Dependency means weakness and that children can be forced to do what adults think is right. This position of weakness is usually not related to any real or potential strength a child might have. Only very special talents like child-stars in sports or media are freed from those restrictions.

Another strong reason for protecting children is the concern about negative influences from the media. This is why so many research projects have dealt with the impact of media violence and comparatively few with the possibilities the various media might offer.

Another societal concern is to act in the best interest of children, and to foster a positive development as early as possible. The creation of pre-school programmes in the 1960's brought about a trend to strongly support children's cognitive and social development. Thus, quality and learning would not leave room for negative influences.

Obligations towards children and the right to control their activities are shared by the family and the society. Since the set of values and order of priorities of the family and those of the society are sometimes different, they constantly fall into conflict and need to be negotiated, when negotiation is possible.

Given family arguments about media quality, children accept rules and guidelines and even restrictions on access to films on television, according to an Austrian study with 6- to 14-year-olds.[7] The most obedient age group is the 6- to 8-year-old children. Those most aware of what is good for them are the 9- to 10-year-olds and those most strongly opposed are the 11- to 12-year-olds. Young teenagers no longer care so much. About half of them (46%) say that if they want to see something on television they will mange to do so even if their parents disagree (Figure 5).

The situation concerning going to the movies is a little different, since the legislative power is stronger. But ways to escape the restrictions at the cinema are obvious: Especially the younger kids say that they can wait until the film comes out as a video or it is shown on television – then they can watch anything (52% of 6- to 8-year-olds and 60% of 9- to 10-year-olds). Among older children about half say they oppose and circumvent restrictions for seeing movies at the cinema (46% of the 11- to 12-year-olds and 52% of the 13- to 14-year-olds) (Figure 6).

An additional reason for protecting children is the intention to foster awareness about children's needs, vulnerability and suggestibility. We must create an environment where children are well accepted and safe.

Still another reason is to enable the audience to make informed choices, i.e., using measures that classify or label media products, and to motivate consumers to use their power to demand what they want and need from the media and to refuse what they do not want or find offensive.

In Austria, the percentage of persons who would like to have more information about media contents is, as we have seen, generally high and they would like to find such information in previews, magazines or at the beginning of a movie. People are not uncertain about when this sort of information should

Figure 5. Austrian 6- to 14-year-olds' reactions to information about television films unsuitable for them (%)

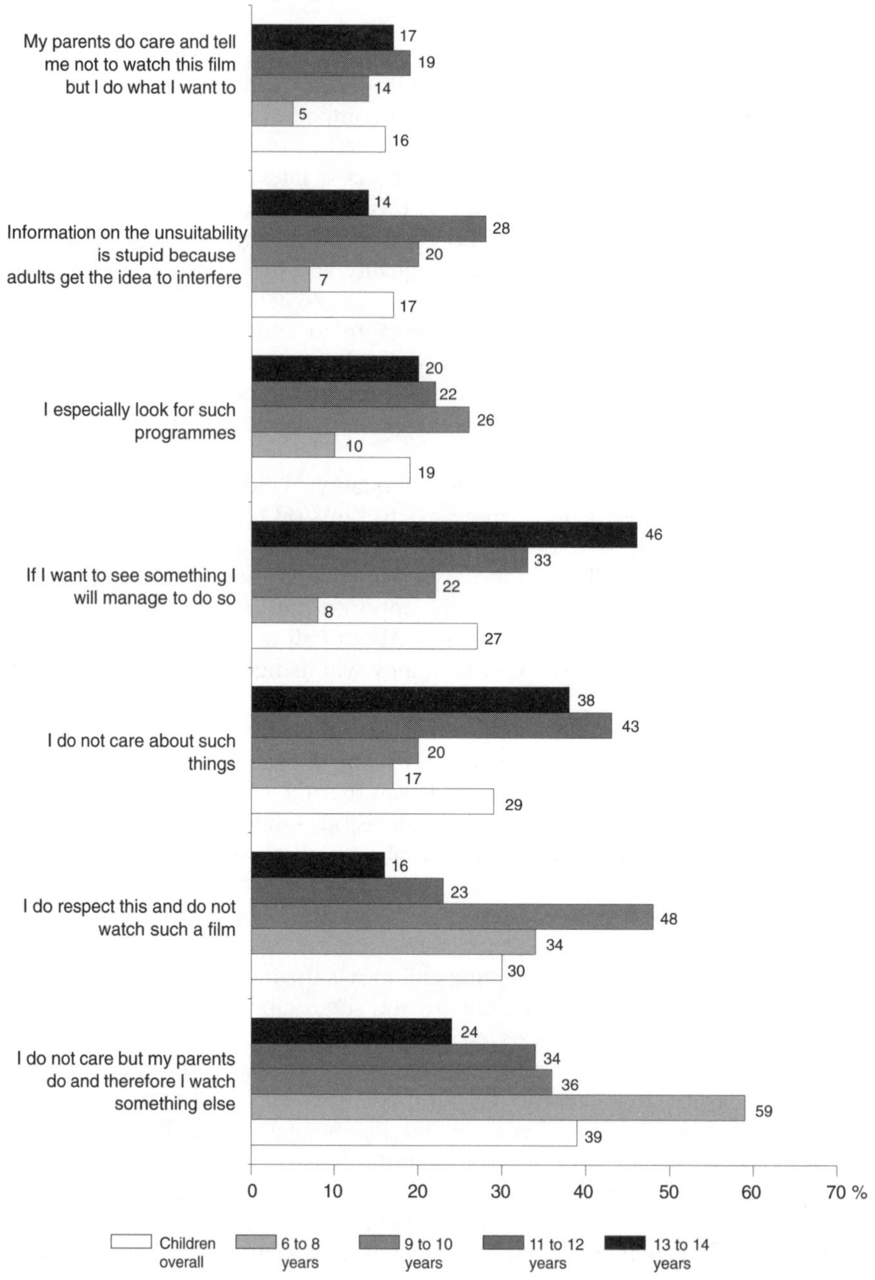

Figure 6. What a given age restriction for seeing a movie at the cinema means for Austrian 6- to 14-year-olds (%)

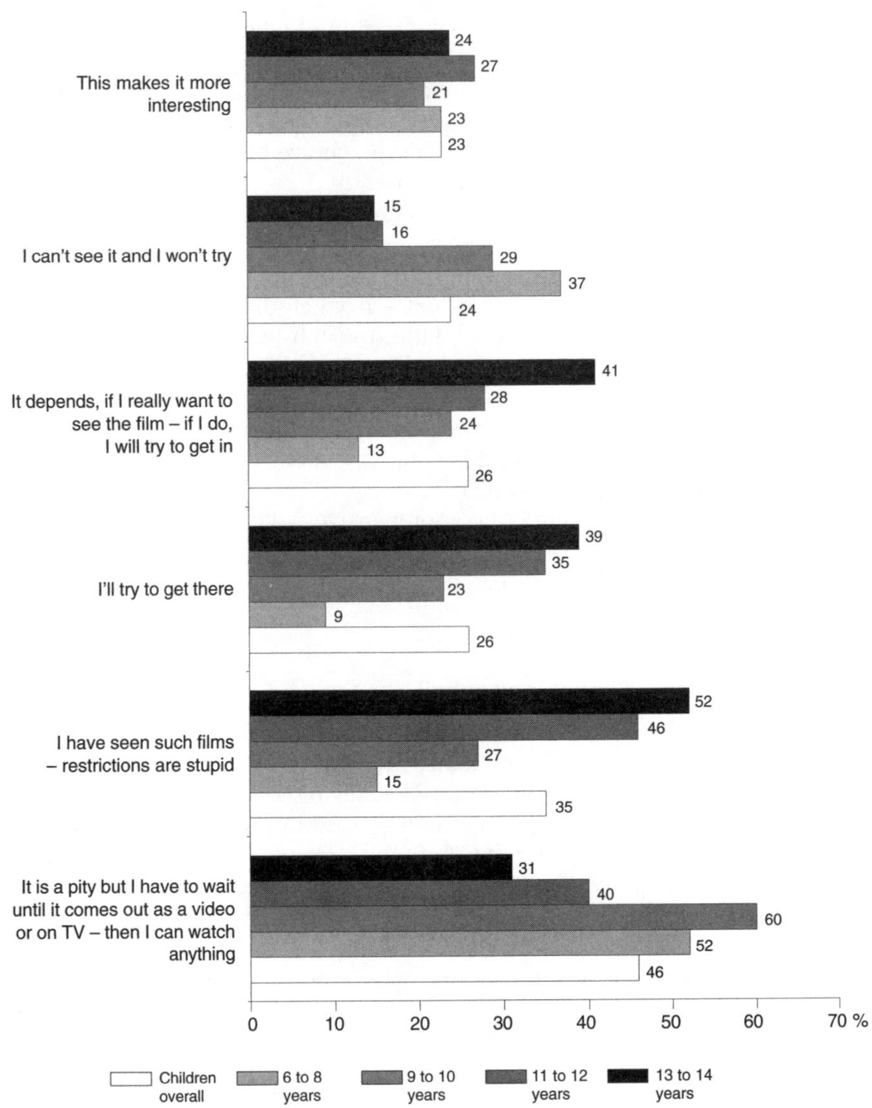

be given. One-third check the previews and TV guides prior to viewing – at least they say so. However, this is doubtful, as the existing means of protecting children and youngsters are hardly familiar. Even the very well-announced introduction of "X" and "0" labels for movies on television after 10 p.m. (introduced two months prior to the survey) was only known to every second person in the adult survey. And the traditional – 50-year-old – Austrian Board of Film Classification was familiar to only one-fourth of the respondents. This indicates clearly that there is not enough information, given that the current need is felt so strongly. But this is also a question of whether the public can be made to actively search for information. In any case, information on media products – particularly information on harmfulness for children as well as content description in the areas people are concerned with – should be made more easily available, e.g., via teletext whenever the choice of a programme is to be made. But we are far from such a situation.

The knowledge we have and use in order to argue in favour of the protection of minors stems mainly from developmental theories. It also comes from effects studies with various results as regards the impact of, e.g., violence in the media, and – but to a much lesser extent – from studies about identification, information processing, etc. However, little research has been done on advertising and children. Advertising is a part of the Western society, and we depend on it for further development. Thus, any negative findings about advertising might be seen as a challenge to the system. The most recent research deals with the effects of using computers. In this context, gender differences are obvious but are still being tackled far too little.

What our society is lacking is a comprehensive policy about children. What is missing – at least in Austria – is especially a media policy including children, and that is based on ongoing research.

What media are of most concern?

Austrian people are especially concerned about certain media (Figure 7). "Films on television", "videos", "computer games" and "Internet services" are the areas people are most concerned about (approximately 65% each). Adults with children under 6 years of age are even more interested in protection in the area of computer games (82% compared to 63% of the average population). To a lesser extent, but still a majority of the Austrians are concerned about "all television programming", and half about "films in cinemas" and "magazines". But in this case we must recall that film in the cinema is the only medium for which effective protective measures are set up by law and for which transgression of the law can be prosecuted. Parents of children aged 6 to 14 have fewer problems with the cinema (46%), but they think protective measures against magazines are important (52%). Their children are the target group of teen magazines containing all sorts of advice for puberty problems, sexual relationships, etc. Also, the Internet is seen as a concern particularly by parents of children under the age of 6 (73% versus 62% in the total population).[8]

Figure 7. Media output that Austrians are concerned about (%)

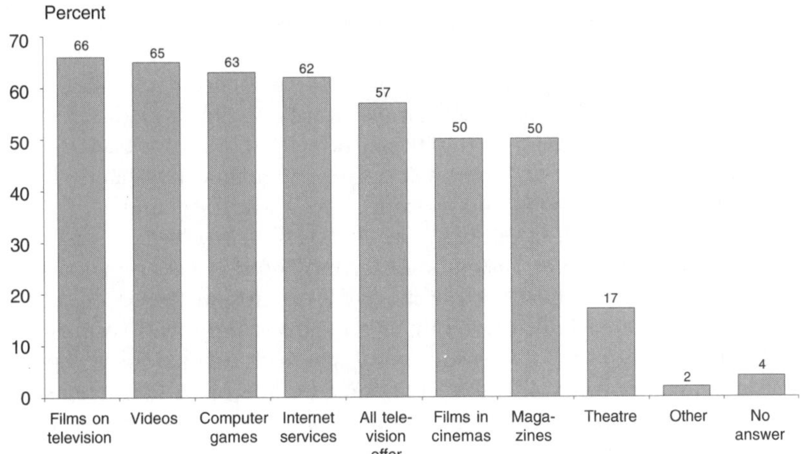

Concluding discussion

Let us try to sum up the situation and needs. International and European policy statements have recommended that the media develop ethical standards and be respectful to children on the basis of codes of conduct with professional guidelines; controlling bodies to back this up have also been recommended. Legislation must be established not just in the best interest of the child, but also related to the actual situation and to the basic law of freedom of information and expression.

This would necessarily lead to

- guidelines for protecting minors to allow for their personal development;
- the provision of quality media contents as stated, for example, in the UN Convention on the Rights of the Child;
- well established media education[9] for every citizen in a democratic society, beginning within the family (supported by information to parents), and in any kind of institutionalised education and teaching.

Guidelines, quality media contents and media education would need to be supported by the dissemination of information on child development, on the development and performance of communication and its media, on ongoing research as well as on the development of appropriate criteria for classification and support systems for production.

However, what are the effects of the policy statements, conventions, etc., so far? This is not easily answered. Among people in areas dealing with children and the media there is little euphoria. The production costs for quality products are increasing, while funds for specific children's media products are diminishing despite increased air time.[10] Children are, of course, an important target group – taken seriously mainly by the advertising industry – but they are becoming increasingly segmented and orientated towards adult productions. Protective measures are being provided, but have not had a sufficient impact on everyday life. We need more demands, more specific and differentiated moral arguments – but as long as traditional powers stay in position and continue to exert their influence, things will only be regulated half-heartedly and not further developed. Why should those in power ask for change?

Recently, some regions ("Länder") in Austria got involved in discussing protection measures with youngsters themselves. There is a tendency towards an integration of youth welfare with protective measures, and media education would seem to be increasingly important as a means to empower youngsters to protect themselves. But until this is successful, we need regulations and protective measures for those in vulnerable situations. On the other hand, legislation concerning minors is now shifting from prohibition and "punishment" of youngsters to putting more emphasis on the responsibility of parents and adults in society as a whole.

The dangers that minors face today are different from those faced by their parents. Therefore, new challenges are to introduce minors to societal structures (including technologies being supplied) and to promote personal development by creating a stimulating environment where minors can learn to deal with potential dangers.

Youngsters – when asked about potential dangers to them – indicate the following range of concerns:[11] alcohol and drugs, credits given by banks, sex shops, loss of family, unemployment and lack of education, friends causing problems, injustice, bullying, unjust treatment by adults, and ignorance of society. Minors ask for limits themselves and, accordingly, for effective protection of children: no alcohol under 15, no credits under 18, no access to sex shops until 18, etc. However, they see no reason for concern about the Internet.

With regard to media, the provincial Austrian government is now suggesting the establishment of training centres to develop a media culture and more concerned usage.

So what have we come up with? Issues about children and childhood are of marginal concern in many scientific and public areas. Even more marginal are issues about children and media in general. The limitation is rooted in a societal tendency to address only a few topical areas – in most cases family and education, sexual abuse, children's television. The current perspectives on children are also very narrow: children as growing up to future members of society (a matter of education) or children in their present immature state, i.e., children as a problem or nuisance (a matter of welfare and social policy).

The policy statements on media mentioned in the beginning of this article offer a starting point and are a relevant background for those who want to get involved. But the UN, the EU, etc., can only give recommendations – though sometimes legally binding – that are open to interpretation. The Council of

Europe asks for a preventive and more positive approach by issuing rewards for quality production, for codes of conduct and internal guidelines from the media, and for parents' and teachers' support of children in the development of a critical attitude towards low quality programming. Independent regulatory bodies ought to be established in the EU member states. These should be obliged to licence media, promote research, protect minors, support media education and support the teaching of appreciation of quality material. Awareness programmes should be developed for a safer use of the digital media.

Today, protection of minors with regard to media in an environment where children are respected, and not just tolerated, must be looked at from at least three angles:

1. keeping out of children's reach those things that might negatively interfere with their development (things for which society and industry are responsible);
2. providing children with a range of worthwhile media products and enabling them to participate in social life, e.g., in media production (thereby creating a stimulating cultural environment);
3. enabling children to cope with the challenges in society and the media environment as a preventive measure through, e.g., media education (i.e., education and personal development).

Notions of childhood and the best interest of the child need to be revisited. We must reflect on the ongoing development and the applied strategies of the media and other interest groups in order to give our children the time and space to find their own way. For our children, the most crucial role is played by us – the men and women who are their parents and who make up society. If we are sensitive and strong enough to ask for proper treatment, then our children will get their share of the recognition, support and protection they need.

Notes

1. Market-Institut für Markt-, Meinungs- und Mediaforschung: *Jugendschutz für Medien. Ergebnisse einer Umfrage repräsentativ für die österreichische Bevölkerung ab 15 Jahre* [Media Protection for Minors. Findings from a survey representative of the Austrian population 15 years of age and over]. Linz, 1999.
2. *Parental Control of Television Broadcasting*. University of Oxford, Programme in Comparative Media Law and Policy (PCMLP), Centre for Socio-Legal Studies, 1999.
3. Little recognition is given to the fact that girls tend to identify with the victim who, at the same time, is often a female character. Thus, girls develop more often a rejection of violent behaviour that is used to keep them under control in real life as well.
4. A goal among boys that puts girls under great strain.
5. Drinking of alcoholic beverages among youngsters from about 12 years of age is increasingly seen as a problem in recent studies.

6. Shamgar-Handelman, Lea (1994): To Whom Does Childhood Belong? In Qvortrup, Jens et al. (eds): *Childhood Matters. Social Theory, Practice and Politics.* Avebury, Aldershot, pp. 250-265, here p. 250.
7. Market-Institut für Markt-, Meinungs- und Mediaforschung: *Altersbeschränkungen für Kinder bei Filmen. Ergebnisse einer österreichweiten Befragung unter Kindern im Alter von 6 bis 14 Jahren im Dezember '97/Jänner '98* [Age Limits regarding Films for Children. Findings from an Austrian Inquiry among Children from 6 to 14 years in December 1997/January 1998]. The study, commissioned by the Austrian Board of Film Classification for minors, was conducted with 497 children representative of the age group 6 to 14 years.
8. Youngsters themselves find it completely absurd to set up protective measures for the Internet, as found in a survey among 1,000 teenagers in Lower Austria.
9. The Vienna Recommendation on Media Education to UNESCO was agreed upon at an international conference in April 1999 in Vienna and was presented to the General Assembly of UNESCO.
10. This is even valid for children's channels where child audiences are supposed to gather and not interfere with other interest groups as occurs with the programmes of the public service broadcasters in Germany.
11. Institut Dr. Brunmayr: *Expertise: Jugendschutz 2000. Anforderungen an einen zeitgemäßen Jugendschutz. Kurzfassung einer Studie auf Basis einer empirischen Erhebung bei 1.058 NÖ-Jugendlichen* [Experts' Report: Protection of Minors 2000. Demands for a modern protection. Summary of a study on 1,058 young people]. Gmunden-St. Pölten, Frühjahr 1999.

Authors

Peng Hwa Ang	Associate Professor School of Communication Studies Nanyang Technological University Singapore
Carlos A. Arnaldo	Chief Communication Policies and Research Communication Division UNESCO, Paris, France
Alexander Ask	Dr. Department of Psychology University of Adelaide Adelaide, South Australia
Martha Augoustinos	Dr. Department of Psychology University of Adelaide Adelaide, South Australia
Erica Biely	Research Assistant University of California Santa Barbara (UCSB) California, USA
Ragnhild T. Bjørnebekk	Researcher National Police Academy Unit of Research Oslo, Norway
André H. Caron	Dr., Professor Department of Communications University of Montréal Montréal, Canada
Letizia Caronia	Dr. Department of Science of Education University of Bologna Bologna, Italy
Bo Carstens	Consultant Know-ware Management Roskilde, Denmark
Ferran Casas	Professor, Coordinator Catalan Network of Researchers for Children's Rights and Quality of Life (XCIII) Research Institute on Quality of Life University of Gerona Gerona, Spain

Children's Express Worldwide	Alicia Aebersold Director of Communications Washington, D.C., USA
Jan Christofferson	Secretary Council on Media Violence Ministry of Culture Stockholm, Sweden
Kirstie Cope	Research Assistant University of California Santa Barbara (UCSB) California, USA
Margaret Cupitt	Senior Research Officer Australian Broadcasting Authority Sydney, Australia
Edward Donnerstein	Professor of Communication, Dean Division of Social Science University of California Santa Barbara (USCB) California, USA
Kevin Durkin	Professor of Psychology University of Western Australia Nedlands, Australia
Tor A. Evjen	Research Engineer SINTEF, The Foundation of Scientific and Industrial Research at the Norwegian Institute of Technology SINTEF Production Engineering Trondheim, Norway
Wendy Farinola	Research Assistant University of California Santa Barbara (UCSB) California, USA
Margareta Forsberg	Master of Social Work Göteborg, Sweden
Ingrid Geretschlaeger	Dr. Medienpädagogik, Medienkultur/Kindermedien Jugendmedienschutz Vienna, Austria
Mark Griffiths	Dr., Head of Psychology Psychology Division Nottingham Trent University Nottingham, United Kingdom

Albert C. Gunther	Associate Professor Department of Agricultural Journalism University of Wisconsin-Madison Madison, Wisconsin, USA
Birgitte Holm Sørensen	Dr., Associate Professor The Royal School of Educational Studies Copenhagen, Denmark
Aletha C. Huston	Dr., Professor Department of Human Ecology University of Texas at Austin Austin, Texas, USA
Carsten Jessen	Associate Professor The Royal School of Educational Studies Copenhagen, Denmark
Stephen Kline	Professor of Communications, Director Media Analysis Lab (MAL) School of Communications Simon Fraser University Burnaby, BC, Canada
Jennifer Kotler	Dr., Postdoctoral Fellow Children & Media Project Department of Psychology Georgetown University Washington, D.C., USA
Dale Kunkel	Dr., Professor of Communication University of California Santa Barbara (UCSB) California, USA
Jason Low	Dr., Lecturer Victoria University of Wellington Wellington, New Zealand
Marcel Machill	Dr., Director of Media Policy Bertelsmann Foundation Gütersloh, Germany
Andrea Millwood Hargrave	Research Director Broadcasting Standards Commission London, United Kingdom
Peter Nikken	Dr., Head Information Center for Children's Television and Media The Netherlands Youth Information Institute Utrecht, The Netherlands

Lilach Nir	Graduate Student Annenberg School for Communication University of Pennsylvania Philadelphia, PA, USA
Rachel O'Connell	Researcher and Lecturer Cyberspace Research Unit Department of Psychology University of Central Lancashire Preston, United Kingdom
Peter Petrov	Media Researcher CID Centre for User Oriented IT Design NADA, Department of Numerical Analysis and Computer Science Royal Institute of Technology Stockholm, Sweden
Emma Rollin	Research Assistant University of California Santa Barbara (UCSB) California, USA
Akira Sakamoto	Dr. Department of Psychology Ochanomizu University Tokyo, Japan
Ronda Scantlin	Dr., Senior Research Associate College of Communication University of Texas at Austin Austin, Texas, USA
Lisbeth Schierbeck	Freelance Journalist and Consultant in Computer Gaming Søborg, Denmark
Veronica Silva	Psychologist, Researcher Research Department Chilean National Television Council Santiago, Chile
Maria Dolores Souza	Psychologist, Director Research Department Chilean National Television Council Santiago, Chile
Joseph Turow	Professor of Communication Annenberg School for Communication University of Pennsylvania Philadelphia, PA, USA

Jens Waltermann	Deputy Head of the Media Division Bertelsmann Foundation Gütersloh, Germany
Ellen Wartella	Professor, Dean of Communication College of Communication University of Texas at Austin Austin, Texas, USA
Anthony H. Winefield	Professor Department of Psychology University of Adelaide Adelaide, South Australia